"The book is an authoritative view of very important research about the psychology of eating and drinking. It serves as a superb overview of scientific literature without hidden agendas. The author makes the material accessible to readers of all backgrounds by relating the research to her own experiences with food and drink. Everyone can benefit from reading this book."—**Linda Bartoshuk**, *PhD, Bushnell Professor, Food Science and Human Nutrition, University of Florida*

"Alexandra Logue is masterful in distilling a mountain of work on eating and drinking into an engaging, coherent, and captivating picture of these essentials of human life."—**Kelly D. Brownell**, *PhD, Dean, Sanford School of Public Policy; Professor of Public Policy, Professor of Psychology and Neuroscience, Duke University*

"Alexandra Logue's now classic text is the place to begin exploring how our psychology—as distinct from genetics—influences human taste preferences, eating behavior, and food choices. Logue deals with the evidence available to help explain anorexia, obesity, alcoholism, and the near universal craving for chocolate. Does psychology matter in food choice? Here's where to answer that question."—**Marion Nestle**, *Professor of Nutrition, Food Studies, and Public Health, New York University; co-author of* Why Calories Count: From Science to Politics

THE PSYCHOLOGY OF
EATING AND DRINKING

This insightful, thought-provoking, and engaging book explores the truth behind how and why we eat and drink what we do. Instead of promising easy answers to weight loss or eliminating picky eating, this book approaches controversial eating and drinking issues from a more useful perspective—explaining the facts to promote understanding of our bodies. The only book to provide an educated reader with a broad, scientific understanding of these topics, *The Psychology of Eating and Drinking* explores basic eating and drinking processes such as hunger and taste, as well as how these concepts influence complex topics such as eating disorders, alcohol use, and cuisine. This new edition is grounded in the most up-to-date advances in scientific research on eating and drinking behaviors and will be of interest to anyone.

Alexandra W. Logue, PhD, is an internationally known behavioral scientist. Her general research area is learning and motivation, with special research interests in higher education, choice behavior, self-control, and food aversions and preferences. She has published over 130 books, articles, and chapters on higher education, quantitative models of choice behavior, and food aversions and preferences, and has served on the editorial boards of many prestigious journals.

THE PSYCHOLOGY OF EATING AND DRINKING

Fourth Edition

Alexandra W. Logue

Routledge
Taylor & Francis Group

NEW YORK AND LONDON

Fourth edition published 2015
by Routledge
711 Third Avenue, New York, NY 10017

and by Routledge
27 Church Road, Hove, East Sussex BN3 2FA

Routledge is an imprint of the Taylor & Francis Group, an informa business

First edition published by W.H. Freeman & Company 1986

Third edition published by Routledge 2004

Library of Congress Cataloging-in-Publication Data
Logue, A. W. (Alexandra W.)
The psychology of eating and drinking / Alexandra W. Logue.—Fourth
edition.
pages cm
1. Food habits—Psychological aspects. 2. Nutrition—Psychological aspects.
3. Drinking behavior. 4. Food preferences. I. Title.
TX357.L67 2014
616.85′26—dc23
2014024509

ISBN: 978-0-415-81708-0 (hbk)
ISBN: 978-0-415-81707-3 (pbk)
ISBN: 978-0-203-38792-4 (ebk)

Typeset in Sabon
by Book Now Ltd, London

To Jamie and Milla, whose preferences
for certain vegetables resulted in
many mealtime discussions

CONTENTS

CONTENTS

PREFACE

When I was a year old I stopped eating everything except bread and milk. For years my diet showed little improvement, and by 15 I was eating mostly meat, milk, potatoes, bread, orange juice, and desserts. I did not eat pizza, spaghetti, or any other food that I considered "foreign." I avoided soda, fresh fruit (except bananas), vegetables (except peas, carrots, and beets), and cheese (except grilled American cheese sandwiches). Fish I regarded as poison.

My parents were not alarmed; I come from a long line of people with unusual food preferences. My mother, by choice, rarely served fresh fruit or fish at our home. She never served liver, which she hates, although my father loved it. He always ate first the food he disliked most, and many times I saw him finish salad and string beans before touching baked potato and steak. When I was a child my mother frequently recounted to me how her grandfather would eat chocolate cupcakes but not cake made from the same batter; he said that the cake gave him indigestion.

At home my parents gave me vitamin pills and basically let me eat whatever I wanted. But everywhere else I had to contend with sticky social occasions in which I was served what I abhorred eating. Just imagine going to a birthday party and not being able to eat the soda and pizza that everyone else was eating.

Food aversions were not the only troubles of my youth. Food preferences also gave me problems. Although I disliked many things, when I did like a food I could eat it at any hour of the day or night. My Southern grandmother was happy to feed me fried chicken, mashed potatoes, and hot biscuits dripping with butter whenever I wished. It was not easy to keep my weight at a reasonable level. One of the most dangerous places for me was the farm of my great-aunt and great-uncle in South Carolina, where the dinner table groaned with a great many things that I loved to eat. One exception was the milk from their cows. Although I relished it when it came back from the packager, I found milk totally unacceptable when it came straight from the cow (even though my great-uncle had pasteurized it).

Two things saved me from an unhealthy preoccupation with eating and not eating certain foods: my husband and my study of experimental psychology.

My husband was known in childhood as the HGP, or human garbage pail, because of his voracious and indiscriminate eating habits. Through example, pleading, and occasional bullying over the 40 years of our marriage, he now has me regularly eating (and sometimes even liking) vegetables, fruits, and different types of ethnic food. (No one, under any circumstances, will ever get me to eat fish.)

Becoming an experimental psychologist, the other saving factor, channeled my former embarrassment into research enthusiasm. As a graduate student, I was continually drawn to research on eating and drinking behaviors. Sometimes I conducted studies that grew out of hypotheses I had about the origins of my own eating peculiarities. Only much later did I realize that a great deal of psychology focuses on eating and drinking.

As a graduate student at Harvard I was encouraged to pursue my interests wherever they led, a strategy that prepared me well for writing this book and its predecessors. As part of my studies I taught a small seminar for sophomore psychology majors. I was expected to come up with a topic for a year-long tutorial that would integrate material from many areas of psychology. I chose eating and drinking.

Later, as an assistant professor at the State University of New York at Stony Brook, I created a new lecture course: The Psychology of Eating and Drinking. Although it was an advanced, nonrequired course, it grew in popularity each year. Toward the end of my years at Stony Brook, literally hundreds of students from many different majors tried to get into the course each time I taught it. Unfortunately I could not take them all. In the first years of the course, the students read only original articles; the only textbooks that were at all relevant covered isolated topics such as hunger or alcoholism. The lack of a suitable text for my course and the enthusiasm of my teaching assistants and students finally convinced me that I should write a textbook for the course. The result was the first edition of *The Psychology of Eating and Drinking*.

The story of my path to writing *The Psychology of Eating and Drinking* would be incomplete without mention of Paul Rozin, the ultimate food psychologist. I first met Paul in 1977 at the University of Pennsylvania, where he was pursuing research on why people eat chile pepper. That first meeting with Paul and his wife, Elisabeth, cookbook writer and culinary historian, and the time we spent in their kitchen, catalyzed my interest in the psychology of eating and drinking, and the effect has not yet worn off. Liz's first cookbook, *The Flavor-Principle Cookbook*, has been my favorite ever since and I doubt if that will ever change.

The present book, similar to the previous versions of *The Psychology of Eating and Drinking*, describes scientific inquiries into eating and drinking behaviors. However, the book does this in such a way that the material is completely understandable to the educated lay person. You need not have had any courses in psychology, or courses in any science for that matter, to understand what's written here. The only requirement for reading and enjoying this book is that the reader be willing to approach psychology as a science. One of my goals in writing all of my books has been to show how much can be learned by applying scientific methods to the study of behavior. Should you wish for further information on any topic, the extensive references listed at the back of the book will assist you. But you can also just read the book through, or selected chapters, without being concerned with the sources of the material.

I have elected to cover only those aspects of the psychology of eating and drinking that seem well researched and interesting, and I have had to cover some of these only briefly. Complete coverage of the psychology of eating and drinking would require many, many volumes. This book is meant only as an introduction. Nevertheless, when possible I describe how the research was conducted—not just the results—so that you can judge that and other research for yourself.

This book covers the major eating and drinking disorders, but it will not tell you precisely how to diagnose or treat your own or someone else's eating and drinking problems. The book describes some of the principles for doing so, but real problem solving requires professional help. The relevant chapters list clinics and self-help organizations that may be useful in obtaining that professional help.

ACKNOWLEDGMENTS

Many people and organizations assisted me in preparing this book and the first three editions of *The Psychology of Eating and Drinking*. For the first edition, James Hassett gave me a great deal of valuable, general advice on how to write a psychology book. My library research assistants, Lawrence Epstein, Pilar Peña-Correal, Telmo Peña-Correal, and Michael Smith, were always ready to run to the library to find source material for me. Herbert Terrace and Columbia University kindly provided me with space and library privileges that helped me finish the book during my sabbatical. Conversations with Alex Kacelnik on foraging and Nori Geary on hunger were also very helpful. Invaluable comments were made on the manuscript by Lorraine Collins, Howard Rachlin, Monica Rodriguez, Elisabeth Rozin, Paul Rozin, Diane Shrank, Ian Shrank, Michael Smith, and Richard Thompson. Their help is greatly appreciated. In particular I thank Camille Logue Orman, whose hours of insightful and witty taped comments kept me company in the lonely hours of revision; she went far beyond the requirements of sibling duty.

In preparing the second edition, the comments made in the many reviews of the first edition were extremely helpful. Several reviewers (Leann L. Birch, John P. Foreyt, Bonnie Spring, and Rudy E. Vuchinich) made many insightful, useful suggestions regarding a draft of the second edition. Many researchers put up with my seemingly endless questions about this or that aspect of eating and drinking. In particular, Kelly Brownell provided much information regarding overeating and obesity, Jasper Brener helped me to identify research on metabolic rate, and the Cuisine Group (most notably Linda Bartoshuk, Barbara Kirshenblatt-Gimblett, Rudolph Grewe, Solomon Katz, Elisabeth Rozin, and Paul Rozin) were a constant source of inspiration.

I also thank James Allison for sending me the Warm Feet powder. (Will the wonders of capsicum never cease?) Lori-Ann Bonvino Forzano and John Chelonis ably word processed and organized the references.

Ann Streissguth at the University of Washington generously supplied the photographs for Figure 13.2 (the children with fetal alcohol syndrome). Twentieth Century Fox provided the photograph of Marilyn Monroe from the movie *Monkey Business* for Figure 9.1a, and Columbia Pictures provided the photograph of Jamie Lee Curtis from the movie *Perfect* for Figure 9.1b. Phototeque, in New York City, was of great assistance in locating these latter two photographs. Jacob Steiner of Hebrew University in Jerusalem, Israel, kindly provided the photographs of newborn infants tasting various solutions (Figures 5.3 and 5.5).

For the third edition of this book I am indebted to John Wahlert for his many insights into and enthusiasm about chocolate, chile pepper, and computer games; David Szalda for assisting me with chemical calculations; and especially to Yenny Anderson and the librarians of Baruch College and the New York Institute of Technology, all of whom take the science of information retrieval to new heights. Yenny Anderson also prepared some of the figures. Kari Scalchunes and Joyce Mulcahy provided able office assistance and food encouragement when needed. Extremely helpful comments on the manuscript were made by Linda Bartoshuk, Amber D. Hoover, Rebecca A. Pearce, Patrice Tombline, Shawna Vogel, several anonymous reviewers, and especially Susan Brennan. My husband, Ian Shrank, and then teenage son, Samuel Logue Shrank, also gave me many excellent comments on the manuscript. (The only problem with having my son read the manuscript is that he now happily recites to me the five research-based reasons why he doesn't like and won't eat certain dark vegetables or fish.) My agent, Al Zuckerman, rescued the manuscript at a critical time and George Zimmar signed it with proper gastronomic flair.

For the fourth edition, I must particularly thank the extensive library resources of the City University of New York system, and the dynamic and super-knowledgeable head of all of these resources, Curtis Kendrick, University Dean for Libraries and Information Resources. Without his guidance, this book would have been far less than it is. I also want to thank Linda Bartoshuk, Jeffrey Robbins, Peter Todd, Brian Wansink, and several anonymous reviewers for their very helpful comments, and Samuel Logue Shrank and Sylvia Stone for their insights into contemporary culture. My agent, Al Zuckerman, my editor, George Zimmar, and several Routledge/Book Now staff (Maureen Allen, Katharine Atherton, Richard Cook, and Elizabeth Lotto) provided wonderful support at all the right moments.

Throughout it all, the Long Island Railroad provided many, many hours of uninterrupted work time. Harvard University, the State University of New York, Baruch College of the City University of New York, the New York Institute of Technology, the central office of the City University of New York, the United States Public Health Services Biomedical Research Support Grants, the National Institute of Mental Health, and the National Science Foundation all provided funds for research that is reported here. I am especially grateful for the study leave from the City University of New York and for the appointment as a CUNY Research Professor that permitted me to finish the fourth edition. Many ideas and much inspiration came from the students and teaching assistants in my undergraduate and graduate courses on the psychology of eating and drinking, as well as from my many academic colleagues. Finally, I want to express my deepest appreciation to Ian Shrank and Samuel Logue Shrank for their constant unquestioning encouragement and support.

1

INTRODUCTION

The Essential Nutrients of the Psychology of Eating and Drinking

SIR TOBY—

Does not our life consist of the four elements [earth, air, fire, and water]?

SIR ANDREW—

Faith, so they say; but I think it rather consists of eating and drinking.

SIR TOBY—

Thou art a scholar; let us therefore eat and drink.

William Shakespeare (1623/1936)[1]

Have you ever noticed just how much of your time is devoted to eating and drinking, or to thinking about eating and drinking? Pick a day and try keeping a record of the total time that you spend preparing or eating meals and snacks, as well as the time that you spend just thinking about the foods and drinks that you will or won't have. You'll likely find that far more time is devoted to these activities than to anything else, including sex. I once used a stopwatch to record how much total time I spent thinking about or touching food. My total was 4 hours and 33 minutes, and I'm not any more obsessed with food than is the average person. A great deal of the behavior of all animals consists of obtaining and consuming foods and liquids.

It doesn't take a scientist to know this. Supreme Court Justice Sonia Sotomayor stated in her autobiography: "And always food at the center of it all."[2] But it does take a scientist to find out what causes these food- and drink-related behaviors. And once we understand the causes, then we may be able to change these behaviors, something that a lot of people would like to do for many different reasons.

For example, I'm sure that you've noticed that a lot of people consume so much of certain foods and drinks that bad things happen—such as weight gain from eating too much chocolate, high cholesterol from eating too much of certain kinds of fats, and liver damage from drinking too much alcohol. Why do people do these things? And, even more intriguing, why do some people overconsume these foods and drinks more than other people or only at certain times? Why do women tend to crave chocolate at certain points in the menstrual cycle, for instance? We need to understand the causes of behaviors such as these. Once we do, we'll have important information to guide us in modifying these behaviors.

Our fascination with such eating and drinking behaviors and their causes has resulted in a huge industry of food-related pop science. Every bookstore, every magazine stand, every grocery store checkout counter is filled with publications about how to get your child to eat vegetables, how to tell if someone has an eating disorder, or, most commonly, how to lose weight. TV programs and movies on these subjects abound. But the degree to which any of these is based on scientific research is very limited. Thus the information and advice offered is, at best, incomplete, and is often simply incorrect. Let's take as an example the advice that to eat less you should drink lots of water. Have you ever heard that? Well, it's completely untrue; people don't eat less when they drink more water. And after you read this book, you'll understand why.

This book is different from what you'll find in most magazines or books. It will introduce you to the scientific study of eating and drinking behavior. It will show you how scientists, particularly psychologists, conduct research on eating and drinking and what they have been able to find out so far. It will tell you many of the latest discoveries in this field. The answers aren't always simple, and they aren't always what we'd like to hear. But if you want accurate information about what causes our eating and drinking behavior, and about what we can and can't do to change that behavior, you'll get that information here. And while you may not always be able to use that information to change your own behavior or someone else's—serious eating and drinking problems require professional help—you will get much immediately useful information.

What's Psychology Got to Do With Eating and Drinking?

Most of the information in this book is drawn from carefully conducted psychology experiments. *Psychology* is the science of behavior, the science of "how and why organisms do what they do."[3] So if your goal is to understand the behavior of people and other animals, as opposed to, say, the reproduction of plant cells, then psychology is your field.

In this book we'll look at a certain set of behaviors—the behaviors involved in eating and drinking—using many different types of psychological approaches, from the physiological to the social. Our strategy will be to use whatever psychological science can tell us about these behaviors. We have something we want to understand—eating and drinking behaviors—and we're going to use every possible tool to gain that understanding.

Psychology is the science of behavior, and therefore the analytical method that you'll see used throughout the entire book is the scientific method. The scientific method assumes that the laws of nature govern all things and that they do so in a consistent manner for all people and other animals at all times. Without this scientific orientation it would be impossible to conduct experiments to determine the causes of behavior. In an experiment, all conditions are held constant except for one aspect that is manipulated by the experimenter. If this change in one factor is followed by a change in the behavior of the subject, the experimenter concludes that manipulating that factor has the observed effect on behavior.

For example, you might take 10 people, ensure that they had eaten and drunk the exact same things for the 6 hours prior to dinner, have half of them drink a quart of water right before dinner, and then measure how much they all ate during dinner. If, on average, the people who drank the extra water ate less than the other people, you could conclude that drinking lots of water decreases how much people eat right after drinking the water. Of course, this experiment wouldn't tell you what might happen at breakfast the next morning; the water drinkers might make up for their smaller dinners by eating larger breakfasts. You would need to do another experiment, or expand your original experiment, to determine that. All psychological scientists assume a scientific orientation in their work.

The study of the psychology of eating and drinking is a huge but fascinating subject. It includes research on how you detect tastes, why you become hungry or thirsty, why you like some foods more than others, how you choose among foods, how certain foods can affect your behavior, and how and why we sometimes eat and drink in less than ideal ways. It would be impossible to cover all of the psychology of eating and drinking in one book. But I hope that this book will give you a good overview or, more appropriately, a good taste of this subject.

Getting There by Degrees: Evolution and Eating and Drinking

In doing any kind of scientific investigation, it helps if you have some conceptual framework that guides where you're going, some theory or theories that suggest how things work, so that you'll have specific ideas to test and ways to describe your findings as a whole. Psychological science, particularly psychological science as it's applied to eating and drinking behaviors, is often organized around the concepts of evolution and natural selection. The reason that the concepts of evolution and natural selection seem particularly appropriate for the psychology of eating and drinking is that every animal, including every person, must eat and drink appropriately or it will die. This means that any animal that has some genetically influenced behavior or anatomical trait that enables it to eat and drink well will be more likely to survive and will have more offspring than will other members of that species. Therefore you would expect the eating and drinking behaviors of all species to have evolved over the millennia so as to be beneficial; you would expect that, by the process of natural selection, individuals who are well adapted with regard to how they eat and drink have survived and reproduced. Repeatedly in this book you'll hear me say that some way in which a species eats or drinks is adaptive and has helped that species to survive.

At this point I hope that you're saying, "Wait a minute. You're telling me that people and other animals have evolved to eat and drink well. But we all know, and you wrote yourself earlier in this chapter, that people eat and drink in all kinds of harmful ways. If we have evolved to eat well, why is it, for example, that people eat so much chocolate that they gain weight?"

Just because natural selection is and has been in operation doesn't mean that all of the behaviors of every species will be perfectly adapted for every situation. In fact, there are several reasons why an animal's eating behavior might not be optimal. Just one such reason is that you may be observing the animal in a situation different from the one to which its species was adapted. We didn't evolve in surroundings where chocolate was easily and cheaply available around every corner, and with our advanced medical techniques, people usually don't die at young ages from overeating chocolate. Therefore, despite the harmful effects of overeating chocolate, those of us who are chocolate-obsessed are still having lots of children. In this book you'll read many explanations such as this of unhealthy eating and drinking behaviors.

Getting Down to the Subject

Now that we have our theoretical framework for experiments on the psychology of eating and drinking, let's suppose that you're a scientist thinking about an experiment that you might do to find out why people like chocolate so much. Let's assume that you've read research suggesting that a particular gene results in people loving chocolate after they've had many years of exposure to it, and you want to find out for sure if that's true. Therefore you design an experiment in which you'll take 50 people with identical genes, give half of them chocolate from birth to age 25 while preventing the others from having any contact with chocolate during those years, and then test all of the participants' preferences for chocolate when they are and aren't hungry. Sound like a great experiment? Well it is, but there are a few practical problems. To begin with, you'll never find 50 people with identical genes. Even finding two (identical twins) is hard. Second, what scientist is going to have the patience to do an experiment that lasts 25 years? Scientists are under great pressure to publish frequently in order to keep getting research grants and to get promoted at their universities. Third, where are you going to get enough money to do this experiment? The participants will expect to get paid for their time, which will be considerable. And 25 years of chocolate for 25 people will also cost quite a lot. Fourth, you might have to deprive the participants of food for a period of time in order to make sure that they're hungry. Is this ethical?

Issues such as these have resulted in scientists often using animals other than people in their experiments, something that you're going to read a lot about in this book. This should give you some concern; after all, only people behave just like people. However, in addition to the practical considerations, when you're trying to understand people's eating and drinking behaviors, there are good reasons for using animals other than people in the experiments. If I've convinced you that evolution has shaped eating and drinking behaviors, then you must also accept that different species will have at least some similar eating and drinking behaviors. One reason for this is that some species have evolved from relatively recent common origins. For example, all mammals have ancestors in common and, therefore, have some genes in common.

Thus the process of evolution ensures that, even if your primary interest is the eating and drinking behaviors of people, you can learn something of value from studying the eating and drinking behaviors of other species. Let's consider some of the advantages and disadvantages of using different species in our hypothetical chocolate experiment. As you read this material, you should be able to see many similarities in the eating and drinking behaviors of different species, while at the same time noting significant differences in the ways that these different species interact with their particular surroundings.

Let's start with the sea slug *Pleurobranchaea*. This slug is a carnivore—a meat eater. It's not much to look at; the beauty of this animal is definitely more than skin deep. *Pleurobranchaea*, similar to people, has specialized cells (known as neurons) in its body that collect information about its surroundings and cause it to move. Together these cells are known as a neuronal system. *Pleurobranchaea*'s neuronal system is less complex than ours. Therefore its neurons are relatively easily identified and manipulated.

Some of *Pleurobranchaea*'s neurons, called food command neurons, are responsible for making *Pleurobranchaea* move automatically in order to eat food that it has detected. This is an example of a reflex, a specific response that occurs reliably following exposure to specific aspects of the surroundings. In such a case no learning is involved. Scientists have been able to determine that what *Pleurobranchaea* has recently eaten affects this reflex—*Pleurobranchaea*'s motivation—by influencing how much certain inhibitory neurons decrease the activity of the food command neurons. Whether or not this slug eats can also be affected by learning—*Pleurobranchaea*'s knowledge about which events occur together. For example, if an experimenter shocks *Pleurobranchaea* whenever it eats, it will be less likely to approach and consume food.[4] Exciting as it is to be able to see the precise changes in neuronal activity that represent changes in feeding behavior, the usefulness of *Pleurobranchaea* as a model of our feeding behavior is limited due to this species' limited behavioral repertoire. To begin with, due to its carnivorous proclivities, *Pleurobranchaea* would be useless in an experiment on chocolate.

Let's consider using a mammal for our experiment. People are mammals—animals that suckle.[5] Therefore, other mammalian species would seem the most likely choices for studies on the eating and drinking behaviors of people. In the early days of physiological investigations of hunger, one mammalian species—dogs—was a frequent choice for experimental subjects. Dogs, although technically considered carnivores, can consume a wide variety of foods,[6] making their eating behaviors more similar to ours than is the case for *Pleurobranchaea*. Dogs will, on occasion, eat chocolate. In addition, their social behaviors and ability to learn quickly can make them useful in studying a number of eating behaviors that are similar to behaviors seen in people. Some of the earliest and best known feeding research with dogs was conducted by one of the most famous parents of psychology, Ivan Pavlov, beginning around 1900.[7] Pavlov showed that if an attendant repeatedly gave a dog food, the dog would come to salivate simply on hearing the attendant approaching. If you have a cat, you have certainly seen something similar. (See Figure 1.1.) My pet cat, like everyone else's, went crazy when he heard any can being opened. Pavlov's research became the foundation of one of the two major branches of learning theory, the branch concerned with learned and unlearned reflexes that is known as classical conditioning. Nevertheless, despite the fact that dogs sometimes eat chocolate, they are rarely used in current research because they are relatively large in size, take a relatively long time to reach maturity, and are popular pets.

Chimpanzees, another mammalian species, are close evolutionary relatives of people. Therefore, not surprisingly, many of their eating and drinking behaviors are similar to those of people. (See Conversation Making Fact #1.) For example, just like people, they're omnivores; they

"Zelda! Cool it! ... The Rothenbergs hear the can opener!"

Figure 1.1 Drawing by Gary Larson. Copyright 1989 FarWorks, Inc. (Reprinted with permission from Gary Larson, *Wildlife Preserves: A Far Side Collection*, Kansas City: Andrews and McMeel, 1989, p. 92.)

can eat fruit, insects, and meat. In addition, similar to people, chimpanzees use spatial memory to find and remember good food sources.[8] Some of the most fascinating information about the eating and drinking behaviors of chimps has come from the pioneering investigations of primatologist Jane Goodall and her colleagues at the Gombe National Park in Tanzania, East Africa. Goodall was the first to discover that chimps make tools for obtaining food and water: twigs, stripped of leaves, to which termites cling when the twigs are stuck into their nests, and chewed-up leaves that can be used as sponges to obtain water from tree hollows (see Figure 1.2). Never before had a species other than ours been seen to construct tools.[9] Goodall was also the first to discover that chimpanzees hunt other animals and consume their meat. Usually males engage in these hunts and they demonstrate elements of cooperative hunting behavior. One chimp creeps toward the prey while other chimps position themselves to block the prey's escape routes. After the hunters

---

Conversation making fact #1

Do you sprinkle salt on your french fries or on your eggs? Some monkeys also "season" their food. Travel to a small island called Kashima in Japan, and you might see a group of monkeys seasoning their sweet potatoes in saltwater using a method that Japanese scientists saw develop about 60 years ago.[10] In 1952, the scientists began giving the monkeys sweet potatoes to eat. The sweet potatoes were frequently covered with sand. In 1953, a female monkey named Imo began to wash the sweet potatoes. Imo would dip a sweet potato into the water with one hand and then brush off the sand with her other hand. By 1958, approximately 80 percent of the monkeys were washing sweet potatoes. During the period that most of the monkeys began to do this, the way that they washed the potatoes began to change. At first the sweet potatoes had been dipped only in fresh water. By 1961, the potatoes were being dipped primarily in salt water. Further, the monkeys would take a bit of a sweet potato, dip it, and then take another bite, "seasoning" the sweet potato—much yummier than plain sweet potato, and just like what we often do with our food.

Figure 1.2 Chimpanzee obtaining termites from a termite nest.

catch and kill the prey, they often share the food among themselves, as well as with other chimps.[11]

The similarities between our and chimpanzees' eating and drinking behaviors are indeed remarkable. Yet it's precisely this close similarity that makes many people consider chimps an inappropriate choice for experiments. Because chimps are so similar to people, ethical constraints that would apply to using people in experiments might also apply to using chimps. There are also several practical disadvantages to using chimps in experiments. Just as with people, chimps are very expensive to maintain, can be difficult to handle, and take a long time to produce sexually mature offspring. For all of these reasons, psychologists have usually not worked with chimps—or other primates—in the investigation of eating and drinking behaviors.

This brings us, finally, to the rat (surprise!). Perhaps the rat isn't your favorite animal, but without question it's the favorite subject for experiments on the psychology of eating and drinking. There are many reasons for this. The rat's diet is diverse and very similar to that of people, which accounts for its ability to flourish for so many centuries in close association with us. Rats, for example, absolutely love chocolate. In addition, except that they can't vomit, the individual and social behaviors that rats use in avoiding poisons and identifying beneficial foods are in many ways similar to those of people. Further, laboratory rats, bred for docility, are easy to handle.[12] They're also relatively inexpensive to buy and maintain, and they reach sexual maturity only about 2 months after birth.[13] Finally, the extensive amount of information that scientists have already collected concerning rats provides a rich framework into which to place the results of any new investigations.[14]

The scientific literature lists these reasons for why the rat has become the favorite experimental subject. However, I've always wondered whether there might be other contributing factors. Having spent many years with laboratory rats, I can attest to the fact that they can be quite cuddly, even affectionate, similar to hamsters or guinea pigs. At least for me, it's a lot harder to imagine snuggling up to a slug or a chimp than to a rat.

Conclusion

In addition to justifying the liberal use of rat research in the rest of this book, I hope that this chapter has given you a sense of the rich variety and also enormous similarities among different species' eating and drinking behaviors. Similar principles govern the behaviors of many species. Yet each species has adapted to a different part of the world, a particular ecological niche. Each species obtains food and drink from its surroundings in its own particular way.[15] Therefore each species has much to tell us about the nature and origins of eating and drinking behaviors. For many reasons, rats are usually the best choice for studies in which the goal is to apply the results to people. Nevertheless, other species have provided and will provide us with much sustenance in our quest to understand the psychology of eating and drinking.

2

DOWN THE HATCH

Hunger and Satiety

No animal can live without food. Let us then pursue the corollary of this: namely, food is about the most important influence in determining the organization of the brain and the behaviour that the brain organization dictates.

J. Z. Young (1968)[1]

Many of you reading this book are, I'm certain, interested in weight control (most likely your own). In order to modify one's weight, it's extremely helpful to understand the basic factors responsible for the starting and stopping of eating. In other words, you need to understand the basic factors responsible for hunger and satiety. This information will help you understand what might be wrong if someone is eating too much or too little, and will also give you ideas about how to change the amount that someone eats. Perhaps most interestingly, this information will tell you what will *not* affect the amount that someone eats. For example, this chapter will explain why filling up with water won't decrease how many calories you eat, something that anyone familiar with the basic laboratory research on eating knows.

Given that the focus of this chapter is on hunger and satiety, its material is more closely related to physiology than that of most of the other chapters. However, particularly toward the end of this chapter, I'll also discuss the relationships of hunger and satiety to aspects of our surroundings. Think of this chapter as providing you with the psychophysiological framework in which to place much of the social and cultural information on eating that you'll read about in later chapters.

The story of the scientific investigation of hunger and satiety reads like a minihistory of psychology laboratory technique. For each time period, the hot theories about what was responsible for hunger and satiety were very much a function of what laboratory techniques had been developed at that time. So, in the early 20th century, scientists investigated the relationship of stomach contractions to hunger because they had a way to measure

11

those contractions. Later, in the 1940s and 1950s, as surgical techniques advanced, the effects on hunger of different types of substances in the stomach, substances that had or had not arrived there via the mouth, were investigated. Also around this time, investigations of the brain's effects on eating began, investigations that still continue and use ever more specific methods to determine which part or aspect of the brain affects which precise type of behavior. Most recently, techniques have advanced to the degree that scientists can show how specific parts of the brain and chemicals elsewhere in the body work together to influence hunger. Now, in the 21st century, the number of different aspects of the body shown to affect hunger and satiety is dazzling and still growing. In this chapter I'll organize all of the major findings so that you'll get an idea of the results and the significance of hunger and satiety research over the past 100 years.

As we progress through these experiments and their results, it'll be helpful for you to keep a few principles in mind. First, many animals, including people, don't eat continuously. Instead, there are periods of time—meals—during which food consumption occurs frequently and periods of time during which there's little food consumption. So this chapter will be looking at what's responsible for a meal starting and stopping. Note that all else being equal, more food will be consumed during a long meal than during a short meal. Therefore, investigations of what causes hunger and satiety are also investigations of what determines how much is eaten.

Second, investigations of how much is eaten have traditionally been classified into two types: investigations of short-term regulation and long-term regulation, that is, animals' abilities to consume both what will satisfy their short-term energy needs and their abilities to maintain fairly constant body weight over long periods of time. Before you scoff at your ability to maintain body weight over a long period, consider this: Suppose every day you eat 2% more calories than you need, approximately the number of calories in one extra pat of butter or margarine. After 1 year, this would be equivalent to a 5-pound weight gain. So, even if you find yourself gaining 2 or 3 pounds each year, you're still doing a pretty good job of eating very close to the amount that your body needs to maintain its current weight.

In both short-and long-term regulation, our bodies have been thought to behave in a way that is similar to a household thermostat. A thermostat is set for a particular temperature, and if the temperature becomes too warm or too cold, air conditioning or heat kicks in to bring the temperature back to the ideal level. Many theories of hunger have postulated that, in our bodies, there's a physiological characteristic (e.g., available energy or stored fat) that has an optimal level, the set point, and whenever there's a deviation from that optimal level, something happens in the body so that the optimal level is restored. Walter B. Cannon, an early

20th-century American physiologist who is mentioned several times in this chapter, coined the term *homeostasis* to describe processes such as these.[2] In the sections that follow, see if you can identify the theories of hunger and satiety that incorporate the concept of homeostasis, as well as the complications for such theories.

One final caution is in order here. In some of the experiments described in this chapter and in subsequent chapters, people are asked to report how hungry they are or what they have eaten. There has been some disagreement about how meaningful such statements are. Do people's hunger ratings correlate closely with how much they eat, and do people report accurately how much they eat? What people say they felt and what they say they ate don't necessarily correspond to their actual behaviors. For example, sometimes people report eating significantly less than they really ate, sometimes significantly more, and sometimes they can be quite accurate.[3] As long as there are at least some situations in which people's self-reports help us predict their eating behaviors, experimenters will continue to use self-report data.

The number of different factors that have been shown to influence hunger and satiety is truly mind-boggling. To make your comprehension of this material easier, I'm going to divide it into two major categories: investigations of peripheral factors and investigations of central factors. However, as we go along, you'll see that researchers have increasingly looked at the relationships between these two types of factors.

Out of Your Mind (and Brain): Peripheral Factors

Peripheral factors that influence hunger and satiety are those factors involving parts of the body other than the central nervous system (the brain and the spinal cord). Let's follow a piece of chocolate cake as it wends its way from your kitchen table into your mouth, down into your stomach and intestine, to see what peripheral factors might contribute to making you hungry or satiated.

Getting from the living room to the kitchen

You're in your living room watching TV. What are some of the factors that might make you start thinking about going into the kitchen to eat the piece of chocolate cake on the table? Thinking about it enough to get up from your nice comfy couch?

Let's suppose that your stomach growls, and it feels as if it's contracting like crazy. Many people believe that a rumbling stomach is synonymous with hunger and a nonrumbling stomach is synonymous with satiation. Such beliefs led scientists to formulate the stomach contraction theory of hunger, which says that the initiation and termination of eating can be predicted on the basis of stomach contractions. Someone whose stomach has been contracting might be more likely to eat and vice versa.

Cannon's 1912 work on this theory with A. L. Washburn was one of the first experimental studies of hunger.[4] Cannon and Washburn developed a technique for measuring stomach contractions, and Washburn was the first lucky person to experience it. First, Washburn had to become accustomed to having a long tube inserted down his throat into his stomach and left there for several hours each day. One end of the tube was in his stomach, and the other end was outside his mouth. During the experiment, air was passed into the outer end of the tube to inflate partially a balloon attached to the end of the tube that was in Washburn's stomach. (Washburn must have been a very dedicated scientist!) Stomach contractions were measured by monitoring changes in air pressure in the balloon. Washburn pressed a telegraph key whenever he felt hungry. His stomach contractions were closely associated with his reports of hunger. Apparently, Washburn would report hunger at the height of a contraction, not at the beginning, which suggested that the stomach contractions caused the feelings of hunger and not the other way around. When Washburn wasn't hungry there were no contractions. Follow-up studies with additional subjects obtained similar results.[5] The stomach contraction theory was the first peripheral theory of hunger to receive experimental support, and it was the dominant peripheral theory for many years.

However, subsequent studies showed that neither stomach contractions nor even a stomach are necessary prerequisites for reports of hunger.[6] Further, as more sophisticated methods of measuring stomach contractions have been developed, the relationship between hunger and stomach contractions has been found to be extremely weak.[7] Therefore the stomach contraction theory of hunger now appears to be primarily of historical interest.

You've still got to get from that living room into the kitchen. If stomach contractions won't get you moving, what might? Suppose, in flipping channels, you happen upon a cooking show about how to make the perfect chocolate cake. All of a sudden you're dying for that piece of chocolate cake on your kitchen table. Have you ever noticed that smelling food, hearing cooking noises, or just looking at food makes you feel hungry? You're not imagining this. What's happening to you is related to what happened to Pavlov's dogs. As you will recall, Pavlov showed that dogs would salivate when they heard or saw something that had previously been associated with food. Similar to the dogs, you also salivate when you hear or see or smell things that have been associated with food. And salivation isn't the only response that your body has to these situations. Even if you haven't yet touched the food, your pancreas may secrete insulin, a chemical involved in the metabolism of sugar. The insulin lowers your blood sugar level, which makes you feel hungry. There are several such reflexes that are related to the ingestion and digestion of food and that occur immediately upon—or, with experience, even prior to—our contact with food.[8]

Understanding how these salivation and insulin responses occur can help in understanding the differences in hunger between Muslim men and women during Ramadan. Ramadan is the month during which devout Muslims fast from sunrise to sunset. Researchers have shown that, during the initial days of Ramadan, women report being significantly more hungry than men. However, during the latter days of Ramadan, women and men report approximately equal levels of hunger. As it turns out, during Ramadan, the men aren't usually at home during the fasting periods. In contrast, the women are at home and are involved in preparing food for the children to eat during the day and food for the adults to eat after sunset. Thus, during the fasting periods, the women are probably exposed to far more odors, sounds, and sights that are associated with food than are the men. However, as the month of Ramadan proceeds, the food-related phenomena to which the women are exposed during the day are never accompanied by the women ingesting food. Therefore those phenomena are no longer associated with food ingestion.[9] This may stop salivation or insulin release and result in decreased hunger.

Getting the cake into your mouth

You've taken the big step and entered the kitchen. Now, with that cake staring you in the face, you're releasing more insulin and are feeling hungrier. But the kitchen's window air conditioner breaks, and because it's July and 95°F (35°C) outside, the kitchen quickly becomes unpleasantly hot and stuffy. Suddenly, you're no longer so interested in that chocolate cake.

The surrounding air temperature is well known to affect hunger. If your kitchen is hot, it's likely that you'll eat less than when your kitchen is a little chilly. One explanation for this influence of the surrounding temperature on the amount eaten is that in cold weather the body needs more fuel to keep itself heated to 98.6°F (37°C), and a major source of heat for any animal is the food it consumes. Therefore it's possible that initiation and termination of feeding are related to the maintenance of a specific, optimally efficient body temperature. If this sounds to you like a homeostatic process, you're exactly right! The temperature theory of hunger was proposed in the late 1940s.[10] Since then, experiments with rats and people have supported it—animals do consume more in cold surroundings. Experiments have also shown that exposure to cold surroundings speeds the movement of previously consumed food from the stomach into the intestine. Such a process would, of course, decrease whatever it is about food in the stomach that normally inhibits feeding,[11] and thus this finding helps to explain why animals eat more in the cold.

Cake in the mouth

Let's suppose that you felt hungry enough that you've now put the chocolate cake into your mouth. Does the food's stimulation of your mouth affect your hunger and satiety?

In order to determine whether oral factors by themselves contribute to hunger and satiety, over 50 years ago researchers developed a particular type of surgery called an esophagostomy. You may find the description of this surgery difficult and unpleasant to read. Performing an esophagostomy was one of the few then-available techniques that could be used to separate the influence of oral and gastric factors on hunger and satiety. This surgery involves first bringing the subject's esophagus—the tube through which food passes from the mouth to the stomach—out through the neck. The esophagus is then cut, forming an upper and a lower piece. If an animal that has had this operation eats, the food consumed passes out through the animal's neck instead of continuing to its stomach. This is known as sham feeding. An animal that is sham fed has all of the usual oral experiences that accompany feeding but none of the sensations that originate in the stomach. The subject tastes, chews, and swallows the food, but the stomach never receives it.

Scientists Henry D. Janowitz and M. I. Grossman were among the first researchers to use this surgical technique. They reported that sham fed dogs eventually stop eating, but before they stop they consume much more food than usual.[12] Over many sham feedings, the amount of food eaten increases.[13] Once the animals learn that food in the mouth is no longer associated with food reaching the stomach, the satiating ability of food in the mouth ceases. Thus, oral factors can contribute to the cessation of eating, but by themselves oral factors don't precisely regulate food intake. (See Conversation Making Fact #2.)

Conversation making fact #2

Chewing gum (sugar-free or regular), or just chewing your food more, can decrease both how hungry you then feel and how much you then eat.[14] In middle school my teachers told me that chewing gum would make me look like a cud-chewing cow and I've never been able to chew gum since, which now seems very unfortunate!

Assuming that you're not engaging in sham feeding, what characteristics of that piece of food in your mouth might affect whether or not you feel hungry? One food characteristic that has been widely investigated in this regard is whether the food is sweet. Both rats and people eat more of sweet than nonsweet foods, even if the number of calories in these foods is equal. In other words, even if a food is made sweet using a noncaloric sweetener, animals will eat more of it than had it not been sweet. One possible explanation of these findings is that the presence of a sweet taste causes more insulin to be released than if there's no sweet taste, thus lowering blood sugar to a greater degree and making someone feel hungrier. Another possible explanation is that when we eat food that is sweet, the body makes less of what's eaten available for immediate use and stores more of it than if what was eaten weren't sweet. Therefore, when we eat sweet food, in order to have enough energy for our immediate needs, we have to eat relatively large amounts. There may be similar explanations for the fact that we eat lots of any good-tasting food.[15]

The cake in the gastrointestinal tract

You've chewed up and swallowed that piece of cake and now it's in your stomach, on its way to the small and large intestines. What effects does the presence of food within the gastrointestinal (GI) tract have on your feeling hungry or full? In a survey of college students, most said that the reason they stop eating is because they feel full.[16] But what's responsible for that feeling? What can increase or decrease it?

Investigation of GI effects is complicated because, ordinarily, food gets to the GI tract by way of the mouth. Therefore, effects of food in the GI tract could be due to either the oral or the GI stimulation provided by the food, or both. Nevertheless, just as with oral factors, researchers have come up with ways to isolate the effects of GI factors. For example, researchers can insert food directly into the lower portion of the esophagus following an esophagostomy, thus bypassing oral factors. Alternatively, they can make a hole by which food or an undigestible substance such as an inflated balloon can be inserted directly into the stomach from outside the body. When what's inserted is food, this process is known as intragastric feeding.

Several scientists, including sham feeding researchers Janowitz and Grossman, have investigated the effects of intragastric feeding on dogs' eating behaviors. These researchers have put different amounts of food and other substances directly into the stomach. For example, they have studied the effects of inserting an inflated balloon into the stomach. One finding from this research is that intragastric feeding decreases sham feeding only when intragastric feeding is large and occurs at the same time as sham feeding. Further, a balloon has no effect on feeding unless the balloon is so inflated that it causes nausea and retching. Finally, dogs with holes directly into the stomach or with esophagostomies can eventually learn to eat less when they have been fed intragastrically.[17]

In addition, we now know that foods that are very high fat or that have a lot of fiber are more satiating. The precise reasons for this increased satiety aren't known. It may be that a food's viscosity or amount of fiber affects absorption of that food's nutrients or the speed with which that food passes through the GI tract.[18] Further, even with the total number of calories consumed held constant, higher volumes of food are more satiating than lower volumes if the foods contain at least some calories.[19]

If you're a good detective you'll have put all of these pieces of evidence together into a fairly consistent story. Here's my version. Putting something in the stomach so that the stomach stretches isn't very influential in getting us to stop eating unless the stretching is extreme or is accompanied by nutrients in the GI tract.[20] This explains why drinking lots of water or inserting an inflated balloon into the stomach aren't very effective in decreasing food consumption. Although these substances stretch the stomach, they contain no nutrients, and thus they won't increase satiety effectively.

Effects of digestion and storage of the cake

You've eaten the cake. Now it'll be digested, and some of it may be stored as fat. What effects might these processes have on hunger and satiety?

When you digest food, including chocolate cake, the amounts of certain chemicals in your body increase. Some of these chemicals are the products of the digestion of food. Others are the chemicals produced by the body to aid in the digestion of food. The presence of high levels of chemicals in either group can act as a signal to your body that food has been consumed and so eating should stop. Conversely, when the levels of these chemicals are low, this can signal your body to start eating. A large number of such possible signals have been investigated.

A good chemical signal of currently available energy would be one that increases quickly following feeding and slowly decreases with time until the next feeding. Internationally known physiologist and nutritionist Jean Mayer realized that there was such a signal when he formulated the glucostatic theory of hunger in 1953.[21] The glucostatic theory postulates that hunger is related to blood sugar level and that information about the energy available to an animal is indicated by the level of sugar in the blood. In addition to rising quickly and then decreasing slowly following feeding, blood sugar is known to be the primary energy source for the central nervous system. Therefore, you would expect animals to have evolved so as to use eating to ensure that adequate levels of blood sugar are maintained.

As a refinement to his model, Mayer proposed that it wasn't the absolute level of blood sugar that was important in the initiation and termination of feeding, but the difference between the levels in the arteries and veins. Arteries take blood to the body's tissues, and veins return blood from those same tissues. If the blood sugar level is high in the arteries but low in the veins, sugar is being removed from the blood as it passes from the arteries through various tissues and then into the veins. In such cases the body is receiving a fair amount of sugar. If the blood sugar level in both the arteries and veins is low, then the body isn't receiving much sugar. In support of his theory, Mayer found that the difference between the blood sugar levels in the arteries and veins correlated well with people's reports of hunger.[22]

Mayer realized that his glucostatic mechanism would make errors on a daily basis and that some long-term mechanism would be needed to correct those errors. A mechanism related to the fat stores in the body was the obvious choice. Our bodies store excess energy as fat. One pound of fat is equivalent to 3,500 calories. In order to use this storage system to correct errors made by the glucostatic mechanism, the body must have a way of detecting the extent of its energy stores. Lipostatic theories propose that a circulating chemical related to the amount of the body's stored fat is responsible for long-term regulation of stored fat; when the chemical indicates that fat stores are low or decreasing, eating should increase, and vice versa. In this way, the glucostatic and lipostatic mechanisms could work together to regulate the body's food intake on both a daily and a long-term basis. Mayer was among the first to propose a lipostatic theory of long-term regulation.[23]

Over the years since lipostatic theories were first developed, researchers have proposed several candidates for the chemical that signals the amount of stored fat, including leptin, a hormone found in the blood and manufactured by the cells that store fat. The level of leptin in the body is related to the amount of stored fat.[24]

In the meantime, while lipostatic theories were developing, the glucostatic theory of hunger encountered some bumps. Unfortunately, there hasn't been extensive evidence supporting the difference in blood sugar between the arteries and veins as a primary determinant of hunger.[25] Therefore, researchers have proposed alternatives. One of the most frequently used has become the glycemic index. The glycemic index score for a given food has to do with your body's metabolic response to that food (see Table 2.1). More specifically, when you eat a certain number of calories of a particular type of food, the glycemic index measures how much total glucose is subsequently added to your blood during a specified period of time (see Figure 2.1).[26]

Table 2.1 Typical glycemic index scores for sample foods

Food	Glycemic Index
Bread	100
Rice Bubbles (Rice Krispies) cereal	116
Porridge oats (oatmeal)	60
All-Bran cereal	43
Eggs and bacon	24

Source: S. Holt, J. Brand, and C. Soveny, "Relationship of Satiety to Postprandial Glycaemic, Insulin, and Cholecystokinin Responses," *Appetite* 18 (1992): 129–141.

If a particular food results in a lot of added blood sugar, then that food gets a high glycemic index score and vice versa. High glycemic scores are associated with hunger and low scores with satiety.[27] This is an explanation of satiety and blood sugar that takes into account how blood sugar changes over time. (What a daunting thought. It appears that it is not just the amounts of many body chemicals that are involved in hunger and satiety, but the temporal patterns of these chemicals as well.)

Figure 2.1 Effects of high and low glycemic index foods on blood glucose over time. (From S. B. Roberts and A. G. Pittas, "The Role of Glycemic Index in Type 2 Diabetes," *Nutrition in Clinical Care* 6[2003]: 73–78. Reprinted with permission from S. B. Roberts and A. G. Pittas.)

20

Many factors contribute to the glycemic index score. These factors include the chemical structure of a food, the amount of fiber in that food, and how the food has been processed. For example, oatmeal, which is high in fiber, has a lower glycemic index score than Rice Bubbles(Rice Krispies) cereal, which contains finely milled grains.[28] Similarly, adding salad to your meal or flax seed to your food can also help to increase satiation.[29]

In an intriguing experiment, scientists J. H. Lavin and N. W. Read gave 10 young men a radioactive, 300-calorie, orange-tasting, glucose drink and then measured the amounts of glucose and insulin in the men's blood for the next 3 hours, as well as the men's hunger ratings, fullness ratings, and amounts of radioactivity in the men's stomachs. Each man came to the laboratory twice; on one day he had the basic glucose drink, and on the other day he had that drink with the addition of guar gum. Guar gum is an inert substance that isn't digested. The results showed that after consuming the guar gum as compared to the regular drink, the participants' glycemic index scores, plasma insulin levels, and hunger were all lower. These results indicate that slowing the absorption of glucose, in this case by the use of guar gum, makes people feel more full. Lavin and Read also showed that there were no significant differences over time in the changes of the amounts of radioactivity in the stomach; there was no difference in how long the drink stayed in the stomach with and without the guar gum. Based on this evidence, the researchers believed that the guar gum drink was more satiating because it extended the contact between the molecules of glucose and the glucose receptor cells in the small intestine, the next location after the stomach on the drink's trip through the gastrointestinal tract.[30]

I do have one question about this experiment, however. Did the guar gum change the taste of the drink? We know that eating good-tasting foods results in the release of more insulin than eating not-so-good-tasting foods. Perhaps the guar gum drink resulted in a lower glycemic index score because the drink didn't taste as good with the guar gum. The authors don't discuss this possibility or report any data on the taste of the two drinks, so unfortunately, at present, there's no answer to my question.

Among the chemicals produced by the body to aid in food digestion, three of the most investigated in terms of their import for hunger and satiety are insulin, cholecystokinin (CCK), and glucagon. There is a great deal of evidence that insulin outside of the central nervous system is a satiating agent—insulin produced by the pancreas during the digestion of food does reduce subsequent food intake.[31] Experiments also suggest that CCK, which is produced in the small intestine during digestion, may help to terminate feeding.[32] In one experiment, rat pups were first administered a chemical that causes the release of CCK from the small intestine. These experimental rats subsequently ate less than untreated rats.[33] Similar to insulin, glucagon is produced in the pancreas. One experiment gave small doses of glucagon (like the levels that occur naturally after food consumption) intravenously to people. These people subsequently ate less food than if they had not been given glucagon.[34] Therefore glucagon may be another naturally occurring substance that plays an influential role in satiety.

Types of foods

By this point, you're probably pretty well satiated with the effects on hunger and satiation of different levels of your body's different chemicals. So let's turn to something else. What sorts of foods increase and decrease hunger? You already know that foods that have a lot of fiber are more satiating. Does a food's caloric density affect how much we eat? A gram of one food can have a lot more, or a lot fewer, calories than a gram of another food. Consider our infamous piece of chocolate cake. The cake could be made with a high proportion of fat (which contains 9 calories per gram) or with a high proportion of sugar (which contains 4 calories per gram). Will we eat different amounts of chocolate cake (or other food) depending on the relative proportions of fat and sugar in it? This is a question to which I would personally like an answer because I have been known to buy and eat low-fat, low-calorie chocolate truffle cake.

A great many experiments have been conducted to answer this question. In general, these experiments find that, when single meals are examined, eating a high-calorie food can cause us to eat less afterward.[35] Similarly, over the long term and many meals, if animals are fed foods that are relatively low in caloric density as part of their regular diet, they will eat more so that their total caloric intake remains the same.[36] This is disappointing news—after all, what's the point of buying that low-calorie chocolate truffle cake? But this news shouldn't be that surprising. When we were evolving, in order to maintain adequate fat stores, our bodies had to be able to compensate by eating more when food supplies were relatively poor in calories.

Nevertheless, psychologists repeatedly tantalize us with experiments showing that certain foods under certain conditions result in more short-term satiation than other foods. For example, with calories held constant, eating a meal of meatballs is more satiating that eating a meal of pasta; tomato soup is more satiating than crackers with cheese or than melon; prunes are more satiating than low-fat cookies; protein is more satiating than carbohydrates; and eating the exact same food in liquid form isn't as satiating as eating it in solid form (perhaps because there's less chewing—see Conversation Making Fact #2).[37]

In general, these sorts of experiments seem to indicate that the lower the glycemic index score, then the less insulin released, the more cholecystokinin released in the small intestine, the higher the satiety, and the less food that's eaten. Certain foods fill us up faster. Enjoy a meal of dehydrated tomato soup with meatballs and prunes for dessert!

Conclusion to peripheral factors

I hope that, by learning about the many different factors that contribute to our starting and ending meals, you're also learning to appreciate how exquisitely constructed our bodies are. Eating the right amount of food is absolutely essential to survival. Therefore it's not surprising that our bodies have apparently evolved with a number of different, sometimes redundant, mechanisms that each help to ensure that the correct amount of food is consumed. Should one of these mechanisms fail for any reason, another will still be in effect so that we are unlikely to starve or eat ourselves to death. These different mechanisms work together to guarantee that eating is basically within normal limits. You'll see more examples of our bodies' exquisite construction and redundancy as we now turn to the central nervous system factors that are involved in hunger and satiety.

Food on Your Mind: Central Factors

Ever since scientists began investigating the influence of the central nervous system on the initiation and termination of feeding, they have viewed the brain as first receiving information about what's going on inside and outside of the body and then causing the body to take some action. The initial experiments tried to identify the many individual parts of the brain, each made up of millions of neurons, that were responsible for these sorts of central functions. In recent years, investigations of the role of the central nervous system in hunger and satiety have grown far more complex. These more recent investigations include examinations of the combined effects of activity in several parts of the brain, as well as examinations of the effects of a variety of chemical substances present in the brain. What follows is a semihistorical review of the highlights of the research on central factors.

Hunger and satiety centers

This story begins with a now famous case of obesity in an adolescent boy with a large tumor of the pituitary gland around 1900:

R. D., a boy, was born in 1887.... Since March 1899 the patient, who previously had been slim, had been rapidly gaining weight. In January 1901 he complained about diminishing eyesight on the left.... Later, vision in the right eye also began to fail.... Since the patient suffered from severe headaches and his eyesight was rapidly decreasing, an operative procedure appeared justified. The operation by the nasal route was performed by von Eiselsberg on June 21 [1907]. In the depth of the sphenoid sinus the whitish membrane of a cyst the size of a hazelnut was encountered. After incision in the midline, several spoonfuls of a fluid resembling old blood drained out. By measuring with the finger and comparison with the roentgenogram, it could be ascertained that the cyst which contained this fluid corresponded to the hypophysis [the pituitary gland, connected to and near the hypothalamus]. The walls of the cavity were cut away as far as could be done without damaging the optic chiasm and the carotid arteries.... The postoperative course was favorable.... There was considerable improvement in the general condition.[38]

Information such as this suggested that the hypothalamus might be involved in satiety; interference with the hypothalamus apparently resulted in overeating and obesity.

By 1940 science had advanced far enough that scientists A. W. Hetherington and S. W. Ranson were able to conduct a detailed physiological study of the brain and the control of feeding.[39] They inserted small electrodes into the brains of anesthetized rats, more specifically, into the area of the hypothalamus. When an electrode was in the proper place, an electrical current was passed through it, thereby destroying the surrounding cells. Several such small lesions were made in each rat's brain. The rats subjected to this procedure usually recovered after the operation and appeared fairly normal. However, they ate excessively and became obese, behavior known as hyperphagia. The most likely place, if lesioned, that would result in obesity was the ventromedial hypothalamus (VMH). Therefore the researchers concluded that the VMH was involved in the control of satiety. Additional research showed that stimulation of the VMH (activating the cells with an electrical current, rather than destroying them with lesions) inhibits eating,[40] which seemed to confirm that the VMH functions as a satiety center. Further, it was discovered that there are cells in the VMH that are sensitive to one kind of sugar, glucose, and that destroying these cells caused rats to behave similarly to VMH-lesioned rats.[41] This suggested that the VMH receives information about blood sugar levels, thus allowing it to serve as a central collection center for information about the body energy level. (See Figure 2.2.)

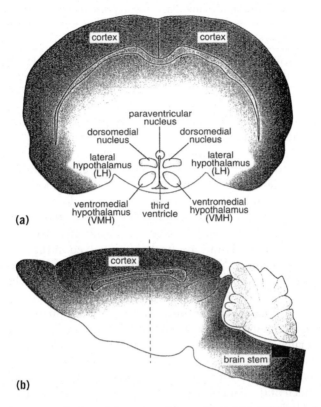

Figure 2.2 Diagram of some of the parts of the rat brain that have been found to be important in the initiation and termination of feeding. The top panel (a) is a vertical cross section of the brain. The bottom panel (b) gives a side view of the brain in which the front part of the brain is to the left. The vertical line drawn through this side view shows the location of the cross section. The shaded rectangle in panel b is the part of the caudal (that is, posterior) brain stem containing the area postrema. (Adapted from R. J. Martin, B. D. White, and M. G. Hulsey, "The Regulation of Body Weight," *American Scientist* 79[1991]: 528–541.)

During the next decade, scientists reasoned that if there were a location in the VMH that controls satiety, there might also be a location in the hypothalamus that's involved in hunger. Physiologists Bal K. Anand and John R. Brobeck's 1951 report[42] identified such a location as the lateral hypothalamus (LH). Their research seemed to show that destruction of this specific area of the hypothalamus resulted in rats that would never eat again, rats that eventually die of starvation. Further, it was shown that stimulation of the LH induced rats to eat.[43]

Together, the data that had been collected through the 1950s seemed to form a tidy package, as indicated in Table 2.2. Based on this evidence,

Table 2.2 Summary of findings involving the hypothalamus in the mid-1950s

Area of Hypothalamus	Lesion	Stimulation
Ventromedial hypothalamus	Increases eating	Decreases eating
Lateral hypothalamus	Decreases eating	Increases eating

in 1954 psychologist Eliot Stellar formally proposed that the VMH is the brain's satiety center and the LH is its hunger center.[44] According to Stellar, these centers, essentially little brains within a larger brain, gather information about, for example, the body's temperature and blood sugar level using a variety of sensory receptors in the hypothalamus; synthesize this information; and then may cause the body to do something, such as eat. Stellar saw brain centers as major locations in the brain that integrate information. However, he stated specifically that areas of the brain other than the hypothalamus are probably involved in the initiation and termination of feeding. Note that Stellar's concept of brain centers did not eliminate the peripheral theories that we talked about earlier. Instead, Stellar's concept of brain centers integrated peripheral theories with central theories of hunger. The brain centers theory dominated study of the initiation and termination of feeding for many years.

Unfortunately, in the 55 years since Stellar first proposed the hunger and satiety centers hypothesis, a number of research findings have revealed problems with it. One major problem concerns the methods that were used to collect much of the data on which the hypothesis was based. These experiments used lesions or stimulation of particular parts of the brain. It can be very difficult to be precisely certain about what particular behavior has been affected by lesions or stimulation. Every action consists of many component actions. The act of eating a forkful of peas after being instructed to do so by one of your parents involves hearing and understanding the instruction, seeing the peas, bringing the fork to the peas, balancing the peas on the tines of the fork, bringing the fork to your mouth, scooping the peas into your mouth, chewing the peas, swallowing them, and in some way finding this act worth doing (if only to avoid your parent's wrath). A brain lesion, or brain stimulation that interfered with eating peas, might do so by interfering with any one or several of these components of the act of pea eating. Psychologists are now aware that interfering with what seems to be a very small part of the brain can have profound effects on general arousal or on complex sensory functions.[45] Thus, with regard to the brain centers theory of hunger, it's possible that the brain lesions and/or stimulation affected motor or sensory behavior instead of interfering with hunger and satiety.

Another major difficulty with the hunger and satiety centers hypothesis is the degree to which the lesions and stimulation were actually limited to the parts of the brain where they were supposed to be. These manipulations may have affected larger areas than were intended. In part this may have been due to the shape of neurons; a neuron can have a central part (the cell body) and extensions (fibers) as long as 1 meter. As a result, the lesions and stimulation may have affected neuronal fibers passing through the lesion/stimulation areas, and not just cell bodies at those locations. There seems to be some validity to such criticisms. For example, it appears that lesions strictly confined to the VMH are less effective at inducing the VMH syndrome than lesions not strictly confined to the VMH.[46]

Still another problem with the hunger and satiety centers hypothesis is that experiments have shown that other parts of the brain, including all of those named in Figure 2.2, are also very important in detecting aspects of the surroundings and initiating behaviors related to feeding.[47] Research has shown how these areas of the brain work together in starting and stopping eating. For example, it's now believed that areas of the brain, such as the paraventricular nucleus, monitor and regulate what's going on in the body and then pass their information to the lateral hypothalamus. The LH then influences the brain's frontal cortex, which then affects how the animal plans and performs specific behaviors.[48] Recent research has also been pointing to a part of the brain called the amygdala, which sends projections to the hypothalamus, as essential in the control of feeding.[49]

Not all experimental results have been incompatible with the hunger and satiety centers hypothesis. For example, data from one study[50] showed that putting food in the small intestine quickly results in less activity in the LH and more activity in the VMH. These changes in brain activity were probably the result of information conveyed by the vagus nerve, which projects between the intestine and the part of the brain containing the hypothalamus.

The hypothalamus is one of the major integrators of information about what's going on inside and outside of the body, and of activity from higher and lower brain structures.[51] However, the little brains within a brain that would have so neatly explained the initiation and termination of eating simply don't exist.

Chemical substances in the brain

It's not just the anatomy of the brain that influences the initiation and termination of feeding; the chemical substances present in the brain are also very important. In fact, the effects of brain chemistry on feeding may be particularly intriguing because a thorough understanding of the influence of brain chemistry on feeding might allow us to develop drugs that would be highly effective in treating anorexia or overeating. One group of brain chemicals that has received intense scrutiny is the neurotransmitters, the chemical substances released in the small gaps between two adjoining neurons. These chemicals are necessary for the occurrence of the electrical impulses by which neurons communicate. Two types of neurotransmitters that have been extensively investigated are dopamine and serotonin. It has been known for many years that both of these neurotransmitters inhibit feeding.[52] Recent experiments have examined how these two neurotransmitters might work together in this regard. For example, a review of data from several studies indicated that the interaction of dopamine and serotonin within the LH affects the size of the meals that an animal eats, and that the dopamine and serotonin within the VMH affect the frequency with which an animal eats. These aren't the only mechanisms by which meal size and meal frequency are determined, but they're important ones.[53]

Other chemical substances present in the brain can also affect the initiation and termination of feeding. One example is neuropeptide Y. This substance modulates the effects of neurotransmitters. Ultimately, it increases eating, primarily by affecting the hypothalamus. Research suggests that when excess neuropeptide Y is present for extended periods, significant overeating and obesity can result. In contrast, inactivation of neuropeptide Y inhibits eating.[54] Another example is a protein called apolipoprotein A-IV, which is naturally present in the fluid within the central nervous system. When this protein is infused into the third ventricle of the brain, eating decreases.[55] These are just some of the great many chemical substances involved in the initiation and termination of feeding within the central nervous system.

Putting It all Together: Combinations and Interactions of Different Factors

We've spent most of this chapter pulling apart and examining separately the various peripheral and central factors that affect hunger and satiety. Now it's time to try to put things back together. How do different mechanisms work as a team to determine when we start and stop eating? The answers are complex, and continuously developing. It's extremely exciting research because we can finally see how influences inside and outside of the body combine in determining how much and how frequently we eat.

Combinations of peripheral and central factors

You've already been given some hints about how peripheral and central factors can work together. One such case was when we discussed how the hypothalamus detects the presence of blood sugar, thus integrating the glucostatic (peripheral) and the VMH (central) theories of hunger. Lots of other similar connections have been investigated.

For example, several researchers now believe that insulin links both peripheral and central control of feeding (see Figure 2.3a). As you'll recall, the level of insulin released by the pancreas increases either when an animal eats food or experiences things, such as the smell of chocolate, that have been previously associated with food consumption. An additional fact is that, when nothing associated with food is present, insulin levels are higher in individuals with more body fat. Finally, insulin circulating in the peripheral blood supply can enter the brain, and the more insulin that enters the brain, the less the central nervous system causes eating, and body weight decreases. Together, all of this information indicates that insulin level is an important factor in the short-term initiation and termination of feeding as well as in the long-term control of body weight, with both peripheral and central mechanisms at work.[56]

Figure 2.3b shows another pathway that links peripheral and central controls of feeding. The more fat someone has, the higher the level of leptin in that person's bloodstream. It's believed that special cells in the brain (e.g., in the paraventricular nucleus in the hypothalamus) detect these leptin levels. Further, leptin inhibits the production of neuropeptide Y. Therefore, when leptin levels are high, levels of neuropeptide Y decrease, causing decreased eating.[57]

Finally, let's consider the example of CCK (Figure 2.3c). When first we met CCK in this chapter, it was described as an intestinal chemical involved in the peripheral control of hunger and satiety. We now also know that there are special cells both in the periphery and in the brain that are sensitive to—in other words, behave differently in—the presence of CCK. Further, it appears that CCK released in the periphery affects the vagus nerve, which then sends information to the brain, resulting in the termination of feeding.[58]

The effects of our surroundings, memory, and learning

It's essential, in all of this discussion of anatomy and chemicals, not to forget the influence of our surroundings on eating behavior. The presence or absence of food and things associated with food ultimately cause all of the bodily reactions that we've been discussing. Furthermore, the act of eating, or of not eating, is by definition an act that involves interaction with the world around us. At least partly for these reasons, it has been argued that the only way to determine an animal's homeostatic set point is to know what's going on around that animal. For example, even though hens eat 20% less than usual when they're incubating eggs, we shouldn't describe this behavior as nonhomeostatic. There are so many ways in which our surroundings affect what should be considered homeostatic behavior that it has been suggested that the whole concept of homeostasis be abandoned.[59]

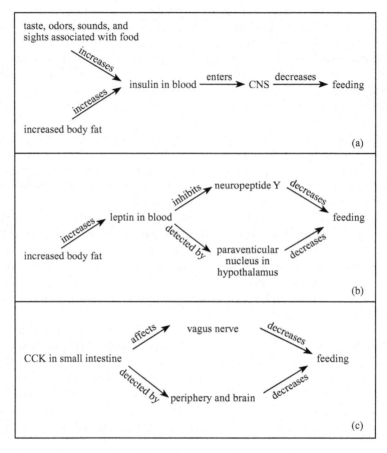

Figure 2.3 Three examples of combinations of peripheral and central factors:
(a) insulin; (b) leptin; (c) CCK.

Not only current surroundings, but experience with past surroundings (memory and learning), greatly influence hunger and satiety. In fact, similar memory and learning processes that operate in other contexts also affect when we start and stop eating. For example, reminders of the previous meal—of how much and what was eaten—influence the next meal.[60] Brain-damaged patients with no memory for events more than 1 minute ago will eat a second lunch 10 minutes after a first lunch, but people with no brain damage won't.[61]

For an example involving undamaged memory processes, consider an experiment conducted by Suzanne Higgs and Jessica E. Donohue. These researchers asked some female undergraduates to focus on the sensory aspects of their food while eating lunch, other female undergraduates to read a food-related newspaper article while eating lunch, and a third group to just eat lunch. Higgs and Donohue measured each student's cookie eating later that afternoon. As it turned out, students who were in the food-focused group ate significantly fewer cookies than those in the other two groups. Not surprisingly, students in the food-focused group also remembered their lunches better than students in the other two groups. Thus, activities that increase memory of a meal may also serve to decrease food intake following a meal.[62]

As another example, I've already explained how odors, sounds, and sights previously associated with food can affect what goes on in the body concerning hunger and satiety. More specifically, you'll recall that just as food you've eaten will cause insulin to be released, so will aspects of your surroundings that have been previously associated with food. Such an explanation can help us understand the differences between men's and women's hunger levels during Ramadan. These learned reactions of the body to upcoming meals have been described as the body's way of anticipating and decreasing the large, potentially harmful, ups and downs in homeostatic functions that are caused by eating food.[63]

As a fourth example, if rats have learned to associate a particular odor such as almond or violet with the later stages of a meal of a highly caloric carbohydrate solution, they will drink less of another carbohydrate solution if that odor is present than if a novel odor is present.[64] The rats apparently learn that the odor indicates that they have consumed a lot of calories. Thus learning associated with an odor can help to control meal volume.

As a final example, psychologist Leann Birch and her colleagues first repeatedly gave preschool children snacks in a specific location where they could see a rotating red light and hear a certain song, but not in another location with other sights and sounds. Later, even if the children had been recently fed, they were more likely to eat in the presence of the sights and sounds that had been associated with eating in the past than in the presence of cues that had not.[65]

Some psychologists, known as psychodynamic theorists, believe that although hunger has a physiological basis, it's immediately affected by learning. They believe that an animal learns how to regulate its intake properly according to its energy needs based on its early eating experiences.[66] As a result of learning, eating can become associated in early life with experiences that usually accompany feeding, such as a parent's attention and warmth. It's therefore easy to see how "love" could become associated with food ("the way to a man's heart is through his stomach"), although love and food might have originally been independent. Psychodynamic theories postulate that eating can come to stand for many things and thus can occur inappropriately. According to this view, it's understandable that a child might come to eat when frightened or lonely, since he or she has associated feeding with security and a mother's love.[67] Alternatively, if early caregivers are wise in feeding a child and respond well to the child's biological needs, they can teach the child to consume food only when it's really needed. Although the psychodynamic approach seems an eminently reasonable one, we have little in the way of research findings to make its conclusions significant for experimental psychologists.

Conclusion

Now you should have a pretty good idea about many of the factors involved in your wanting to eat that piece of chocolate cake, and about how chewing and swallowing that cake affects your wanting to eat more of it. Although, contrary to what was originally thought, stomach contractions and stomach distention per se don't appear to play a leading role in the starting and stopping of eating, many other factors do. These include peripheral factors such as the surrounding air temperature, oral factors, food volume, and blood sugar level changes. You've also learned about the influences of the levels of certain chemicals in the GI tract and in the central nervous system, as well as the importance of certain parts of the central nervous system. You've even learned how peripheral factors and the central nervous system might work together. Finally, you've learned about how important it is to know what's going on in an animal's surroundings, and to know what experiences an animal has had with its surroundings, if you want to do a good job predicting whether or not it will start or stop eating. In sum, there has been ample opportunity for you to see how beautifully people and other animals have evolved—with multiple mechanisms designed to ensure that the right amounts of food are consumed.

The challenge for the future is to continue to investigate the initiation and termination of feeding on many different levels and to show how the results of those different investigations interrelate.[68] The world around us and many different parts of our bodies work together in determining whether or not we eat, and, therefore, so should our investigations. Such research will require the efforts of scientists whose work is interdisciplinary or who are skilled in more than one area. What's so exciting is that many scientists are capable of rising to this challenge.

3

"YOU NEVER MISS THE WATER TILL THE WELL RUNS DRY" [1]

Thirst

> Paul swallowed, suddenly aware of the moisture in his mouth, remembering a dream of thirst. That people could want so for water they had to recycle their body moisture struck him with a feeling of desolation. "Water's precious there," he said.
> From the novel *Dune* by F. Herbert (1965) [2]

Just as an animal can't live without food, so too can it not live without water, a fact that Frank Herbert used to enormous effect in his classic work of science fiction, *Dune*. When I first read this book and journeyed with Paul and the other characters across the sands of the desert planet of Arrakis, I repeatedly felt thirsty. Herbert's absorbing prose helped me to become aware of the enormous role that water and thirst play in our lives.

Beyond being simply essential for life, having enough water is essential to good athletic performance. It is also essential to the prevention of many diseases, such as exercise asthma, urinary tract infections, and hypertension. [3]

There are several reasons that we may not always be aware of the prominent role of water and thirst. First, for most of us in the United States most of the time, water is easily and abundantly available. Schools, businesses, and public parks have water fountains; grocery stores and street vendors sell bottled water and other thirst-quenching beverages; restaurants serve water; and virtually every house and apartment contains a water faucet. Second, because many foods contain at least some water, eating can help to satisfy thirst. For example, a person is unlikely to feel thirsty after eating large amounts of lettuce—lettuce is 96% water. [4] Thus we may not always be aware of how much water we need or of how powerful thirst can be; we rarely reach a state of extreme thirst.

Nevertheless, loss of water can occur very quickly. For example, when sweating, people typically lose about 1 quart of fluid per hour, which is

33

about 2% of the total fluid contained in our bodies.[5] Given this fact, and given that water is essential to life and isn't always available in nature, you would expect people to have evolved powerful mechanisms to ensure that we drink appropriate amounts of water. You would also expect people to have evolved multiple, redundant mechanisms responsible for drinking water appropriately, similar to what seems to have evolved for hunger. This chapter will tell you about some of these mechanisms. But first, when do you and other animals drink because you really need water, and when do you drink for other reasons? What are the drinking behaviors that any theory of thirst needs to explain?

How we Drink

In some ways thirst is easier to study than hunger because it involves the intake of only one substance: water. Despite this simplicity, an astonishing number of different types of drinking behaviors can be observed. These behaviors can be divided into two major categories: homeostatic and nonhomeostatic drinking. Homeostatic drinking restores an animal's water balance when the amount of water in the animal's body isn't optimal. Nonhomeostatic drinking encompasses all other types of drinking. Both categories of drinking are common, as you've probably observed. A truly comprehensive theory of thirst needs to address both homeostatic and nonhomeostatic drinking.

Homeostatic drinking

The concept behind homeostatic drinking, just as for homeostatic eating, is that there's an optimal physical state (the set point) and when there's a deviation from this state, the body does something to restore the set point. There are several different types of drinking behaviors that seem to occur according to a homeostatic model.

For example, one type of homeostatic drinking is the drinking that occurs when you eat. Deprived of food, an animal consumes less water.[6] Similarly, an animal deprived of water consumes less food.[7] This interdependency of food and water consumption may be due to animals' needing to keep a certain ratio of the weight of food to the weight of water in their gastrointestinal (GI) tracts. In rats this ratio is approximately 1 to 1 in their stomachs, and approximately 1 to 3 in their intestines.[8] Maintenance of these ratios is optimal for digestion and absorption of nutrients. Therefore animals, including us, that haven't eaten will drink relatively little, and animals that have eaten a great deal will drink a lot. This helps to maintain the set point, the optimal physical state, for the ratio of food and water in the GI tract.

Much other homeostatic drinking involves the maintenance, within fairly narrow limits, of the overall volume of the blood plasma and of the plasma's concentration of certain substances, such as salt. When the volume is less than optimal and/or the concentration of these substances is greater than normal, drinking will increase in order to restore the optimal states, and vice versa.[9]

These sorts of set point deviations can be caused by loss of water in either of the two main fluid compartments of the body: the water inside cells and the water outside cells. The latter consists of the water between the cells and in the blood plasma.[10] The two types of water loss can occur alone or together. For example, a hemorrhage, such as the sudden loss of blood following a car accident, causes loss of the fluid only outside the cells. When this happens, medical personnel usually administer fluids intravenously. If this isn't done, and if the blood loss is 10% or more, thirst will develop.[11] As another example, if there's a high concentration of salt in the fluid outside the cells, which can occur if salty food is eaten, water will be drawn out of the cells, causing a loss of the fluid only inside the cells.[12] A loss of only 1–2% of the water inside cells is enough for thirst to occur.[13] Finally, simply being deprived of water causes loss of water both from inside and outside the cells and again causes thirst. Drinking water restores water both inside and outside cells.[14]

However, it's important to remember that water won't be restored by the drinking of just any fluid. For example, fluids containing alcohol or caffeine cause the kidneys to increase their manufacture of urine. Therefore, drinking such beverages isn't the best way to counter water deprivation.[15]

Nonhomeostatic drinking

Despite these many examples of homeostatic drinking, much drinking that people and other animals do does not alleviate a water deficit. For example, the amount that rats drink depends greatly on the time of day, independent of when the water is actually needed. Rats receiving 50% of their food during the day drink only about 25% of their water during that time; they drink most of their water at night even though they aren't getting most of their food then.[16]

Let's consider an example that you may be able to relate to more directly. If you keep a record, you'll see that you do most of your drinking while you're eating a meal.[17] Why do you think that's the case? One possible reason might be that you need the water to help digest your food, to maintain the optimal food to water ratio in your GI tract, as was already discussed. Another possible reason might be that you need the water because the food is salty and you need to replenish the water that

35

the salt draws out of your cells. Both reasons are, however, only partly correct. You don't actually need the water until several hours after you eat. When you drink during a meal, you're anticipating a need for water and taking advantage of available water to prevent a deficit.[18] Animals drink, as well as eat, before there's any actual need for doing so, following the maxim, "Dig a well before you are thirsty."[19] This is an excellent way to prevent any serious deficits from occurring.

There are many other examples of anticipatory drinking. People traveling in the desert with no means of carrying water will consume as much water as possible at each water hole before moving on. In general, when water is scarce, animals drink when it's available, as opposed to drinking only when they're thirsty.[20]

There's another kind of nonhomeostatic drinking that's quite intriguing. It's called schedule-induced polydipsia (SIP). It's the excessive drinking that results from delivering rewards according to certain schedules. For example, a rat that had been deprived of food but not water, that is then given food once per minute for 3 hours, and that has continuous access to water, will consume a reasonable amount of food but will consume half its body weight in water[21] (just imagine the effect on the shavings in the rat's cage). This is far more water than the rat could possibly need.

SIP isn't seen just in the laboratory. Here's an example I saw some years ago. I was walking in New York City's Chinatown and went into an

Figure 3.1 Diagram of a tic-tac-toe game played by a chicken inside of a box. Each time a human opponent marks an X on an outside tic-tac-toe grid, the X appears on both the inside and the outside grid, and the chicken pecks at the round button on the right wall of the chamber. An O then appears in a square of both grids, and the chicken receives a reward of food through the opening at the bottom of the box's right wall. Water is continuously available in the cup on the left of the chamber.

arcade. In one game, the customer could play tic-tac-toe with a chicken in a box (see Figure 3.1). Each customer put money in a slot in the box and then selected a square for the first X. The chicken pecked to place its O. As the game continued, the chicken received a little bit of food after each peck. In the back of the chicken's cage was a cup of water. Each time the chicken received food it ran over to the cup and drank large amounts. I heard people watching this say that the chicken must be very thirsty, that the poor chicken must not get enough to drink. But the chicken had had plenty of water; what we were seeing was SIP. By the way, the game was fixed so that the chicken always won.

SIP can also be seen in people. When people in the laboratory were given money from a slot machine every 90 seconds, they consumed about 1.2 cups of water in a 30-minute period. These people had no water deficit and there was no food available, yet they still consumed a large amount of water.[22]

Theories of Thirst

Now you should have a pretty good idea of the many types of drinking that a good theory must explain—a difficult task. The rest of this chapter will tell you about some attempts to construct such theories. As was the case with theories of hunger, theories focusing on peripheral physiological cues generally developed before theories focusing on central physiological mechanisms. And, as was the case with theories of hunger, the most recent theories are quite complex.

Out of your mind (and brain) again: dry mouths and gastrointestinal tracts

I'm sure that you remember physiologist Walter B. Cannon's stomach contraction theory of hunger, described in Chapter 2. Around 1920, Cannon also constructed a theory of thirst based on peripheral cues. The result, the dry mouth theory of thirst, dominated research on thirst for many years.[23] According to this theory, animals drink when their mouths feel dry and don't drink when their mouths feel wet. A large amount of evidence has been amassed both supporting and attacking this theory.

You've probably experienced yourself the strongest evidence in support of the dry mouth theory. Have you ever noticed that when you're greatly in need of water, you have less saliva? Perhaps your mouth feels rather gummy? Salivary flow correlates closely with water deprivation. If someone's water deprivation increases, their salivary flow decreases.[24] I remember one time in junior high school when I had to go to the dentist right after playing several hours of field hockey in the hot sun without anything to drink. The dentist's hand practically stuck to the inside of my mouth and he said that I had the thickest saliva he'd ever seen. Although proud of having exceeded the dentist's expectations, I realized that he wasn't exactly giving me a compliment.

There's more evidence that supports the dry mouth theory. Many ways of removing the sensation of a dry mouth also remove the sensation of thirst. For example, hospital patients awaiting surgery aren't permitted to drink, but their thirst can be decreased if they simply rinse their mouths with a liquid. As another example, applying cocaine to the mouth of a person or a dog anesthetizes the mouth and also decreases thirst. People in the desert provide a final example. They sometimes increase their salivation and thus decrease their thirst by putting small amounts of acidic fruit juices or insoluble objects such as rocks in their mouths[25] (this probably isn't good for their teeth, but their overriding immediate concern is thirst).

Some additional evidence supporting the dry mouth theory comes from studies of both rats and camels. When half an ounce of water is put directly into a rat's stomach, the rat will subsequently drink almost as much as if no water had been put directly into its stomach. In contrast, if a rat is allowed to drink the half ounce of water normally and is subsequently permitted to drink as much as it wants, it will drink much less than if the initial water had been put directly into its stomach or than if there had been no initial water at all.[26] When camels have been severely deprived of water, they can consume the amount that they need, more than 30% of their body weight, in a scant 10 minutes. They stop drinking before much of this water could possibly be absorbed from the gastrointestinal tract.[27] Together these findings suggest that water passing through the mouth does help to slake thirst. Therefore it's possible that a sensation of a very wet mouth is necessary in order for thirst to decrease.

But before you become too enamored of Cannon's dry mouth theory of thirst, there's also a great deal of evidence that seems contrary to it. First consider an incident described by psychologists Barbara J. Rolls and Edmund T. Rolls in their book on thirst. Apparently, in 1925, a man tried to commit suicide by cutting his neck. However, he missed his arteries and veins and instead managed to cut his esophagus, thus giving himself what was, in essence, an esophagostomy. Consequently, when he drank water through his mouth, the water didn't reach his stomach and he remained extremely thirsty. However, if he put water into the lower half of his esophagus, his thirst decreased.[28] This appears to be clear evidence against the dry mouth theory.

The incident described by Rolls and Rolls is a real-life example of the phenomenon known as sham drinking. Sham drinking is similar to the sham feeding described in Chapter 2. In a sham drinking procedure, the water consumed by the experiment's participants is prevented from reaching the participants' stomachs, for example by means of an esophagostomy. Experiments using esophagostomies usually find that, similar to sham feeding, sham drinking isn't very effective in suppressing future drinking. The experiments' participants drink much larger amounts of water than they would ordinarily.[29] Thus, even though the mouth is continually moistened, thirst isn't satisfied.

Additional evidence against the dry mouth theory comes from cases in which animals, including people, have no salivary glands. These animals still consume relatively normal amounts of water. This has been shown both in experiments in which the salivary glands of a member of a non-human species were removed and in clinical cases of people who have had no salivary glands since infancy.[30] In all of these cases the mouth is never moistened, but thirst functions fairly normally.

Further, I should point out that an increase in thirst as a result of a dry mouth or a decrease in thirst as a result of a moistened one would apply mainly to homeostatic drinking. The dry mouth theory has little to say about nonhomeostatic drinking. For example, the dry mouth theory cannot explain the nonhomeostatic anticipatory drinking that occurs when you eat. And, when you see or smell food you salivate,[31] just like Pavlov's dogs. Yet, despite your mouth being moistened, you still drink significant amounts when you eat. Thus, the drinking that occurs with eating isn't only not needed, as explained previously, but occurs despite the presence of a moist mouth, in contradiction to the dry mouth theory. (See Conversation Making Fact #3.)

Conversation making fact #3

We all tend to drink cold beverages when we're really thirsty. But do cold beverages really quench your thirst better than warm ones? The dry mouth theory has nothing to say about this. As it turns out, drinking cold water decreases thirst significantly more than drinking warm water, although this effect apparently lasts for only a few minutes. After that point, thirst is most affected by how much water has been drunk.[32] So if you're one of the people who thinks that a cold drink is the best way to quench your thirst, that's only true for a very short period of time after you drink. Over the long term, the best way to quench your thirst is to drink more water.

In general, scientists now agree that a dry mouth is a signal of thirst but not a cause. When the mouth is moistened, there's an immediate but temporary decrease in thirst. For a lasting decrease in thirst, it's necessary to drink fluids that reach the stomach.[33] In fact, there's research indicating that it's the volume of liquids reaching the gastrointestinal tract—whether that volume is due to drinking plain or salty water—that's important in how much you drink.[34]

Once more into the brain: the lateral hypothalamus

Again, similar to research on hunger, researchers have also sought central, neural mechanisms as the causes of thirst, looking for a particular location in the brain that satisfies two criteria. First, the location should collect and integrate information about how much fluid there is in the animal. Second, using this integrated information, the location should then be responsible for the animal starting or stopping drinking.

There's a fair amount of evidence supporting the lateral hypothalamus as the part of the brain best satisfying these criteria. For example, B. Andersson showed in the early 1950s that injections of salt water into the hypothalamus initiated drinking in goats.[35] Apparently, cells in the hypothalamus are sensitive to salt water, a substance that causes loss of liquid from within cells. Andersson also showed that electrical stimulation of cells in the same area causes drinking.[36] Other researchers have shown that lesions in the lateral hypothalamus interfere with drinking behavior.[37]

A further indication that the hypothalamus is the central area for regulation of the amount of water in the body is the hypothalamus' role in the release of a substance called antidiuretic hormone (ADH). When the hypothalamus releases ADH, water is retained by the kidneys, thus helping to compensate for any water deficit. The hypothalamus releases ADH under two types of conditions. First, ADH is released when pressure sensors in the hypothalamus indicate a loss of fluid from within the cells. Second, ADH is released when pressure sensors in the blood vessels indicate that there has been a decrease in blood pressure, which can be caused by a loss of fluid from outside of the cells.[38] Further, when the hypothalamus detects a decrease in blood pressure, thirst and drinking result.[39] In general, blood pressure is kept very close to optimal through neural as well as hormonal mechanisms, mechanisms in which the amount of fluid excreted by the kidneys plays a significant role.[40]

Together, all of these results seem to suggest that a location within the hypothalamus is responsible for thirst and for the regulation of the amount of water in the body. This conclusion, however, is subject to many of the same criticisms that have been made of the brain centers theory of hunger and satiety, discussed in the previous chapter. These criticisms have pointed to the possibility that neither the experimental manipulations of the brain nor the modified behavior that results from them are specific enough to prove the theory. For example, a lesion in the hypothalamus may appear to affect drinking but may actually affect some other aspect of motivation or behavior.

Angiotensin

It's also possible to explain some types of drinking behavior using physiological mechanisms that aren't completely focused on the central nervous system. One such major contribution to the understanding of drinking behavior was the discovery of the role of the hormone angiotensin around 40 years ago.[41] (See Figure 3.2.)

Figure 3.2 A model of the way in which angiotensin may link peripheral indicators of water deprivation with central control of drinking.

41

As indicated previously, water deprivation causes physiological changes in the body outside of the central nervous system, such as decreased arterial blood pressure and increased salt concentration in the blood. These changes in the fluid outside of the cells are detected by specialized cells in the kidney, which then secretes an enzyme called renin. When renin comes into contact with blood, angiotensin is produced. Therefore the concentration of angiotensin in the blood is greater under conditions of greater water deprivation.[42] Experiments have shown that the presence of angiotensin in the brain increases drinking.[43] Similar to the way that blood sugar level affects eating, the level of angiotensin in the blood may increase drinking by acting on centrally located sensory receptor cells. Thus angiotensin may function as the link between peripheral indicators of water deprivation and central control of drinking. Angiotensin also helps compensate for fluid loss using three additional physiological mechanisms: (1) it causes constriction of the blood vessels, which raises blood pressure; (2) it causes increased release of a hormone important in the regulation of sodium reabsorption by the kidney; and (3) it causes increased release of ADH.[44] The renin–angiotensin system appears to be quite similar across all mammalian species, probably reflecting the fact that all species need water and that need is relatively independent of individual species' particular diets.[45]

Explanations of nonhomeostatic drinking

The theories of thirst that I've discussed so far can basically account only for homeostatic drinking behavior. For example, the hypothalamic theory proposes that thirst is caused when a specific part of the brain detects inadequate fluid levels in the body. But, as you know, much drinking is nonhomeostatic; animals often drink even though they have no water deficit. Therefore we need to consider some alternative theories.

Remember the tic-tac-toe chicken? What might explain its behavior and the behavior of other animals (including people) that demonstrate SIP? One explanation that's widely accepted makes no reference whatsoever to specific physiological factors. According to psychologist John L. Falk,[46] animals exhibit SIP when they're motivated to eat but cannot do so. Their motivation to eat is displaced to another drive, another motivational system, whose satisfaction is available—in this case, thirst. Falk suggests that such displacement increases the probability that animals in the wild will take advantage of whatever rewards are available. However, under laboratory conditions, SIP results in quite unadaptive behavior— greatly excessive amounts of drinking.

What about anticipatory drinking? Scientists don't know for certain what causes all anticipatory drinking. One explanation relates to a substance called histamine that is produced by the vagus nerve. Histamine is produced during mealtimes prior to food being absorbed or even entering the stomach, and it elicits drinking.[47] There's also some research indicating that the insulin that's released during a meal and its associated decrease in blood sugar can elicit thirst.[48] Thus the body may have several mechanisms by which anticipatory drinking occurs as an automatic reflex. However, some other cases of anticipatory drinking, such as people who drink a great deal before crossing a desert, are clearly the result of learning. This has been shown in the laboratory by exposing animals to sights, sounds, and odors that normally elicit no response but, after having been paired with a subsequent need for water, come to elicit drinking.[49] In all of these cases, animals consume water before they're seriously impaired by water deprivation, which is very adaptive behavior. This is a useful illustration of the fact that examples of behaviors that appear similar and have the same function can arise from very different causes.

There is as of yet no unified theory of nonhomeostatic drinking, or of homeostatic drinking for that matter. One way that scientists might overcome this lack would be for them to cease constructing theories for particular kinds of homeostatic or nonhomeostatic drinking behaviors and instead construct complex models incorporating a variety of physiological and nonphysiological factors that influence drinking behavior, similar to recent trends in attempts to explain hunger and eating behaviors.[50]

Thirst and Water Regulation in Specific Groups of People

Thirst and water regulation aren't identical in all groups of people. For example, many elderly people don't drink enough water to compensate for the amounts they lose following water deprivation, or as a result of exposure to heat, or as is needed with accompanying food ingestion. They can therefore develop potentially dangerous water deficits.[51] Even without water deprivation, the total amount of water in the body decreases with age. Therefore when elderly people don't drink sufficient amounts of water it's more serious than when younger people fail to do so. The result can be a higher than intended, possibly toxic, concentration in the body of any medication that the elderly person is taking; a decreased ability to withstand changes in the surrounding temperature; and impaired memory and decision making.[52] It's for reasons such as these that I increasingly worried about my aging mother's alcohol intake; the concentration of alcohol in her body may have been higher than would have occurred years previously when she drank the same amount of alcohol.

Another group of people about whom there's been concern with respect to water regulation is those people who are obese. It has been hypothesized that obesity enhances the activity of the renin–angiotensin system discussed earlier, thereby increasing blood pressure.[53] In other words, obesity affects the body's water regulation and, therefore, blood pressure. Therefore a decrease in the prevalence of obesity should result in a decrease in chronic high blood pressure. However, losing weight is easier said than done, as will be explained in depressing detail in Chapter 10.

As you have repeatedly seen, research on thirst is of more than laboratory interest. Thirst research can benefit our health, as well as inform basic theories of thirst.

Conclusion

Using an approach similar to that taken in investigating hunger, scientists began by trying to explain thirst according first to peripheral, and then to more central, physiological factors. Although these peripheral and central factors clearly are influential in the initiation and termination of drinking, much drinking is nonhomeostatic and therefore isn't fully explained by this type of approach. More recently, researchers have turned to models that include the many different factors that influence drinking behavior, such as an animal's interaction with its surroundings.

I hope that you were able to get through this whole chapter without repeatedly feeling that you had to have something to drink. My typist was apparently not so lucky. When he was midway through the manuscript for this chapter, I heard him announce that he had to take a break to get some juice, that he was very thirsty. He never made the connection to the chapter, but I did.

4

THE NOSE KNOWS
(AND SO DOES THE TONGUE)

> When it comes to food tastes, we all speak in different tongues.... People inhabit separate taste worlds.
>
> L. Bartoshuk (1980)[1]

> "Every time I smell her perfume I think of the day we met and all our many days to come." If a picture is worth a thousand words, then your sense of smell is worth a million.
>
> From a 1995 advertisement by The Fragrance Foundation[2]

You're at a restaurant that serves an enormous buffet dinner and you're starving. Does that mean that you stuff yourself on whatever food is first in line? Probably not. You'll try to choose the best foods from the buffet. This chapter is the first of several to consider how we choose which foods or drinks to consume. In order to make such choices, you have to be able to tell the difference between various foods and drinks. In making these discriminations, you use the senses of taste and smell. In fact, taste and smell are the two senses most involved in eating and drinking. The present chapter will tell you some of what scientists have learned about how taste and smell work. You may be surprised to learn that not everyone tastes and smells in the same way. It's for this reason that, in the first quotation at the beginning of this chapter, psychologist Linda Bartoshuk states that we "inhabit separate taste worlds." You may also be surprised to learn about some of the many different ways that taste and smell enrich our daily lives, as expressed so ably by The Fragrance Foundation in the other quotation. We are creatures greatly influenced by what enters our noses and mouths.

The Chemistry of Survival

Both taste and smell are what we call chemical senses. They operate by detecting minute amounts (molecules) of chemical substances. The sense of taste, also known as gustation, operates by detecting molecules

45

dissolved in liquids, and the sense of smell, also known as olfaction, operates by detecting molecules in the air. Both taste and smell function in ways designed to help us survive.

Although you may be quick to acknowledge dogs' powerful sense of smell or toddlers' sometimes too-discriminating sense of taste, you may not realize that men and women also have extremely sensitive senses of taste and smell. The average person can detect as little as $1/3$ teaspoon of salt in 1 gallon of water.[3] This average person can also detect the scent of perfume when as little as one drop is diffused into the air of the average-size house.[4]

When we are enjoying a food, such as a hamburger, we usually don't think about the taste and smell of the food as separate entities. Instead, we tend to think about the flavor of the food, a sensation that combines taste and smell, as well as the touch, temperature, and any pain provided by the food.[5] To some degree, this makes sense. Taste and smell aren't necessarily independent. Chemicals that affect taste can also affect smell, and vice versa. For example, chemicals in the air from chewed food can reach the nose via the back of the mouth. However, taste and smell don't operate identically, and they serve and protect the body in overlapping, but somewhat different, ways.

In nature, an essential task for any omnivore is determining which foods and drinks are not only safe but good to consume. Omnivores have the difficult job of avoiding poisonous substances and finding the foods and drinks that nourish them best.[6] Taste and smell play very important roles in this effort, both in terms of identifying and promoting the ingestion of nourishing substances and in terms of helping us to reject poisonous substances. Jean M. Auel described some of this process in her 1980 book of historical fiction, *The Clan of the Cave Bear*:

> Part of every woman's heredity was the knowledge of how to test unfamiliar vegetation, and like the rest, Iza experimented on herself.... The procedure for testing was simple. She took a small bite. If the taste was unpleasant she spit it out immediately. If it was agreeable, she held the tiny portion in her mouth, carefully noting any tingling or burning sensations or any changes in taste. If there were none, she swallowed it and waited to see if she could detect any effects. The following day, she took a larger bite and went through the same procedure. If no ill effects were noticed after a third trial, the new food was considered edible, in small portions at first.[7]

Once a food or drink has entered the stomach, removing it from the body may be difficult or impossible. People can vomit if they swallow something poisonous, but even so, some of the poison may remain in the body. Rats are worse off; they lack the muscles necessary for vomiting,[8] so once they've swallowed something poisonous, they're stuck with it.

Rather than dealing with poison in the stomach, it would be better if a poisonous substance could be ejected from the mouth before it's swallowed. That's where the sense of taste becomes helpful. The fact that the taste receptors are located on the tongue helps prevent any undesirable items from reaching the stomach. In addition, in most species, including people, the sense of taste is linked to the gag and vomit reflexes.[9] It's for this reason that when someone eats something that tastes really bad, such as a piece of horseradish hidden in a dish of ice cream, that person is likely to immediately eject the offending item from his or her mouth.

Tastes can also be good and rewarding. These sorts of tastes cause the occurrence of certain reflexes that aid in digestion, such as salivation.[10]

Let's turn back to poisonous substances. Even better than ejecting them from the mouth before they get to the stomach would be detecting them before they enter the mouth, so that there's no possibility of any effect of the poison on the body whatsoever. This is where the sense of smell becomes helpful. Similar to the sense of taste, the sense of smell is also linked to ejection reflexes and helps to identify desirable and undesirable foods and drinks.[11] You can avoid tasting a bad bottle of wine by smelling the cork the waiter gives you; and who hasn't turned away from spoiled milk because of its distinctive odor?

Our bodies have evolved in such a way that any substance must pass several tests before we judge it acceptable and ingest it. The senses of taste and smell are both part of this testing process, with smell being an earlier line of defense and taste being a later line of defense.

Finding the "Secret" Code for Taste and Smell

Now you should have a pretty good understanding about why taste and smell are important to us and the harm that their malfunctioning could cause. In order to prevent or remove any such harm, we need to know precisely how taste and smell work. We need to know how chemicals in the air and chemicals in liquids get perceived by us as particular odors and tastes, what happens when they come into contact with our bodies, and how messages concerning them reach our brains. Scientists call this process coding, and although this type of coding may not be exactly secret, it hasn't been at all easy to decipher.

Several factors have made quick progress in understanding taste and smell coding difficult. One is that it's hard to deliver a taste or an odor in isolation, without any other contaminating tastes or odors. A second factor is that the chemicals that constitute specific tastes and odors vary in a myriad of different ways. For example, there are many different chemicals that taste sweet. A third is that it can be difficult to compare different people's taste and smell sensations—how do we know, for example, that when two people each say that they are experiencing a moderately strong taste that they are experiencing the same thing?[12] For all of these reasons it can be very difficult to figure out which aspects of which chemicals are responsible for a particular substance having a specific smell or taste.

Ever since the beginning of scientific investigations of taste and smell coding, researchers have tried to identify what are called the taste and odor primaries. These are the smallest number of tastes and odors that could be used to describe all other tastes and odors. For example, if the primaries for taste consisted of sweet, sour, salt, and bitter, as many scientists have believed to be the case, then it would be possible to describe the taste of, for example, a hamburger, as a combination of various proportions of only these four tastes. Don't confuse the way these primaries work with the way that color primaries work. Scientists aren't proposing that any taste could actually be made from different combinations of substances having one of the primary tastes, only that any taste could be described as consisting of different proportions of the primary tastes.

Scientists have hoped that, if they could identify the taste and odor primaries, they would then be able to see what chemical characteristics distinguish substances that have those tastes or smells. This information would then give scientists significant clues about what sort of physical processes are involved in taste and smell coding. Now let's see how successful scientists have been in this coding investigation, first concerning taste, and then smell.

Taste coding

Investigations of the four taste primaries of sweet, sour, salt, and bitter began about a century ago. Because these primaries described most tastes fairly well,[13] scientists reasoned that the physiological coding of taste must somehow be organized according to these primaries. Bolstering this view was the fact that many substances tasting mainly like one of the four taste primaries have distinctive chemical properties. For example, substances that taste sweet often contain a certain configuration of the elements oxygen or nitrogen bonded to hydrogen, those that taste bitter can often be dissolved in fats, those that taste salty usually ionize easily, and those that taste sour are often acids.[14] Scientists also realized that at least three of the four taste primaries are critical to the survival of omnivores. A sweet taste such as the taste of an apple often indicates a good source of carbohydrates. In other words, foods that taste sweet are usually good sources of energy. Poisonous foods are sometimes bitter. Salt is necessary for maintaining the body's proper physiological functioning.[15] Thus it would make sense that the body would have evolved to give special attention to these tastes. Given all of this evidence, scientists reasoned that taste coding must be directly related to the taste primaries of sweet, sour, salt, and bitter.

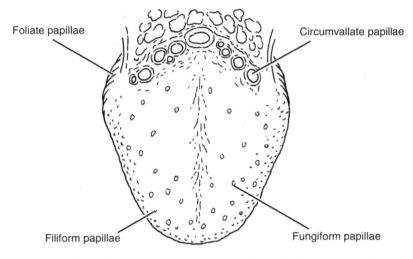

Foliate papillae

Circumvallate papillae

Filiform papillae

Fungiform papillae

Figure 4.1 Diagram of the surface of the tongue, showing the four types of papillae and their locations. (Adapted from P. L. Williams and R. Warwick, *Gray's Anatomy*, Philadelphia: W. B. Saunders, 1980.)

One hypothesis about the nature of this relationship was that there are four types of sensory cells on the tongue, with each type being maximally sensitive to one of the four taste primaries. Even before there were microscopes, it was easy to see that there are four types of bumps—the taste papillae—on the surface of the tongue: the foliate, filiform, circumvallate, and fungiform papillae (see Figure 4.1). If you've got a mirror or a friend handy, you can check this out yourself.

However, until techniques were developed to allow investigations of the responses of single neurons, it wasn't possible to determine what role these four types of papillae had in taste coding, including whether they were or were not related to the four taste primaries.

And there was still another coding question whose answer awaited the technology for investigating the responses of individual neurons. Suppose that there are four types of taste primaries that are somehow associated with four different types of sensory cells on the tongue. How would the information from these cells proceed from the tongue to the brain? One possibility is that each type of sensory cell is connected to different neurons, and the brain distinguishes different tastes by determining which of the four types of neurons are most active. This is what's called a labeled line theory, because it postulates that there are specific lines (i.e., neurons) that are labeled for specific tastes. The other possibility is that there aren't separate neurons for each of the taste primaries, and that the different tastes are coded by a complex pattern of response of many different neurons. The overall frequency of response

49

of the neurons indicates the concentration, or intensity, of the substance that is being tasted. This is what's called a pattern theory.[16]

About 70 years ago, scientists developed the techniques to start investigating precisely how taste coding works. Here's one example of the sort of experiment that could then be done. Kristina Arvidson and Ulf Friberg used suction to draw individual fungiform papillae into tiny tubes. (Please don't try this at home!) The researchers then stimulated these papillae, one at a time, with various chemical substances. Next, each papilla was cut off the tongue (don't worry; they're very small, so the pain is minimal). Then the papillae were examined under a microscope to see how many taste cells were located in each one. The results showed that a papilla containing a single taste cell could be sensitive to more than one of the four primary tastes. Further, the number of primary tastes that a papilla could sense was greater in proportion to the number of taste cells located in it.[17]

Based on a great many experiments, including this one, we now know that the parts of the tongue that actually sense tastes aren't necessarily cells associated with papillae. Fungiform papillae do have taste cells located on their top surfaces. However, the filiform papillae aren't associated with sensory cells in any way. Circumvallate papillae have taste cells located in the trenches around their sides, and taste cells are located in the folds between foliate papillae.[18]

In addition, we now know that the taste cells don't simply sit on the topmost surface of the tongue. The tongue has openings on its surface that are known as taste pores. Underneath a taste pore is the taste bud made up of many different types of cells, including taste cells (see Figure 4.2).

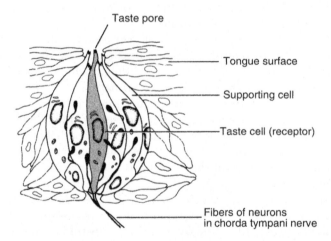

Taste pore

Tongue surface

Supporting cell

Taste cell (receptor)

Fibers of neurons
in chorda tympani nerve

Figure 4.2 Anatomy of the area surrounding a taste receptor cell. (Adapted from V. F. Castellucci, "The Chemical Senses: Taste and Smell," in *Principles of Neural Science*, 2nd ed., eds. E. R. Kandel and J. H. Schwartz, New York: Elsevier, 1985.)

Each taste cell is connected to one of the neurons that make up the chorda tympani nerve. This nerve is the first stage in transmission of information from the tongue to the parts of the brain cortex that are involved in taste. Individual neurons that make up the chorda tympani nerve can be connected to one or more taste cells.[19]

When chemicals dissolved in liquid on the tongue come into contact with the surface of the taste cells, various chemical changes occur in the taste cells. The nature of these chemical changes depends on the particular nature of the chemical substance, which is, as you would imagine, related to how that substance tastes.[20] In other words, substances that taste salty result in one sort of chemical change in the taste cells, sour another kind of chemical change, and so on. As a result of one or more of these types of chemical changes, certain taste cells respond and, ultimately, so do the neurons in the chorda tympani nerve that are connected to those taste cells.

Although we now know a great deal about how taste coding takes place, whether it does so according to the labeled line or the pattern theory continues to be discussed. Some experiments indicate that receptor cells, nerves, and/or specific parts of the brain cortex are particularly responsive to specific tastes, and other experiments indicate that these cells, nerves, and parts of the brain cortex are more broadly responsive. Techniques, such as specific types of brain activity imaging techniques, are continuing to be developed that are providing additional information concerning this issue.[21] However, the most likely outcome is that taste coding does not operate strictly according to a single method. The monkey tastes a sweet banana, and much of its neuronal system increases its activity, but some parts—the sweet detection neurons and cortical areas—do so more than others.

Detecting specific tastes

To figure out more about how taste coding works, let's consider some very specific, unusual cases. For example, consider what happens when a substance called gymnemic acid is applied to the surface of the tongue. Gymnemic acid is a chemical derived from the leaves of a plant native to India. Its effects were first noted in the scientific literature in 1847 when a British officer, Captain Edgeworth, told the Linnaean Society that if he chewed some leaves from this plant, his tea tasted as usual except that he could not taste the sugar that he had put in the tea. Apparently, when gymnemic acid is applied to the tongue, the chorda tympani nerve no longer responds to sweet substances on the tongue, although it continues to react to other tastes.[22] The fact that the reaction to only sweet substances is affected by gymnemic acid is part of the evidence indicating that the tongue has a specialized mechanism for the detection of sweet. Gymnemic acid somehow blocks these receptors.[23] The idea that a chemical in leaves could selectively decrease the enjoyment of dessert while leaving intact enjoyment of the rest of the meal is quite appealing.

On the flip side we have the aptly named West African miracle fruit, a berry about the size of a small grape. This fruit was first brought to scientists' attention by an American named David Fairchild who explored West Africa in the 1930s. Miracle fruit has the opposite effect of gymnemic acid. Although this berry does not have a particularly wonderful taste itself, after it has been eaten, sour foods (such as lemons and rhubarb) taste sweet. The active substance in miracle fruit is named miraculin[24]—and miraculous it is. When placed on the tongue, this substance, similar to gymnemic acid, selectively affects the taste of sweet, again suggesting that the tongue has a specialized mechanism for detecting sweet. But just think how attractive all foods would be to someone who had been "miraculinized." Miraculin is something that I definitely want to stay away from; there could be heavy consequences for encountering it!

Let's turn to the detection of bitter, beginning with a very simple experiment that you've probably done yourself without knowing it. Have you ever tasted distilled water? Some machines can only operate with distilled water, which has absolutely nothing in it except H_2O. Distilled water often tastes bitter. The reason for this is that your saliva contains various substances such as sodium, a component of table salt.[25] Your tongue adapts to those substances in the sense that, because they're continuously present, it reacts less to them. As a result, when you fill your mouth with distilled water, water that contains nothing but H_2O, and taste it, that adaptation is not in effect and your response to bitter is much stronger than when your saliva is continuously present (see Conversation Making Fact #4). The effects on bitter taste when switching between liquids with different concentrations of minerals suggest that the tongue has a specialized mechanism for detecting bitter. Very recently, scientists have been making significant progress in determining

---

Conversation making fact #4

The adaptation of your tongue to the substances in your saliva explains why the "pure" designer waters that you drink aren't really so pure. Even the most expensive brands must contain small amounts of minerals such as sodium. Otherwise the water would taste bitter.

precisely how the taste cells detect bitter tastes. Their evidence suggests that there may actually be many different types of bitter taste.[26]

So far in this chapter we've assumed that there are only four taste primaries. However, in recent years, many people have agreed that there's a fifth, which scientists have called *umami*, a Japanese word meaning meaty or savory. Umami is the taste of glutamate, an amino acid present in many foods, including monosodium glutamate (MSG).[27]

In all of this taste detection discussion, you may be wondering how we detect the presence of fat in food, a substance that many people crave. Some taste cells may respond in a particular way to free fatty acids (one of the products of the metabolism). However, odor and texture cues are also very important in the detection of fat.[28] Isn't it wonderful that we have all kinds of cues to detect fat, making it easy for us to find it and eat it?

Odor coding

Just as they did with taste coding, scientists have tried to identify the odor primaries, which they hoped would provide cues regarding how odor coding works. However, unlike the outcome for taste, it has not proved possible to identify a small set of odor primaries.

Scientist John E. Amoore tried to identify the odor primaries by looking for what are known as specific anosmias. A specific anosmia is the inability to smell a particular odor when all other odors can be smelled normally. Specific anosmias can be due to genetic effects, infection, or exposure to certain types of chemicals. The existence of a specific anosmia suggests that the nose has a special way of detecting that particular odor, and therefore that odor is a primary. Using this approach, Amoore identified what he believed were eight odor primaries: sweaty, spermous, fishy, malty, urinous, musky, minty, and camphoraceous. (I certainly would never have volunteered for one of his experiments!) In any case, Amoore believed that these eight would only be a starting point, that many more odor primaries would be found.[29]

Recently, a particularly intriguing anosmia was discovered, one that might indicate the identity of yet another odor primary. Scientist Marcia Levin Pelchat and her colleagues have now shown that some people are genetically unable to smell the sulfurous odor (similar to cooked cabbage) in the urine of some people who have recently eaten asparagus. (Providing an odoriferous justification for those of us who prefer not to eat said vegetable!)[30]

Researchers now believe that people have about 350 different types of cells that are at the front line of detecting odors.[31] These cells are located on what's called the olfactory epithelium, the tissue up inside your nose that detects odors. Chemicals in the air come into contact with the olfactory epithelium, more specifically with the tiny hair-like entities on the olfactory epithelium, and this causes the special odor receptor cells to respond. The different types of receptor cells seem to be randomly distributed within different regions of the olfactory epithelium.[32]

But what of that wonderful mucus with which your nose is often filled? This mucus covers the olfactory epithelium. Only certain chemicals can pass through the mucus, and some chemicals change as a result of this passage.[33] So your mucus is actually an important part of odor coding.

Turning to the receptor cells, these are essentially neurons that can each extend 3 to 4 centimeters in length toward the brain. The projections from some 10 million of these neurons converge in an area of the brain called the olfactory bulb. In the olfactory bulb, these neurons form groups of about 10,000 neurons each. The neurons within each group tend to be most sensitive to the same small set of molecular features, and particular odors are coded by the spatial pattern of activation of the neuron groups. Finally, the receptor cell neurons in the olfactory bulb are connected with the rest of the brain by additional neurons.[34]

Thus, the olfactory system, similar to the gustatory system, seems to contain elements of both the labeled line and the pattern theories of coding. There are a great many different types of odor receptor cells, as would be the case with a labeled line theory. However, within the olfactory bulb, it appears that odors are coded by the pattern of activity of the neuron groups, consistent with a pattern theory.

As you can see, both odor detection and taste detection are exceedingly complicated. For this reason, construction of electronic devices that will detect tastes or odors—in other words, artificial tongues and noses—has proved very difficult. This is unfortunate because such devices could be employed, for example, to detect smoke or gas to see if a location such as a mine shaft were safe for people to enter. Although artificial noses are now being constructed, so far they can distinguish among only a very limited set of odors.[35]

Recent research interest in the sense of smell has undoubtedly been stimulated by the awarding of the 2004 Nobel Prize in Physiology or Medicine to scientists Richard Axel and Linda Buck for their work in olfaction. These researchers have been responsible for establishing the foundations of much of what we know about odor coding.[36] Some of the subsequent exciting work on olfaction that has been reported includes how the brain detects combinations of odors and how it detects odors emanating from different locations,[37] two activities that are both essential to our living full and healthy lives with regard to food.

We're Not All the Same

Up until now, everything that I've told you about the senses of taste and smell applies to pretty much everybody, including most mammals. But, as I indicated at the beginning of this chapter, we're not all the same when it comes to smelling and tasting. Sometimes someone's taste and smell sensitivities change, due to a variety of factors, and sometimes different people's sensitivities differ even though these people are all tasting and smelling under the same conditions.

To begin with, species differ in terms of how sensitive they are to different tastes and smells. These differences help enable more than one species to exist in the same geographical area, with the different species consuming different foods in that area.[38]

For example, mosquitoes are extremely good at detecting odors emitted by people, such as the odors of CO_2 (found in people's breath) and lactic acid (found in people's sweat), and at using those odors to find a highly desirable food: human blood. DEET, a common and effective mosquito repellent, works by blocking the responses of the mosquitoes' odor receptor cells that detect human odors. Together this information may be useful in helping us to develop new ways to prevent itchy mosquito bites.[39]

In addition to there being differences in taste and smell sensitivity among different species, there can also be differences in taste and smell sensitivity among individuals of the same species. You already had a hint of that when I discussed Amoore's investigations of specific anosmias. Only some people have these specific anosmias.

It has been difficult to get a handle on just how much variation in taste and smell sensitivity there is among people. A truly mammoth attempt was the 1986 smell survey conducted by *National Geographic*. This magazine inserted into one of its issues a scratch-and-sniff smell test. Readers of the magazine were asked to scratch and sniff each odor patch and answer several questions about each odor. A total of about 1.5 million people participated from many different countries, although by far the largest number were from the United States, suggesting that the results would have been even more varied if a truly global sample of people had been obtained. The survey revealed some significant differences in odor sensitivity and odor preferences between men and women, and among people from different countries. For example, on average, women, no matter what the country, rated odors as more intense than did men. And although odors such as banana, peppermint, lemon, and vanilla were preferred by everyone, preference for other odors differed according to the country in which a study participant currently resided. For example, the scent of cloves was much less preferred by people living in Asia than by people living in the United States.[40]

Ways in which taste and smell sensitivities can differ for the same people under different circumstances include the finding that doing other things at the same time as tasting decreases people's taste sensitivity.[41] Another finding is that men (but not so much women) show less brain activity to tastes when the men are full than when they are hungry.[42]

In the following sections we'll consider in depth some additional ways in which people differ in terms of how they taste and smell, beginning with material about my own peculiarities.

The taste of bitter

Now we come to what is my most favorite subject in all of the psychology of eating and drinking—the subject that may very well have been responsible for my interest in psychology and food in the first place, although I didn't realize it until well into my adulthood. This is the study of sensitivity to the taste of phenylthiocarbamide, otherwise known as PTC, and its chemical relative 6-N-propylthiouracil, otherwise known as PROP. I'm sure you're saying, "phenyl-what? 6-N-prop-what? How can they be relevant to anything?" Well, some people taste very low concentrations of PTC and PROP as bitter, and those same people—adults and children—also tend to taste as bitter substances such as saccharin, caffeine, beer, grapefruit juice, and dark green vegetables including brussels sprouts, among others.[43] Perhaps you can see where I'm going with this.

To be more specific, people seem to divide roughly into three groups— those who can taste relatively low concentrations of PTC and PROP, those who need a somewhat higher concentration of PTC or PROP in order to taste them, and those who can taste PTC or PROP only if the concentrations are relatively high. These three groups are known as supertasters, tasters, and nontasters, respectively. Whether you're a supertaster, taster, or nontaster is determined by your genes.[44] About one-third of Northern Europeans are nontasters. The proportion of nontasters in other groups is much smaller.[45] For example, among university students in China it's about 10%.[46]

If you've read this book's preface, you should have a pretty good guess as to which group I fall into. Yes, I'm a supertaster. This may very well explain why I've never liked vegetables, beer, coffee (even coffee ice cream), grapefruit juice, or saccharin. I abhor brussels sprouts. Apparently many things taste bitter to me that don't taste bitter to many other people. Research has also shown that supertasters seem to be more sensitive to pain in the mouth.[47] This may explain why I've never liked soda—from the time I was a child I felt that the bubbles hurt my mouth. Similarly, especially as a child, I never liked raw fruit because I felt that it was just too acidic and hurt my mouth. The one exception was bananas, which I've always liked (similar to other primates). I also prefer my water to be room temperature, not ice cold as most Americans do. Finally, the findings on pain and supertasting can also explain why I've never been able to eat food that contains a great deal of chile pepper.

How I discovered my supertaster status is a story worth telling. In the late 1980s I was part of something called the Cuisine Group, a small informal group of psychologists, historians, anthropologists, and the like who were interested in food and cuisine. The group was organized by the food psychologist nonpareil, Paul Rozin, a professor at the University of Pennsylvania. About one Saturday a month, we would meet in the Manhattan loft apartment of Barbara Kirshenblatt-Gimblett, a professor at New York University. At a typical meeting, we would gather at noon, each having brought something interesting to share for lunch. Usually the other members of the group, who were all interested in food because they liked to eat everything (and I do mean everything), would bring all kinds of strange things for lunch. Much of lunch would be spent by the other attendees trying to get me to eat whatever strange things they had brought (they were never successful). Then we would have discussions and perhaps a lecture during the afternoon, during which we would snack. As the afternoon drew to a close, we would all go out to dinner at some interesting place.

Each meeting had a theme. At one meeting, psychologist Linda Bartoshuk—then an otolaryngology professor at Yale University (now at the University of Florida), Cuisine Group regular, and the top expert on taste in the world—brought her little taste-testing papers. These are very small squares of what look like plain white paper. One in particular was doused with PROP. She asked each of us to taste a PROP paper. The other Cuisine Group members were chomping down happily on theirs. I touched my tongue to the tip of one corner of the PROP paper and *bam*! It was incredibly bitter. Linda dubbed me a supertaster on the spot. I asked for an extra paper to take home to test my husband, who, as a child, as you may remember from the preface, was known as the HGP (human garbage pail). That night I gave him the paper to taste. He tasted one corner and said, "It tastes like paper." "Put the whole thing in your mouth," I growled. He complied and said again, "It tastes like paper." This was definitely not a match made in heaven. I had managed to pair myself with someone who was as different from me in food preferences as possible—a nontaster! Well, at least now I knew it was genetic, and so all of my husband's nasty comments about how supposedly intelligent people don't turn up their noses at delicious vegetables could be deflected with a quite authoritative statement that they *really* do not taste so delicious to *me*. Facilitating détente, we were glad to discover that our son is a taster, occupying the middle ground between the extremely different taste worlds inhabited by my husband and me.

Some years ago I was able to put the information on PTC tasting to a very practical use. Two friends of mine, Liz and Rich, had been going out together for years. It wasn't a smooth courtship, to put it mildly. One complaint that Liz had about Rich was that he was a very picky eater— he didn't like to eat vegetables and many other foods. Liz thought that this pickiness was evidence of Rich being egocentric. Liz's opinions made Rich very angry. One night, when we were all out to dinner together, I questioned Rich about his food preferences and realized that they fit the PTC/PROP supertaster pattern. I explained this to both Liz and Rich, and it was as if a light went on in Liz's head. She immediately stopped being upset with him about his food preferences, and it wasn't too long after that they decided to get married. They now have three children and live happily together in New Jersey.

Being a supertaster has sometimes been a public matter. In 1991, Linda Bartoshuk was president of the Eastern Psychological Association (EPA), and she gave her presidential address at EPA's annual meeting. The subject was my favorite—PTC/PROP tasting. As Linda discussed the latest information on supertasters, she repeatedly used me as an example, pointing me out in the audience. In 2002, the music group They Might Be Giants immortalized supertasters in their song "John Lee Supertaster." The Web sites pickyeatingadults.com and wickipedia.com contain information about supertasters. Finally, Paul McFedries's Web site, The Word Spy (www.wordspy.com), a site devoted to "'lexpionage,' the sleuthing of new words and phrases that have appeared in print and online," lists the word *supertaster* as one of its entries. After quoting Linda Bartoshuk, the entry goes on to state that the earliest citation of the word *supertaster* is contained in my description of my supertaster status in the first (1986) edition of this book. Who would ever have predicted that my eating habits would become part of a dictionary?

Memory

One way in which people vary significantly is in their ability to recognize an odor or a taste and to identify its source correctly. This ability seems to depend on the experiences that people have had. How well you can remember an odor or a taste depends on the circumstances under which you previously experienced that odor or taste, as Marcel Proust realized so well:

> And once I had recognized the taste of the crumb of madeleine soaked in her decoction of lime-flowers which my aunt used to

give me ... immediately the old grey house upon the street, where my room was, rose up like the scenery of a theatre ... and with the house the town, from morning to night and in all weathers, the Square where I was sent before luncheon, the streets along which I used to run errands, the country roads we took when it was fine ... so in that moment all the flowers in our garden and in M. Swann's park, and the water-lilies on the Vivonne and the good folk of the village and their little dwellings and the parish church and the whole of Combray and of its surroundings, taking their proper shapes and growing solid, sprang into being, town and gardens alike, from my cup of tea.[48]

When people try to learn to identify the odors of many different chemicals, such as pyridine, butanol, and acetone, even if they're given a great deal of practice and feedback, they can learn to identify at most 22 odors. However, if, instead of consisting of chemicals with little significance for ordinary people, the odors consist of those likely to occur frequently in everyone's daily lives—substances such as chocolate, meats, bandages, and baby powder—then people on average can identify 36 substances.[49] In general it appears that it's easier for people to identify an odor if it has been encountered frequently, if they have associated that odor with a particular name for a long period of time, and if they're given feedback when they try to identify an odor. These principles may help explain why we sometimes recognize an odor but cannot recall the circumstances in which we smelled it before. Such odors are usually ones for which we had no names when we smelled them previously.

Memory for odors and tastes can also be influenced by emotion. For example, the odor receptor cells of mice become sensitive to odors that have been paired with shock (i.e., fear).[50] As another example, suppose a college student is in a good mood and is given several baby foods to taste, some that taste good and others that don't. The college student will then, when faced with a large set of baby foods, have an easier time picking out the good-tasting previously tasted baby foods than the bad-tasting previously tasted baby foods. On the other hand, if the college student is in a bad mood when originally tasting the baby foods, that student will subsequently have an easier time picking out the bad-tasting previously tasted baby foods than the good-tasting previously tasted baby foods.[51] In other words, it's easier to remember good tastes when you've experienced them in a good mood, and it's easier to remember bad tastes when you've experienced them in a bad mood. Something to think about the next time you're contemplating checking the temperature of your crying child's baby food by taking a little taste.

Age and health

Our abilities to taste and smell are affected by how old we are. As we age, our abilities to taste and smell low concentrations of chemicals and to discriminate among various chemicals decrease. More than 75% of people over age 80 have a major olfactory impairment.[52] Further, people in their 70s and 80s are less able to taste salt in their food than are young adults and middle-aged people.[53] Age-related decreases in olfactory sensitivity may explain why older people, on average, are more willing to try new or unpleasant-smelling foods than younger people.[54]

However, the age-related decrease in the ability to taste and smell does not appear to occur identically for these two senses. For example, decreases in odor sensitivity are more likely to occur with age than are decreases in taste sensitivity. In fact, there is evidence that the ability to smell starts to decline when people are in their 50s.[55] However, it's important to keep in mind that there are many people of advanced age who show no diminution whatsoever in the ability to smell.

We don't know what causes the decreases in taste and smell ability with age. They could be an inevitable part of the aging process; or they could be due to the fact that people, as they age, are more likely to have experienced some physical trauma, some disease, or some toxic substance in their surroundings that has damaged the ability to taste or smell.[56] One thing that we are sure of is that these age-related decreases in the ability to taste and smell have strong implications for the health of elderly people. Elderly people who can't taste and smell well don't enjoy their food as much as they used to and are less likely to eat a nutritionally balanced diet. They're also less likely to show the reflex responses such as salivation that normally accompany eating. These reflexes aid in digestion; impairment of such reflexes can therefore impair digestion.[57] In addition, elderly people who can't taste and smell well are less likely to detect the odors of smoke and gas, making them more likely to succumb in a fire or when there is a gas leak.[58] Family members and health professionals need to be aware of these potential dangers so that they can take steps to help the elderly avoid them. For example, family members can ensure that their elderly relatives have working smoke and gas alarms. Extra flavorings can be added to their elderly relatives' meals.[59] However, such a strategy can backfire in the case of food tasting salty. One study showed that, as compared to people aged 18–30 years, a group of adults aged 69–87 years needed more than two times as much salt in their tomato soup in order to experience its taste as slightly salty.[60] Therefore, problems in the ability of the elderly to taste salt could result in an excessive, unhealthy intake of salt.

It's not just diseases associated with aging that can take their toll on taste and smell. As you surely know without my telling you, a simple cold can decrease the ability to smell. But you probably don't know the whole story. T. Hummel and colleagues examined the ability of men and women to smell during a cold. As expected, smelling was impaired. Then each participant used a nose spray containing the decongestant oxymetazoline, the active ingredient in the over-the-counter nasal decongestant Afrin. Unexpectedly, although mucus secretion was greatly decreased, the participants still couldn't smell as well as when they didn't have a cold. This suggests that having a cold can adversely affect smell independent of any nasal congestion that may be present.[61] So even if you use a decongestant while you have a cold, you may not be in tip-top shape when it comes to detecting odors.

One case of taste disability that got some publicity was the temporary inability to taste experienced by Raymond D. Fowler, then chief executive officer of the American Psychological Association. In 1997 he suddenly was unable to taste. Food not only didn't taste good, it seemed to be foreign matter, something that he didn't want to put in his mouth. As a result, he ate very little. His regular physician didn't have a clue as to what was going on. Finally, Fowler went to see Linda Bartoshuk, taste expert extraordinaire. She gave him every possible test, including painting his tongue bright blue and videotaping it, and anesthetizing various parts of his mouth while taste tests were done. After conducting the tests, Bartoshuk was able to suggest that Fowler's problem was a respiratory virus that had gotten into his inner ear and attacked the chorda tympani nerve. Luckily, Fowler soon spontaneously recovered from his very debilitating taste problem.[62]

There are several places to which someone with a possible taste or smell abnormality might turn. One involves contacting Dr. Bartoshuk at the University of Florida Center for Smell and Taste (352–273–5119; lbartoshuk@dental.ufl.edu). Another involves contacting the Monell Chemical Senses Center in Philadelphia (www.monell.org). A third source of assistance is the website of the National Institute on Deafness and Other Communication Disorders (www.nidcd.nih.gov/health/smell-taste/Pages/Default.aspx).

Conclusion

If there's one concept that you should take away from this chapter it's that we live in a world richly populated by food tastes and odors, a world that isn't the same for everybody. Our individual abilities to taste and smell play extremely important roles in eating and drinking; it's these senses that largely determine which foods and drinks we will consume, or whether anything will be consumed at all. Taste and smell provide critical information that the body needs in order to distinguish among various foods and drinks.[63] Food preferences and aversions are often based on this information, as we will see in the next two chapters.

5

GENES RULE—OR
DO THEY?

"I used to drink milk all the time when I was young, but now I hardly ever do. Why did I change?"

"Why can my wife never seem to get enough sweet or salty snacks, even though she knows they're bad for her?"

"Five years ago I ate a hot dog and a few hours later got really sick to my stomach. I still can't stand even the thought of hot dogs. Will this ever go away?"

"Our son won't eat vegetables, but the rest of the family eats them. How did this happen? What can we do?"

Do any of these questions sound familiar? It seems that almost everyone has a food preference or food aversion of mysterious origin, or one that he or she would like to change. Parents worry about what their children like to eat and what they refuse to eat (see Figure 5.1). Adults worry about their own eating preferences too (see pickyeatingadults.com). All of these worries are for good reason. Not only is a balanced diet synonymous with good nutrition, but what you eat is known to influence the incidence and course of many diseases. For example, eating what is known as a Mediterranean diet, with lots of olive oil, nuts, vegetables, fish, beans, etc., can decrease heart attacks and strokes in people of high cardiovascular risk.[1] Food preferences and aversions clearly have medical as well as social consequences.

The previous chapter explained how people and other animals tell one food and drink from another. Given that animals can tell foods and drinks apart, and assuming the foods and drinks are all equally and easily available, which ones do animals prefer and which ones do they dislike and why? This chapter and the next one cover what scientists have discovered about the nature and causes of food aversions and food preferences.

"Let's review the whole picture, Janine. You don't like milk. You don't like chicken. You don't like anything green. Now, you tell me, Janine—what does that leave us with?"

Figure 5.1 Drawing by Saxon. (Reprinted from *The New Yorker* [August 10, 1981]: 37, with permission from Conde Nast.)

There's a huge amount of research on this topic. Therefore, to make it more comprehensible, I've divided up the discussion. This chapter focuses on the contributions that genes make to food preferences and aversions. The next chapter focuses on the contributions that our experiences make to food preferences and aversions. Nevertheless, as you read this material, please remember that no trait is entirely determined by your genes or your experience. For example, if I asked you what determines whether someone is male or female, you'd say it was entirely due to the person's genes, wouldn't you? But it turns out that if the necessary amount of male hormone isn't present at the appropriate time during pregnancy, a genetic male can develop into a person who is, to all outer appearances, female.[2] In other words, what happens during fetal development can affect whether someone has a male or female body. Consider another example. If I asked you what determines whether someone can sing a particular song, you'd probably say it was entirely due to the person's experiences. But without vocal cords and a mouth, which are genetically determined, singing that song would be impossible.

Knowing the extent to which food preferences and aversions are genetically influenced can help us understand how to change them. If an animal's food preference or aversion is determined primarily by the genes, it will be difficult to change it by manipulating the animal's surroundings. If an animal's food preference or aversion is determined primarily by experience, it will be much less difficult to change it by manipulating the animal's surroundings.

This chapter begins with discussion of three specific food preferences: the preferences for sweet foods, salty foods, and milk. Describing them will introduce you to many of the themes and problems common to all studies of food preferences. These three food preferences were chosen because, at least to some degree, most people prefer them at some point in their lives. The fact that these preferences are virtually universal, despite the varied circumstances in which people grow and mature, suggests that they're substantially genetically determined and that possession of these preferences has helped animals to survive. The last section of this chapter presents more general information about how genes contribute to food aversions and food preferences. You're about to discover that what you like to eat is controlled a lot more by your genes than you thought.

Our Sweet Teeth

The preference for sweet is stronger and more prevalent than the preference for any other taste. No matter who you are, no matter what your origins, you usually can find room for almost anything that is sweet, even after a satisfying dinner. In addition to people, many species (including horses, bears, and ants) are likely to pick sweet foods over others.[3] Common laboratory lore holds that if you're having trouble training your rat to press a lever, smearing a little milk chocolate on the lever will solve the problem.

It's not surprising that many species seek out sweets. Sweet foods and drinks tend to have a high concentration of sugar and, therefore, of calories. Calories provide energy for the body and are necessary for the body to function. In the natural surroundings of most species, including people, digestible calories are frequently not freely available in sufficient amounts. Therefore a preference for a concentrated source of calories is likely to help animals to survive.[4] One example of such a source would be ripe fruit, which, in addition to providing sugar, provides many vitamins and minerals necessary for body function and growth. It was very advantageous for our ancestors to prefer the taste of sweet, thus ensuring that they consumed ripe fruit whenever it was available.[5]

Now, thanks to advanced industrial technology, most people in developed countries can count on having a huge variety of cheap, readily available foods and drinks that contain sugar but very little else. From cupcakes to cola, candy to Honey Smacks cereal (almost two tablespoons of sugar in every cup), we are confronted at every turn with foods whose main nutritive value consists of the calories they provide. As a result, we tend to consume these foods and drinks instead of healthy others, such as milk, which contains the important nutrients protein and calcium. For example, the preference for cheap, easily available, sweet soft drinks is blamed, in large part, for the huge numbers of calories that Americans now consume in the form of added sugar—an average of 15% of our total daily calories. These many hundreds of daily empty, sweet calories promote cardiovascular disease, obesity, and diabetes.[6] It's essential for our health that we understand what causes our preference for sweet foods and drinks and what factors do and can affect that preference. (For an example of how soft drinks affect our nutrient consumption, see Figure 5.2.)

At face value

One way that you might be able to tell if the preference for sweet is primarily due to genes or to experience is to see how people react when they first encounter a sweet taste. One such approach has involved examining the reactions of newborn babies to a sweet taste. For example, Teresa R. Maone and her colleagues gave newborn infants two kinds of nipples to suck: gelatin-based nipples that had sugar embedded in them and standard latex nipples. As an infant sucked the sugar nipple, very small amounts of the sugar—just enough to provide a sweet taste—were released into the infant's mouth. The results showed that even premature babies who never before had food in their mouths sucked more often and stronger when there was sugar in the nipple.[7] These findings provide strong evidence that the preference for sweet is inborn and isn't dependent on experience with sweet foods or drinks.

Another similar approach that has been used to see if the preference for sweet is inborn is to examine the facial expressions of newborn babies' reactions to sweet and other substances. Scientist Jacob E. Steiner has shown that when babies, tested before any breast or bottle feeding, taste a sweet liquid, they show a facial expression very similar to that of adults when they taste something sweet (see Figure 5.3). The sweet stimulus leads to a marked relaxation of the face, resembling an expression of "satisfaction." This expression is often accompanied by a slight smile and was almost always followed by an eager licking of the upper lip, and sucking movements. This licking and sucking is almost "aloud" sucking. The facial play elicited by the sucrose stimulus was labeled by the observers of the films and pictures as an expression of appreciation, liking or enjoyment.[8]

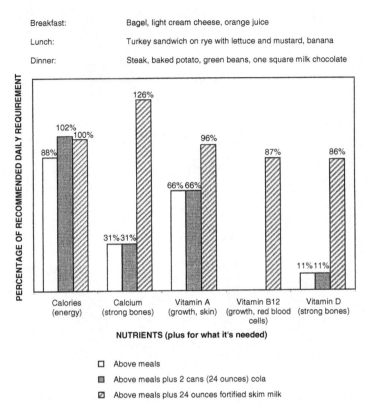

Breakfast: Bagel, light cream cheese, orange juice

Lunch: Turkey sandwich on rye with lettuce and mustard, banana

Dinner: Steak, baked potato, green beans, one square milk chocolate

NUTRIENTS (plus for what it's needed)

☐ Above meals

▨ Above meals plus 2 cans (24 ounces) cola

▧ Above meals plus 24 ounces fortified skim milk

Figure 5.2 Intake of various nutrients when meals are consumed with two cans of cola versus the equivalent volume of fortified skim milk. The top part of the figure shows what foods someone who was eating in a very healthy way (for an American) might consume in a typical day. Note the absence of snacks, fried foods, alcohol, and sweets (except for one square of chocolate after dinner). The bottom part of the figure shows what percentage of the recommended daily requirements these foods would constitute for five important nutrients, as well as the percentages when, in addition to these foods, the person consumed two cans of cola or the equivalent volume of fortified skim milk. Note the inadequate daily intakes of calcium, vitamin A, vitamin B12, and vitamin D when the cola, as opposed to the milk, is consumed. The calculations are for an adult who needs 2,000 calories per day to maintain his or her current weight. The cola provides 40 calories more than the milk. This would translate into a weight gain of approximately 4 pounds in 1 year. Note that children usually consume much less than 2,000 calories per day. Therefore, assuming no weight gain, two cans of cola would leave very few calories to be consumed as nutritious foods.

Figure 5.3 Facial expressions of newborn infants in reaction to sweet liquid. Typical facial expressions of newborn babies between birth and the first feeding: 1, resting face; 2, reaction to distilled water; 3, response to sweet liquid. (Reprinted by permission from J. E. Steiner, "Facial Expressions of the Neonate Infant Indicating the Hedonics of Food-Related Chemical Stimuli," in *Taste and Development*, ed. J. M. Weiffenbach, Bethesda, MD: U.S. Department of Health, Education, and Welfare, 1977.)

Rats also make facial expressions of satisfaction when a sweet substance is placed on their tongues, and both normal rats and rats missing the upper portions of their brains do this.[9] Note that these characteristic responses to a sweet taste, as described by Steiner, result in the sweet substance being taken into the mouth and swallowed. It appears that the acceptance and consumption of sweet substances is, in many cases, an inborn reflex that can occur without conscious awareness.

It's also possible to look at people's first experience of sweet. There have been several documented cases in which a culture that lacked sweet foods and drinks (with the exception of milk, which is slightly sweet) came into contact with a culture that regularly consumed sweet foods and drinks. In these cases none of the cultures previously without sugar rejected the sugar-containing foods and drinks of the other culture.[10] The Eskimos of northern Alaska are an example of such a sugar-adapting culture.[11] Once again, these findings seem to point to the preference for sweet being inborn, and not the result of experience.

Age and sex

Let's take another tack in our investigation into the origins of the preference for sweet by seeing what happens to that preference as people age and become sexually mature.

Some people have speculated that exposing babies to a sweet taste very early in their lives would predispose them to preferring sweets later in life. Early exposure to a sweet taste happens in many cultures in the form of what's called prelacteal feeding, a feeding that is given to a newborn infant before that infant begins to consume milk. Prelacteal feeding usually consists of a solution of sugar and water[12] and is much sweeter than breast or cow's milk. Does prelacteal feeding predispose people to prefer sweet later in life? We know that 6-month-old babies who are being fed sweetened water prefer that water more than 6-month-olds who aren't being fed sweetened water,[13] but this could be due to a number of reasons. For example, perhaps the 6month-old babies who are being fed sweetened water like it more simply because they're more familiar with it.

Some helpful information comes from an experiment with rats performed by Judith J. Wurtman and Richard J. Wurtman. They fed rat pups, 16 to 30 days of age, one of three nutritionally equivalent types of food containing either 0, 12, or 48% sugar. Between 31 and 63 days of age, the rats were given simultaneous access to all three types of food. During this period of simultaneous access, the rats' total consumption of sugar was unrelated to their previous exposure to sweet.[14] Therefore it appears that, at least for rats, early exposure to sweet does not influence later preference for sweet.

Let's consider still another approach to finding out whether experience can modify sweet preference. If exposure to sweet increases the subsequent preference for sweetness, then you would expect people's preference for sweetness to increase as they age. However, the opposite appears to be true.

Many studies have found a greater preference for the taste of sweet among younger, as opposed to older, people and rats.[15] Given that it's not clear how this change could be due to experience, other explanations must be sought. One possibility, although it has not yet been proven, is that younger animals prefer sweet substances because these animals are growing and thus have larger caloric requirements.[16]

Most of the studies examining the change in the preference for sweet from young to older ages have compared people and rats pre- and post-puberty. Therefore, perhaps the change in the preference for sweet due to age has something to do with the hormones of puberty. If this were true, then you might expect to find differences between men and women in their preferences for sweet. I'm sure you've heard people say that women like sweets more than men. As it turns out, there are no such clear differences. Among the studies that have been done, some have found a greater preference for sweet foods in men, and others in women.[17] Because the methods of all of these studies were so different, it's difficult to say whether their results are contradictory. The only firm conclusion that can be drawn regarding sex differences in the preference for sweet is that, as yet, no consistent, striking differences have been demonstrated.

Body basics

Let's look at some more physiological aspects of consuming sweet foods and drinks to see what they might tell us about the causes of the preference for sweet tastes.

You'll recall from the previous chapter that there's fairly substantial evidence that the tongue has special mechanisms for detecting the taste of sweet. In fact, we now know that there is genetic determination of several taste receptors important in the preference for sweet. In addition, as it turns out, in many species, including people, the chorda tympani nerve, the nerve that relays taste sensations from the tongue to the brain, contains more fibers maximally sensitive to the taste of sweet than to any other taste.[18] These findings suggest that the taste of sweet is more important to the body than any other taste, providing additional support for the hypothesis that the preference for sweet has a substantial genetic component.

However, it's still possible that early exposure to the taste of sweet could permanently increase the sensitivity of the chorda tympani fibers to sweet and thus be responsible for there being more chorda tympani fibers maximally sensitive to sweet than to other tastes. In rats, early exposure to an odor has been shown to increase neural responses to that odor.[19] To eliminate this possibility for the taste of sweet, experiments are needed that investigate the sensitivity of the chorda tympani nerve in either newborn babies or older people who have no previous exposure to the taste of sweet.

There's another physiological aspect of the consumption of sweet foods and drinks that can be used to explore whether the preference for a sweet taste is largely determined by the genes or by experience. Some people are unable to digest a particular kind of sugar called fructose, a sugar that is found in fruit and honey. If they consume it, they may vomit and develop convulsions. Such people are referred to as fructose intolerant. Because one of the products of the digestion of sucrose (table sugar) is fructose, people who are fructose intolerant can eat neither table sugar nor fruit. Just imagine becoming seriously ill each time you ate a cookie or even an apple. People who are fructose intolerant learn to decrease their consumption of sucrose and fructose. Nevertheless, some fructose-intolerant individuals persist in eating small amounts of fructose and sucrose and risking the consequences.[20] Apparently, in at least some cases, although being fructose intolerant can decrease the consumption of sweet foods and drinks, it doesn't decrease liking for the taste of sweet. The inborn preference for sweet may be so strong that even though tasting sweet is associated with severe illness, people may still prefer to ingest sweet foods and drinks.

Siblings and other relatives

Now let's consider some direct examinations of the contribution of genes to the preference for sweet tastes.

One way to do this is to try to breed animals that have different levels of preference for sweet. This has been done successfully with rats by selectively breeding together those rats that have the greatest and least preferences for sweet.[21] These findings suggest that genes can play a role in the preference for sweet in rats. But these results don't, of course, indicate that genes must play a role in the sweet preferences of other rats or, for that matter, in the sweet preferences of people.

The most traditional way of assessing the contribution of people's genes to some trait is to do twin studies. Twin studies look at how similar the members of fraternal twin pairs are, as compared to the members of identical twin pairs. Fraternal twins arise from two eggs, each fertilized by a different sperm. Thus, on average, they have half of their genes in common, just as any two siblings. Identical twins, on the other hand, arise from a single egg and sperm that split into two developing embryos very soon after conception. Thus, identical twins have identical genes. This means that if a trait has a substantial genetic component you would, on average, expect a pair of identical twins to be more similar with regard to this trait than a pair of fraternal twins would be. Twin studies that have looked at the preference for sweet have consistently failed to find greater similarity in sweet preferences for identical twin pairs than for fraternal twin pairs.[22] However, if you were to say that this means that the preference for sweet isn't largely due to genes, you would be jumping to conclusions.

Consider the study done by Lawrence S. Greene, J. A. Desor, and Owen Maller. In this study, both identical and fraternal twins ranked their preferences for different concentrations of sugar. As I previously indicated, the identical twins were no more similar in their rankings than the fraternal twins. But let's look at the ratings themselves. All of the twins tended to give very similar ratings for the different sugars.[23] I hope you can see that, if everyone gives the same ratings, it isn't possible for some pairs to be more similar in their ratings than other pairs. Thus, Greene and his colleagues' failure to find greater similarity in sweet preference for identical versus fraternal twin pairs doesn't necessarily mean that genes have little to do with the preference for sweet tastes. Greene and his colleagues' data could still be explained by saying that everyone easily learns a similar preference for sweet tastes. However, the virtual universality of this preference suggests a strong genetic component in the preference for sweet tastes.

Together, all of this early evidence is very suggestive of a strong influence of the genes on the preference for sweet, a preference that shows little variation among people.

In recent years, the available evidence has become more definitive. For example, scientists have been able to identify specific genes involved in sweet taste sensitivity and the frequency of sweet food and drink consumption.[24] There is no question that our genes play a significant role in our consumption of sweet foods and drinks.

A widespread, genetically influenced, strong preference for sweet is actually not that surprising. As I previously mentioned, the taste of sweet is often a good indicator of available calories. Therefore you would expect evolution to result in a preference for sweet tastes that is strongly influenced by genes and that shows little variation. And what this means is that it's going to be very difficult for you, or anyone else, to decrease your preferences for sweet foods and drinks.

The role of experience

Surely there are some experiences that can at least modify people's preferences for sweet foods and drinks. As is discussed in detail in the next chapter, we know that, in general, rats learn to prefer the foods that other rats prefer, and young children learn to prefer the foods that other people, including both children and adults, prefer. In addition, we know that young children develop an increased preference for foods that are given as rewards or that are accompanied by attention from adults.[25] Couldn't some of these influences be at least partly responsible for the preference for sweet? How many times have you heard a parent say to a child, "If you're really good you can have some candy"? However, none of this past research has been specifically directed at the preference for sweet. We don't know whether these sorts of manipulations of rats' and young children's experiences can modify their preferences for sweet. It may very well be the case that the preference for sweet is so strong to begin with that nothing can make it stronger.

We do know that, as the economy of a country develops, per capita consumption of sugar increases.[26] This would seem clear evidence of the effects of our surroundings on the preference for sweet. However, such an increase in sugar consumption might not be due to an increase in the liking for sugar. If more people can afford foods and beverages with a high sugar content as the economy of a country develops, those foods and drinks would probably be consumed more. But this change in consumption doesn't have anything to do with how much the people in that country actually like sweet foods and drinks.

Some scientists think that the greatest influence of experience on the preference for sweet isn't on the preference for sweet itself, but on the particular foods that we prefer to be sweetened.[27] We adults don't want a sugar coating added to our pot roast or fried eggs, but we would often prefer to eat ice cream or cake rather than pot roast or fried eggs. Our culinary experiences, which may be very different for different cultures, determine which foods we expect to be sweet. For example, in the United States, chocolate is usually sweetened, but in traditional Mexican cuisine it is not. As adults, it's by means of our preferences for commonly sweetened foods that we demonstrate our preferences for sweet.

When my son was young, I tried really hard to decrease his preference for sweet foods and drinks by controlling his contact with them. Basically, from the time he was born, I tried to keep him away from sweet foods and drinks, even when we were out and about, and I kept this up as long as possible. Until he was old enough to have learned on his own what cookies, ice cream, cake, candy, and soda were, I never let him have these foods or drinks, and I never mentioned them to him. It has never been clear to me why parents often go out of their way to give their children these foods and drinks, particularly when the children are too young even to know what they really are. Although the children may look happy eating them, their health may, as a result, be compromised. Wouldn't it be much better if parents made their children happy just by playing with them?

Getting back to my son, restricting his access to high-sugar foods and drinks at home wasn't much of a problem when it came to soda, because neither my husband nor I like it and so we never have it in the house. However, I love cookies, ice cream, cake, and candy and allow myself one of these most days. For example, I usually have a box of cookies in the house and frequently I'll have a couple after dinner (my current favorite is Snackwell's fat-free Devil's Food cookies). At about age 2, my son began noticing that I was eating things after dinner that he wasn't eating. He'd watch me take the cookies out of the cabinet and eat them. Once he had learned to ask questions, he began asking me what I was eating. "Brown things," I'd say. "Oh," he'd reply. This worked for a year or two until, thanks to *Sesame Street* and Cookie Monster, he figured out that there was another name for the brown things I was eating. Then I started hiding them on a high shelf, and only taking some when I thought he wasn't watching. Unfortunately, in later years, he grew taller than I am, became more inquisitive, became determined to have whatever dessert I was having, and navigated New York City on his own with money in his pocket. The days of my restricting his access to sweets have been over for quite a while now, and he seems to like sweets as much as anyone else. So much for that grand experiment!

Salt Licks

The preference for salty tastes is, similar to the preference for sweet tastes, extremely strong and prevalent. With the exception of newborn babies, all people, and many other species, prefer salt. What's more, animals—including people—show a strong preference for salt the first time that they taste it.[28] Newborn babies appear not to be able to detect salt, possibly due to the taste mechanism for salt not yet being mature. However, after 4 months of age, the story is very different, and these babies, similar to older people and to other species, show a preference for salty water over plain water.[29]

It wouldn't be surprising for natural selection to result in an innate preference for salt in most species. Similar to calories, salt is essential for the body to function properly, in people as well as many other species. Many bodily functions depend on the presence of salt and even on a particular concentration of salt.[30] For example, the concentration of salt in the blood must be kept at a specific level. However, small amounts of salt are lost continually through sweat and through the action of the kidneys. If someone ceased to ingest salt, eventually the body would excrete water in an attempt to keep the concentration of salt in the blood at the optimal level, and that person would die of dehydration.[31]

Salt isn't easily available in the wild. Prior to industrialization, people sometimes had great difficulty obtaining enough salt. Many species must constantly seek salt in order to have sufficient amounts. In such situations, an inborn preference for salt would be extremely useful.[32] In the following sections we'll consider more direct evidence regarding the extent to which the preference for salt is due to genetic factors.

When salt is really needed

There has been a great deal of research concerning how animals, including people, seek out salt when they're deprived of it. Under such conditions, the preference for salt is increased (see Conversation Making Fact #5).[33] You'll recall from Chapter 4 that, in general, people show more sensitivity to tastes when they are hungry. In the case of salt deprivation, one factor that may be involved in this increased preference is the release of angiotensin,[34] which you learned earlier in this book occurs during conditions of water deprivation and has several consequences that increase drinking. Recall that, when an animal is salt deprived, the body of that animal will excrete water in an attempt to keep the concentration of salt in the animal's blood at optimal levels. This essentially deprives the animal of sufficient water, and therefore should result in the release of angiotensin. The possibility that angiotensin increases the preference for salt is based entirely on automatic physiological processes that are independent of an animal's experiences.

Conversation making fact #5

Have you ever wondered why, at certain times of the year, you often see small animals by the sides of rural roads—alive or dead? For example, the summer presence of porcupines near roads in the Catskill Mountains in New York State appears to be due to a need for salt. These porcupines must maintain approximately equal amounts of the chemicals potassium and sodium (a component of table salt) in their bodies in order to remain healthy. However, the summer vegetation in the Catskills generally contains at least a 300 to 1 ratio of potassium to sodium. As the porcupine's body works to remove the excess potassium, it also removes the sodium, and the porcupines cannot keep sufficient amounts of sodium in their bodies. Therefore the porcupines seek out sources of salt, which contain sodium but no potassium. The locations of two such sources are the salt left on the sides of roads from the previous winter and the wood on the sides of barns. Seeking out salt in either of these two locations is extremely dangerous for the porcupines, because in the one case they're likely to get run over and in the other they're likely to get shot by an angry farmer. Yet the majority of porcupines are driven to areas of human habitation by their need for sodium.[35]

Psychologists Robert J. Contreras and Marion Frank did an experiment investigating another reason why the preference for salt increases when animals are salt deprived. These researchers first deprived rats of salt for 10 days, so that the rats' preferences for salt increased. They then measured the responses of various neuronal fibers in the chorda tympani nerve to different concentrations of salt. They found that, although the lowest concentration of salt that would induce a response in the nerve did not change, a higher concentration of salt was necessary to make the nerve respond as vigorously as before deprivation.[36] Similarly, neurons in the brain that respond to the presence of salt respond much less after salt deprivation.[37] Both of these findings suggest that, after deprivation, the rat would perceive a particular concentration of salt as equivalent to a lower concentration prior to deprivation and would therefore prefer foods with a relatively higher concentration of salt. Once again, these mechanisms for increasing the preference for salt seem to be based entirely on automatic physiological processes that are independent of an animal's experiences.

Evidence for the influence of physiological state on the preference for salt has also been seen in people. For example, in 1940 L. Wilkins and C. P. Richter published a letter written to them by the parents of a boy who had an unusual preference for salt due to a tumor in his adrenal gland:

When he was around a year old he started licking all the salt off the crackers and always asked for more. He didn't say any words at this time, but he had a certain sound for everything and a way of letting us know what he wanted.... [H]e started chewing the crackers; but he only chewed them until he got the salt off, then he would spit them out. He did the same with bacon, but he didn't swallow the pieces.... In an effort to try to find a food that he would like well enough to chew up and swallow, we gave him a taste of practically everything. So, one evening during supper, when he was about eighteen months old, we used some salt out of the shaker on some food. He wanted some, too. We gave him just a few grains to taste, thinking he wouldn't like it; but he ate it and asked for more.... [T]his one time was all it took for him to learn what was in the shaker. For a few days after that, when I would feed him his dinner at noon, he would keep crying for something that wasn't on the table and always pointed to the cupboard. I didn't think of the salt, so I held him up in front of the cupboard to see what he wanted. He picked out the salt at once; and in order to see what he would do with it, I let him have it. He poured some out and ate it by dipping his finger in it. After this he wouldn't eat any food without the salt, too. I would purposely let it off the table and even hide it from him until I could ask the doctor about it.... But when I asked Dr. [ ] about it, he said, "Let him have it. It won't hurt him." So we gave it to him and never tried to stop it altogether.... [B]ut he wouldn't eat his breakfast or supper without it. He really cried for it and acted like he had to have it.... At eighteen months he was just starting to say a few words, and salt was among the first ones. We had found that practically everything he liked real well was salty, such as crackers, pretzels, potato chips, olives, pickles, fresh fish, salt mackerel, crisp bacon and most foods and vegetables if I added more salt.[38]

Tragically, the boy had died in a hospital because the hospital diet did not give him the salt that he craved and his body needed.

There are several other special situations in which the body's needs may increase the preference for salt. For example, similar to what has been found with the taste of sweet, 9- to 15-year-old children prefer saltier liquids more than do adults.[39] We can speculate, as with sweet, that these findings are related to the evolutionary history of humans. If, during this history, there was generally an increased need for salt by younger, growing people, some automatic mechanism that results in relatively higher preferences for salt among young people might have increased their chances of survival and therefore have been passed on to future generations.

In another special situation, traditional Bedouin women in the Negev desert consume about 50% more salt than other women (including urban Bedouin women).[40] This increased preference for salt is presumably due to the women's increased need for salt in the desert.

And finally there's recent research on exercise and salt preference that I find particularly intriguing. I'm a big fan of physical fitness and sweat quite a bit when exercising. I've always wondered whether the resulting lost salt affects my preference for salt. Psychologists M. Leshem, A. Abutbul, and R. Eilon have shown that, immediately after exercising for 1 hour, male university students preferred a higher concentration of salt in tomato soup than did students who had not exercised. The students were allowed to add as much salt as they wanted to the soup, and the exercisers added 50% more than the nonexercisers. In fact, even 12 hours after exercising, the exercisers still preferred a higher concentration of salt in their soup than the nonexercisers.[41] Further, with experience, people learn to prefer saltier drinks that they consume around the time when they exercise.[42] It appears that people, and not just other species, are quite good at finding ways of obtaining extra salt when some of their bodies' salt content has been lost.

How much is too much?

Salt isn't just consumed when people and other animals are deprived of it; it's also consumed when there's no need for it whatsoever.[43] Similar to sweet foods, salty foods are more easily and inexpensively available now than when people first evolved. Consequently, the preference for salt has resulted in consumption of salt in amounts far exceeding the body's needs—an average among U.S. adults of at least 3,450 mg of sodium per day in comparison to a recommended level of less than 2,300 mg per day. This excess salt consumption contributes to high blood pressure, although there is disagreement about what to do about that.[44]

No matter what you think about this controversy, it has sparked much interest about whether it's possible to modify people's preferences for salt so that they eat less of it. We've known for many years that, similar to the preference for sweet, after the age of 2 years, children learn which foods are supposed to be salty and reject foods that don't contain the customary degree of saltiness. But can adults' preferences for the amount of salt in a food be modified?

In fact, in contrast to findings with sweet, there is some evidence that the preference for salt can be directly modified. A salt-deficient rat will eat less of a salt-enriched diet if it has recently interacted with other rats that aren't salt deprived.[45] In other words, social interaction can affect a rat's food preferences.

Salt preference can also be modified in adult humans. If people are put on a low-salt diet for several weeks, they will begin to prefer foods that have less salt.[46] Similarly, men and women on a low-salt diet given salt tablets to swallow subsequently add less salt to unsalted tomato juice.[47] Other evidence of modified salt preference seems related to very recent experience with low or high amounts of salt. For example, if men and women are first given lunch and then, immediately afterward, are given vegetable broth to eat, they prefer the broth to have a lower concentration of salt if the lunch has been high-salt (cheese sandwich plus high-salt chicken noodle soup) as opposed to if the lunch has been low-salt (low-salt chicken sandwich and low-salt chicken noodle soup).[48] Thus there have been several experiments showing that experience can modify the preference for salt. Unlike the situation for sweet, there's some possibility that you might be able to decrease your preference for salt.

However, it would undoubtedly help in decreasing our salt consumption if the foods we buy in the store had less of it. You might be surprised to know that one of our largest sources of salt consumption is bread,[49] and that a single piece of pizza can contain more sodium than you're supposed to eat in a whole day. You might also not know that many food manufacturers have been striving to decrease the salt content of their products, but consumers often don't prefer, and thus won't buy, the low-salt versions of these products.[50] It seems that we need a two-pronged effort of decreasing salt preference along with decreasing the salt in available foods if we want to decrease our salt consumption.

Beyond Mother's Milk

Milk contains calcium, essential to building and maintaining strong bones. Nearly every newborn baby avidly consumes milk—not surprisingly given that milk contains a type of sugar, lactose. However, this isn't the case for every adult. Some groups of people, such as Northern Europeans, drink a lot of milk and also eat a great deal of milk products, such as cheese. Other groups, such as the Chinese, consume neither milk nor its products.

It turns out that these groups differ not only in terms of how much milk they drink, but also in what's called lactose intolerance, the inability to digest the sugar present in milk. Whether someone is lactose intolerant depends on whether his or her body has sufficient lactase, a chemical that breaks down lactose during digestion. When people without lactase drink milk, the resulting symptoms include diarrhea and flatulence. Lactose intolerant people can, however, usually consume some milk.[51]

Many groups of adults tend to be lactose intolerant, including many groups in the United States (see Figure 5.4). In fact, by 1.5 to 3 years of age, many people around the world become largely unable to manufacture lactase, a loss that is shared with all adults of all other species.[52] This means you shouldn't give your cat milk! Men and women who can digest milk are such an exception in the animal kingdom that it raises the question as to how such people could have come to exist.

One possibility is that, if you always drink milk from the time you're born, your body adapts by continuing to produce lactase beyond early childhood.[53] No other species could be in such a situation because, in other species, young animals are weaned to make way for subsequent offspring. But people have kept cows and goats for thousands of years and so can continue to drink milk into adulthood without jeopardizing the nutrition of their younger siblings. If this explanation of lactose tolerance

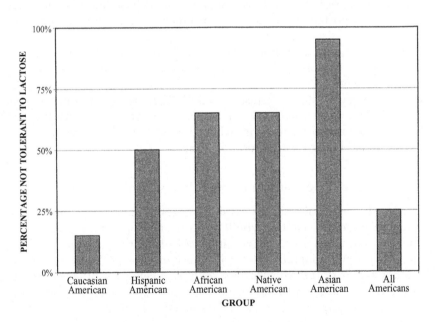

Figure 5.4 Percentage of various groups who are not tolerant to lactose. (Adapted from D. France, "Groups Debate Role of Milk in Building a Better Pyramid," *The New York Times* [June 29, 1999]: F7.)

in adults were correct, you would predict that intolerant adults given milk to drink over a period of time would start to manufacture lactase and be more able to digest milk. However, such experiments have shown very little, if any, increases in lactase activity.[54]

Therefore we must look elsewhere to explain lactose tolerance in adult humans. Given the title of this chapter, you won't be surprised to learn that that explanation lies in the genes. Whether someone can manufacture lactase as an adult is genetically determined.[55] But why did people, and not other species, evolve this ability?

It is now thought that people first domesticated cattle for their meat and for the work they could do. Then, during periods of inadequate food, people who could successfully consume the milk from these cattle were more likely to survive and reproduce than other people. In this way people who were lactose tolerant became more common in the population.[56] This evolutionary process would have been particularly likely to occur with people living far from the equator. There's more cloud cover and less sunlight away from the equator than near it. Sunlight on the skin of people results in the synthesis of vitamin D, a vitamin that assists in the necessary absorption of calcium into the body.[57] Therefore people living far from the equator aren't able to synthesize lots of vitamin D. Because the digestion of lactose by lactase also assists with the absorption of calcium, consumption of lactose accompanied by lactase manufacture may have been important in the survival of human adults living away from the equator.[58]

Once again, please keep in mind that even though lactose intolerance may result in certain men and women not drinking milk, this doesn't necessarily mean that these people don't like milk; many of them would drink it if a magic pill would just prevent the diarrhea and flatulence (and such pills do, in fact, exist). We have here another case in which genes seem to affect the frequency with which a food or drink is consumed, but not the actual liking for that food or drink.

The Bitter End and Other Points for the Genes

Several other areas of research implicate genes as important contributors to food preferences. First, as you'll recall from the previous chapter, the ability to taste very low concentrations of phenylthiocarbamide (PTC) and 6-N-propylthiouracil (PROP) is determined by genes. And, as you also know, PTC/PROP supertasters are more likely than other people to taste food as bitter and therefore dislike substances such as saccharin, caffeine, beer, grapefruit juice, and dark green vegetables.

In recent years, scientists have been able to link PTC/PROP supertasting—including the specific taste receptors and genes responsible—to a number of additional aspects of food preferences. For example, supertasters have a lower preference for virtually every kind of vegetable that contains a thyroid toxin. These vegetables include watercress, mustard greens, turnips, broccoli, rutabagas, and horseradish. An example of a vegetable that does not demonstrate this preference pattern is radicchio.[59] In addition, we now know that being a supertaster is associated with a greater preference for salt and with greater salt consumption.[60] When you combine this information with the fact that bread is a significant source of salt in our diets, and with my PTC/PROP status as a supertaster, my lifelong huge preference for bread and its relatives (as a child I would happily sit and eat a huge pile of nothing but saltines or oyster crackers), my inability to eat more than the tiniest pinch of horseradish at Passover, and my strong dislike of every vegetable in the preceding list are not at all surprising. Nor is the fact that I don't mind radicchio in my salad any more than I do baby lettuce. It is wonderful when science explains the genetic underpinnings responsible for some of your seemingly peculiar behaviors!

Before we leave evidence concerning the taste of bitter, look at the pictures of the babies in Figure 5.5. This figure shows what babies' faces look like when they taste bitter. This expression has been described as follows:

> Stimulation with the bitter fluid leads to a typical arch form opening of the mouth with the upper lip elevated, the mouth angles depressed, and the tongue protruded in a flat position. This expression involves primarily the mouth region of the face and ... was typically followed by spitting or even by the preparatory movements of vomiting.[61]

When adults watched babies making this expression they described it as a rejection response.[62] This facial expression is similar to the rejection response that rats make when they're given an aversive substance to taste.[63] This information, together with that on the characteristic facial response to sweet, suggests that there are two distinct inborn taste response systems: an acceptance system and a rejection system. These two systems are apparently universally present in at least two species (people and rats) and probably other species as well, and they appear to be genetically linked to certain tastes—the acceptance system to the taste of sweet and the rejection system to the taste of bitter. These two systems increase the chances that newborn babies without taste experience, or animals experiencing new foods, will take in substances that provide calories but won't take in substances that could be poisonous.[64]

The evidence continues to accumulate regarding genetic contributions to food preferences. A relatively new area of inquiry along these lines is the preference for sour foods and drinks. Scientist Outi Törnwall and her

1   **2**   **3**

Figure 5.5 Facial expressions of newborn infants to bitter liquid: 1, resting face; 2, reaction to distilled water; 3, response to bitter liquid. (Reprinted by permission from J. E. Steiner, "Facial Expressions of the Neonate Infant Indicating the Hedonics of Food-Related Chemical Stimuli," in *Taste and Development*, ed. J. M. Weiffenbach, Bethesda, MD: U.S. Department of Health, Education, and Welfare, 1977.)

colleagues compared identical and fraternal twins' preference for sour tastes. The research participants drank and rated orange juice that varied in sourness due to the addition of citric acid, and they also rated (using a questionnaire) how much they liked 21 foods of varying degrees of sourness. The 21 foods included such items as lemons, bananas, plain yogurt, and flavored sweet yogurt. For both the tasted juice and the questionnaire items, identical twins were more similar in their ratings than were fraternal twins, and that increased similarity found in the identical twins had a significant genetic component.[65] Given that sour preference can be strongly related to how much fruit someone chooses to eat,[66] and that the consumption of fruit can significantly contribute to health, Törnwall and her colleagues' findings can help us understand the causes of, and possibly how to promote, healthy eating behavior.

Finally, I would like to tell you a little bit about a personality trait called sensation seeking and its relationships with food preferences. Research on sensation seeking was pioneered by psychologist Marvin Zuckerman, who has described sensation seeking as the tendency to seek out new or unusual experiences.[67] How much of a sensation seeker someone is can be measured by asking that person to choose between such statements as "I like 'wild' uninhibited parties" and "I prefer quiet parties with good conversation."

Several studies have shown strong relationships between sensation seeking and certain food preferences. Michael E. Smith and I found that people who scored high on sensation seeking tended to report a greater preference for spicy foods, and people who scored low on sensation seeking tended to report a greater preference for bland and sweet foods. We also noted that people who scored high on sensation seeking tended to prefer items such as alcohol and shellfish, foods that are often reputed to cause illness; but people who scored low on sensation seeking tended to prefer items such as bread and corn, foods that are rarely reputed to cause illness.[68]

Because there appear to be many relationships between sensation seeking and food preferences, there may be a common basis for some aspects of sensation seeking and some food preferences. Further, based on studies examining sensation seeking and food preferences among identical and fraternal twins, Zuckerman has argued that there's a genetic component to sensation seeking.[69] Therefore Zuckerman's research raises the possibility that there may be genetic influence on whether someone likes strong-tasting foods.

You'll remember that I used to belong to the Cuisine Group described in the previous chapter. At one meeting, I gave everyone a sensation seeking questionnaire. I got one of the lowest scores possible, and everyone else (these people who would eat *anything*) got among the highest scores possible. So it appears that I have at least two factors with genetic input that have contributed to my food finickiness: I'm a PTC/PROP supertaster and I'm unusually low in sensation seeking, an unfortunate double whammy.

Conclusion

In the world in which we evolved, eating sweet things and salty things was virtually always good for us, as was drinking milk, if we could digest it. Therefore it would have helped people to survive if they liked to consume these things the first time that they encountered them, with no learning period. Under such conditions, survival is more likely if preferences for these substances are strongly influenced by the genes. Now we live in a world where there's too much of these substances, a world in which advertisers try to get us to buy and then consume things that we shouldn't. Even our college campus vending machines contain almost nothing but high-sweet and/or high-salty and/or high-calorie items, including twice as many sugar-sweetened beverages as no-calorie beverages.[70] Now our genetic tendencies can get us into deep trouble. Unfortunately, even when food preferences and food aversions can be modified by experience, this doesn't necessarily mean that the resulting eating is ideal, as you'll see in the next chapter.

6

ONE PERSON'S MEAT IS ANOTHER PERSON'S POISON

The Effects of Experience on Food Preferences

> No other fundamental aspect of our behavior as a species except sexuality is so encumbered by *ideas* as eating; the entanglements of food with religion, with both belief and sociality, are particularly striking.
>
> Sidney W. Mintz (1996)[1]

The previous chapter may have convinced you that much of what you do and don't like to eat has a strong genetic basis, but that's by no means the whole story. There's a great deal of variation in what people like to eat that clearly has no genetic basis. Take entomophagy (insect eating). Many insects are highly nutritious and are widely consumed. For example, someone has to eat only 100 grams of caterpillars in order to get all of his or her daily recommended protein, iron, and vitamins.[2] Dozens of different insect species are on the menu in countries such as Cambodia and Mexico.[3] In the United States, the government officially approves of entomophagy; the Food and Drug Administration permits as many as 30 insect parts in every 100 grams of peanut butter.[4] Nevertheless, in the United States most people, no matter where they immigrated from, think eating insects is disgusting. Why are there such huge differences in food preferences? Do these differences in food preferences help us and other animals to survive?

Suppose you must live in the wild without any of the benefits of civilization, under the sort of conditions in which people evolved. Think about how many food choices you would have. There would be many different kinds of plants and animals that you could conceivably put into your mouth and swallow. Which ones will taste good to eat and which ones won't? Which ones will keep you healthy and which ones won't? Which combination of foods will give you all of the nutrients that you need? And if you move from, say, an open savanna to a shady woodland, the food choices available to you will completely change. How do you decide what to eat in your new surroundings?

When people are born, they consume only milk. But usually by the time a child can walk, the child is eating a large variety of foods. How do young children and other animals learn what foods they should be eating when their parents are no longer around?[5]

For omnivores such as us, our genes just can't preprogram all of our food preferences. There are too many choices and the choices change too much. Somehow, omnivores have to learn what foods are good to eat and what foods aren't, and they had best do that as quickly and efficiently as possible and as often as necessary. Eat the wrong thing and you'll die; there are plenty of poisonous plants and animals.

Fortunately, we and other omnivores figure out pretty well what is and isn't good to eat under changing conditions. In the laboratory, psychologist Paul Rozin showed that thiamine (vitamin B_1)-deficient rats preferred a food with thiamine over a food without thiamine.[6] In classic research known as the cafeteria experiments, psychologist Curt P. Richter showed that rats given a wide choice of nutritive substances—such as sugar, olive oil, cod liver oil, and baker's yeast—did quite well at selecting all of the nutrients that they needed.[7]

But what about people? Do our preferences also result in our eating a balanced diet? If you've raised a child, some well-meaning person probably told you at some point not to worry about your child's finicky eating, that over a period of time children choose to eat the nutrients that they need. My own parents were convinced that, as long as they gave me vitamin pills, I'd be fine. Many people, including some pediatricians, have believed this because of famous research done in the 1920s and 1930s by physician Clara M. Davis. Davis's research used 15 healthy babies between the ages of 6 and 11 months who, at the time the experiment began, had little experience with foods other than milk. All of the babies lived in a hospital for the 6 months to 4½ years that they participated in the experiment. (Such an experiment would never be permitted now.) At meal times a nurse presented each child with a tray containing a variety of foods, such as different meats, cereals, eggs, milk, fruits, and vegetables. The nurse would give the child any item to which the child pointed. The children sometimes went on binges during which they consumed large amounts of particular foods for extended periods, but these binges eventually stopped. Over long periods of time the children ate fairly well-balanced diets and grew well.[8]

So parents should just stay out of it and let babies choose their own foods, correct? Unfortunately, it isn't that simple. There were two major problems with Davis's experiment. First, even though they were told not to, it's possible that the nurses who were giving the foods to the babies unconsciously—or perhaps even consciously—affected the babies' choices. Suppose a baby you were taking care of ate nothing but beets for five meals in a row. Could you just ignore this and not nudge the baby to eat something else? Second, the sweetest choices available to the babies were milk and fruit and, not surprisingly, those items were also the ones chosen most often. These babies showed the sweet tooth described in the previous chapter. Luckily the sweetest choices available to them, milk and fruit, were also quite nutritious. It seems unlikely that Davis's subjects would have chosen an equally nutritious diet if candy and soda had been available.

This all means that, unfortunately, unless you remove the nonnutritious foods from your child's surroundings, you can't rely on your child to choose a nutritious diet. And as a parent, I can testify to how difficult ensuring a healthy food world for your child can be. Once he started visiting friends' homes, my son (who is now 28) was repeatedly offered candy, soda, chips, and other wonderful but nonnutritious foods, which a great deal of our culture seems to think appropriate to have available for children at all times of the day or night. This gave my husband and me three choices: (1) call the relevant parents and nicely ask them to change their ways (what do you think is the probability of an enthusiastic response to a call like that?); (2) tell our son that he can't go places where unhealthy food is available, thereby isolating him from just about everybody; or (3) try to educate our son about what foods he should eat, and then grin and bear the situation. You can guess which one we picked.

Nevertheless, in many situations, people, similar to rats, choose fairly balanced diets. But we still need to know how they do that and what's responsible for the huge variety in our food preferences. How do our experiences influence these preferences? Why is it that some people learn to like eating insects and others don't? Perhaps if we knew the answers to these questions we could help our children to eat healthier foods. The rest of this chapter will tell you some of the highlights of what scientists have learned about the effects of experience on food preferences.

Tried and True: Experience With Particular Foods

There are many ways in which experience with a particular food can increase or decrease your subsequent preference for that food. At least in the world in which people evolved, most of these food preference changes helped people to survive.

Familiarity with a food

You're at a dinner party and your hosts serve you a plate of what is supposedly food, but there's nothing on the plate that you recognize. There's a mound of something green and squishy and some things shaped like sticks that are purple, complemented by a pile of small orange ovoids.

Most likely you wouldn't feel terribly enthusiastic about eating this dinner. Such feelings have been immortalized in college students' description of certain cafeteria dishes as "mystery meat." Our disinclination to like and eat foods with which we are unfamiliar isn't unique. In general, people and other animals have a fear of new things, which is known in the scientific literature as *neophobia*.[9] In general we prefer foods and situations that are familiar.[10]

Some people are more neophobic than others. When it comes to food, neophobic people don't just avoid trying new foods. If they're persuaded to try them, they tend to rate them lower than do neophilics (people who enjoy trying new things, including new foods).[11]

How neophobic someone is appears to have a genetic component and to be fairly consistent in an individual from when he or she is a toddler until at least young adulthood.[12] Even so, if we are afraid of new foods and prefer familiar ones, then simply exposing someone to a new food should increase that person's preference for the food. Many experiments have shown that this is indeed the case. For example, psychologist Patricia Pliner gave male college students between 0 and 20 tastes of individual novel fruit juices, such as guava, mango, and soursop. Juices that had been tasted more frequently received higher preference ratings.[13] As another example, psychologist Leann L. Birch and her colleagues repeatedly asked 2- to 5-year-old children to just look at some fruits and to both taste and look at other fruits. All of the fruits that they used were novel ones such as kiwi, papaya, lychee, and sugar palm. Preference for a fruit's appearance was greater the more times that a child had seen that fruit. Preference for a fruit's taste was increased only if a child had tasted that fruit. Therefore, Birch and her colleagues concluded that in order to increase preference for the taste of a food, experience with the actual taste of the food is necessary.[14]

If familiarity increases preference for a food, then why do we not end up eating, say, bananas, day after day, year after year? The more you eat them, the more you should like them as compared to something else, until finally you're eating nothing but bananas. This wouldn't be very adaptive because almost no natural food contains all of the nutrition that a grown person should have. Fortunately, after we eat something, there's a short-lived decrease in preference for that particular food. This *sensory specific satiety* appears to occur whether or not the food is swallowed, as opposed to being chewed. In other words, exposure to simply the appearance, taste, and texture of a food appears to cause a temporary, short-term decrease in preference for that food, as well as a long-term increase in preference for that food.[15]

A number of experiments on food preferences have demonstrated this phenomenon. In psychologist David J. Stang's experiment, women repeatedly tasted 15 spices, including chile powder, mustard, cloves, and marjoram. The preference ratings for the spices decreased with repeated tastings but recovered after a week without tastings.[16] In another experiment, psychologist Barbara J. Rolls and her colleagues showed that female student nurses would consume more sandwiches if the available sandwiches had four different fillings (cheese, egg, ham, and tomato) as compared to if the available sandwiches had only one of these fillings.[17]

This tendency of people and other animals to prefer familiar foods coexists with a tendency to avoid recently consumed foods. For omnivores such as us, this combination of strategies is very useful, ensuring that a variety of familiar foods, and thus a variety of nutrients, is eaten.[18] When it comes to food preferences, familiarity does appear to breed (some) contempt, while absence makes the heart grow (somewhat) fonder.

It's good and good for you!

At the beginning of this chapter you learned that rats, and sometimes even people, are fairly good at selecting foods that have the nutrients that they need. In fact, many species of animals can do this, including beetles and spiders.[19] When an animal that needs a particular nutrient shows a preference for a food containing that nutrient this is called a *specific hunger*.[20] (See Conversation Making Fact #6.) Researchers have some good ideas about what causes specific hungers.

Conversation making fact #6

One type of specific hunger has been of particular concern to physicians. Some children and pregnant women repeatedly consume nonnutritive substances such as paint, plaster, and dirt. Because such food cravings sometimes appear in people who need a lot of nutrients, it has been proposed that at least some of these cravings are the result of specific hungers for minerals such as iron.[21]

Rozin's experiments with thiamine-deficient rats, which were described at the start of this chapter, give us some clues. The rats spilled the thiamine-deficient food from their dish, the same way that they treated a food to which quinine, a very bitter substance, had been added. Even when no longer thiamine deficient, the rats preferred to eat nothing when they were hungry if the only choice was the old, deficient food.[22] Thus the rats appeared to have an aversion to the thiamine-deficient food.

Based on evidence such as this, a good explanation for specific hungers is that animals develop aversions to nutritionally deficient foods.[23] In other words, animals may appear to like a nutritional food solely because they don't like the other deficient food that is available, and the nutritional food is all that is left. This is similar to when I eat broccoli because the only other available vegetable is brussels sprouts; this does not mean that I *like* broccoli. However, there's also evidence that animals can learn a preference for a particular food that makes them healthier, a food tasted right before an animal recovers from illness. Such a learned preference is known as the *medicine effect*.[24]

Nevertheless, before you think that the existence of specific hungers will allow all animals to select a perfect set of foods to eat, there are two cautions. First, it has been very difficult to demonstrate specific hungers in rats fed diets deficient in certain nutrients, such as vitamins A and D.[25] Second, the experiments on specific hungers give the subjects a very limited choice of foods. In situations more similar to real life, when there are lots of foods available, it might be quite difficult for people and other animals to choose the nutritionally best foods. Once again, we can't count on having great bodily wisdom.

Often what you need to eat isn't a particular nutrient but simply calories. Every animal needs a certain number of calories to fuel its activity. In the world in which people evolved, calories were much more scarce than they are now. So it's not surprising that being hungry makes people rate foods—including specific odors and tastes—as more pleasant.[26] However, taking our calorie-seeking mechanisms one step farther, we and other animals have actually evolved to learn to prefer foods that are dense in calories.

A great many experiments support this conclusion. For example, E. L. Gibson and J. Wardle showed that the best way to predict how much 4- to 5-year-old children would prefer different fruits and vegetables was not how sweet they were, or how much protein they had, or whether the children had tried them, but how dense in calories they were. When I read this study I was fascinated by the fact that the most calorie-dense fruits and vegetables turned out to be, in order, bananas, potatoes, peas, and grapes,[27] very similar to my fruit and vegetable preference order when I was growing up.

As another example, psychologists Elizabeth H. Zandstra and Wael El-Deredy gave hungry young men and women one of two types of a plain yogurt drink on alternate days (5 days total for each drink). The two types of drinks had the same volume (200 ml), and looked and tasted the same, but, unbeknownst to the experiment's participants, one drink had 57 calories and the other had 255 calories. For some participants the high-calorie drink always had a blue label and the low-calorie drink had a pink label, and for other participants it was the reverse. When participants were subsequently given a choice between blue- and pink-labeled drinks, they were much more likely to choose the drink with the color label that had been associated with more calories.[28]

But, you might say, always preferring foods that have lots of calories isn't always the best goal. In order to consume an appropriate number of calories, you should show a large preference for a high-calorie food when your body needs calories, and a small preference for a high-calorie food when your body does not need calories. This does happen sometimes. Psychologist D. A. Booth and his colleagues showed that if men and women are hungry when they eat meals containing a lot of disguised high-calorie starch, their preference for these meals increases. However, if people are full when they eat these meals, they later show less preference for them. Further, people will even learn to eat smaller meals when they contain a lot of disguised high-calorie starch.[29] Psychologists Leann L. Birch and Mary Deysher got similar results with preschool children. The preschoolers learned to eat smaller amounts of cookies or crackers following a snack (vanilla or chocolate pudding) that had regularly contained a large number of calories, and larger amounts of cookies or crackers following a snack (vanilla or chocolate pudding) that had regularly contained a smaller number of calories.[30]

I can hear your puzzlement. If people adjust their meal size depending on how many calories they have eaten or are eating, why does anyone become overweight? Keep in mind that the research shows that people eat fewer, not necessarily few, calories when they're full or when they're consuming other calories. Someone could be eating fewer calories when full than when hungry, but enough calories to gain weight in both situations.

Now that you understand how our preferences for foods are affected by their caloric densities, you should also understand our obsession with foods that are high in fat, for example, french fries, ice cream, fried chicken, scrambled eggs, butter—the list goes on and on. Fat is much denser in calories than are protein or carbohydrate; fat contains 9 calories per gram, but protein and carbohydrate each contain only 4 calories per gram. Therefore we have a learned strong preference for high-fat foods. Because of this preference, and because, for most people in the United States, high-fat food is easily available, many of us end up consuming much more fat than is recommended.[31] This tendency to learn to prefer high-fat foods, combined with our largely genetic preferences for sweet and salty foods, though originally useful, gets us into a lot of trouble in our current environment.

When eating a food makes you sick
(or seems to)

Have you ever eaten something, become sick, and then did not want to eat that food again? Perhaps one night you drank too much champagne, became sick, and now you cannot stand the thought of even tasting champagne? If so, you're not alone. A questionnaire given by Iris Ophir, Kerry E. Strauss, and myself to over 500 college students found that, on average, each student reported one food aversion of this sort. In general the aversions were strong and had persisted a long time; 62% of the aversive foods had never been eaten again, even though the aversions had been acquired an average of about 5 years previously.[32] Many of the students wrote quite explicit derogatory comments about the aversive food in the margins of the questionnaire. For example, one student wrote that hot dogs, a food that popped up relatively frequently on the questionnaire, "are 100% s_ _ _!'"

This type of learning, known in the research literature as taste aversion learning, is extremely powerful. Usually, a person has to get sick only once after eating a particular food in order for a taste aversion to form, and taste aversions can last an extremely long time. The illness needs to be gastrointestinal in order for this type of learning to occur. Taste aversions are more likely to form to novel, as opposed to familiar, foods. Taste aversion learning occurs similarly in a huge variety of different species, including people and rats. In fact, the food aversions described in the previous section, the aversions to nutritionally deficient foods that make it appear that animals have specific hungers, are thought to be taste aversions.[33]

Taste aversions were first observed by farmers trying to get rid of rats. The farmers found it was difficult to kill rats by putting out poisoned bait. The rats would take only small samples of any new food, in this case the bait, and if they then became ill, they would subsequently avoid the bait. For this reason, farmers called the taste aversion learning phenomenon bait shyness.[34]

Another report of taste aversion learning in nature comes from a well-known psychologist at the University of Pennsylvania, Martin E. P. Seligman (president of the American Psychological Association in 1998). In 1972 Seligman described how he ate sauce béarnaise on steak and subsequently became ill with what was definitely stomach flu; his work colleague who had not eaten the steak came down with the same affliction, and his wife who had eaten the steak did not. Yet, even though he was absolutely convinced that the sauce béarnaise did not cause his illness, Seligman acquired an aversion to it. Because of this famous story, taste aversion learning has also been called the sauce béarnaise phenomenon.[35]

Psychologist John Garcia and his colleagues were the first to study taste aversion learning in the laboratory. Garcia noticed that his rats ate less after being irradiated. Apparently the irradiation made the rats gastrointestinally ill and they associated the illness with the food, resulting in a taste aversion to the food.[36] Since Garcia's original discovery, most of the research on taste aversion learning in rats has made the subjects sick by means of injection.[37]

You may wonder how taste aversion experiments are done with people—how are people made sick? It's obviously a challenge because researchers don't want to inject people unless there's an extremely good reason. Therefore a variety of other techniques have been used. One uses a large rotating cylinder whose inside is painted with vertical stripes. The participant sits inside the cylinder and, while it rotates, tilts his or her head to the right and then to the left. This procedure really works, and if vomiting seems imminent, a participant can simply close his or her eyes.[38] If you're wondering why anyone would volunteer for such an experiment, the participants tend to be neophilic and/or sensation seekers (I'd never be in one of these experiments).

By far the most famous paper on taste aversion learning was published in 1966 by psychologists John Garcia and Robert A. Koelling. The design of their experiment, shown in Figure 6.1, was very clever. In the first part

Figure 6.1 Garcia and Koelling's procedure showing the tendency of rats to associate taste with illness and audiovisual stimuli with shock. (Adapted from J. Garcia and R. A. Koelling, "Relation of Cue to Consequence in Avoidance Learning," *Psychonomic Science* 4[1966]: 123–124.)

of the experiment, Garcia and Koelling allowed thirsty rats to lick at a spout. With each lick, all of the rats got flavored water and there was a light flash and a click. Half of these rats were shocked whenever they licked. The other half, while licking, were made ill, either by irradiation or injection. Several days later, in the second part of the experiment, after all of the rats had recovered, the rats were again allowed to drink from a spout. But this time, for half of the rats, the water was flavored but there were no light flashes or clicks. For the other half of the rats, there were light flashes and clicks after each lick, but the water was unflavored. The results showed that the rats that had been shocked in the first part of the experiment drank very little of the water that was accompanied by light flashes and clicks in the second part of the experiment, but the rats that had been made ill in the first part of the experiment drank very little of the water that was flavored in the second part of the experiment. Garcia and Koelling concluded that it's easier for rats to associate taste with illness and audiovisual events with shock than vice versa.[39] Due to results such as these, the term *taste aversion learning* has been more popular in the research literature than *bait shyness* or *the sauce béarnaise phenomenon*. Subsequent experiments have suggested that, in addition to tastes, odors may also play an important role in food aversions linked to illness,[40] yet the term *taste aversion learning* has persisted. The fact that tastes and odors are more easily associated with illness than with other sorts of events helps us to survive. The presence of a poison is more likely to be indicated by a particular odor or taste than by a particular appearance or sound.

Many subsequent experiments have found that taste aversion learning has some other unusual properties that may help animals to survive. For example, taste aversions can be acquired with up to 24 hours between consumption of the food and illness.[41] This is helpful because it may take hours before a poison will result in illness. In addition, in taste aversion learning, the taste actually seems to acquire aversive properties.[42] Remember how the rats treated the thiamine-deficient food in Rozin's experiments on specific hungers, overturning the food dish and in general behaving toward the thiamine-deficient food as they would to a bitter, aversive food? Remember how some of my research participants felt about hot dogs? This characteristic of taste aversion learning helps us to survive because a poison should be avoided no matter under what circumstances it's encountered. Finally, the fact that taste aversions are more likely to form to novel foods, and often form after just one pairing of a taste with illness, helps to ensure that, as much as possible, we stay away from foods that are likely to make us sick.

Lest you think that the only current interest in taste aversion learning is by laboratory researchers, I should point out that taste aversion learning has been used to help understand and treat many eating and drinking disorders. Understanding how taste aversion learning works may have other practical implications as well. For example, Carl R. Gustavson and his colleagues tried to use taste aversion learning to prevent coyotes from attacking sheep on sheep ranches in the western United States. Many ranchers choose simply to kill the coyotes. Coyotes are a valuable part of the ecosystem, however. For example, they help to keep the rabbit population under control. Gustavson and his colleagues reasoned that if they could train the coyotes to avoid sheep but not rabbits, this would disrupt the ecosystem much less than killing the coyotes. Gustavson and his colleagues therefore placed lamb bait laced with an illness-inducing drug on the range in areas frequented by wild coyotes. The coyotes appeared to acquire an aversion to eating or even approaching sheep.[43] In fact, after the aversion training, coyotes behaved submissively toward sheep, running the other way when a sheep approached. I've seen this amazing sight myself on film. The coyote in the film actually cowered when the sheep was near.

"You can have candy only if you eat your spinach"

There are a number of other interesting ways that you can increase or decrease a preference for a taste by pairing it with something. One way is to pair a taste with a better or worse taste, which will increase or decrease the preference for the first taste, respectively.[44]

Psychologists believe that this type of learning is responsible for our learning to like initially aversive substances such as coffee and tea. Think back to the first time that you tasted coffee or tea. If there was nothing added to it, most likely you did not particularly enjoy the experience. A new coffee or tea drinker usually adds sugar or milk. Gradually, as the taste of the coffee or tea becomes associated with the taste of the sugar or the milk, the coffee or tea can be drunk with less, and finally no, sugar or milk. Psychologist Debra A. Zellner and her colleagues did an experiment demonstrating this. They varied the numbers of times that college students (both men and women) drank several different types of sweetened herbal teas. The more times that a student drank a particular sweetened tea, the more the student's preference for that tea increased.[45]

An experiment by psychologists Karen Ackroff and Anthony Sclafani showed that not all sweet tastes are equally effective at increasing preference when they're paired with another taste. Ackroff and Sclafani's experiment used rats and two types of sugar: glucose (one of the products of the digestion of table sugar) and fructose. When almond- or vanilla-flavored laboratory chow (in the same family as dog chow and cat chow) was paired with unflavored glucose or fructose, preference for a particular flavor of chow increased more when it was paired with glucose than when it was paired with fructose. Also, although the rats initially preferred the fructose, with experience they came to prefer the glucose. Therefore something about the postingestion physiological effects of the glucose must have been relatively more positive for the rat than was the case with fructose. Two possible explanations are that glucose remains in the stomach longer than fructose and that glucose produces a greater increase in insulin after it has been absorbed than fructose.[46] One conclusion that you might draw from Ackroff and Sclafani's experiment is that, at least for rats, regular table sugar is in some way more pleasurable to eat than fruit. Many people would agree with the rats!

Let's consider situations in which a taste is paired with doing something rather than with another taste. L. L. Birch and colleagues have conducted experiments of this sort with children. For example, Birch and her colleagues let preschool children engage in a specific play activity, such as drawing or tricycle riding, only if they drank a specific type of fruit juice, such as apple or grape. This decreased the child's subsequent preference for the fruit juice.[47] The flip side of this phenomenon, also demonstrated by Birch's research group, is that if you give children a particular snack only if they behave well in the classroom, preference for that snack can increase.[48]

Think what this means for parents. If they want their children to eat more spinach and not to eat so much candy, they may be doing exactly the wrong thing if they tell the children that they can have candy only if they eat spinach. According to Birch's research, this would decrease the preference for spinach and increase the preference for candy, making it even more difficult to get the children to eat spinach and to stop eating candy. How many parents do you know who tell their children that they can have dessert only if they eat their dinner? Just about everybody.

Nevertheless, it seems doubtful that telling children that they can eat spinach if they first eat their ice cream would result in the consumption of more spinach and less ice cream. The bitterness of spinach (for some people) and the sweetness of ice cream (for practically everyone) would make it difficult to use such methods to change people's extreme feelings about spinach and ice cream. Birch did not use highly liked or highly disliked foods in her experiments. Even so, parents may want to keep Birch's findings in mind when setting guidelines for their children's eating behaviors.

On the other hand, there is evidence that using praise and some other nonfood rewards can result in long-lasting increases in choice of and preference for certain foods. Therefore it is possible that congratulating your child or giving your child stickers may help in establishing healthy eating habits.[49] Further research is going to have to continue to tease out when making something contingent on eating a certain food increases or decreases preference for that food.

Researchers Brian Wansink and his colleagues took this line of research one step farther, reasoning that eating certain foods under unpleasant circumstances—simple temporal proximity of a food and unpleasant activities—would decrease preference for those foods. These researchers were able to show that American World War II veterans who had experienced high levels of combat in the Pacific had a lower preference for Chinese and Japanese food than American World War II veterans who had experienced high levels of combat in Europe.[50] The circumstances under which we are exposed to certain foods can affect our preferences for those foods many decades later.

Two other experiments conducted by Birch and her colleagues also have sobering messages for parents. If day care workers restricted 3- to 6-year-old children's access to snack foods such as fruit bar cookies and fish-shaped crackers, the children later tried harder to get those snacks as opposed to other snacks.[51] Further, simply telling preschool children to "Finish your soup, please," resulted in their eating less soup and making far more negative comments about it.[52] In other words, my attempts to keep my son when he was young away from unhealthy snacks and to tell him to eat healthy foods (yes, I did that too) may have done the exact opposite of what I intended and contributed to the unhealthy snacking that he sometimes does today.

"I'm not Sure What to Order for Dinner… What are you Having?"

The fact that animals' experiences with food can modify their food preferences clearly helps us to survive. But wouldn't it be much more efficient, not to mention safer, for animals to share their information about which foods are good to eat and which are not? Wouldn't it make great sense for animals to eat what they see other members of their species eating safely?

Perhaps you remember the commercials for Life cereal some years ago. Three brothers are in their kitchen faced with a box of cereal that they have never seen before. The youngest brother is named Mikey. "Let's get Mikey to try it!" the two older brothers exclaim. If he eats it and likes it, then they will eat it too. This is a very smart move on the part of the older brothers. If the cereal is deadly poisonous, only Mikey will die.

As it turns out, there are many different ways in which members of a species influence one another's food preferences. We have all had the experience in a restaurant of getting advice from our table companions or the waiter before ordering. Researchers have now done a fair amount of experimentation on such effects. Sometimes these sorts of effects involve one animal directly influencing the food preferences of another member of the same species. There are also more indirect ways in which people influence the food preferences of other people through the effects of our culture.

"Are you telling me what to eat?"

Sibylle K. Escalona was one of the first to record observations of changes in people's food preferences due to social interactions. She worked as a psychologist in the Massachusetts Reformatory for Women during the 1940s. The women then incarcerated in that institution were often permitted to keep their children in the institution if the children were under 3 years of age. The children lived in the prison nursery, and their mothers could frequently visit and care for them. Other inmates as well as reformatory employees also cared for the children in the nursery.[53]

On many occasions Escalona observed what she believed to be cases in which the caretakers influenced the children's food preferences subconsciously. For example:

> It came to attention accidentally that many of the babies under four months of age showed a consistent dislike for either orange or tomato juice. (These juices were offered on alternate days with equal frequency.) The number preferring each kind of juice was about equal. Furthermore, such preferences seemed to change and a baby who had refused orange juice for about three weeks occasionally would reverse his preference within two or three days, accepting orange juice and refusing tomato henceforth. A checkup revealed that where there was a sudden change in preference the baby's feedings had been re-assigned from one person to another. Next we determined the preference of the students who took care of these babies in such a way that they could not know why the question had been asked, in fact, were not aware of its having been asked. In the fifteen cases we were able to investigate in this matter, the student in charge of a baby showing a decided preference had the same preference, or rather the same dislike, as the baby. That is, babies who refused tomato juice were found to be fed by adults who also expressed a dislike for tomato juice. In three cases we were able to establish the fact that a baby reversing a preference had been changed to a student who possessed the dislike acquired by the baby subsequent to the change in personnel.[54]

These are sobering observations, especially for parents. Perhaps adults can influence children's food preferences without any awareness whatsoever that they're doing so.

But how might this happen? What unconscious signal could an adult give a child about whether a food is good to eat? One possibility is related to the acceptance and rejection responses shown by many species, including people, discussed earlier in this book. These responses are present at birth.[55] In addition, babies as young as 36 hours are apparently able to imitate the facial expressions of adults.[56] Perhaps adults who are feeding young children consciously or unconsciously make faces of acceptance or rejection, depending on their own preferences for the food being fed, and the children then imitate the expressions and consume more or less food accordingly. This could explain why people feeding babies so often intone "open the hangar" while simultaneously opening their own mouths and directing a spoonful of food at the babies' mouths.

Escalona's research wasn't a controlled experiment, so her results and her interpretations of them aren't conclusive. For many years, very little properly controlled research was done to find out to a high degree of certainty whether someone's facial expression when eating a food could influence someone else's preference for that food. However, experiments have now shown that a child or an adult making a facial expression of disgust can decrease a peer's preference for a particular food.[57]

Birch has done several intriguing experiments showing other ways in which social context can affect children's food preferences. For example, she has shown that if an adult repeatedly gives a child a snack food such as canned unsweetened pineapple or cashews while being very friendly to the child, the child's preference for the food will increase.[58]

In another intriguing experiment, this one conducted by psychologist Janette Greenhalgh and her colleagues at the University of Bangor in Wales, children (called the target children) were individually exposed to a new food (e.g., blue bread) while in the presence of four, slightly older, children (called the confederate children, who were acting on instructions from the experimenter). In some cases the confederate children said the novel food was wonderful and ate it, and in other cases the confederate children said the novel food was not wonderful and did not eat it. The target children increased their consumption of the novel food in the former case and decreased it in the latter.[59]

Laboratory research has also demonstrated that young children are more willing to try something new if they first see an adult try it[60] (similar to what happened in the Mikey commercial). Along the same lines, the likelihood that a college student will eat a new, as opposed to a familiar, food depends on what the student sees someone else do. For example, if the other person, faced with a choice between potato chips and cassava chips, picks the cassava chips, then the student will be more likely to pick the cassava chips, and vice versa.[61]

These experiments with people illustrate some of the fascinating ways in which we influence one another's food preferences. Experiments with rats have investigated these sorts of effects in much more detail. By far the most accomplished at conducting such experiments has been psychologist Bennett G. Galef. He has performed a great many ingenious experiments designed to identify the mechanisms that are involved in the social transmission of food preferences among rats. We don't know to what degree these mechanisms also operate in people. But Galef's research certainly points to some intriguing possibilities.

For example, Galef has shown that rat pups learn to choose adult rats' preferred food. Further, he has identified three ways in which this preference is transmitted: odor or taste cues at the feeding site, such as might be contained in feces, which attract pups to the site; the presence of adult rats at the feeding site, which attracts pups to the site; and a particular odor or taste cue, specific to a mother rat's preferred food, which is present in her milk and which increases the preference for that food in her nursing pups.[62]

Apparently, then, there are at least three ways in which food preferences can be transmitted from adult rats to rat pups. This means that if rat pups don't learn appropriate food preferences one way, they will learn them another way. It's clearly safer for rat pups to learn food preferences by these multiple, redundant mechanisms of social transmission rather than by their own trial and error.

Galef and his colleagues have also shown that long-lasting food preferences can also be transmitted between adult rats. Preference for Food A is increased in an "observer" rat after the observer interacts with a "demonstrator" rat that has previously eaten Food A.[63]

In other species, the young also learn to eat what the adults of their species eat. For example, wild vervet monkey infants prefer a pink, nonbitter food over a blue, bitter food, neither of which have they ever encountered before, when their mothers demonstrate that preference.[64] On the flip side, a rat can acquire a taste aversion if it eats a food and is then exposed to a sick rat.[65]

Apparently there are a large number of different mechanisms by which rats and other species, including people, learn food preferences and food aversions from members of their own species.

When in Rome, eat as the Romans do

You've already learned a great deal about how one person can influence another person's food preferences. Given this information, you would expect that a culture's attitudes toward certain foods would also influence people's food preferences. After all, a culture consists basically of the views held by and the practices of a group of individual people. There appear to be many ways in which our culture influences our food preferences.

For example, consider advertising, a ubiquitous part of our culture. By age 2, children are viewing, on average, over 4,000 TV food advertisements per year. For teenagers 13–17 years of age, that value increases to, on average, over 6,000 TV food advertisements per year. And most of these commercials are for foods low in nutrition.[66] Good nutrition is critical to good health. Therefore, if people are indeed influenced by advertisements, advertisements could be seriously harming their health.

Those of us with children have all had the experience of their asking for some totally nonnutritious food that they saw advertised on TV. For my son it was usually some revolting cereal that consisted primarily of sugar. Therefore it will also not surprise you that research has indeed shown that when children and young adults are exposed to commercials and other advertisements for foods poor in nutrition (such as soda), the research participants then say that they like those foods more and they are more likely to eat them.[67] And it isn't just explicit advertisements that may be influencing our food preferences. Children's TV programs, even on public television, are much more likely to depict unhealthy than healthy foods.[68] What this all means is that the advertisements and TV we're seeing are very likely encouraging us to prefer foods that are poor in nutrition.

Another way that our culture can affect our food preferences is by affecting the types of things that are considered appropriate to eat. As you learned in the previous chapter, this can include such preferences as which foods should have salt or sugar added to them (after all, why shouldn't we sprinkle salt on our ice cream and sugar on our fried eggs?), the temperature at which certain foods should be served (warm soda is considered good only for upset stomachs), which foods should be eaten at certain times of the day (we don't eat green beans at breakfast or Danish at dinner), whether or not we should eat insects, and which foods are considered ethical or moral to eat. People learn through their culture to prefer foods with certain characteristics.[69] Cultures exert these effects by means of the sorts of food preference mechanisms described earlier in this chapter, for example food familiarity and observational learning.

Our culture also repeatedly tries to tell us what's healthy to eat; these days the relative health benefits of eating different types of foods is a popular subject in the media. This information does appear to have some effect on our food preferences, at least under some conditions. For example, researchers Erica van Herpen and Hans C. M. van Trijp showed that putting on the front of a food package a bright logo with a big checkmark that indicated the food was healthy increased choice of that food more than did putting a nutrition label on the food package.[70] But does this mean that preference for the food was actually changed by the packaging? Several people I know, after starting to take medication that dramatically lowers your cholesterol no matter what you eat, immediately began consuming large amounts of fatty beef and other high-cholesterol foods. Information about foods' convenience and nutrition may primarily affect the amount eaten of a food, but not the degree to which that food is liked; food liking may be more affected by the sorts of factors discussed earlier in this chapter and in the previous chapter.

Finally, let's consider the effects of religion. Many religions have rules about what may or may not be eaten, and these rules may be consistent with the food preferences of the members of the religion. For example, many Jews don't enjoy the taste of pork.[71] This lack of a preference for eating pork is probably due to members of the religion influencing one another in the ways described earlier in this chapter. Some people have also claimed that a religion's beliefs about what should and should not be eaten may have helped the members of that religion to survive. You'll hear more about that in a later chapter.

How to Have a Healthy Plate

The United States Department of Agriculture recommends that half of the food on each of our plates consist of fruits and vegetables (see choosemyplate.org), but many people in the United States fail to achieve that. On average, children and adults consume about 80% and 60%, respectively, of the recommended amounts of fruit, 40% and 60% of the recommended amounts of vegetables, and 0.5% and 40% of the recommended amounts of greens and beans (see information on the Healthy Eating Index at www.cnpp.usda.gov/healthyeatingindex. htm). In fact, there is even a word to describe the fear that many of us have of vegetables: *lachanophobia* (see Encyclo, the online encyclopedia, at www.encyclo.co.uk). To help increase our consumption of fruits and vegetables, during the past couple of decades a great many experiments have now been conducted employing the preference modification principles described earlier in this chapter. There have been multiple experiments showing that, for example, preference for fruits and vegetables can be increased simply by exposing children to the fruits and vegetables (though six exposures may be needed and some children may show no increase in preference at all); or by pairing vegetables in children and adults with a highly preferred taste, such as sucrose; or by an adult and children simply interacting positively, including talking about a vegetable. The reference list gives a few examples of these experiments.[72]

Let's consider one in detail. In perhaps her best-known experiment, Birch arranged for certain 3- to 5-year-old children (called the target children) to eat lunch repeatedly with other children the same age. They ate in groups of four or five (one target child and three or four other children) that did not change during the experiment. Adults came by with serving plates to each group's table. The adults asked the children to choose between a vegetable preferred only by the target child at a given table and a vegetable preferred only by the other three children at the same table. The same pair of vegetables was served to each table for the 4 days of the experiment. On the first day the target child chose first, but on days 2, 3, and 4, the other children chose first. Not only did the target children increase their choices of their nonpreferred vegetables during the latter days of the experiment, but their reported preferences for those vegetables also increased. These effects were stronger for the younger children.[73] Peers don't just affect such matters as wearing the latest styles and what TV shows to watch!

Putting all of the research together, I'd recommend the following for anyone trying to get a child to eat more fruits and vegetables:

- Expose the child to the target food items under very relaxing, pleasant circumstances.
- Make sure that other people in the room are talking about and/or eating the target items with great enjoyment.
- Ensure that alternative, highly preferred, but less healthy foods are not present.
- At least initially, combine the target food items with a highly preferred flavor, or present them in a very tasty sauce.
- Praise the child and give the child stickers or other nonfood rewards for making contact with and/or eating the target items.
- Repeat this process many times.
- Do not make eating a highly preferred item contingent on the child eating the target items.
- Limit, to the degree possible, the child's exposure to advertisements for and other media about unhealthy foods, including exposure to TV, and increase, to the degree possible, the child's exposure to advertisements and other media about healthy foods.
- Finally, do not get discouraged if the child's preference for the food items does not change. What the child perceives when tasting the foods may be quite different from what you perceive—what the child perceives may actually be quite negative (see Chapter 5).

Classifying Different Types of our Food Aversions: How Much Can you Stomach?

By now you've heard a lot about what causes people to like and dislike certain foods. Much of the information on food aversions can be summarized using psychologists Paul Rozin and April E. Fallon's classification of the four different types of food aversions shown by people: foods that are rejected because they're distasteful, dangerous,

Table 6.1 Classification of food aversions in people

Type of Aversive Food	Description	Example	Possible Origins
Distasteful	Not aversive if cannot be tasted	Warm milk	Aversive taste, smell, or texture; consumption of the food may have been followed by gastrointestinal illness
Dangerous	Could cause physical harm	Poisonous mushrooms	Consumption of the food has been followed by, or has been reputed to be followed by, a nongastrointestinal illness
Inappropriate	Not considered to be food	Tree bark	Genetically based aversive taste, or direct experience with food, or information from other people indicates that food cannot be consumed and/or digested
Disgusting	Aversive even if cannot be tasted or if in very small quantities; substances paired with a disgusting food also become disgusting (i.e., contamination occurs)	Urine	Direct or indirect contact with other people who consider the food disgusting, or contact with another disgusting food, or similarity to another disgusting food

inappropriate, or disgusting.[74] (See Table 6.1.) Some of these types of aversions seem to involve contact with other people, and others seem to be due just to experience with the food itself. While I describe each of them in the following paragraphs, see if you can figure out how to classify my aversion to eating seafood (or your own favorite food aversion).

Distasteful foods are those that most people would not mind eating if the taste of the food were covered up by another taste or if they only discovered what they had been eating after they had finished. An example of a distasteful food is warm milk, whose fulsome aroma and taste many people find quite unpleasant. Taste aversion learning, in which the taste of a food is paired with gastrointestinal illness (principally nausea), usually results in a distaste for the food. A genetically based reaction to the taste of a food (e.g., if a food is very bitter) may also result in a food aversion that is categorized as a distaste.

On the other hand, if eating a food is paired with another type of illness, such as difficulty in breathing, as can happen with an allergic reaction, this will result in a food aversion in which the food is classified as dangerous. Dangerous foods are those that could cause physical harm if eaten. With this sort of food aversion, someone would be glad to eat the food again if a magic pill would just prevent the illness. An example of a dangerous food is a poisonous mushroom. Someone may consider a food dangerous because of direct experience with the food or because of information received from other people.

Inappropriate foods are those items that aren't considered food. An example is tree bark (and for me, items such as lettuce, which to me seems very similar to grass). Someone may consider a food inappropriate due to a genetically based reaction to the food's taste, due to direct experience with the food (have you ever tried to chew tree bark?), or due to information from other people.

And now we come to by far my favorite category: disgusting foods. These are foods that most people would never want in their stomach no matter how the foods were disguised and no matter how small the amount. Some examples are urine and feces. Disgust has been described as an emotion that helps to maintain and emphasize the distinction between people and other animals. It's certainly the case that foods become disgusting in large part because of direct and indirect contact with the reactions to these foods by other people. Thus as children age and acquire increased experience with adults' reactions to certain potential foods that adults tend to treat as disgusting, such as, in some cultures, insects, the children themselves come increasingly to treat those potential foods as disgusting. Foods may also be classified as disgusting because they have come into contact with something disgusting, or because their appearance is similar to that of something disgusting. For example, a milkshake that once had, but no longer has, a cockroach floating in it is disgusting, as is fudge shaped to look like dog feces. This makes sense according to traditional learning theory, which says that we tend to associate events or aspects of our surroundings that have been paired together or that are similar to each other.[75]

Now take a guess into which category my aversion to eating seafood falls? If you guessed "disgusting" you were correct! I cannot stand the thought of touching seafood nor of having even the tiniest particle of seafood in what I eat. Once, on a trip to a friend's house in Martha's Vineyard off of Cape Cod, Massachusetts, I was served lobster and had no choice but to try and eat it. I managed to get down a small amount. That night, in bed, I kept tasting the lobster, and it was horrible. Finally, I got up, went to the bathroom, and put a huge amount of toothpaste into my mouth—that helped some. Paul Rozin, the world's leading expert on food aversions, has tried mightily to figure out what's responsible for my aversion to seafood. The fact that it's classified as a disgust has puzzled him; he would have expected it to be a distaste.

What Rozin did not know, and what I learned only relatively recently, is what my early food surroundings were like when it came to fish. Some years ago, my mother uncovered a set of instructions the pediatrician wrote out for her concerning how I should be fed when I was 9½ months old: "Offer baked and broiled fish—cod, flounder, halibut. Shred well to avoid bones. Try tuna fish and salmon." I asked my mother if she could remember if she did this. "Oh, I'm sure I didn't," she said. "I can't stand the smell of cooking fish." Further interrogation of my mother revealed that, at the time, she herself ate only lobster and shrimp. She had no tuna fish in the house. She never, ever cooked fish at home with the exception of, when I was child, steaming shrimp. She said that this odor seemed different to her than the odor of cooking fish, that the shrimp odor did not bother her. On the other hand, I can remember vividly as a child the odor of her steaming shrimp and finding it so horrible that I had to retreat to my third-floor room next to the attic.

Thus it appears that, similar to me, my mother was extremely sensitive to the odors of fish and seafood. As it turns out, my father did not like these odors either. So I probably got my fish-odor sensitivity from my parents' genes. However, in addition, my parents never exposed me to the taste of fish when I was young, so it did not become a familiar, preferred food. Further, it's possible that I may have observed my mother's aversive reactions to the taste or smell of fish, thus resulting in my disgust for fish.

Conclusion

Armed with this chapter's and the previous chapter's scientific information about the origins of various food preferences and aversions, we can now try to answer the questions posed about various food-preference and food-aversion problems at the beginning of the previous chapter. Some of these problems, for example the decreased preference for milk with age and the extreme preferences for sweet foods and for salty foods, are probably due largely to the effects of genes. In most people milk becomes largely indigestible after the age of 3, and people show a genetic preference for sweet and salty foods. However, the degree to which an animal (including a person) prefers to eat sweet foods, salty foods, and milk can be modified by experience.

The acquired aversion to hot dogs after hot dog consumption has been followed by illness probably is due primarily to the effects of experience. Animals associate food consumption with subsequent nausea, resulting in eating that food less.

Finally, a child's—and my—aversion to eating vegetables may result from a number of different factors. Some people (such as me) may find some vegetables bitter tasting because of a genetically based taste sensitivity to certain chemicals. In addition, vegetables, when eaten by themselves, are low in salt and sugar (both of which are innately preferred) and are also low in fat (which we learn to prefer due to its high concentration of calories). Finally, as Birch's research has shown, children can learn to prefer certain vegetables by observing other children eating them. If someone does not see other people eating vegetables, or sees people eating them although clearly not liking them (and I always saw my father eat his vegetables first, knowing full well that he ate the food on his plate in reverse order of preference), then a preference for eating vegetables is unlikely.

Therefore it would probably be easier to change, for example, the hot dog aversion than the sweet preference. In the case of the hot dog, research indicates that preference is likely to be changed by repeated consumption of the food in a familiar, good-tasting sauce, under pleasant circumstances, and in the company of others who apparently enjoy hot dogs. Gradually, the sauce can be eliminated.

To a large degree, the ways in which our food preferences and aversions arise and change reflect our evolutionary heritage. Not only have we evolved to like certain tastes and to dislike others, but we have evolved to learn to like certain foods under certain conditions and to learn to dislike them under other conditions. All of this greatly helped us to survive in our original surroundings in which calories and salt were scarce and nutritious, nonpoisonous food sources had to be identified. That world no longer exists, but our preferences for salty, sweet, caloric food and our aversions to foods associated with illness continue. This legacy of our past can cause serious problems.

Now that you've read this chapter and the previous ones, you may enjoy an exercise involving Figure 6.2. For each of the panels, see if you can explain why the different people feel the way they do about the various foods. In addition, you probably now understand America's—and increasingly, other countries'—obsession with fast food such as McDonald's; much fast food is high in salt, fat, sugar, and/or calories, and is very familiar. Finally, you won't be surprised by *Time* magazine's report of what some executed criminals chose for their last meals: "TED BUNDY: Serial killer; electrocuted Jan. 24, 1989; Starke, Florida. Last meal: steak, eggs, hashed brown potatoes, coffee. GARY MARK GILMORE: Murderer; shot by firing squad Jan. 17, 1977; Point of the Mountain, Utah. Last meal: hamburgers, eggs, potatoes, coffee, whiskey. PERRY SMITH AND RICHARD HICKOCK: Murderers; hanged April 14, 1965; Lansing, Kansas. Last meal: shrimp, French fries, garlic bread, ice cream, strawberries and whipped cream."[76]

Figure 6.2 Drawing by Lynda Barry. (Reprinted from *The New York Times Magazine* [March 10, 1996] 55.) Every effort has been made to trace and acknowledge the copyright holder of this drawing. Acknowledgement will be granted upon request.

7

THIS OR THAT

Choosing What We Eat and Drink

It's early Saturday morning, you're lying in bed, and you realize that there's no food in your house. You've got to go to the grocery store. You've also got to visit your elderly parents and take your teenage children to soccer practice that afternoon, so you have limited time for grocery shopping. You decide to do the grocery shopping right away because, although you'll be able to spend less time lying in bed, the really good grocery deals sell out by 10 a.m. on Saturdays, so in the long run, you'll be able to buy more food if you get out of bed now. And, because you spent all but $40 of your cash last night playing bingo and you've maxed out your credit card, there's a limited amount of food that you can buy; you'll need to get as much food as you can per dollar. It needs to be enough to provide dinner for your children and a few of your nephews and nieces who will be coming over after soccer practice, absolutely starving. Although $40 probably won't buy enough food to stuff all of them, it will buy enough so that your children and their cousins won't die before morning.

So you drive to the grocery store and race down the aisles. You, your children, and their cousins eat all kinds of things, so choosing what to buy is more complicated than if, for example, you were koala bears eating only eucalyptus leaves. And you can't just buy what you and your children like best (caviar and lobster) because $40 won't buy enough of that. You also can't buy just foods or just drinks; consuming food without drink, or vice versa, isn't at all appealing. You have to figure out the right combination. In addition to these problems, you wish that you could remember which aisle the soda is in so that you wouldn't have to spend your precious time looking for it. While you're looking for the soda, it occurs to you that maybe you should just spend the whole $40 on food for yourself. After all, you're the one who earned it in the first place, not your children and not their cousins. And $40 doesn't buy a whole lot of food these days. But then you remember how much you love your children and their cousins and you decide to buy food for everybody.

There are just a few other shoppers this morning. Suddenly, there's a loudspeaker announcement: There are marketing demonstrations in aisles

B and F. In aisle B, the demonstrator is making miniature waffles with a new type of waffle iron that does a great job, but takes about 5 minutes to make each waffle. In aisle F, another demonstrator is making hors d'oeuvres on a new type of cracker, averaging one per minute. Given that there was no food in your house when you woke up, you haven't had breakfast, and you really like both miniature waffles and hors d'oeuvres, so these demonstrations sound great. But you've got limited time—which demonstration do you go to? And if you have time to get some more free food while you're grocery shopping, do you keep going to the same or a different demonstration? Maybe you should go to aisle F five times as often as aisle B, because the hors d'oeuvres are ready five times as often as the miniature waffles. Or maybe you should calculate the time for each trip to aisles B or F, as well as calculating when the next waffle and hors d'oeuvre will be ready, and visit the two demonstrations in such a pattern as to get the most total food.

Is this all sounding really complicated? Well, maybe you don't consciously think about all of these issues when you go grocery shopping. However, whether you're aware of them or not, psychologists would contend that it's just these sorts of factors that are involved any time you choose one food or another to eat, and that very similar factors were involved when our ancestors foraged for food in jungles and savannahs, and are still involved in the food choices of other animals in the wide world.

What you actually choose to eat and drink is the ultimate focus of the psychology of eating and drinking. So far, this book has provided a lot of information about how we distinguish among different foods and what causes us to like or dislike certain foods. But knowing all of that won't tell you everything you need to know to predict whether someone will consume a particular food or drink at a particular point in time. You need to know what else is available, how hungry the person is, what else is going on in the person's surroundings, and how much work, time, and money it's going to take to get a particular food or drink as compared to something else. This chapter will tell you about some of these other factors and how they influence eating and drinking.

Choosing to Survive

What can help us understand how and why people and other animals choose certain foods? You've already heard a lot about how eating behaviors have evolved in ways that, at least originally, helped us all to survive, such as the innate preferences for sweet and salty foods. Perhaps thinking about the relationships among food choice, survival, and evolution can increase our understanding of the factors involved in animals—including people—choosing different foods.

It shouldn't surprise us if animals choose foods or drinks in ways that appear to help them survive. Think about the major food problem facing an animal living in the wild: It has to find and consume enough food and water to meet its energy needs and reproduce. And this animal must do this no matter in what surroundings it finds itself. A uniform, steady food supply is unusual in the animal kingdom. Things change, both over time and through space, and therefore the best food choices for an animal also change.[1] Even grocery stores that are members of the same chain can carry different items in different locations at different times.

Given that animals' surroundings aren't fixed and uniform, one particular set of choices of what to eat and drink won't, in the long run, be best for an animal. Instead we would expect that evolution has resulted in various strategies that animals employ to make their choices, strategies that would, over time, best help the animals to survive. Thus the most important questions for this chapter are what sorts of choice strategies will best help us to survive? And do we and other animals follow those best strategies?

It's important to remember that evolution of food choice strategies is multifaceted and continuous. Not only do choice strategies per se evolve, but so do the cognitive abilities needed for those choice strategies—abilities such as memory. Here's one example.

Two species of monkey, golden lion tamarins and Wied's marmosets, perform differently on memory tasks in the laboratory. The marmosets do better than the tamarins when they have to remember something for only 5 minutes, but the tamarins do better than the marmosets when they have to remember something for 24 or 48 hours. As it turns out, the marmosets, but not the tamarins, obtain a lot of their food in the form of gum from trees, which they gouge with their teeth. The gum is rapidly replaced by the tree, sometimes in less than an hour. Therefore the marmosets confine their food search to a small area involving a few trees to which they return several times in a day. In order not to waste time going to a tree without much gum, the marmosets need to remember well where they have been for only a few minutes or hours. In contrast, the tamarins eat little tree gum. Instead, they eat small animals (primarily insects) and plant parts such as ripe fruit. These foods are widely spread out over a large area. In order to locate good food sources, tamarins need to remember well over large distances and periods of time.[2] In a nutshell, these monkeys' cognitive abilities and their food choices have evolved to be well suited to each other.

Now let's consider how food choice strategies and cognitive abilities might have evolved together in people. Some scientists believe that the excellent cognitive abilities of people are actually a result of food-related evolution. Scientist Katharine Milton has speculated that, when people were evolving, they were caught in a sort of dietary squeeze because specialized carnivores and herbivores were evolving at the same time, increasing the competition for certain foods. To survive, omnivorous humans had to become good at finding all kinds of different food sources

111

in different locations at different times. They needed to remember well and to learn quickly, contributing to the evolution of a large brain. In fact, according to Milton, "Overall, I would say that the collected evidence justifiably casts the evolutionary history of primates in largely dietary terms."[3] Milton believes that in addition to people's cognitive abilities, certain physical abilities, such as our highly manipulative hands, evolved to serve food choice needs. Our hands allow us to obtain and consume all kinds of food items that we otherwise could not.[4]

Before we leave the topic of evolution and food choice, there's one particular aspect of food choice that has occupied the attention of many researchers interested in evolution: food sharing. If evolution results in individuals choosing foods that maximize their survival, why would anyone ever share food? Particularly in times of food scarcity, such behavior would make it less, not more, likely that you would survive. Nevertheless, there have been several documented instances of food sharing in species other than people. For example, when a young raven finds a good food source such as a dead moose, it will leave to find other young ravens, and then they will all return to the carcass and eat it together. As another example, vampire bats will regurgitate blood that they have eaten and give some to a roostmate. There may be very good reasons for the individual young ravens and bats to share food. In the case of the young ravens, ravens must eat on a fairly regular basis to survive, and one young raven by itself cannot gain access to a carcass in the territory of older ravens. By inviting many other young ravens to share, the finder ensures that it will get something to eat.[5] In the case of the bats, bats that go two nights without consuming blood will die. Bats that roost together tend to be related to one another. This means that when bats share food they ensure that their relatives, and thus other copies of their genes, will survive.[6] Therefore food sharing in bats helps to ensure that the genes of the sharer will be multiplied in the future, a factor that may also be at work when we feed our children and other relatives.

Model Choice Behavior

The previous material should have given you a fairly good idea of the general strategies that animals, including people, use to choose among different foods, and the general relationships between those strategies and evolution. This section examines more extensively particular food choice strategies that different scientists believe animals use.

Some scientists have tried to specify in great detail the strategies that animals use in choosing among different foods—such detail, in fact, that it's possible to predict exactly how much time or energy an animal will devote to choosing one food versus another food. These scientists believe that if you know everything about an animal's history and current surroundings, and if you have a good idea of what choices will best help an animal to survive, then you'll be able to predict those choices very closely. Such predictions could be extremely useful in helping us find ways to modify undesirable eating behaviors. But scientists have disagreed over what strategy they think that animals are most likely to use in making their food choices. So they construct elaborate mathematical models of these strategies and then test to see how closely animals' actual food choice behaviors do or don't conform to these models. Here we'll look at two of the most popular models of animals' food choice behaviors: the matching law and optimal foraging theory. We'll look at each of these models' advantages and shortcomings to see what each can contribute. You've already had an introduction to each of these models at the beginning of this chapter when I described two possible strategies that you might use in choosing between the two free sources of food in the grocery store: visiting the hors d'oeuvre source five times as often as the miniature-waffle source (the matching law) or calculating which source will get you the most energy consumed for the least energy expended (optimal foraging theory).

The matching law

The matching law assumes that animals follow one simple rule that often results in maximizing the total amount of food that they obtain. If you're mathematically inclined, it's possible to learn a great deal about the matching law in the form of equations. However, given that some readers of this book may not be particularly enamored of equations, I'm going to describe this law without resorting to any mathematical intricacies. Let's go back to the free food available in the grocery store and see what the matching law has to say about it.

The question is how should you, during the limited time that you have to get food in the grocery store, choose to distribute your time between the miniature-waffle and hors d'oeuvre demonstrations? What strategy will result in your obtaining the most free food? When you first hear the announcement about the two demonstrations you should choose the hors d'oeuvre demonstration, because food is available there more frequently. However, if it has been at least 5 minutes since you've been to the miniature-waffle demonstration, then you should go there, because a waffle is likely to be available. If you then spend 1 minute at the waffle demonstration, obtaining any waffles available there, you should return to the hors d'oeuvre demonstration, because another completed hors d'oeuvre is likely to be waiting there for you, and so on.

The matching law, first formulated by Harvard University psychologist Richard Herrnstein, states that, on average, animals, including people, distribute their choices in proportion to the distribution of the foods available.[7] They "match" the distribution of their choices of foods to the distribution of those foods. Thus, according to the matching law,

113

you should choose to spend five times as much time at the hors d'oeuvre demonstration as at the miniature-waffle demonstration because hors d'oeuvres are available five times as often as waffles.

Scientists have tested the matching law in many different species, including cows, people, pigeons, and rats. These experiments have used many different kinds of food, including hay, snack foods, grain, and laboratory rat chow. The results have shown that, in general, the behavior of all of these species conforms well to the matching law.[8] The matching law has even described well the food choice behavior of a flock of wild pigeons: The total number of choices the members of a flock of wild pigeons made of each of two food sources matched the frequency with which food was available at those two food sources.[9] There are very few psychological principles that can predict precisely how someone will behave. Much of my own research has made use of the matching law in one way or another.

Optimal foraging theory

To *forage* means to "wander or rove in search of food or other provisions."[10] Therefore optimal foraging theory, also known as optimization or maximization,[11] refers to a set of theories about the best way to find food or other items. Most likely, if you had to forage in nature, and food was scarce, you would try to find the most food you could while expending as few calories as possible. Such a strategy would best enable you to survive. Not surprisingly, one version of optimal foraging theory assumes that evolution has shaped us to behave in this way;[12] animals that follow such a strategy would be likely to reproduce successfully.

Similar to the matching law, optimal foraging theories are often expressed in the form of extremely complicated mathematical equations. Once again, although I personally enjoy such equations, I'm not going to present them here; the equations aren't necessary for you to understand the basic concepts of optimal foraging theory. The optimal foraging theory equations calculate everything in terms of energy—energy consumed via foraging and energy expended via movement and metabolic processes. They essentially treat optimal foraging as analogous to the earning and spending of money. Consumed food can be thought of as income, and energy expended in order to obtain that food can be thought of as cost. As you might therefore guess, many scientists draw parallels between optimal foraging research and the theoretical framework for economics.[13]

Using the framework of economics to understand eating and drinking choice behavior can be very helpful in a number of ways. One way is that it can help scientists to understand the consumption of different food and drink combinations. For example, consider a typical meal in which an animal both eats food and drinks water. If you try to figure out separately how much food and water an animal will consume, you'll have trouble because each depends on the other. In Chapter 3 you learned that most animals require food and water in specific combinations of so much food and so much water. Therefore food is worth little to a hungry and thirsty animal unless water is also available. This is why, when you go to the grocery store, you're unlikely to buy just food or just drinks. The matching law has no way to describe or predict such findings. However, the economics framework of optimal foraging theory can help us to understand such situations because economics contains concepts for items whose worth is affected by the presence and absence of other items.

Within the economic framework of optimal foraging theory, researchers have considered the specific effects of money, time, and effort on how people make food choices. Probably the greatest amount of this work has been done on money. For example, does being poor or being in a recession make it more likely that you will purchase junk food that contains little nutrition other than that it has a high density of calories? And does junk food actually give you more calories per dollar? Although researchers' views are not unanimous, the weight of their opinions seems to be that the answers to both of these questions is yes.[14] Future research on food choice will undoubtedly have to take into account some additional cost-related variables that can now affect people's food choices, such as whether the food is or is not locally sourced and the carbon footprint of each food.

Here's an intriguing example of how the cost of food can strongly affect college students' foraging behavior. A Carnegie Mellon student created a computer program that helped identify sources of free food on his campus (see www.food-bot.com). He did this by subscribing to several thousand campus email lists and then filtering the emails he received, isolating the ones that contained food words. Using this program, he was able to go 5 months without paying for food (http://chronicle.com/blogs/wiredcampus/for-free-food-on-their-campus-hungry-students-consult-food-bot/31135), and he subsequently expanded the program to other universities.

However, all of these calculations and even computer programs can't always result in optimal behavior. There are limits—constraints—on animals' (and computer programs') physical and cognitive abilities. All animals' foraging behaviors are constrained to at least some degree.[15] One example is when you're in the grocery store and can't remember which aisle the soda is in and, as a result, you don't take the route to the soda involving the least steps and the least energy expenditure.

Let's consider some specific examples of the application of optimal foraging theory. You may have heard of microeconomics and macroeconomics. These areas of study involve applying the principles of economics to individual people and to groups of people, respectively. These two types of economics are both used in studies of optimal foraging.

For an example of foraging and the microapproach, let's consider first experiments conducted by biologist Graham H. Pyke.[16] If you like to watch birds, perhaps you've wondered why, in obtaining food, some birds hover but other birds perch. Pyke investigated this question with two bird species that both obtain nectar from flowers: hummingbirds, which hover, and honeyeaters, which perch. He conducted three types of studies. One type involved observing the birds' behaviors under natural conditions, measuring as many of the relevant aspects of the birds' surroundings as possible. For example, he measured the distance the birds traveled between flowers, the time they spent at each flower, and the birds' body weights. Pyke conducted the second type of study in an aviary. He constructed artificial "flowers" consisting of surgical needles filled with sugar water so that he could control the exact amount and spacing of available food. For the third type of study, Pyke fed into a computer information about the birds' actual foraging behaviors as well as certain assumptions about how the birds foraged. Together, these three types of studies showed that the actual foraging behaviors of the two species of birds—hovering for the hummingbird and perching for the honeyeater, as well as the birds' patterns of movement between the flowers and the amount of time that they spent at each flower—were approximately optimal. For example, hovering allows a bird to move more quickly and easily between flowers, but hovering requires more energy than does perching. Thus, hovering is more suited to a smaller bird that requires less energy to hover, such as the hummingbird, than to a larger bird that requires more energy to hover, such as the honeyeater. (See Conversation Making Fact #7.)

Conversation making fact #7

Optimal foraging theory and the microapproach can give you a new perspective on your favorite couch potato. Consider what happens to an animal's behavior when it has to expend increased energy to obtain food. Psychologists Suzanne H. Mitchell and Jasper Brener have shown that rats pressing levers for food will press the levers harder if it's the only way to get food. However, while pressing the levers harder in order to get food, the rats will expend less energy on other activities so as not increase their total energy expenditure.[17] Similarly, couch potatoes, and all of us from time to time, will take advantage of opportunities to expend little energy.(Hence the success of the TV remote control!) This would have been adaptive when we were evolving in surroundings containing limited food, but now can result in some people being labeled as lazy. As you can now see, the word lazy may not be the most accurate way to describe such behavior.

Now let's consider some examples of the macroapproach—using economic principles to describe the food choice behavior of groups of animals, including people. Using the macroapproach makes sense if you believe, as many scientists do, that the behaviors of groups of individuals, in addition to the behaviors of individuals, follow the principles of economics. Another reason that the macroapproach is often used is that group data are often the only data available.[18]

Do you remember reading in the section on sweet preference that when the price of sugar products went down and the availability of these products went up, consumption of sugar products increased? That's an example of how economics and a macroapproach can explain choice of sweet foods and drinks. Increasing sugar consumption is a common pattern as countries industrialize.[19]

The macroapproach has also been used frequently in anthropological studies of different cultures. For example, it has been used to explain how groups of people forage together and the degree to which they share food.[20] As a more specific example, both the Ache foragers in Paraguay and the Hiwi foragers in Venezuela work together to obtain food from a particular source, but only when that food will provide them with more energy than they will use to obtain that food.[21] As another example, the relatively low amount of energy involved in obtaining calories and protein from insects may explain the popularity around the world of insects as a food source.[22]

Having Your Cake and Eating It too: Self-control and Impulsiveness

Let's now consider one of the most important types of choice of foods and drinks: self-control—the choice of a larger or better piece of delayed food (or another reward) over a smaller or worse piece of immediate food (or another reward)—and its opposite, impulsiveness.[23] How would the matching law and optimal foraging theory explain and predict these sorts of choices?

First, let's talk a bit more about what we mean by self-control and impulsiveness. One of the most famous psychologists of the 20th century, B. F. Skinner, gave the following example of self-control involving food: "A principle of self-control: In looking at a menu, ask not what will taste good but what will feel good an hour or so from now."[24]

Consider now the following example:

> Suppose a child's mother tells him on a Tuesday evening that if he eats all of his vegetables at dinner that night he can have three cookies for dessert. [I know you learned in the last chapter that this would only make the child like cookies more and

117

vegetables less, but remember I'm trying to give an example similar to what people actually do, not what they should do.] He eats his vegetables, but then the mother discovers that there's only one cookie in the cookie jar. (The father secretly eats the cookies in the cookie jar, always leaving one cookie because he thinks that way no one will notice what he's been doing.) Because she believes that it's important to keep promises to children, and because she feels badly that she does not have the cookies immediately available, she tells the child that he has two choices. He can either have the one cookie after 1 hour or he can wait until tomorrow, Wednesday, and when she goes to the store she will get him three cookies for dessert after tomorrow night's dinner. But he cannot have both.

If the child chooses the one cookie Tuesday evening, this would be an example of impulsiveness; a choice of the three cookies Wednesday evening would be an example of self-control. In order to get the most cookies, the child should show self-control. However, we all know that many people, adults as well as children, would show impulsiveness in such a situation.

What does the matching law predict would happen in such a situation? The matching law states that the greater the amount of food, the more you should choose it, and the more a food is delayed, the less you should choose it. The delay decreases the value of the food—the greater the delay, the more the value of the food is decreased. In the above example, one choice offers 3 times as many cookies as the other, but 24 times as much delay. Therefore, the overall value of the choice of three more delayed cookies is less than the overall value of the choice of one less delayed cookie, and the matching law predicts that the child will be impulsive and choose the one cookie. In the laboratory, people as well as other animals are frequently impulsive when choosing among foods of differing amounts and delays.[25]

What does optimal foraging theory have to say about choosing between events that can occur only some time in the future? About self-control and impulsiveness? First let's think about what might happen when you're waiting for food, such as the free miniature waffles in the grocery store. During the delay period, you might be interrupted and never get any waffles because (a) you got a call on your cell phone that your child just tried to wash the family dog using laundry detergent, (b) you collapsed with a heart attack, (c) the waffle iron was opened by some ravenous children who ate all the half-cooked waffles, or (d) a waffle iron malfunction caused the waffles to burn up. This example shows that waiting for food can be a risky proposition; for many different reasons, you may or may not end up getting the food.

As psychologist Edmund Fantino put it, "The future is uncertain; eat dessert first."[26]

Most species, including people, evolved in surroundings in which food was scattered and not reliable. In such surroundings, taking any immediately available food could give an animal a definite survival advantage, particularly if the animal is hungry. In nature, if you're hungry, and if there aren't lots of reliable food sources, the most sensible thing you can do is to eat anything that you can get your hands or paws or beak on right now; to do otherwise is to risk not having enough energy to find better food, and even to risk death.[27] Therefore, particularly if an animal needs some food quickly in order to survive, the optimal choice, the choice that would be predicted by optimal foraging theory, may be for an animal to choose a smaller, immediate food item (impulsiveness) over a larger, delayed food item (self-control). And the advantages of immediate food aren't limited to the jungle and the savanna, as illustrated by this section of the play *Annie*:

WARBUCKS: The New Deal, in my opinion, is badly planned, badly organized and badly administered. You don't think your programs through, Franklin, you don't think of what they're going to do to the economy in the long run.

FDR: People don't eat in the long run.[28]

On the flip side, you would expect that, in an environment in which there is lots of food, animals would be more likely to engage in risky food-seeking behavior. This is just what anthropologists Ian Gilby and Richard Wrangham found. These researchers demonstrated that chimpanzees in Uganda are more likely to engage in the only-sometimes-successful behavior of hunting Colobus monkeys when there is plenty of vegetarian food around than when there is not.[29]

Whether you are taking a matching law or an optimal foraging theory approach to self-control, an understanding of the physiological underpinnings of this sort of behavior can be very useful in predicting and modifying it. Scientists don't yet know precisely the physiological basis of self-control and impulsiveness, but we have some clues. For example, the neurotransmitter serotonin seems to play a role. In one experiment, the level of serotonin was decreased in various parts of the brains of some rats, including the hypothalamus. When compared with other rats that hadn't had this treatment, the treated rats were less likely to wait for delayed food.[30] In people, it has long been observed that patients with damage to the frontal parts of their brain cortex are very likely to behave impulsively.[31] Similarly, the part of the brain known as the ventromedial prefrontal cortex seems to be critically involved when people make choices about foods of different amounts and delays.[32] Thus we seem to have some idea of the anatomical and chemical elements of the brain that are important in demonstrating self-control.

You may be saying to yourself, "Well, all of this information is fine and good for explaining self-control, but can it help us to increase self-control?" The matching law and optimal foraging theory analyses of self-control and impulsiveness actually suggest a number of different ways that self-control can be increased. Many of these self-control techniques are used in treating eating and drinking disorders, as you'll learn about in Chapters 10 and 11. For now, let's just go over some of the techniques that have been demonstrated in basic research laboratories, and you can begin thinking about how these techniques might be used to increase or decrease food and alcohol consumption in clinical cases.

One way to increase self-control is for the choice to be made as early as possible before any food can be obtained. In the cookie choice example described earlier, if the choice is modified so that the child can have one cookie tomorrow evening or three cookies the evening after, he will be more likely to choose the three cookies than with the original choice between one cookie in an hour and three cookies tomorrow evening. With the modified choice, in addition to discounting the value of the three cookies a great deal because of their delay, the child also discounts the value of the one cookie because of its extended delay, and so the three cookies are worth more to the child than the one cookie.

But what happens as time marches forward? Gradually, as time passes, the child, if allowed to, will change his choice to the one cookie; he will reverse his preference. This occurs because, as time passes, the choice becomes the original one between the one cookie delayed 1 hour and the three cookies delayed 24 hours. Therefore, to make sure that self-control is maintained, the child's early choice must be irrevocable; the child must not have a way to change his choice. For example, once the child makes his choice, he could ask his mother to write a big note and put it on the refrigerator stating that choice and that nobody (father, babysitter, grandparents, etc.) is to let him change his mind. When people do something to prevent themselves from changing from self-control to impulsiveness, that act is known as a precommitment device.[33] Precommitment devices are perhaps the most useful of all methods for enhancing self-control. I use them all the time, such as when I take to work a lunch that I packed the night before and am thus stuck eating a lunch consisting of yogurt, crackers, and fruit, as opposed to the leftover chocolate cake that I might have been tempted to eat if it were near me at lunchtime.

Describing how the child's choice might change suggests another way in which self-control might be increased. Suppose the child were first given the choice between one cookie tomorrow evening and three cookies tomorrow evening, and the child chooses the three cookies. Suppose further that the choice is irrevocable and the child gets and eats the three cookies. Now suppose that the child is given a similar choice twice a week, each week for 26 years, and that with each subsequent choice, the delay to the one cookie is decreased by 30 seconds. Finally, after 26 years, the child is choosing between an immediate cookie and three cookies delayed until tomorrow evening. Experience with such a procedure, in which the delay to the small reinforcer very gradually fades away, results in both pigeons and impulsive children showing far more self-control than if they had not been exposed to this procedure.[34]

What goes on during the delay periods also affects self-control. You've probably noticed yourself that if you're hungry and you focus on how good something tastes, it's harder to wait for it. But if you're hungry and you distract yourself with some absorbing non-food-related task, it's easier to wait for a good-tasting food. Columbia University psychologist Walter Mischel and his colleagues, in their experiments with children, collected much evidence showing that thinking about the motivating qualities of foods, such as how good cookies taste, makes it harder to maintain self-control. But thinking about other characteristics of foods, such as cookies' round shape and the little specks in them, makes it easier to maintain self-control. These types of thoughts can be termed *hot* and *cool thoughts,* respectively. Playing games during the delay period or even falling asleep, both of which presumably decrease hot thoughts, increase self-control in children.[35] Performing the equivalent of distracting behaviors during the delay of a food item may also help pigeons maintain self-control.[36] The effects on self-control of reminders present during the delay periods have also been studied. For example, when colored lights are present during food delays for pigeons, and the color of the lights indicates whether a self-control or an impulsive choice has been made (when the pigeons have a "reminder" of which choice they have made and thus which food item they're waiting for), they show more self-control.[37]

It's possible that there may be a single physiological explanation for the effects of hot and cool thoughts, reminders and distracting behaviors. Recall that Chapter 2 showed that some aspects of our surroundings that are associated with food cause the release of insulin and increase hunger. Given that increased hunger can increase people's impulsiveness, perhaps the hot and cool thoughts are equivalent to events that do or don't result in the release of insulin. You see yummy chocolate cake in front of you, you release insulin, and, despite having just finished lunch and being on a diet, you can't resist eating some of the cake. Additional evidence seems to support the hypothesis that insulin release is related to self-control and hot and cool thoughts. For example, both dieters and pigeons seem better at self-control for food in the laboratory when they can't always see the food .[38]

121

B. F. Skinner obviously had an inkling about the role of visual cues in self-control for food and how to control those cues when he wrote his provocative, prescient, and amusing 1948 novel *Walden Two* about a utopian community founded on psychological principles:

> "Take the principle of 'Get thee behind me, Satan,' for example," Frazier continued. "It's a special case of self-control by altering the environment. Subclass A 3, I believe. We give each child a lollipop which has been dipped in powdered sugar so that a single touch of the tongue can be detected. We tell him he may eat the lollipop later in the day, provided it hasn't already been licked. Since the child is only three or four, it is a fairly diff—"
>
> "Three or four!" Castle exclaimed.
>
> "All our ethical training is completed by the age of six," said Frazier quietly. "A simple principle like putting temptation out of sight would be acquired before four. But at such an early age the problem of not licking the lollipop isn't easy. Now, what would you do, Mr. Castle, in a similar situation?"
>
> "Put the lollipop out of sight as quickly as possible."
>
> "Exactly. I can see you've been well trained. Or perhaps you discovered the principle for yourself. We're in favor of original inquiry wherever possible, but in this case we have a more important goal and we don't hesitate to give verbal help. First of all, the children are urged to examine their own behavior while looking at the lollipops. This helps them to recognize the need for self-control. Then the lollipops are concealed, and the children are asked to notice any gain in happiness or any reduction in tension. Then a strong distraction is arranged—say, an interesting game. Later the children are reminded of the candy and encouraged to examine their reaction. The value of the distraction is generally obvious. Well, need I go on? When the experiment is repeated a day or so later, the children all run with the lollipops to their lockers and do exactly what Mr. Castle would do—a sufficient indication of the success of our training."[39]

Adults also use such self-control techniques, as described in *Blue Shoes and Happiness*, a book in Alexander McCall Smith's *No. 1 Ladies Detective Agency* series:

> As the others ate the pudding she had prepared for them— banana custard with spoonfuls of red jam in the middle, she sat as if fixed to her seat, watching them enjoying themselves.

"Are you sure you won't have some of this custard, Mma Ramotswe?" asked Mr. J. L. B. Matekoni.

"No," she said. And then said, "Yes. Yes, I am sure that I won't. Which means no."

Mr. J. L. B. Matekoni smiled. "It is very good," he said.

This is how we are tempted, thought Mma Ramotswe. But at least some of us are strong.

She closed her eyes. It was easier to be strong, she thought, if one had one's eyes closed; although that would only work to a limited extent. One could not go around indefinitely with one's eyes closed, especially if one was a detective.[40]

And just in case you think descriptions of how to train self-control are limited to tales of fiction:

[At] a reunion dinner with Philippe's university friends [in France].... other children were already gathered at a respectful distance. Their eyes were on the crackers, but no one dared touch them. Later, a French friend hinted at how this self-control is achieved. Starting at age 3, all the children at her *maternelle* (preschool) had to sit still with their hands on their knees while the lunchtime dessert was served. Only when the *maitresse* gave permission could they begin to eat; anyone who gave in to temptation had her dessert promptly removed.[41]

There is additional support for the hypothesis that insulin release is related to self-control. Both people and pigeons do better at self-control in the laboratory when they're working for tokens that can be exchanged for food after many choices have been made, rather than when they're working for food that they get before they make their next choice.[42] We could easily surmise that more insulin is released—with the animals becoming hungrier and therefore more impulsive—when food is always visible or is available after every choice, rather than when food isn't always visible or when it's available only after many choices have been completed.

In possibly related research, psychologist Roy Baumeister has postulated that self-control functions as a limited resource that can be depleted, and that giving someone a sweet drink (which provides energy) can increase self-control. Nevertheless, some researchers have found that a sweet taste increases self-control whether or not there is an increase in blood sugar, and it has not always been possible to replicate any of these findings.[43] Therefore additional research is needed to determine precisely how self-control might or might not function as a limited resource, and whether or not this relates to blood sugar levels.

Finally, research suggests that the passage of time by itself can affect self-control. For example, if you fall asleep while you're waiting for the three cookies, time will pass very quickly for you. If time seems to pass very quickly, then you'll discount the value of the three cookies very little due to their delay. Thus, anything that makes time seem to go faster should increase self-control. Doing something fun, taking certain drugs, having certain reminders present, as well as falling asleep, might all make time seem to pass quickly and thus increase self-control. The afternoon before I was to go to Europe the first time and was terribly excited and felt that I couldn't wait to leave for the airport, my now husband took me to see the movie *The Godfather*. The time waiting to leave for the airport flew by while we were in the theater. In contrast, being hungry, staring at good food, taking certain other drugs, or doing something that isn't fun might all make time seem to pass less quickly and thus decrease self-control. The matching law has ways of mathematically expressing, and even predicting, the differences in individual animals' sensitivities to the passage of time that result from these sorts of factors.[44]

I hope that you can see that research on self-control suggests many different ways for increasing and decreasing food and alcohol consumption.

What Are the Options?

You've already read about some of the ways in which self-control and impulsiveness regarding food choices can be modified by changing different aspects of the environment. For example, people are more likely to show self-control and not eat food immediately if the food is hidden.

Researchers have investigated many other methods for changing food choices by means of making modifications in the environment. The goal of all of these interventions is not to change whether someone likes a particular food or not, but to change whether that person actually chooses that food or not. Professors Richard H. Thaler and Cass R. Sunstein describe many of these types of interventions in their excellent book *Nudge: Improving Decisions about Health, Wealth, and Happiness*.[45]

Some examples of these types of interventions include where a food is placed in a cafeteria or vending machine, publicly posting nutritional information about restaurant items, increasing the price of or tax on certain foods, and whether a food is offered as a choice at all.[46]

Cafeteria layout modification effects are well illustrated by two clever experiments conducted with university students by Herbert L. Meiselman and his colleagues. These scientists manipulated the difficulty of obtaining candy and potato chips in a university cafeteria that served a full range of foods. In the first part of each experiment, large displays of candy (Experiment 1) or potato chips (Experiment 2) were placed at each of the four main locations where students paid for their meals. In the second part of each experiment, the candy or potato chips were available only at a location that was some distance away from where the students usually paid for their meals, and the students had to stand in another line and pay separately for anything bought at that location. The cafeteria cashiers told the students the new candy or potato chips location only if the students asked about it. The experimenters found that when it was harder to get candy or potato chips, the students were much less likely to buy these items. Under these conditions, the students tended to buy foods such as fruit and other desserts instead of candy and other starches instead of potato chips.[47] Apparently it's possible to use effort—the amount of energy required to obtain a certain food—to influence what sorts of food someone chooses. Just imagine the effects on the eating behaviors of all of the office workers of America if vending machines containing junk food were banished to the basement instead of being right down the hall.

The strategy of simply eliminating an item as a choice made big news in New York City when then-mayor Michael Bloomberg attempted to ban certain establishments from selling large-size sodas. There were many people and organizations that were supportive of this move, and many that were opposed to it. There were repeated stories about the controversy in *The New York Times* and other media.[48] The June 18, 2012, issue of *The New Yorker* even featured a drawing by Owen Smith, entitled "Soda Noir," that depicted a man and a woman on a shadowy city corner holding a super-size soda with utter terror on their faces. The proposed soda ban (which has not gone into effect due to legal challenges) was one of Mayor Bloomberg's last public health initiatives.

Opponents of such moves as the soda ban have stated that people should be free to make their own choices—that giving them information is all right, but changing access to certain foods, and even more extreme, not offering them as choices at all, is excessively paternalistic and controlling. Supporters of such moves have pointed out that food manufacturers and distributors spend enormous amounts of time and money to display their foods in such a way, and to provide other cues about these foods, as to maximize people's purchase and consumption of these foods. So why should food manufacturers and distributors be allowed to do everything possible to influence our choices of their wares, even when this causes us to have an unhealthy diet, but other people and organizations are prevented from taking similar steps to promote a healthy diet? You can probably guess which side of this controversy I come down on. As I have stated previously in this book, our bodies are adapted for a very different environment than the unhealthy one in which we now live, an environment that we have ourselves created. Thus, in my opinion, it is completely appropriate that we take steps to modify our self-created, unnatural, environment in order to maintain our health.

Conclusion

You've seen many examples of how studying choice behavior can help us to understand why we consume particular foods and drinks. In particular, you've seen how two very specific models of choice behavior—the matching law and optimal foraging theory—try to describe and predict choice behavior. The matching law postulates that animals rely on a (relatively) simple rule of thumb when choosing among different foods, a rule of thumb that sometimes, but not always, coincides with choosing so as to maximize food or drink intake. In contrast, optimal foraging theory postulates that animals choose in accordance with many different aspects of their surroundings, assessing, within the constraints of the animals' capabilities, energy output, and energy input, in order to determine which choices will result in maximizing food or drink intake. Thus the focus of optimal foraging theory is on energy input and output and survival. Nevertheless, under some conditions, the matching law and optimal foraging theory make the same predictions. For example, both predict that when you go to the grocery store with the free demonstrations you should choose to get the hors d'oeuvres five times as much as the miniature waffles. And both involve animals using heuristics to make good choices.[49] Also, both can help us to understand how particular changes in the environment can affect food choice.

Although many scientists have conducted tests to see if the matching law or optimal foraging theory is better at describing animals' food choice behaviors,[50] it's important to realize that there may not be one single correct model of food choice behavior. For example, both models have particular contributions to make to our knowledge about self-control. This is helpful because the study of self-control is of paramount importance to understanding and modifying all kinds of eating and drinking behavior, including eating and drinking disorders. You'll learn lots more about this in future chapters.

8

YOU ARE WHAT YOU
EAT AND DRINK

A full belly counsels well.

French proverb

CAESAR:

Let me have men about me that are fat;
Sleek-headed men and such as sleep o' nights;
Yond Cassius has a lean and hungry look;
He thinks too much: such men are dangerous.

William Shakespeare (1599/1936)[1]

We've spent a lot of time so far in this book examining the factors that affect what we eat and drink. Now we're going to turn things around—how does what we eat and drink affect our behavior? In the extreme case, when someone eats or drinks nothing for a long period of time, all behavior ceases and the person dies. But what about situations in which at least some food and drink are being consumed? Under such circumstances can what is or isn't consumed affect specific aspects of a person's behavior? And what sorts of effects occur? Clearly the French, as well as Shakespeare, have expressed the opinion that eating well makes people easier to live with. Are opinions such as this correct?

Consider the fact that every single part of our bodies originated as some sort of nutrient that we or our mothers consumed. As with other mammals, the nutrients might have come to us through our umbilical cords or through our mouths. If everything about our bodies has originated as consumed nutrients, and if our behavior is entirely a function of our bodies (as opposed to some nonphysical entity or entities), then what we do must be affected by what we have eaten and drunk. As stated by Alice in what's perhaps the best-known published work on how you can be affected by what you eat or drink (*Alice's Adventures in Wonderland*),

"I know *something* interesting is sure to happen...whenever I eat or drink anything."[2]

In this chapter we'll be looking at two basic types of situations: situations in which something missing from an animal's usual intake causes it to behave abnormally, and situations in which something present in an animal's usual intake causes it to behave in specific ways. One example of the latter that we won't cover in the present chapter is alcohol, because that subject is covered extensively in Chapter 11.

I'm sure that you've heard or read that it's okay to take such and such pill or drink for some illness or psychological problem because the pill or drink is "all natural." Such beliefs are part of our awareness that what we eat and drink can affect our behaviors, that foods and drinks can function as drugs or medicines. Foods and drinks that can prevent disease and increase health are known as functional foods. Functional foods have been used by many cultures for millennia. For example, one traditional Chinese belief is that diabetes can be treated with stewed duck egg and green tea. Functional foods represent a growing part of the United States food industry.[3] But what many people don't seem to realize is that just because something is "natural," it isn't necessarily good for you. In fact, although there are plenty of foods in our natural surroundings that can ameliorate symptoms of illness, our surroundings also contain plenty of poisons and toxins, substances that can cause abnormal behavior.

Because there has been so much hype and pop psychology about the effects of natural substances on our behaviors, I'll be spending some time in this chapter trying to show you how scientists investigate these effects and whether these effects really exist. It is by no means an easy process.[4] I hope that by the time that you finish reading this chapter you'll have a new respect for how what you put in your mouth can affect your behavior and that, at the same time, you'll be better prepared to evaluate what you hear others say those effects may be.

Garbage in, Garbage out: Effects of Missing Nutrients

Some nutritional deficiencies affect virtually everyone, but other deficiencies cause problems in only some people's behaviors. We'll discuss both of these types of cases.

Effects seen in everyone

There are a number of different ways that we can look at how deprivation of certain nutrients affects behavior—deprivation of all nutrients versus just one nutrient, deprivation for a short or a long period of time, and deprivation of nutrients during pregnancy and early childhood or later. Let's start with early general malnutrition, beginning before or soon after birth. Malnutrition during infancy and early childhood can hinder children's cognitive development with accompanying brain abnormalities. However, nutritional supplements, if begun early, can eliminate some of these effects.[5]

Some scientists believe that there isn't a simple relationship between malnutrition in children and subsequent impairments in their cognitive development. Instead, scientists believe that a child's nutritional status interacts with other aspects of the child's surroundings and that interaction can impair cognitive development. Adequate nutrition by itself isn't enough for a child to develop well intellectually—a child needs both adequate nutrition and intellectually stimulating surroundings.

Tufts University nutritionist Ernesto Pollitt and his colleagues examined such interactions among poor children in a village in Guatemala. For 8 years, beginning in 1969, children in two villages were given Atole, a high-calorie, high-protein nutritional supplement, while children in two other villages we were given Fresco, a relatively low calorie, sweet drink that contains no protein. Some 20 years later, Pollitt showed that the children (now adults) who had received Atole performed significantly better on most cognitive tests than the children who had received Fresco. Pollitt also showed that the differences between the Atole and the Fresco children increased the greater the amount of education that these children had had. It was as if the better nutrition provided by the Atole allowed the children to take advantage of the educational opportunities available to them.[6] Malnutrition may decrease children's energy levels, curiosity, or responsiveness to changes in their surroundings, all effects that can inhibit their ability to learn.[7]

Now let's consider malnutrition in older adults. For many reasons, people of advanced age are relatively more likely to suffer from nutritional deficiencies than younger adults. One of these reasons, as you read about in Chapter 4, is that elderly people often have impaired senses of taste and smell and consequently don't eat well. The resulting nutrient deficiencies can impair memory, as well as cause other psychological problems. Therefore nutritional supplements can be extremely important for elderly people.[8]

The absence or presence of a single meal can also affect the cognitive abilities of children, as well as of adults. The usual nighttime fast, followed by missing breakfast, can cause both children and adults to perform less well on memory tests.[9] However, in one experiment, psychologist Andrew Smith and his colleagues showed that there were no differences in the number of errors that women made on tasks requiring focused attention if the women had a lunch sized appropriately for their caloric needs or if they had a lunch 40% smaller than that. In other words, eating a little was as good cognitively as eating a normal amount.

In contrast, if the women had a lunch 40% larger in calories than what they needed, they made significantly more errors on the focused attention tasks.[10] It therefore seems that if you want to work well in the afternoon, you need to eat just a small amount and should stay away from those big business lunches.

Even more intriguing, hungry university students—men and women—say they support social welfare beliefs to a greater extent than do nonhungry university students. Nevertheless, the hungry students aren't more likely to share their own resources than are nonhungry students. It therefore seems possible that the hungry students' increased support of social welfare beliefs may be (most likely unconsciously) designed to increase the probability that the students themselves will be the beneficiaries of others' largesse.[11]

Now let's consider the effects of depriving children or adults of specific nutrients over long periods of time. Can such situations affect people's behaviors? In many cases, the answer is yes. You already know from Chapter 5 that being deprived of certain nutrients such as salt can automatically, without any experience, increase preference for that substance. But what about deprivation of certain nutrients affecting other sorts of behaviors? Studies have shown that children with deficiencies in folate, iron, and vitamin B_{12} do worse on cognitive tasks. Luckily, in many such cases, providing children with sufficient amounts of the previously inadequate nutrient will remove the cognitive deficiency.[12] In adults, one example concerns the consequences of eating a very low-cholesterol diet. Such a diet can apparently make people more likely to engage in suicide or violent behavior, which is a concern given many people's obsession with low-cholesterol eating.[13] Is this what Caesar was thinking when he was speaking about Cassius? I've always known that trying to eat a low-fat diet makes me feel cranky, but I've never thought that I might go so far as to kill myself or someone else!

Effects seen in some people

Some researchers believe that, for a variety of reasons, some people, even though their intake is considered normal, have bodies that are deficient in one or more nutrients. These researchers reason that such deficiencies can cause the nutrient-deficient people to behave abnormally, and that the abnormal behavior can be treated or prevented by removing the deficiencies. The Nobel Prize–winning scientist Linus Pauling called this approach orthomolecular psychiatry.[14]

One example of such a deficiency has been known for quite some time—the irreversible memory disorder that has been called Wernicke–Korsakoff syndrome. People who suffer from this disease have difficulty remembering recent events. The syndrome is caused by two factors. One factor is a genetic abnormality in the activity of a particular chemical substance in our bodies that normally, among other actions, helps us to digest glucose. The other factor is food intake that is deficient in thiamine. When both of these factors are present, the syndrome will develop. This syndrome tends to be seen in alcoholics because they're frequently malnourished, but it can also occur in nonalcoholics if they have the genetic abnormality and a thiamine deficiency.[15]

The symptoms of Wernicke–Korsakoff syndrome were dramatically demonstrated to me when I was only 17 years old. For my high school senior project I worked as a nurse's aide in a psychiatric hospital in Philadelphia. During one of my first days at the hospital, a nurse asked me to take a middle-aged woman patient for a walk. The patient was attractive looking and well dressed. The hospital grounds were quite nice and it was a beautiful day. I didn't know my way around very well and the patient repeatedly told me she was new there also and had no idea which way to go. We walked to the greenhouse and the patient said that she was delighted to find out that this hospital had a greenhouse. We also passed an old tree with huge, twisting roots, which the patient said looked like snakes. We had a very pleasant conversation during our walk and I kept trying to figure out why she was in the hospital—could it be related to her thinking that the roots looked like snakes? When we got back to the ward, I checked her chart. She had been there for many weeks and had been to the greenhouse many times. She was an alcoholic and had been diagnosed with Wernicke–Korsakoff syndrome. She could not remember that she had seen the grounds and the greenhouse before. I was told that, even if she stopped drinking alcohol, her memory would never improve.

Pauling conceived of orthomolecular psychiatry as much more than disorders such as Wernicke–Korsakoff syndrome. According to Pauling, many people are suffering from nutrient deficiencies that can be cured by changing what they eat. For example, he contended that schizophrenics suffer from a deficiency of vitamin C and that schizophrenia can be successfully treated by giving large doses of vitamin C. However, firm scientific results for such beliefs, as well as the belief that large doses of vitamin C help to cure or prevent other diseases, have not been forthcoming.[16]

Some researchers have claimed that the amounts of some neurotransmitters such as serotonin are deficient in some people with resulting psychological abnormalities. Researchers have repeatedly shown that low levels of serotonin in people as well as other animals are associated with high levels of impulsive behavior, including aggression and suicide.[17] In fact, it's believed that low levels of cholesterol in the body may decrease the level of serotonin, and that is why, as you just read, low cholesterol levels are associated with violent behavior in some people.[18]

Other researchers believe that low levels of serotonin cause depression in some people.[19] Now how does this relate to what you eat? Amino acids, the building blocks of proteins, are also important building blocks of neurotransmitters. You get amino acids into your body by eating protein. Behavior is influenced by the levels of the neurotransmitters, which in turn are influenced by the levels of amino acids, which in turn may be influenced by what you eat each day.[20]

If all of this is correct, then increasing the levels of serotonin in people who are impulsive, violent, and depressed should decrease their problem behaviors. There have been attempts to do this using medication as well as by modifying what people eat. The latter, although somewhat more speculative, is of greater interest to us here. We know that, theoretically, it should be possible to affect serotonin levels by manipulating people's food intake. Serotonin is made in the body from its precursor tryptophan, which is an amino acid. As it turns out, the concentration of tryptophan in the blood can be increased by eating a high-carbohydrate meal. Note that I didn't say that you increase tryptophan in the blood by eating a high-protein meal. If you've been following this section closely, you should be saying, "How can that be? Tryptophan is a component of protein, not carbohydrate." Let me explain.

Protein foods contain very little tryptophan, although they do contain a great many of the other amino acids. After an animal, such as you, has eaten a high-protein meal, the tryptophan and the other amino acids that you've eaten enter your blood. From there, they compete to enter your brain. Also present in your blood at this time is insulin, because you've probably also eaten at least some carbohydrate, and the body produces insulin to digest the carbohydrate. The insulin transports some of these other amino acids (but not tryptophan) to the muscles that move your bones. Yet there will still be enough of these other amino acids left to compete with the tryptophan in the blood around the brain so that many more of these other amino acids will enter the brain than will tryptophan. (See Figure 8.1.) On the other hand, if you eat a high-carbohydrate meal, the amounts of tryptophan, other amino acids, and insulin in your body are such that there end up being very few amino acids other than tryptophan competing to enter the brain, and so much more tryptophan enters the brain.[21] This should then increase the levels of serotonin in the brain. I say *should* because experiments don't usually directly measure levels of brain serotonin, at least not in people, so researchers don't usually know for sure that what they were doing affected the brain.

Let's take an example of all of this in people. Dutch scientists C. R. Markus, G. Panhuysen, A. Tuiten, and colleagues did an experiment to examine people who were and weren't prone to stress. The researchers were specifically interested in finding out whether stress-prone people would be

Figure 8.1 Conceptual diagram of how tryptophan may enter the brain and thus affect behavior. Tryptophan (T) in the blood competes with other amino acids (A) for access from the blood to the brain. After a high-protein meal is eaten, many amino acids enter the bloodstream; few of these are tryptophan. Therefore, because of competition, relatively little tryptophan enters the brain, and therefore tryptophan does not affect behavior. However, after a high-carbohydrate meal, very few amino acids enter the bloodstream. In addition, insulin is released. Insulin transports most of the amino acids, but not tryptophan, to the muscles that move your bones. Therefore, because there's little competition, a relatively great amount of tryptophan enters the brain. In the brain tryptophan increases serotonin, which may affect behavior. (Adapted from H. R. Lieberman, S. Corkin, B. J. Spring, J. H. Growdon, and R. J. Wurtman, "Mood, Performance, and Pain Sensitivity: Changes Induced by Food Constituents," *Journal of Psychiatric Research* 17[1982/1983]: 135–145.)

less likely to get depressed in performing a stressful task if they ate a food rich in carbohydrates prior to doing the task. These researchers assumed that people more prone to stress reactions would have deficient levels of serotonin in their brains, and therefore eating significant amounts of carbohydrate would increase their brain serotonin levels and make them less likely to demonstrate stress reactions.

During the experiment, in addition to measuring the participants' mood levels, the researchers measured the participants' stress levels (e.g., by measuring pulse rate) and blood levels of tryptophan and other amino acids. The stressful task that the participants were asked to perform consisted of doing mental arithmetic—arithmetic without the benefit of pencil, calculator, or computer. Further, during the mental arithmetic, loud noise was present, and the participants were led to believe that they were repeatedly getting the questions wrong (sounds pretty stressful to me!). Participants were tested on the task both after eating food that was rich in carbohydrate and after eating food that was rich in protein. The number of calories and the amount of fat were kept constant. Thus, there were two kinds of participants (stress-prone and non-stress-prone participants) and two kinds of meals (rich in carbohydrate and rich in protein); everything else was kept constant. The results showed that, for the stress-prone participants only, there was less of a stress response, including no increase in depression, when they performed the task after eating the carbohydrate-rich food. Also, the ratio of tryptophan to other amino acids in the participants' blood after they had eaten the carbohydrate-rich food was significantly higher than after they had eaten the protein-rich food. These results suggest that, if you've a tendency to get stressed out, you may do better if you eat mostly carbohydrates, and that effect may be due to increased serotonin in your brain.[22]

"One Side [of the Mushroom] Will Make You Grow Taller, and the Other Side Will Make You Grow Shorter"[23]

But what about people who have no demonstrable nutritional or neurotransmitter deficits? Can what such people eat affect their behavior? There's a lot of good evidence indicating that, at least in some cases, it can.

Effects seen in everyone

A large number of experiments have demonstrated that simply eating a meal can affect your level of activity, mood, performance of a task, and the speed with which you think time is passing. Sometimes eating a meal increases these aspects of behavior and sometimes it decreases them, depending on the time of day that the meal is eaten and what it contains.

For example, a high-carbohydrate meal, which, you'll remember, increases tryptophan and therefore probably also serotonin, can make you feel more tired, improve your mood, and can make time seem to pass more slowly.[24] And eating a healthy breakfast can keep your cognitive functions in good shape throughout the morning, whether you are a child or an adult.[25]

There is also now a fair amount of converging evidence that a high-fat diet can impair memory and learning.[26] Even exposures to symbols associated with high-fat diets, such as the logos for fast-food chains, can impair memory and self-control.[27]

As a more specific example, in an experiment performed by psychologist Bonnie Spring and her colleagues, women reported feeling tired after a single high-carbohydrate meal, but not after a single high-protein meal or a single meal containing both carbohydrate and protein. In addition, Spring and her colleagues showed that the fatigue following the high-carbohydrate meal wasn't related to blood sugar level; instead, the onset of fatigue coincided with the elevation of tryptophan in the blood.[28] This is interesting because serotonin is important in the regulation of sleep, and many studies have shown that direct administration of tryptophan improves sleep in adult and newborn humans.[29] Spring and her colleagues have also shown that people tend to perform worse on a task requiring sustained attention following a high-carbohydrate meal than following a high-protein meal.[30]

What all of this says to me is that, if I'm having trouble sleeping, my dinner should consist of nothing but carbohydrates. And if I want to be alert, it's a good idea to eat some protein, as opposed to snacking on cookies and crackers, or even on vegetables and fruit (all of which consist primarily of carbohydrates). But my reading of this literature probably resulted in an even larger impact on my son's life than on mine. When he was a teenager and described what he ate for lunch at school, he always had to listen to me intone, "Where was the protein?" (His favorite lunch was pasta with meatless tomato sauce washed down by juice, a meal containing virtually no protein.) At every breakfast, from the time that my son started attending preschool at age 2 until he left for college, I obsessed about his having some protein—be it in the form of milk in his cereal, yogurt, or cheese (all of which contain the calcium that I also insisted that he have). If none of these were available or were, heaven forbid, refused, I even resorted to giving him his favorite leftover—takeout sesame chicken. Anything, as long as he had some protein in his stomach for his morning classes.

But if protein makes you relatively more alert, and carbohydrate makes you feel more tired, what about the sugar high that everyone talks about, especially in kids? Sugar is 100% carbohydrate, but kids go crazy when they eat lots of candy, correct? This is one of the most cherished beliefs of American parents and teachers: When kids are wild, it's not them or how they're treated; it's the sugar they ate. Yet carefully conducted experiments have repeatedly failed to show that sugar significantly affects children's behavior.

For example, pediatrician Mark L. Wolraich and his colleagues published an analysis of a group of 16 previously published studies of the effects of eating sugar on children's behavior. To be included in the examined group of studies, a study had to have several characteristics. First, it had to give children a specific, measured amount of sugar. Second, it had to compare the effects of giving sugar to giving an artificial sweetener. Third, in order to ensure that whatever behavioral changes were seen were due only to the actual effects of the sugar, and not due just to what someone thought the sugar should do, the children, their parents, and the researchers monitoring the children's behavior could not know when sugar (as opposed to artificial sweetener) was given. After the sweet substance was given to a child, and the child's behavior measured, only then could a qualifying study have revealed to the participants when a child had been given sugar or an artificial sweetener. The analysis of all of the studies meeting these criteria showed that, no matter what aspect of the children's behavior was measured, be it activity level or performance on a learning task, there was no significant change in the children's behavior due to sugar. The authors do admit, though, that there may be some children whose behavior is somewhat affected by sugar. However, there's no question that the behavior of at least the large majority of children isn't affected by sugar.[31] So, all those times when your kids seem to go crazy at Halloween, it's probably the holiday that's exciting them, not the candy that they've eaten.

Aspects of food and drink consumption other than ingesting protein or sugar can also affect your behavior. A flavonoid substance in green tea has been shown in a carefully designed experiment to decrease self-reported stress along with congruent changes in brain activity.[32] Even just drinking water can improve memory and other types of cognition in both children and adults. Similarly, being even slightly water deprived impairs cognition.[33]

Food odors, by themselves, can also affect your performance. For example, smelling a sweet caramel odor can increase your tolerance for pain.[34] As another example, Glade Spiced Apple air freshener can significantly enhance performance in a high-stress word task.[35] Reading this last experiment made me seriously consider spraying some air freshener around my office staff (to whom I undoubtedly cause stress) for my own version of aromatherapy. But I was afraid that the staff might have been so surprised to see me spraying the office that their astonishment would counteract any positive effect of the air freshener!

Effects seen in some people

Some scientists have contended that some people's bodies are sensitive to particular nutritive substances present in normal food, and that if these sensitive people eat these particular substances, they will behave abnormally. The study of these food sensitivities is part of what's called clinical ecology, the study and treatment of animals' reactions to what's present in their surroundings.[36]

A well-documented food sensitivity that results in psychological symptoms is shown by children with PKU (phenylketonuria). Approximately 1 in every 20,000 children born in the United States has this disease. These children are born missing the gene that plays an important role in the metabolism of the amino acid phenylalanine. Phenylalanine therefore accumulates in the body, resulting in very severe and permanent retardation. Fortunately, in the United States, newborns are now tested for PKU. If an infant with PKU is given only low-phenylalanine foods immediately after birth, he or she will usually develop normally.[37] However, this dietary treatment may need to continue indefinitely. In fact, continuing the treatment may be particularly important if a woman with PKU becomes pregnant. If treatment isn't continued throughout pregnancy, the resulting baby may have low IQ, low birth weight, and brain and heart abnormalities.[38]

Experiments are scanty on more subtle food sensitivities. One study was conducted by scientist David S. King.[39] He examined participants' reactions to substances to which they were likely to be sensitive. First he asked the participants how frequently they ate various substances, how much they craved them, and how they felt after they ate them. Based on those reports, he selected for his study the substances to which he thought his participants would be most likely to be sensitive: extracts of wheat, beef, milk, cane sugar, and tobacco smoke. King placed these extracts under the participants' tongues and compared the subjects' reactions to when a placebo (distilled water) was used instead. He took many precautions to make sure that participants' responses were solely a function of the actual substances under their tongues and weren't affected by what they believed was under their tongues. For example, he didn't tell the participants which extract he was using when, or even that sometimes a placebo was used. The participants reported significantly more cognitive-emotional symptoms (such as depression and irritability) following administration of the extracts than following administration of the placebo. However, they did not report significantly more bodily symptoms (such as nasal congestion and flushing) following the extracts. Therefore King's results appear to provide support for the hypothesis that some food substances can cause psychological reactions in people. But it isn't clear to what extent these reactions are characteristic of only some people, as opposed to the general population. Also, it's important to keep in mind that King used food extracts, not natural foods, and so his results might not apply to natural eating conditions.

Put a Tiger in Your Tank: The Effects of Nonnutritive Substances in Foods

What we eat and drink often contains substances that don't provide any nutrition. These substances include artificial colors, flavorings, and preservatives, as well as unintended contaminants and toxins.

(See Conversation Making Fact #8.) To the extent that these substances affect our behavior, they're of concern to us here. I'll be discussing three examples: caffeine, lead, and the food additives that some people believe make some children hyperactive.

Conversation making fact #8

History is replete with examples of nonnutritive substances that have been present in food and that have contributed to events of major historical significance. Let's consider two examples. First, some researchers believe that a type of food poisoning, ergotism, was responsible for the 1692 Salem witch trials. The symptoms of ergotism include temporary deafness or blindness, sensations of pinching or of ants crawling under the skin, and convulsions. Ergotism is caused by ergot, a fungus that grows on grains, particularly rye. It's likely that a great deal of rye contaminated with ergot was eaten in Salem around 1692, and, probably not coincidentally, those accused of being bewitched in the Salem witch trials complained of symptoms almost identical with ergotism.[40] As another historical example, if you're a Van Gogh fan, you should know that his paintings may have been influenced by his addiction to a pale green liqueur called absinthe. Absinthe was popular in France in the late 19th and early 20th centuries and was contaminated with a toxin called thujone. Thujone causes hallucinations, mental impairment, and, eventually, irreversible brain damage. Some people believe that Van Gogh's addiction to absinthe contributed to his psychosis and suicide.[41] Van Gogh was so enamored with absinthe that in 1887 he even created a still life painting entitled A Glass of Absinthe and a Carafe.

Caffeine

One nonnutritive substance that can strongly affect behavior and that many Americans consume frequently is caffeine. Caffeine is present in chocolate, many soft drinks, coffee-flavored yogurt, and, of course, tea and coffee (see Table 8.1). Among United States adults who regularly consume caffeine, the average consumption of caffeine per day is equivalent to the amount in about three cups of regular coffee (280 mg),[42] but keep in mind that some people never consume any and other people regularly consume a great deal more that 280 mg. It's also important to remember that many Americans, including children, currently get their caffeine in the form of soft drinks. In fact, the marketing of the "energy"

Table 8.1 The amount of caffeine in some foods and drinks

Food/Drink	Amount of Caffeine
Starbucks coffee, 12 ounces	190 mg
Brewed coffee, 6 ounces	100 mg
Red Bull Energy Drink, 8.4 ounces	80 mg
Mountain Dew, 12 ounces	56 mg
Dannon coffee yogurt, 8 ounces	45 mg
Tea, 6 ounces	40 mg
Hershey chocolate bar	20 mg

Sources: American Psychiatric Association, *Diagnostic and Statistical Manual of Mental Disorders* (Rev. ed.), 4th ed., Washington, DC: APA, 1994; E. O'Connor, "A Sip into Dangerous Territory," *Monitor on Psychology* (June 2001): 60–62; energydrink-us.redbull.com/content/caffeine.

soft drink Red Bull is based, in part, on its high caffeine content—one 8-ounce can has almost as much caffeine as a cup of coffee.

As you certainly know yourself if you've ever drunk a cup of coffee, consumption of caffeine, in moderate doses, increases feelings of alertness and energy, as well as increasing attention and positive mood.[43] Many people find these effects pleasant, so that they're willing to expend effort to obtain caffeine. For example, in the laboratory, psychologist Suzanne H. Mitchell and her colleagues showed that habitual coffee drinkers, whether or not they were caffeine deprived, would repeatedly move a computer mouse and click it at specific locations in order to obtain points exchangeable for coffee.[44] In another experiment, scientists Nicola J. Richardson and her colleagues compared people who regularly did and didn't consume a caffeinated beverage after lunch. Only those who did showed greater increased preference for a novel-flavored fruit juice after drinking it with a caffeine capsule as compared to if the capsule were a placebo. Such findings can help us understand why some people who have decided to stop consuming caffeine will still drink black decaffeinated coffee, a bitter substance. They have previously associated the positive effects of caffeine with the taste of coffee, resulting in an enduring preference for the taste of black coffee.[45]

There has been some controversy as to whether caffeine can have adverse health effects. Certainly in high doses it can. For example, high doses can cause panic attacks and palpitations, as well as aggravate stomach ulcers and disturb sleep.[46] Caffeine can also increase metabolic rate, so that more calories are burned, which sounds like a good thing if you're concerned about your weight. However, that possible benefit may be counteracted by the decrease in blood sugar level caused by caffeine, which in turn increases hunger.[47] In addition, in some people consumption of as little as one cup of coffee can result in a disorder called caffeine intoxication, which is marked by "restlessness....nervousness.... insomnia....diuresis [excessive discharge of urine]....gastrointestinal disturbance....muscle twitching....rambling flow of thought and speech.... [and] cardiac arrhythmia."[48]

Lead

Lead is a toxin that, throughout the course of human history, has been all too often present in what we've eaten or drunk, and whose effects have been extensively investigated. There is much evidence that ingesting lead can cause behavioral problems. In one experiment, a group of rats began consuming lead-containing liquids as soon as they were weaned. The liquids given to another group of rats contained no lead. Then as adults, all of the rats, while hungry, were tested on a task in which a fixed number of lever presses would result in the rats getting a food pellet. In addition, if a rat waited a specified amount of time after receiving a pellet before beginning to press the lever again, that rat would receive extra pellets. As it turned out, the lead-exposed rats responded more quickly on the lever and were less likely to wait after receiving a pellet. Thus, although they still received a lot of pellets, they ended up making many more lever presses per pellet.[49] These results seem to suggest that lead exposure can increase nonefficient, impulsive behavior.

We also know that large doses of dietary lead hinder children's learning and even cause IQ deficits. Further, there are indications that children whose bodies contain significant amounts of lead may be more likely to have decreased attention and be aggressive[50]—tendencies that can also be described as impulsive.

Lead poisoning has been affecting our behavior for much of history. Because lead has a sweet taste, people, since the time of the Roman Empire and continuing through the 18th century, added various lead-containing substances to wine to preserve or sweeten it. In the 18th century, the powder used to whiten wigs contained lead.[51] Just imagine how much of that got on people's hands and in their food! Another example of how, in the past, lead entered the food supply concerns the 134-member Franklin expedition of 1845. This expedition left England for the Arctic with the task of mapping the Northwest Passage. During the course of the expedition, many of the expedition's members began to behave strangely, and all of them died before they could complete their mission. Examinations of their bodies have indicated that their deaths were caused by lead in the expedition's food supply. The recovered bodies contained high amounts of lead, and the cans that contained the expedition's food supply were probably made with large amounts of lead.[52]

We know enough now to make our food cans without lead and to keep lead out of our wine, and, thank goodness, we no longer wear powdered wigs. In fact, knowledge about the damaging effects of lead poisoning has resulted in the United States banning lead from house paint and gasoline for many decades. As a result, the number of severe lead poisoning cases has been significantly decreasing.[53] However, public health officials have become more sensitive to the negative effects of even low lead levels in children, and in 2012 cut in half the permissible lead blood level (to 5 micrograms per deciliter of blood; see www.cdc. gov/nceh/lead/ACCLPP/20131024_POCguidelines_final.pdf). Concern has been increasing that permissible levels in adults, some of whom are particularly susceptible to lead exposure due to their working conditions, also need to be lowered.[54] Our unhealthy interactions with lead are not yet over, and require continued vigilance to prevent.

Hyperactivity

There have been many claims that food additives cause psychological abnormalities in some people. The most thoroughly investigated as well as the most controversial claim of this nature concerns attention-deficit/hyperactivity disorder (ADHD). This disorder is characterized by "a persistent pattern of inattention and/or hyperactivity-impulsivity that interferes with functioning or development, as characterized by [inattention] and/or [hyperactivity and impulsivity]." Examples of inattention are "makes careless mistakes in schoolwork, at work, or during other activities [or] does not follow through on instructions"; and examples of hyperactivity-impulsivity are "often talks excessively [or] often interrupts or intrudes on others." Before you get too upset thinking, "But I do that!" keep in mind that all of us, particularly children, engage in these sorts of behaviors some of the time. In order to be diagnosed with ADHD, someone must show many of these behaviors in several settings, and these behaviors must clearly interfere with the person's ability to lead a successful life. Please also keep in mind that no one description characterizes all people diagnosed with ADHD. There are a number of different subtypes, and even within one subtype the same symptoms aren't shown by all people.[55]

Several different treatments have been tried with hyperactive children. Stimulant drugs called amphetamines have been used for many years. Although amphetamines seem to speed up adults' behavior, they seem to slow down the behavior of children, including hyperactive children. Apparently, for both adults and children, amphetamines increase attention to cognitive tasks. Because sustaining attention on a cognitive task is particularly difficult for children, and because activity and attention are incompatible, hyperactive children administered amphetamines are less active.[56] Various behavioral procedures have also been used as treatments. For example, there have been attempts to teach boys with ADHD to speak in a group only after raising their hands.[57] However, in general, trying a wide variety of treatments is the most effective strategy for this disorder with many different subtypes.[58]

Now we should return to the reason that ADHD is included in this book—the possibility that some cases may be caused by eating certain things. Some research has shown that consumption of the toxins PCBs causes hyperactivity and a deficit in attention.[59] However, far more discussed is the possibility that ADHD is caused by sensitivities to food additives. Approximately 40 years ago, physician Ben F. Feingold proposed that hyperactivity in some children is due to their increased tendency to react to certain substances in their food. These substances include artificial flavors, artificial colors, the preservatives BHT and BHA, and salicylates, substances that occur naturally in foods such as almonds, apples, and tomatoes. Feingold reasoned that if all of these substances were removed from what's consumed, the hyperactive behavior should significantly decrease. Thus was born the Feingold diet for hyperactive children.[60]

Over the ensuing years, many experiments have been conducted, with people and other animals, to find out whether the above substances are responsible for ADHD symptoms. Although scientists do not agree that these substances cause ADHD, they do seem to agree that for a small number of children with ADHD symptoms, removing these substances from their diets can help alleviate their symptoms.[61] However, it can be difficult for parents to determine if removing these substances from their child's diet has a positive effect—on average with the passage of time, some children might, without any specific treatment, show improvements in their behavior. For these reasons, there's no consensus on using approaches such as the Feingold diet. Further, it's important to remember that there are definite costs to using something like the Feingold diet. If this diet isn't effective at treating ADHD, the result can be loss of money, wasted effort, disappointment, and the possible avoidance of other more effective treatments. On the other hand, ensuring that ADHD children have sufficient zinc, iron, and certain fatty acids in their diets can be an important adjutant to other ADHD therapies.[62]

The Sticky Case of Gum

And now we come to gum, chewing gum, that is. For many of us our primary contact with gum is as a nuisance on sidewalks and on the undersides of desks and restaurant tables. However, in the past 10 years there has been an astonishing amount of published empirical research on the effects on our behavior of the act of chewing gum. In the journal *Appetite* alone there have been some 20 articles on gum chewing published during this period. This research concerns how chewing gum might affect appetite, attention, memory, and mood, in both children and adults. Questions that arise as part of this research include whether or not there are any reliable effects of gum chewing, whether or not the gum must be sweet or contain calories in order for any of the effects to occur, and how what is found is or is not dependent on what the chewer thinks will happen as a result of the chewing.[63]

You'll recall from Chapter 2 and Conversation Making Fact #2 that chewing gum—sugar-free or regular—decreases appetite. Generally the findings of the research on gum chewing also seem to indicate positive effects for gum chewing on cognition and mood. It is possible that many of the results are due to the chewer becoming aroused by the act of chewing[64] (perhaps a mechanism similar to that responsible for the improvements in cognition that result from the simple act of drinking water). Future research will undoubtedly focus more on the possible physiological mechanisms for the positive effects of chewing gum.

Although there have at this point been multiple experiments demonstrating that gum chewing does, for example, enhance attention, results have been no means uniform, causing scientists to discuss what might be responsible for that lack of uniformity.[65] Yet the positive findings are frequent enough to warrant those of us who are not gum chewers to reconsider our chewing habits. Perhaps what I was taught as a child constitutes cow-like behavior will be a part of my future, or at least when I'm in private!

Food for Thought: Conclusion

Scientists have made some dramatic discoveries in the past several decades about the effects of food consumption on our behavior. Although what we eat and drink may not influence hyperactivity in children to any great degree, it may influence how sleepy we are, how well we learn, how depressed we are, and whether we feel as if ants are crawling under our skin. To some degree, you are indeed what you eat and drink. The future will undoubtedly bring additional speculations and research that will test statements such as the following by Galileo who, in this interpretation by Bertolt Brecht, is a dedicated scientist who believes that plentiful supplies of food and drink are essential to his doing his research:

> How can I work, with the tax collector on the doorstep? And my poor daughter will never acquire a husband unless she has a dowry, she's not too bright. And I like to buy books—all kinds of books. Why not? And what about my appetite? I don't think well unless I eat well. Can I help it if I get my best ideas over a good meal and a bottle of wine? They don't pay me as much as they pay the butcher's boy. If only I could have five years to do nothing but research! Come on. I am going to show you something else.[66]

9

"HUNGER TALKS A MOST PERSUASIVE LANGUAGE"[1]

Anorexia and Bulimia

You are at an outdoor cafe on a pleasant summer evening. A young woman is sitting at a table with two other people. You look at her face. She has very prominent cheekbones and a sharp chin. She raises her right arm to reach for her water glass. You see that the arm is a mere stick with skin on it; her arm looks like a skeleton's with a flesh-colored covering. A waiter brings plates of food to the young woman and her companions. She uses her fork to push the food around her plate. Very occasionally she brings a small forkful of food to her mouth and chews and swallows the food. When the waiter takes her plate away, most of the food is still there.

This chapter and the next will discuss situations in which we eat inappropriate amounts of food—either too little or too much. The present chapter focuses on cases in which someone, such as the young woman just described, eats too little. Such behavior is described as *anorexia*, which literally means "lack of appetite." However, this definition is somewhat misleading because, as you'll learn, people with anorexia sometimes have a significant appetite; they just don't eat. This chapter is a very serious one, including discussion of life-threatening eating disorders. I hope that the information will be useful to you in understanding and dealing with these extremely difficult disorders.

When you read about the young woman at the start of this chapter, you may have immediately assumed that her anorexia was a symptom of anorexia nervosa, an eating disorder that will be discussed later in this chapter. However, the young woman's anorexia could actually have been due to many different factors. Anorexia is sometimes caused by infections, certain types of gastrointestinal diseases, decreases in taste and smell, Alzheimer's disease, and AIDS.[2] Some drugs, such as amphetamines, also decrease the amount eaten.[3] In addition, anorexia can be associated with mood, but the relationship is complex. For example, if someone is not a dieter and that person becomes depressed, then that person will tend to eat less than usual. On the other hand, if someone is a dieter and that person becomes depressed, then that person will tend to eat more than usual.[4] (For more information on mood and appetite see Chapter 10.) This chapter will review in detail one type of anorexia that has been investigated a great deal, the anorexia associated with cancer, as well as anorexia nervosa. Finally, because anorexia may occur as part of bulimia nervosa, an eating disorder characterized by intermittent periods of excess eating, the present chapter also includes information on bulimia (however, binge eating disorder, which does not include periods of food restriction, is covered in the next chapter).

But what about voluntarily not eating in order to improve your health? You have probably seen in newspapers and magazines reports of research showing health benefits of severe calorie restriction. Experiments with mice and monkeys have shown that these animals may live longer and be less likely to become ill if, for many years, they eat a diet that is nutritionally balanced but contains about 70% of the calories that the animals would ordinarily eat, and caloric restriction seems to improve memory in aging people.[5] Research has begun elucidating some of the physiological mechanisms responsible for these effects.[6] Not surprisingly, there is an organization called the Caloric Restriction Society whose mission "is dedicated to understanding and promoting the Calorie Restriction... diet"(www.crsociety.org).

However, before you begin drastically cutting back on your calories for the next 10 or 20 or 30 years, a couple of caveats are in order. First, it's possible that the reduced-calorie diet must continue for many years in order for there to be health benefits. Would you be able to do this? The rats and monkeys had no choice, but you would constantly have to defy temptation. Also, it's very difficult to achieve a balanced diet with that kind of calorie intake, and much time and care may be involved in doing so.[7] Further, research suggests that a fluctuating weight has negative health consequences.[8] Therefore trying—and repeatedly failing—to restrict severely calorie intake could be worse than never trying to restrict calories at all. Perhaps most concerning of all, recent research reported by the National Institute of Aging has *not* found an increase in lifespan among monkeys as a result of calorie restriction, and the reasons for these different results are not yet clear.[9] For all of these reasons, at this time people should use extreme caution in contemplating any sort of long-term calorie restriction for the purpose of increasing lifespan.

When dealing with anorexia, as well as when dealing with overeating (see the next chapter), it becomes critical to have good ways of measuring weight gain, loss, and the percentage of body fat. Over the years, many ways have been suggested and have gained and lost popularity. Currently the most popular method is the body mass index, or BMI. Your BMI is equal to your weight (measured in kilograms) divided by the square of your height (measured in meters). A higher BMI means that someone has more body weight for a given height. In other words, if two people are the same height, the heavier one will have a larger BMI value. For example, someone who is 5 feet 4 inches tall (1.63 meters) and weighs 124 pounds (56 kilograms) will have a BMI of 21. There are online calculators for easily determining your own BMI (e.g., www.cdc.gov/healthyweight/assessing/bmi/adult_bmi/english_bmi_calculator/bmi_calculator.html and www.nhlbi.nih.gov/guidelines/obesity/BMI/bmicalc.htm). However, it should always be remembered that two people can have the same BMI and have very different proportions of fat and muscle—BMI is only a rough (but convenient and useful) method for measuring whether someone is under- or overweight.

There has been a lot of research conducted about which weights are and aren't healthy. Many studies have been done to determine if, assuming everything else is held constant, people are more likely to become ill at certain weights than others. It does appear that, all else being equal, being very thin (BMI below 18.5) can decrease lifespan, as can being obese (BMI greater than or equal to 30.0). For people who are overweight (BMI 25.0–29.9), the results do not appear to be consistent.[10] For the purposes of this chapter, it is important to note that being very thin can inhibit the immune system,[11] in addition to being associated with malnutrition. Anemia (due to inadequate iron intake) and osteoporosis (due to inadequate calcium and vitamin D intake) are two likely correlates of being very thin.

Cancer Anorexia

All too many of us have seen cancer patients who are terribly gaunt and who eat very little. Perhaps 50% of cancer patients lose large amounts of weight, a process known as wasting, with perhaps 10–25% of all deaths from cancer actually being due to wasting.[12] Possible explanations of the anorexia and weight loss accompanying cancer include changes in, for example, cancer patients' taste sensitivities, food preferences, breakdown of stored fat, and metabolisms. These changes may result from the cancer treatment or from the cancer itself.[13]

One approach that has been extremely helpful in understanding and treating some types of cancer anorexia makes use of the research on taste aversion learning, which was described in Chapter 6. Psychologists Ilene L. Bernstein and Mary M. Webster conducted an imaginative and difficult series of experiments showing that children or adults given a novel-tasting ice cream prior to their chemotherapy acquired an aversion to that ice cream. Apparently illness resulting from the chemotherapy was paired with the taste of the ice cream, and taste aversions developed.[14]

Knowing that taste aversions can form during chemotherapy has helped clinicians figure out ways to minimize the adverse impact of such aversions, for example by use of the "scapegoat technique." This technique is used to prevent cancer patients from developing aversions to the foods that they usually eat. In one example, a patient is given a strong-tasting piece of candy prior to his or her chemotherapy session. The aversion then forms to the candy rather than to one of the last foods eaten prior to the chemotherapy.[15]

Close to half of cancer patients have reported nausea and even vomiting in anticipation of chemotherapy.[16] This apparently happens because, in the past, nausea caused by the chemotherapy treatment has been repeatedly associated with aspects of the patients' surroundings. Learning theory has been helpful in suggesting treatments for this type of anticipatory nausea and vomiting. One such treatment involves systematically exposing patients, while they are completely relaxed, to gradual approximations of the objects or aspects of their surroundings that are causing them problems. In the case of cancer chemotherapy nausea, patients are taught to relax while imagining the aspects of their surroundings that induce their nausea. This technique has been helpful in reducing patients' reports of nausea preceding chemotherapy. Therefore it should also be helpful in decreasing the learned taste aversions that contribute to cancer anorexia.[17]

"Enough Is as Good as a Feast":[18]
Anorexia Nervosa

Hazel as a young teenager had enjoyed being popular and was quite flirtatious. She heard her father say, "Is she now going to be a teenager?" and this sounded to her as if he were disgusted and might reject her. Background for this anxiety was a much older half-sister who, according to the family saga, had been her father's declared darling but who had disappointed him.... [Hazel] wanted to deserve her father's love and admiration by excelling academically and in sports, and she restricted her food intake more and more. For her the issue became "mind over body," and she practiced it in the most literal sense. She expressed it: "When you are so unhappy and you don't know how to accomplish anything, then to have control over your body becomes a supreme accomplishment." You make out of your body your very own kingdom where you are the tyrant, the absolute dictator.[19]

Sarah was the only child of rather elderly parents who were both somewhat obese. She had herself been plump from infancy and by the time she was sixteen she weighed [154 pounds]. She was used to being called "fatty" or "the lump" at school and was always embarrassed when she had to undress to change for games. She was a keen horsewoman and had some success in competition. Her occasional attempts at dieting became more determined after she came to the conclusion that her increasing weight was becoming a handicap to her riding. She dieted with the encouragement of her parents and set out to lose [30 pounds]. However, she passed this weight after less than three months, but continued to avoid fattening foods. After a further three months she weighed less than [98 pounds] and was unequivocally in a state of anorexia nervosa.[20]

[Grace] was the youngest of three girls, and the two older sisters had begun to menstruate at eleven. The sister next to her was very heavy and was continuously criticized for not having the willpower to diet. Grace weighed [110 pounds] when her eleventh birthday approached; she was taller than most of her classmates and knew of no others who menstruated. She became alarmed when she noticed the first bloodstains, knowing that this was a harbinger of menstruation, and she felt unable to cope with the responsibilities involved, was fearful of being teased or having an odor or spotting her clothes. She wanted to postpone this event until she was fourteen or fifteen. Her determination to do something about it became even greater when a film about sexual development was shown in school. She dropped [27 pounds] within six weeks, and the signs of approaching puberty disappeared; she did not begin to menstruate until two years later.[21]

These case histories illustrate some of the many varieties of anorexia nervosa, a devastating eating disorder known all too well in the United States and in many other parts of the world. The American Psychiatric Association's diagnostic criteria for anorexia nervosa include "restriction of energy intake relative to requirements, leading to a significantly low body weight....intense fear of gaining weight or of becoming fat.... [and] disturbance in the way in which one's body weight or shape is experienced."[22] Anorexics usually have BMIs less than 18.5, and they tend to perceive their bodies as larger and heavier than they really are. Further, many women with anorexia nervosa have become so thin that they don't menstruate.[23]

Officially, the American Psychiatric Association recognizes two subtypes of anorexia nervosa: the restricting subtype in which "weight loss is accomplished primarily through dieting, fasting, and/or excessive exercise," and the binge-eating/purging subtype, in which "the individual has engaged in recurrent episodes of binge eating or purging behavior (i.e., self-induced vomiting or the misuse of laxatives, diuretics, or enemas).[24] Keep in mind that the second subtype refers to someone who sometimes engages in binging and purging, but also engages in anorexic behaviors; someone whose eating disorder consists primarily of binging and purging would be diagnosed as having bulimia nervosa, a disorder discussed in more detail later in this chapter.

Anorexia nervosa is a disorder seen mostly in young women. About 90% of anorexics are female. This disorder generally develops in adolescence or early adulthood, but there's considerable variation around that age range. In any given year, about 1 in 200 young women will demonstrate the characteristics of anorexia nervosa. It's a very dangerous disorder. About 5% of women demonstrating the characteristics of anorexia nervosa will die from it or will commit suicide in any 10-year period. Some anorexics remain too thin and abnormally concerned about their weights into their later years. Anorexia nervosa is much more common in industrialized countries where food is abundant, and is now being reported in countries such as Japan, in addition to Europe.[25]

Even though a defining characteristic of anorexia nervosa is a lack of eating, and despite the literal meaning of anorexia (without appetite), anorexics are completely obsessed with food and food consumption. They carefully calculate just how many calories they can and do consume. They think and dream about food constantly, saying such things as: "Of course, I had breakfast; I ate my Cheerio," and "I won't even lick a postage stamp—one never knows about calories."[26]

When I was in college I was friendly with another student who I suspected was anorexic. She ate very little, was very thin, and was constantly referring to herself as being overweight. She knew that I was interested in psychology and eating and she knew about my suspicions that she was anorexic. However, she told me, she couldn't be anorexic because she thought about food all the time. This same woman mistakenly believed that someone would never have more fat cells than he or she had in the first 2 years of life. Therefore, when she had her first baby, she restricted his food. She proudly told me that his being thinner than other babies allowed him to stand up and walk earlier. She also told me that, when some friends were visiting, one exclaimed "What's wrong with that baby? Why is he so thin?" But the visitor's comment didn't seem to bother my friend. Unfortunately, her treatment of her baby isn't unique. Psychologist Kelly D. Brownell, one of the best known obesity researchers, has reported a number of cases in which infants of affluent parents failed to grow and develop properly because their parents restricted the infants' food in the hope of preventing them from becoming overweight.[27]

In addition to eating abnormally small amounts of food, research suggests that anorexics may tend to eat certain kinds of foods more than others. For example, anorexics have been shown to have lower preference for high-fat foods than nonanorexics.[28] Further, being a semivegetarian (no red meat, but occasional fish or poultry) and exhibiting eating disorder symptoms tend to go together.[29] Therefore, vegetarian girls and women should be scrutinized carefully for the presence of eating disorders. It may be that girls and women who are excessively concerned about their weight, the sort of people who develop eating disorders, tend to become semivegetarians in the belief that this will help to keep their weight down.

Other aspects of anorexics' eating behaviors are also unusual. For example, anorexics tend to estimate food portions as larger than do nonanorexics, and anorexics' preference for food and how hungry they say they are decrease unusually quickly after eating.[30] In addition, anorexics who restrict food (as opposed to anorexics who occasionally binge and purge) take longer to eat their food and spend more time during a meal doing things such as pushing the food around on their plates.[31]

Origins

For a good number of decades now scientists have been investigating, sometimes in minute detail, characteristics of people with anorexia nervosa, as well as characteristics of people who might develop anorexia nervosa, to try to find out what causes this disorder. If what causes anorexia nervosa were known, then it might be possible to use that information to prevent this disorder or to improve its treatment. A huge number of different explanations for this disorder have been proposed, and many of these possible explanations have received some research confirmation.[32] Anorexia nervosa probably doesn't have one single cause, which would help to explain why anorexics don't all appear to have exactly the same characteristics.

A prime suspect for one cause of anorexia nervosa is the culture in which we live. Have you ever heard the expression, "You can never be too rich or too thin"? Much research has demonstrated that the fashion image of thinness that has prevailed since the 1960s is a significant contributing factor to the high incidence of anorexia nervosa and other eating disorders.[33] This culture of thinness is far more prevalent among the many different ethnic groups in the United States than was previously realized.[34] Just look at the differences among three "perfect" figures from the 1950s, 1980s, and the 2000s: Marilyn Monroe, Jamie Lee Curtis, and Keira Knightley (see Figures 9.1a, b, and c). A quick comparison of past and current fashion magazines will demonstrate

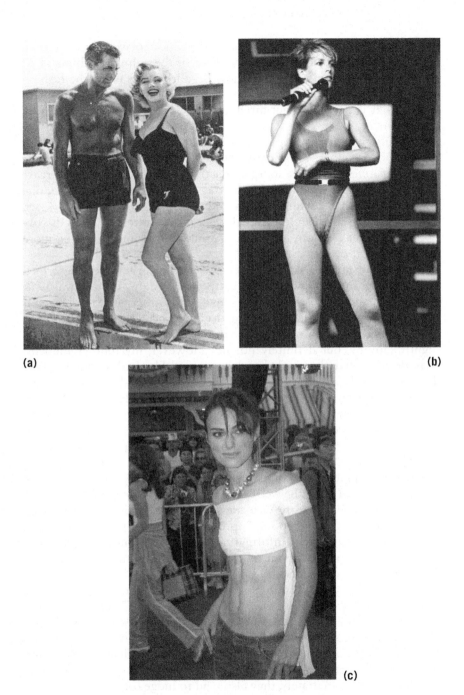

Figure 9.1 (a) A "perfect" figure from the 1950s: Marilyn Monroe (with Cary Grant). (b) A "perfect" figure from the 1980s: Jamie Lee Curtis. (c) Today's "perfect" figure: Keira Knightley. Copyright: Featureflash/Shutterstock.com.

the same point. Fashionable women 60 years ago were heavier than fashionable women now. We see evidence of the culture of thinness all around us. And despite what are now decades of pleas for the fashion industry to change its image of the ideal female body, being super-thin is still what is needed to get hired as a model, sometimes with deadly consequences.[35]

Our culture has not always demanded that women be so thin. Historian Joan Jacobs Brumberg's fascinating book, *The Body Project: An Intimate History of American Girls*, states that active attempts by girls to decrease their body weights didn't start until the 1920s. Prior to that time, one improved oneself by helping others and showing self-control. However, during the early 20th century, the calorie was discovered, and that discovery, plus greater freedom for women, resulted in women focusing more on their own appearances.[36]

My mother appears to have been one of the early dieters described by Brumberg. In 1935, when she was 13 years old, my mother was with another girl and two boys. The boys invited the other girl to a dance but told my mother that they weren't inviting her because she was too fat. I've seen pictures of my mother at that time and she wasn't fat—perhaps slightly chubby, but definitely not fat. However, my mother immediately decided that she needed to lose weight. She had a vague notion that some foods were fattening and these she avoided. She remembers sometimes eating only lettuce. She also exercised. Her family had no scales at home so she used her small change to pay to weigh herself on scales in drugstores. During the next year she lost 20 pounds and grew 6 inches, turning into what she described as a bean pole. She proudly told me this story many, many times, ever since I was quite young.

Ideals of thinness, as well as methods for achieving those ideals, are being popularized using the web in ways that were unimagined in decades past. For example, there are Web sites devoted to "pro-ana" (promoting anorexia nervosa) and "pro-mia" (promoting bulimia). These Web sites provide, along with other information, dieting and purging tips. There has been much concern about these Web sites promoting what are very dangerous eating disorders.[37]

Given the ever-present culture of thinness, it's not surprising that many women have an exaggerated view of their body size. This misperception is one of the defining characteristics, and possible causes, of anorexia nervosa. (See Conversation Making Fact #9.) More girls and young women are dissatisfied with the appearance of their bodies than are boys and young men.[38] Further, women with eating disorders not only judge their own body sizes inaccurately, they also tend to judge other women's body sizes as thinner than their own, a likely motivating factor for demonstrating an eating disorder.[39]

Conversation making fact #9

We would feel better about people dieting if we thought that the right people—that is, those who weigh too much—were primarily the ones doing it. Unfortunately, at least among young women, that may not be the case. Psychologist Caroline Davis and her colleagues made a disturbing discovery when they studied what physical characteristics of young women undergraduates were associated with dieting and body weight dissatisfaction. They found that whether a woman undergraduate dieted and was dissatisfied with her weight were best predicted by whether she had a large body frame. In contrast, knowing a woman's BMI or percentage of body fat did not result in as good a prediction of whether the woman dieted or was dissatisfied with her body weight. In other words, these results suggest that young women tend to be dissatisfied with their bodies and tend to diet, not because they're fat, but because of something that they can't change: their body frame size. These results are disturbing because they indicate that, even if the dieting is successful, these young women will still not be satisfied with their bodies. Further, given that they're dieting even when they're not overweight, these young women can gain no health benefit from the dieting, only possible health risks.[40]

Differences in body dissatisfaction between women and men are amply illustrated in a landmark study by psychologists April E. Fallon and Paul Rozin. This research involved 475 male and female undergraduate participants. The participants used sets of male and female figure drawings ranging from very thin to very heavy to indicate (a) the figure that looked most similar to their current shape, (b) the figure they most wanted to look like, (c) the figure they felt would be most attractive to the opposite sex, and (d) the figure of the opposite sex to which they felt they would be most attracted. The men chose very similar figures as representing their ideal figure, their current figure, and the figure that they thought would be most attractive to women; the women, however, chose a heavier figure as representing their current figure, and a thinner one as both their ideal and the one that they thought would be most attractive to men. In addition, although the male figure judged by the men to be most attractive to women was heavier than what the women actually preferred, the female figure judged by the women to be most attractive to men was thinner than what the men actually preferred. (See Figure 9.2.)

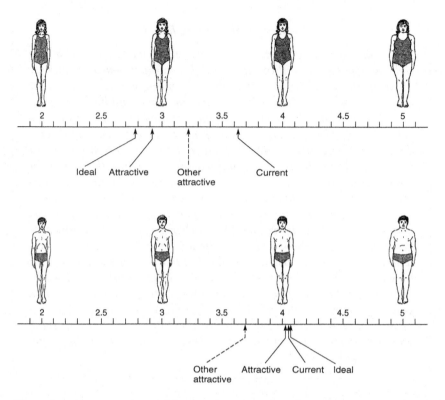

Figure 9.2 Average ratings of figures. Average ratings by women (top) and men (bottom) of current figure, ideal figure, and figure most attractive to the opposite gender; average ratings by men of the female figure that they find most attractive (top, labeled *other attractive*) and equivalent average ratings by women, on the bottom. (Adapted from A. E. Fallon and P. Rozin, "Sex Differences in Perceptions of Desirable Body Shape," *Journal of Abnormal Psychology* 94[1985]: 102–105.)

Altogether, this study's findings show that most of the women, but not most of the men, were dissatisfied with their current figure in such a way that could encourage them to diet and to become anorexic.[41]

Differences in body size satisfaction also appear to be related to how people spend their time. For example, athletes such as distance runners, dancers, and gymnasts—athletes for whom being thin is thought to help performance and thus for whom appearance is extremely important—tend to have a higher prevalence of eating disorders than nonathletes.[42] The National Collegiate Athletic Association (NCAA) devotes a section of its Web site to eating disorders, including a discussion of the "Female Athlete Triad," which consists of "eating disorders, menstrual dysfunction and bone mineral deficiency, which can cause osteoporosis" (www.ncaa.org/health-and-safety/medical-conditions/disordered-eating-and-eating-disorders). Specific occasions, such as your upcoming spring break or wedding, can also inspire inappropriate food restriction, with some women even purchasing a too-small wedding dress to provide themselves with additional incentive to lose weight.[43]

On the plus side, there are some indications that, due to the increasing involvement of women in athletics, there may now be a new female body ideal. Until some years ago there were only two such ideals—how women wanted to appear (extremely thin) and how men wanted them to appear (with more curves). However, athleticism among women may have created a third popular alternative: a sleek, muscular body, the sort of female body seen in fitness magazines,[44] similar to the body of Jamie Lee Curtis in Figure 9.1b. Unfortunately, even an athletic ideal can be taken to extremes. The newest (5th) edition of the American Psychiatric Association's *Diagnostic and Statistical Manual of Mental Disorders* now contains an entry entitled "muscle dysmorphia: The individual is preoccupied with the idea that his or her body build is too small or insufficiently muscular."[45] People with this disorder engage in unhealthy behaviors such as steroid abuse and obsessive exercising.[46] It seems as if there's some sort of disorder custom fit for every situation.

Scientists have been studying families to try to figure out both which sorts of children might be likely to develop an eating disorder later on in life and what sorts of early experiences might be associated with the later development of an eating disorder. From this research we know, for example, that mothers who tend to restrict their own eating also tend to restrict the eating of their children;[47] that children as young as 5 years old can develop inhibited eating, secretive eating, and overeating-induced vomiting;[48] that, in a large sample of 431 children aged 7 to 10 years, 23% of the children (most of them girls) said that they had dieted or were dieting;[49] that 9- and 10-year-old children, particularly girls, are significantly influenced by their parents' (especially their mothers') comments about their weights;[50] and that girls' peers can also significantly influence the girls' likelihood of dieting.[51] Thus it appears that abnormal eating behaviors can occur well before adolescence and that both mothers and peers can influence the development of those behaviors.

I remember vividly how, when I was about 12 and was at the pediatrician's office for my annual checkup, my mother suddenly started telling the pediatrician that she was concerned about my weight. She had made similar comments to me at home. She told the pediatrician that she was concerned that I was going to end up with a body similar to my overweight father's. The pictures of me around that time show a girl who was neither skinny nor small (my feet were size 8½ by the time I was 11), but who was also definitely not fat or even chubby. Although I had some vague sense that I'd like to be thinner, the greatest impetus for me to lose weight was coming from my mother and, unlike some other girls of that age, I didn't value what she had to say too terribly much. Now that I look back on it, perhaps that was a good thing. Otherwise, with my large frame and a mother who took active steps to control both her weight and mine, I might have ended up with an eating disorder.

Several other explanations of the development of anorexia nervosa have focused on the interactions of girls with their surroundings. For example, anorexics have been seen as using anorexia as a way of gaining attention, as an attempt at individuality, as a denial of sexuality (in addition to not menstruating, girls who are severely underweight lack breasts and other secondary sexual characteristics), and as a way of dealing with problems caused by overdemanding parents.[52]

Let's consider more physiologically based possible explanations or causes of anorexia nervosa. To begin with, let's think about the fact that anorexics often exercise a great deal, supposedly to help remove the caloric consequences of what they eat. However, it's possible that the tendency of anorexics to exercise a great deal is an effect rather than a cause of low body weight. Hyperactivity, a behavior seen frequently in anorexics, has also been observed in people and other animals who have been deprived of food either in the laboratory or under natural conditions. The increase in activity level associated with food deprivation may help animals in nature to survive. If you haven't got much to eat, you may be more likely to find some food if you're active than if you're not.[53] Therefore, when hyperactivity is seen in anorexics, it's possible that it's occurring because of the anorexics' low body weights, and not the other way around.

Scientists have had similar discussions about the physiological abnormalities found in anorexia nervosa. Are these abnormalities a cause of the disorder or an effect of it? The physiological abnormalities include, in addition to menstrual and growth disturbances, low levels of some hormones, low thyroid activity, low insulin levels, low blood pressure, and increased activity of the neurotransmitter serotonin. The stomach also empties more slowly, which is thought to be responsible for the fact that anorexics claim to feel full so easily. Usually all of these abnormalities disappear when an anorexic gains weight, lending support to the argument that these abnormalities are effects, not causes, of anorexia nervosa. However, it's possible that some of these abnormalities, such as the increased serotonin activity, once put in motion by dieting, may have physiological consequences that contribute to the continuation of anorexia nervosa.[54]

In their major review article on the factors which, if present, appear to lead to eating disorders, behavioral scientists Ruth H. Striegel-Moore and Cynthia M. Bulik conclude that both environmental factors, such as the culture of thinness, and biological factors, including genetic contributions, predict the development of anorexia nervosa. Further, investigations of these two types of factors have proceeded largely independently, and making significant progress in understanding and treating anorexia nervosa will require integration of the two approaches.[55] As we have discussed earlier in this book, it can be quite difficult to isolate environmental and biological factors, and an approach that recognizes their interaction can be very productive.

Getting better all the time: treatments

Given that anorexia nervosa is such a dangerous disorder, it's essential that we have effective treatments for it. The treatments for anorexia nervosa can be divided into two types: those designed to obtain an immediate weight gain, and those designed to maintain that weight gain.[56] The treatments designed to obtain an immediate weight gain are important for two reasons. First, some patients may be in danger of dying from starvation. In such cases, an immediate weight gain, which sometimes has to be achieved without the patient's consent, will help to ensure the patient's survival. The second reason that these sorts of treatments are important is based on the fact that, as you've just learned, some of the physiological effects of starvation may help to prolong anorexia nervosa. Therefore, it may not be possible to make any real progress in treating anorexia nervosa without first obtaining a weight gain.

The treatments used to help anorexics gain weight immediately include nurturance, behavior therapy, and drug therapy. Nurturance consists of one or more treatments that attempt to improve the patient's nutrition. A simple example of nurturance is a high-calorie diet combined with bed rest, which decreases the calories used by the patient. If a patient won't comply with this form of nurturance, force feeding may be used; food may be given to the patient through a tube down her throat or through a needle into one of her veins. Force feeding, unlike other treatments for anorexia nervosa, is usually given only in a hospital setting. Nurturance can be extremely successful in obtaining an immediate weight gain in patients.[57] In behavior therapy anorexics aren't allowed to engage in pleasurable activities unless they eat. Behavior therapy is based on principles of learning established in the laboratory. Behavior therapy can be fairly successful in obtaining an initial weight gain, although probably not as successful as nurturance.[58] In drug therapy, any of a variety of medications may be given to anorexics to try to increase the amount that they eat. Based on the evidence of elevated levels of serotonin in patients with anorexia nervosa, physicians have tried to treat anorexia nervosa with medications known to affect serotonin levels. However, so far, no medication has been consistently and significantly shown to improve the treatment of anorexia nervosa.[59]

The sorts of treatments that are used to maintain a weight gain, or at least to prevent further weight loss, include individual, group, and family psychotherapy, as well as self-help groups. All of these treatments aim to maintain the health of a patient over a long period of time. In individual psychotherapy, the patient works with the therapist on a one-to-one basis. In group psychotherapy, a group of patients discusses their problems together with the therapist. In family psychotherapy, the therapist treats the whole family as a unit, rather than just treating the anorexic.[60] With each of these types of psychotherapy, a therapist may use one of many different styles of therapy, such as behavior therapy. Psychotherapy can also vary in length; each of these types of psychotherapy can last for as little as a few weeks or for as long as several years.

One type of psychotherapy that has been frequently used for treatment of anorexia nervosa is cognitive-behavior therapy. Cognitive-behavior therapy is similar to behavior therapy in that it's based on principles of learning established in the laboratory. However, instead of focusing on modifying the patient's eating behavior, the therapist works with the patient to modify the patient's reported thoughts and images. For example, the therapist may work with a patient to modify her reported perception of her body size, helping the anorexic to see herself as too thin, instead of too fat. Unfortunately, there haven't been many controlled studies looking at the effectiveness of cognitive-behavior therapy in treating anorexia nervosa, and its efficacy is unclear.[61]

Family therapy has been used with anorexia nervosa for many years. A particular type of family therapy—what is known as the Maudsley model—has been shown to be quite effective with adolescent anorexics. This method involves working with an anorexic's family, in addition to the anorexic, and transitioning from the parents completely controlling the anorexic's eating at the beginning of the therapy to the anorexic eating independently, contingent on the anorexic demonstrating healthy eating behavior.[62]

Nevertheless, many anorexics are extremely difficult to treat. This fact prompted B. Timothy Walsh, a well-known psychiatrist and eating disorders researcher, to write: "This oldest eating disorder remains impressively resistant to a wide range of interventions, and arguably has the highest death rate of any psychiatric disorder."[63] Yet he remains hopeful, writing in the same paper that "new efforts based on the analysis of genetic factors, on the use of brain imaging and on the detailed analysis of behavioral disturbances hold promise for significantly advancing our understanding of these disorders."[64]

I'll end this section by mentioning self-help groups. These groups serve many functions, including helping anorexics to find therapists, information, social support, and other types of assistance. Self-help groups are popular because they're relatively inexpensive and because they provide a number of services often not easily available through traditional mental health care institutions. Self-help groups have become particularly easy to find because of the World Wide Web. An advantage of the online self-help groups is that participants can use them anywhere and at any time of the day or night; participants aren't limited to preset meeting locations or times. For some examples of relevant Web sites and other types of self-help information, see the section on where to get help and information at the end of this chapter. Research needs to be done to determine the degree to which self-help groups, on the Web or otherwise, can assist in treating anorexia nervosa.

Does She or Doesn't She?: Bulimia Nervosa

Undoubtedly you've also heard of bulimia nervosa, another eating disorder. The American Psychiatric Association characterizes bulimia nervosa as consisting of "binge eating [and]....recurrent inappropriate compensatory behaviors in order to prevent gain, such as self-induced vomiting; misuse of laxatives, diuretics or other medications; fasting; or excessive exercise....[and] the binge eating and inappropriate compensatory behaviors both occur, on average, at least once a week for 3 months."[65] As you can see, there's some overlap in the definition of a bulimic and the definition of a binge-eating/purging anorexic stated in the preceding section on anorexia nervosa. Also similar to anorexics, bulimics tend to be overly concerned with their body size and shape, and about 90% of bulimics are female. However, unlike anorexics, bulimics are usually within the range of normal or overweight BMIs.[66]

In any given year, about 1 in 100 young women will demonstrate the characteristics of bulimia nervosa,[67] about twice as high a frequency as anorexia nervosa. It's possible that when groups of young women live together, such as in college dormitories, information spreads about binging and purging, which at first glance appears to be the perfect solution to dealing with both the wide availability of tempting food in college and the desire to be physically attractive according to prevailing standards. As one patient said, "I thought I had the problem licked; I couldn't understand why everyone didn't eat and then vomit."[68] Unfortunately, this brilliant dieting strategy doesn't work; adolescent girls who engage in bulimic behaviors are more likely to be overweight 4 years later than girls who eat normally.[69]

Bulimia even seems to have become an accepted, if sometimes denigrated, part of our culture. When Christine Quinn, New York City Council speaker, was a candidate for mayor in 2013, she made a public statement about her struggles with bulimia that became a front page *New York Times* story,[70] and singer Demi Lovato accused Lady Gaga of glamorizing bulimia when she had a vomit artist spew green and black liquid all over her at a 2014 music festival in Austin, Texas (www.huffington-post.com/2014/03/22/lady-gaga-demi-lovato_n_5014032.html).

There are many negative physiological effects of binging and purging, and bulimics who persist with these behaviors are risking their health. For example, depending on the purging method used, bulimics may have abnormal body chemistry, fluid retention, and heart muscles.

Obviously, it's extremely important to detect bulimia nervosa and to get immediate professional help for anyone suffering from it. Unfortunately, it can be very difficult for a nonprofessional to detect that someone is suffering from bulimia nervosa. A bulimic can hide her binging and purging. In addition, as you've already learned, a bulimic's outward appearance is often similar to that of someone without an eating disorder. Nevertheless, there are two physiological changes in vomiting bulimics that can help a keen observer to detect the bulimia: those bulimics who induce vomiting by sticking their fingers in their throats develop a callus or scrape on the back of the hand that they use and, due to vomit's acidity, the tooth enamel on the back of the top teeth becomes eroded in most bulimics who have been vomiting for several years.[71] Thus dentists can play a critical role in detecting bulimia nervosa.

You might wonder, given the large amount of vomiting in which many bulimics engage, why it is that they don't develop taste aversions to the foods that they eat during binges. Why isn't the vomiting paired with the food eaten, so that an aversion develops to the food? Instead, bulimics continue to crave their binge foods. One possible explanation is that the vomiting is self-induced and isn't accompanied by nausea, a very different situation than what you find in experiments on taste aversion learning. Another possible explanation has to do with the fact that bulimics sometimes report that they're extremely used to vomiting; it's not aversive to them.[72] Experiments with rats show that nausea that's familiar is less likely to result in a taste aversion than nausea that's novel.[73]

Another very interesting physiological characteristic to examine in bulimics is metabolic rate. Better understanding of bulimics' metabolic rates could help identify ways for bulimics to control their weights other than severely restricting or purging the food that they eat. There have been reports of significantly lower, as well as significantly higher, metabolic rates in bulimics.[74] As you'll learn in the next chapter, metabolic rates are important because they help to determine how easy it is for someone to gain or lose weight. If two people, one with a high metabolic rate and one with a low metabolic rate, eat the same large meals for a week, the one with the low metabolic rate will gain more weight than will the one with the high metabolic rate. We don't understand why bulimics seem to have abnormal metabolic rates, and why some researchers have measured these rates as being abnormally high and others as being abnormally low. However, it's possible that these differing meta-bolic rates are due to the variation in how much bulimics eat. Metabolic rate rises when someone eats a lot and decreases when someone eats very little.[75] Therefore, if a bulimic has recently binged, you would expect her metabolic rate to be high, and if she has recently been restricting her intake, you would expect her metabolic rate to be low. Experiments need to be done in which bulimics' metabolic rates are tracked through several binge-purge and binge-restrict cycles.

As with anorexics, scientists have been carefully studying the eating behaviors of bulimics to look for clues as to why bulimics engage in abnormal eating behaviors. Different from anorexics, as bulimics eat, they generally don't report a sharp decrease in pleasure in the food they're eating. In fact, bulimics report less of a decrease in pleasure as they eat than people without an eating disorder, and they tend to salivate more in the presence of food. Similarly, bulimics, in comparison to nonbulim-ics, don't report as much of a decrease in hunger after having eaten food prior to a meal; and bulimics have a greater desire to continue to eat after a meal is over than do nonbulimics.[76] We don't yet know for sure what causes all of these differences in hunger and satiety between bulimics and nonbulimics. There is evidence that there are strong genetic contributions to the tendencies to binge eat and to engage in self-induced vomiting.[77] However, as with anorexia nervosa, researchers caution that many of the physiological abnormalities found in bulimics may be an effect of the binging and purging, rather than their cause.[78]

Many of the possible explanations and causes that have been proposed for anorexia nervosa have also been proposed for bulimia nervosa. The weights reported as desirable by bulimics are far below healthy weights. Bulimics, similar to anorexics, seem to have a distorted view of their own weights. Further, bulimics, similar to anorexics, are obsessed with controlling their food intake. However, unlike an anorexic, who is suc-cessful at this control, a bulimic will regularly slip and consume huge amounts of food. Once the binge starts, it seems uncontrollable. Then the bulimic attempts to purge herself of the food.[79] Once the binging and purging are over, the bulimic attempts again to continue to restrict her food intake, but slips and binges again. It's a vicious cycle. For the bulimic, the continual struggle with binging and purging results in a preoccupation with food: how much to eat, when to eat, how to do it without the knowledge of others, and how to get enough food for a binge. Thus, bulimia has been seen by some researchers as an adverse consequence of dieting.[80]

Due to the vicious cycle in which bulimics can neither control their restricted eating nor their binging, bulimia has been seen as a problem of impulsiveness. Bulimics repeatedly engage in behaviors that offer them some current pleasure, or at least some decreased displeasure, but at the expense of their long-term health and happiness. With this in mind, some researchers have wondered if there might be some common underlying cause of bulimia nervosa and other impulsiveness disorders such as drug abuse and pathological gambling. Supporting this view is the fact that someone with one impulsiveness disorder is likely to have another, and someone whose family contains someone with an impulsiveness disorder is more likely to develop binge eating. There has been speculation that the common underlying cause of all impulsiveness disorders is a decreased level of the neurotransmitter serotonin.[81] Abnormal serotonin activity has been shown in the brains of recovered bulimics.[82]

The hypothesis that decreased levels of serotonin cause or contribute to bulimia nervosa gains further support from research on depression and bulimia. It has been repeatedly found that, on average, bulimics are more depressed than are nonbulimics, although there are certainly bulimics who aren't depressed.[83] Further, being depressed appears to be related to an enhancement of the neural responses to food, as well as to an enhancement of bulimic symptoms.[84] It's also well known that depression is often associated with low levels of serotonin, as is food craving. Finally, several researchers have shown that bulimics tend to have low levels of serotonin.[85]

These many investigations of the characteristics and possible causes of bulimia nervosa have resulted in a variety of suggestions for possible treatments. In many respects, the treatments parallel those used for anorexia nervosa. For example, various types of psychotherapy and drug therapy have been tried. The drug therapies have been based on the findings that many bulimics are depressed and have low serotonin levels. Therefore the medications used have primarily been ones that ameliorate depression and/or raise serotonin levels. There's now evidence that such medications are effective in treating the associated depression, but not necessarily the bulimic symptoms themselves.[86]

The standard treatment for bulimia nervosa has become traditional cognitive-behavior therapy. This psychotherapeutic approach appears to be the best single method of treating bulimia nervosa, plus it doesn't have the side effects that can accompany drug therapy.[87]

Nevertheless, even with a combination of cognitive-behavior therapy and drug therapy, many patients don't improve.[88] In addition, cognitive-behavior therapy can be expensive and not everyone lives near a qualified therapist. Therefore alternative methods of getting inexpensive care to bulimics have been developed. One method that has apparently proved successful with at least some bulimics involves use of a self-care manual accompanied by occasional therapy sessions.[89] As described for anorexia nervosa, online support groups may also prove helpful,[90] although research is needed to confirm this. I've listed examples of Web sources of help following the conclusion to this chapter.

Enough is Enough: Conclusion

This chapter has described anorexia and bulimia. Learning about these eating disorders can be scary; it seems as if as a group they're extremely common, difficult to cure, and dangerous. Yet researchers have been making enormous progress in understanding and treating all of these disorders. We're no longer helpless when faced with an eating disorder diagnosis. And, although there has been much research on the possible physiological causes of eating disorders, much more is being discovered daily and will continue to be discovered. Combined with carefully conducted studies of the efficacy of different forms of psychotherapy, there's no question that even better treatments lie ahead. There's much to be hopeful about now in the treatment of eating disorders. Of course, a big help in preventing eating disorders would be for the fashion industry and the media to change their standards for attractive body weights. However, such an outcome seems unlikely given that appeals of this sort have now been made unsuccessfully for decades.

Where to Get Information and Help

Books

A great many books have been written about eating disorders. Routledge publishes a long list of them (see www.routledgementalhealth.com/books/subjects/SCBE054033/). Here is a small selection of additional helpful ones:

Am I Thin Enough Yet? The Cult of Thinness and the Commercialization of Identity by Sharlene Hesse-Biber (New York: Oxford University Press, 1996).

Body Image, Eating Disorders, and Obesity in Youth: Assessment, Prevention, and Treatment (2nd ed.) (Washington, DC: American Psychological Association, 2008).

The Body Project: An Intimate History of American Girls by Joan Jacobs Brumberg (New York: Vintage, 1997).

The Eating Disorders Sourcebook by Carolyn Costin (New York: McGraw Hill, 2007).

Fasting Girls by Joan Jacobs Brumberg (New York: Vintage, 2000).

The Golden Cage: The Enigma of Anorexia Nervosa, with a New Forward by Catherine Steiner-Adair by Hilde Brach (Cambridge, MA: Harvard University Press, 2001).

Real Gorgeous: The Truth about Body and Beauty by Kaz Cooke (New York: Norton, 1996).

When Dieting Becomes Dangerous: A Guide to Understanding and Treating Anorexia Bulimia by Deborah M. Michel and Susan G. Willard (New Haven, CT: Yale University Press, 2003).

Organizations and web sites

National Eating Disorders Association, 165 West 46th Street, Suite 402, New York, NY 10036. Phone: 212–575–6200. Helpline: 1–800–931–2237. Provides eating disorder information, referrals, prevention programs, etc. Web site: www.nationaleatingdisorders.org

National Association of Anorexia Nervosa and Associated Disorders (ANAD), 750 E. Diehl Road #127, Naperville, IL 60563. Phone: 630–577–1333. Helpline: 630–577–1330. Provides support groups, referrals, information, etc. Web site: www.anad.org

National Institute of Mental Health: Provides information including about clinical trials. Web site: www.nimh.nih.gov/health/topics/eating-disorders/index.shtml

The Renfrew Center. Provides resources for education and treatment of eating disorders. Phone: 1–800-Renfrew. Web site (live chat available): www.renfrew.org

10

THE BATTLE WITH
THE BULGE
Overeating and Obesity

Here's the chapter that many of you have been waiting for: the chapter on overeating and obesity. Or perhaps you didn't wait. Perhaps you just went straight to this chapter without reading any of the preceding ones—despite their providing much information that would be helpful to you in understanding what's to come next! But prepared or not, here you are, and I'll do my best to explain to you what scientists know about food consumption so excessive that it's considered abnormal (overeating) and about body weight that's significantly greater than average (obesity).

Monitoring your weight in the United States has become big business, as evidenced by the many different apps you can get to do this on your electronic device. And even First Lady Michelle Obama has made preventing and decreasing obesity one of her top priorities with her Let's Move! Campaign, which promotes exercise and healthy eating (www.letsmove.gov).

Given this huge interest in preventing and treating obesity, including among those of you reading this chapter, I feel perhaps a particular responsibility about what I put in this chapter. Exacerbating this feeling is the fact that the published scientific literature on overeating and obesity is absolutely huge, so huge that it couldn't possibly be described by the content of many books, much less one chapter in one book. This means that I have to pick and choose very carefully the studies that I tell you about. And perhaps more importantly, I need to ensure that, when you've finished this chapter, you're an informed scientific consumer who knows the characteristics of a good study and how to interpret carefully the results from a study. In this way, when you encounter, as you certainly will, descriptions of research on overeating and obesity that aren't included in this chapter, you'll be able to decide for yourself what the results of that study may or may not mean.

You're probably going to find what this chapter has to say about overeating and obesity to be fairly depressing. There are, unfortunately, no easy solutions to the problem of weight control, at least not in surroundings such as ours in which there's much tasty food and people need to expend little physical energy. We evolved in very different surroundings, surroundings in which food was scarce and you had to work hard to get it. As a result of this evolutionary history, our bodies have all kinds of methods for getting in, and keeping in, large numbers of calories.[1]

Nevertheless, despite this evolutionary history, you and everyone else will have a far better chance of controlling your weight if you know something about the relevant research than if you ignore that research. Forewarned can be forearmed! To your credit, you've already come this far. So let's see what scientists know about overeating and obesity. I'll begin by telling you a bit about who is obese and who isn't. Then I'll discuss the research concerning what causes overeating and obesity. And finally I'll discuss the research concerning how to decrease overeating and obesity.

Weighing in on Obesity

There have been an enormous number of studies of people who are obese. In order to discuss this research, we first need to define obesity. As stated in Chapter 9, overweight is usually defined as a BMI of 25–29.9, and obese as a BMI of ≥30.0. Methods other than the BMI, such as dual x-ray absorptiometry, can directly determine how much fat someone has.[2] However, BMI has the advantage of being easy and inexpensive to calculate. Recently, some researchers have been advocating for the use of "A Body Shape Index" (ABSI), which is similar to BMI except that it also takes waist circumference into account, thus incorporating an approximate measure of stored abdominal fat. Stored abdominal fat appears to be particularly important in the relationship of obesity to health risk.[3] An online calculator for ABSI can be found at: www.absi-calc.appspot.com. This calculator is, however, similar to the BMI calculator introduced in Chapter 9, only as good as the values that go into it. And when weight is self-reported, it is often incorrect. One recent study found that, on average, female college students underreported their weights by about 8 pounds.[4]

No matter which classification or reporting scheme you use, overweight and obesity are extremely prevalent in the United States. In fact, many researchers and public health officials refer to an "obesity epidemic."[5] More than one-third (35%) of adults in the United States are now classified as obese.[6] The prevalence of obesity is particularly high in certain minority groups, especially non-Hispanic blacks (48%) and Hispanics (43%).[7] In 2011–2012, 17% of 2- to 19-year-old children in the United States were classified as obese.[8] Even our pets are not immune: a 2012 survey conducted of veterinarians found 53% of dogs and 58% of cats to be overweight or obese.[9] Consistent with the statements that there is an obesity epidemic, the American growth in obesity rates among children and adults is now being replicated in countries throughout the world, even in some relatively poor countries.[10]

The increasing worldwide prevalence of obesity is particularly concerning given the health risks associated with being overweight and obese, although researchers now think that that relationship is rather complex. It has been known for years that obese people were more likely to have cancer, cardiovascular disease, diabetes, etc., and that obesity may inhibit cognition. However, it now appears that some obese people, particularly those just above a BMI of 30.0, may be less likely to die than those with normal-weight BMIs. How to explain these apparently discrepant data? One answer may be that the negative effects of obesity can at least partially be negated if the obese person exercises.[11] Another answer may lie in stored abdominal fat. Obese people with stored abdominal fat may be more likely to develop health problems and die, and obese people whose fat is stored elsewhere may be protected from the effects of certain diseases. In addition, people who are obese, as opposed to normal weight, may be more aggressively treated by their physicians for problems such as high blood pressure and high cholesterol.[12] Further research using measures such as the ABSI is needed to confirm these explanations.

Once again, children are no exception to these trends. Approximately 60% of 5- to 10-year-old children who are overweight have at least one resulting health problem, such as increased levels of insulin.[13] What we know for sure is that, at least in the United States, there's a huge number of people who are overweight or obese, and that people who have higher BMIs, particularly in association with stored abdominal fat, tend to have certain diseases.

As a result of the relationships between obesity and various illnesses, the American Medical Association has recently recognized obesity as a disease. However, it is not clear that such a label will help obese people to increase their engagement in healthy behaviors, and may indeed have the opposite effect.[14]

In addition to adverse health consequences, people who weigh more than average may be discriminated against socially and professionally, they may be seen as unintelligent and lacking in self-control, and they may eat more as a result.[15] Further, children may be judged more negatively by their teachers simply because they are obese.[16] Clearly there are many reasons to prevent or remove excess weight. In order to understand how doing that may or may not be possible, we need to understand the causes of overeating and obesity.

Land of the Rising Fat

As you'll see, many different roads lead to overeating and obesity. It's important to understand these different causes because the success of different treatments may vary depending on the cause of a particular case of obesity. Some cases of obesity depend more on genetic or physiological causes, and some depend more on past experience or current surroundings.

Body not so perfect: contributions of your genes and some other body parts

A major issue a few decades ago was whether genes had anything to do with how overweight someone is. Now that we are well into the 21st century, no one questions that genes have something to do with being overweight. Now the issues are what specific gene or genes contribute to someone's being overweight and how those genes exert their effects. There have been enormous advances in these areas. However, as you read this material on the connections between genetics and obesity, keep in mind that, as clear as those connections may be, genes can't possibly explain everything to do with obesity. Obesity has drastically increased in the past several decades, but that's too short a time period for evolution or mutation to have affected the gene pool. In addition, there are significant correlations between the weights of adoptive children and their adoptive parents. Therefore people's surroundings, or how people interact with their surroundings, clearly also have a significant impact on obesity.[17]

Now back to the genes. We've known for many decades that obese parents tend to have obese biological children; approximately 70% of children with two obese parents become obese.[18] However, parents and children share not only some genes, but their home surroundings—ranging from ones containing only low-fat/low-sugar foods to the exact opposite. Thus the tendency of obese parents to have obese biological children, by itself, doesn't prove that genes contribute to obesity, only that they may contribute. More convincing have been studies done with twins. Such studies have shown that the weights of identical twins, those who come from the same egg and sperm and thus have identical genes, are more similar than the weights of fraternal twins, who come from different eggs and sperm and who, similar to any siblings, on average share half of their genes.[19] Identical twins look exactly alike, and fraternal twins look no more alike than do any two siblings. Therefore, if how you look influences how someone treats you (and there is indeed good scientific evidence that this is the case), then identical twins may have more similar weights because people treat them more similarly, not because they have more similar genes. Still better evidence comes from studies of adopted children. The weights of these children tend to be more similar to those of their biological parents than to those of their adoptive parents.[20] It's difficult to conceive of an explanation for these results other than that genes have a strong influence on whether someone becomes obese. Twin studies have also shown that there is a strong genetic component to how much appetite someone has over time.[21]

Scientist Claude Bouchard and his colleagues published a 1990 twin study with an intriguing twist. These researchers overfed 12 pairs of identical twin men. None of the men had ever been obese and all were sedentary. For 120 consecutive days, the men were isolated and under 24-hour surveillance in a special section of a dormitory. Physical activity was limited. For 84 of these days, each man was fed 1,000 calories more per day than was needed to maintain his current weight. When the experiment was over, there were huge differences in how much weight different men had gained: between 10 and 29 pounds. On average, members of a twin pair were a great deal more similar in how much they had gained than were two unrelated men. The greater similarity among the members of the twin pairs applied not only to weight gain, but also to the amount of body fat and the distribution of body fat.[22] These results seem to suggest that there's a significant genetic component to weight gain and to where fat is gained. Unfortunately, the publication describing this experiment doesn't explain how the men were persuaded to participate. Participation in this experiment sounds like a truly miserable experience; I can't imagine what would have persuaded me.

There are many examples of research examining the influence of specific genes on obesity. For instance, a number of scientists have been studying the genes that control enzymes in your body known as JNK. When someone is obese, these enzymes cause an immune response that contributes to the development of certain obesity-related disorders such as Type 2 diabetes (see Chapter 12).[23] Genetic studies have also identified various types of genes associated with cases of severe, early-onset obesity.[24] Still other studies have indicated relationships between a protein in your body called perilipin, whose levels are genetically determined, and which influences body weight.[25]

However, despite all of these intriguing studies showing the influence of the genes on obesity, it's extremely important to remember that none of these genes cause obesity in any simple sense. Instead, they seem to make it likely that the people (or rats or mice) who have them will become obese when exposed to certain conditions in their surroundings.[26] Even if you have lots of genes related to the deposit of excess abdominal fat, if your surroundings contain very little food and you exercise a lot, you'll have no calories to deposit as fat.

In continuing our discussion of the many different physiological bases of overeating and obesity, let's now consider adipose cells, the proper name for what you may have heard referred to as fat cells. These are the cells in your body that store fat. When they're full, you're less hungry; when they're not full, you're more hungry.[27] Thus, your adipose cells contribute to the regulation of your body's set point described in Chapter 2.

Bouchard's study described earlier in this chapter is one of a number of pieces of evidence suggesting that heredity contributes to the number and distribution of adipose cells. In addition, we know that, although the number of adipose cells can increase when you gain weight, the number of adipose cells can never decrease.[28] When you lose weight, the fat cells become empty, but their numbers don't decrease. Therefore if you've been overweight at some time in your life, regardless of whether you're presently overweight, you'll have a relatively large number of adipose cells. Unless these many adipose cells are full of fat, you'll be hungry. In other words, if you've been overweight at any time in your life, you'll tend either to be overweight or hungry. This should help you to understand one of the reasons that it's so difficult for anyone to lose weight and then keep it off.

You'll recall from Chapter 2 that there are a number of possible indicators of the body's level of stored fat and that these indicators interact with other chemicals in the body to influence eating behavior. One of the indicators of stored fat, leptin, a hormone found in the blood and manufactured by the adipose cells, has been the recent focus of many obesity researchers. When there's little stored fat, there's less leptin; and when there's a great deal of stored fat, there's more leptin. It's been shown that people with a genetic disorder resulting in an absence of leptin have huge appetites and become obese. Researchers originally hoped that the role of leptin in controlling weight would be so strong that manipulation of leptin level would lead to straightforward treatments for obesity. However, it now appears that leptin's role is more related to the physiological mechanisms involved in protecting the body against weight loss when fat stores shrink rather than vice versa.[29]

Many other substances involved in your body's ingestion, digestion, and storage of food have also been investigated for their role in obesity. For example, in the past few years there have been a number of studies on ghrelin, a protein produced in the stomach when the energy supply is low, and that is sometimes called the "hunger hormone." Ghrelin increases appetite and the storage of fat. For these reasons, researchers have started investigating drugs that inhibit ghrelin's effectiveness.[30]

A relatively new area of research on physiological contributions to obesity, an area of research that has gotten a lot of attention in the popular, as well as the scientific, press concerns the presence of certain bacteria in the GI tract. These bacteria are collectively known as the microbiota, and one person's GI microbiota can differ from another's. In an experiment published in *Science* in 2013, scientist Vanessa Ridaura and her colleagues reported weight increases in mice who had been transplanted with fecal material (microbiota) from the obese members of human twin pairs in which the other members of the twin pairs were not obese.[31] These findings add to the growing body of research suggesting that the particular bacteria living in our GI tracts can influence our weights, but there is much more research to be done before we can base obesity treatments on these findings.

Slow or quick burn: effects of energy expenditure

Now we come to what is, in my opinion, the most fascinating area of research concerning overeating and obesity—the effects of energy expenditure. The reason that I find this area the most fascinating will become apparent later in this chapter, when I explain how exercise is one of the very few successful methods that we have for losing and keeping off excess weight. As you know from the beginning of this chapter, the percentage of the United States population that is obese is extremely large, both in adults and in children. There are only three possible explanations for these increases: people are eating more, people are expending less energy, or people are doing both of these things. Many researchers have focused on the energy expenditure side of this equation. In the United States, we have become a nation accustomed to not only cars, but elevators, dishwashers, lawn mowers, food processors, washing machines, escalators, and moving walkways. And let's not forget the remote controls available for all kinds of devices. I can now raise and lower my bedroom shades without moving from my bed. Industrialization and technology have allowed us to expend far less energy in living our daily lives (see Figure 10.1).

"Be honest—how much are you exercising?"

Figure 10.1 Drawing by Charles Barsotti. (Reprinted from *The New Yorker* [March 27, 2006], with permission from Conde Nast.)

For a poignant example of the effects of these changes, consider the results of a study, published in 1999, of two native Canadian populations: the Sandy Lake Oji-Cree and the Keewatin Inuit. The researchers observed that the Oji-Cree were living in small houses that had been completely winterized, and that many owned snowmobiles and cars. Although their food supply used to consist of wild animals and plants, at the time of the study their primary food source was a company store. On average, members of this group were extremely sedentary. In contrast, the Inuit still lived an active, fairly traditional lifestyle, including eating large amounts of fish. Not surprisingly, the average BMI of the Oji-Cree was 29.0, whereas that of the Inuit was 25.0. Also not surprisingly, the researchers found significantly more heart disease and diabetes in the Oji-Cree than in the Inuit.[32]

Before discussing some of the experiments on energy expenditure in lean and obese people, and how different situations can affect that energy expenditure, it'll be helpful to understand a bit about the different types of energy that we all expend. Your total energy expenditure is composed of (a) your basal metabolic rate, which is the energy expended for basic metabolic functions such as respiration and circulation; (b) the extra energy your body uses as a result of voluntary and nonvoluntary physical activity such as walking and fidgeting; and (c) the extra energy your body uses following food consumption.[33] A low value for any of these three types of energy expenditure could increase your tendency to gain weight and to become obese. Let's review what scientists have to say about each of these three types of energy expenditure and their relationships with weight gain and obesity.

We'll begin with metabolic rate. It will probably not surprise you to know that even people who weigh exactly the same can have different metabolic rates. We all know people who seem to be able to eat a lot and not gain weight and vice versa. There are many different reasons for this. For example, fat supports a lower metabolic rate than muscle or bone.[34] Therefore if two people weigh the same but one person has a higher percentage of body fat than the other person, you would expect the first person to have a lower metabolic rate. An insidious factor contributing to low metabolic rates is decreased eating. When less food is eaten, metabolic rate goes down, and this lowered metabolic rate may continue for months after the level of food intake has returned to normal. This is why, when you're dieting, losing weight is much easier at the beginning and why, when you stop dieting, it's so easy to regain the lost weight. Such changes in metabolic rate were adaptive when people's food supplies were erratic and often inadequate; lowered metabolic rate as a result of food deprivation helped to prevent starvation. However, now, in the United States, low food intake is frequently due to people trying to lose weight.[35]

Lest you despair, there's a way to increase metabolic rate. It turns out that, in addition to exercise using energy in and of itself, under certain conditions exercise can increase metabolic rate. Even more importantly, that increase can last for hours beyond when the exercise has ceased, such as after a strenuous game of football, or after 45 minutes of vigorous exercise on a stationary bike.[36] However, we don't yet know very much about what type or duration of exercise will result in an increase in metabolic rate of a specific amount or duration. Further, there are individual differences in the degree to which exercise affects weight. Bouchard conducted an exercise study with twins that was similar in design to his overfeeding study with twins, and once again very challenging for the participants.[37] There were seven pairs of identical twin men in this study. Each man exercised two times a day for most of 93 days, using up about 1,000 calories per day. This is the equivalent of jogging about 45 minutes twice a day. During the 93 days, the amounts of nutrients and calories that the men ate were kept constant. The average amount of weight lost was 11 pounds. However, on average, the amounts of weight lost by members of a twin pair were more similar than for pairs of men who weren't related. You may also be interested to know that the lost weight was apparently due to the loss of fat, not due to loss of bone, muscle, and so forth.

One concern that people often have when considering the effects of exercise on metabolic rate is the possibility that exercising more can also make you eat more, thus countering any calorie-expending effects of exercise. The results on this issue have been mixed, with some studies finding that more food is eaten after intense exercise, and other studies finding that there is no change. Some findings seem to suggest that exercise temporarily decreases hunger, but that in the long run people eat more as a result of exercise, thus compensating for the calories burned by exercise.[38]

One of the most disturbing areas of research on exercise and obesity concerns the positive association between obesity and television watching.[39] Several hypotheses as to the origins of these relationships have received some support in both adults and children: people eat more of foods advertised on TV; people eat more when watching TV, even when there aren't any food commercials; and people expend less energy when TV watching. Further, these findings may extend to sedentary video game playing and computer use as well.[40] Together all of these results suggest that TV watching and sedentary video game playing and computer use may be a major contributor to the huge problem of obesity in the United States. As a result, recent research has been exploring whether interventions such as adding a physically active component to video games can help compensate for the extra calories children eat while gaming. (The answer is yes, but unfortunately not enough to completely negate the effects of the extra calories.)[41]

There is one other aspect of energy usage that has received recent research attention: the relationship between the amount we sleep and obesity. At first blush you might think that people who sleep less would also be less likely to be obese. After all, such people are the opposite of couch potatoes and are in an active state for much more time than other people. But the opposite turns out to be true—both adults and children who sleep less and are sleep deprived are more likely to gain weight. The explanation for this seemingly counterintuitive finding is that when people sleep less their appetite increases more than does their energy expenditure.[42] I can remember in high school and college staying up past midnight (yes, even when I had class the next day) and seeing that as good justification for some post-dinner pizza or a run to the local diner for some eggs, toast, and bacon. Regular sleep habits can assist weight control.

This brings us to the third component of total energy expenditure: the extra energy your body uses following food consumption. This energy is larger following a high-carbohydrate than a high-fat meal, but it is apparently similar regardless of whether the food eaten tastes good or not.[43] If food consumption is greater than usual, the energy used is also greater. Similar to the decrease in metabolic rate that accompanies food deprivation, this increase in energy used following increased food consumption helps animals to stay at a constant weight. However, if rats' weights are increased by continued free access to a high-fat diet, their adipose cells increase in number, and eventually the increased energy effect disappears; a new set point has been reached.[44]

Scientists James A. Levine, Norman L. Eberhardt, and Michael D. Jensen followed Claude Bouchard's lead by examining energy usage in 16 nonobese male and female volunteer participants who were fed extra food. Each of the 16 participants was fed 1,000 calories per day in excess of their energy requirements for 8 weeks. As in Bouchard and his colleagues' study, there was wide variation in how much weight each participant gained: between 3 and 16 pounds. On average, the participants' energy expenditure tended to increase, although again there was wide individual variation, with energy usage increasing more in people who gained less. By measuring or controlling each of the different aspects of energy expenditure, Levine and his colleagues were able to determine that the participants' energy usage probably increased due to increases in the participants' nonvoluntary activity, such as fidgeting and posture maintenance.[45] Therefore how much someone gains when overfed may be due to how much the person fidgets. However, several questions remain. First, why does overfeeding increase such activities as fidgeting in some people but not others, and which sorts of people are likely to show the fidgeting effect? Also, we know that fidgeting in response to overfeeding would help people stay at a certain weight, but why would that trait ever have helped anyone to survive? Why did we evolve to do this? Finally, what precise mechanism is responsible for the increase in fidgeting or similar activities following overeating?[46] Answers to these questions could be extremely useful in helping us to control weight gain.

Who's counting? What's eaten and how it's eaten

We've talked about influences on obesity that focus primarily on what's going on inside the body. But what about how people interact with their surroundings, including the food in their surroundings? How does what people eat and how they eat it contribute to overeating and obesity?

Let's begin by looking at the eating behavior of the obese. Do they eat differently from other people? There have been a great many experiments done on this subject with all kinds of results. These results show that, in many ways, the eating behavior of obese people and nonobese people is similar.[47] However, some of the recent differences that have been identified include fast eaters gaining more over an 8-year period than slow eaters, obese people eating chocolate pudding more quickly than nonobese people, and people with higher BMIs being more likely to take a large as opposed to a small plate, and leave less food on that plate, at a Chinese buffet.[48] But note that we don't know if these eating behavior differences actually cause weight gain, or are just correlated with other factors that cause weight gain.

Now what about the types of food that are available to us? How might that contribute to obesity? First, remember from earlier chapters that we prefer the tastes of salt and sweet, as well as highly caloric, high-fat foods. These preferences helped us to survive when food was scarce and low in fat and energy content prior to the agricultural revolution and industrialization. Our food supply was simply very different back then. For example, in the Paleolithic period, people ate meat in the form of wild game, which had a fat content of about 4%, as compared to the approximately 30% in our meat today.[49] Currently in the United States, sweet, salty, and high-fat foods are widely and cheaply available. The combination of this availability and our preference for these foods results in our consuming them to excess, which contributes to obesity. Experiments with both rats and people have shown that when large amounts of good-tasting food are available, they'll overeat and become obese.[50]

In addition to there now being many more kinds of good-tasting food, the relatively low level of fiber in what we eat, as compared to prior to industrialization, may be contributing to our obesity. Some researchers believe that eating little fiber results in the secretion of more insulin, and that this increased insulin increases weight gain.[51] (See also the discussion of the glycemic index response in Chapter 2.)

Adding to the effects of wide availability of relatively unhealthy food is a variety effect. Increasing the variety of foods available in a single meal can also increase the amount eaten.[52] Such variety is another common characteristic of industrialized countries such as the United States. Although some diets may decrease eating by decreasing food variety, as soon as the diet is over a huge array of foods will again be available to most Americans.

Food availability and variety can also affect the development and maintenance of obesity through the types of food that are present in the stores and restaurants of particular neighborhoods and in schools. Public health experts have long been concerned that the relative lack of fresh fruits and vegetables and other healthy foods in poor neighborhoods, and the prevalence of many unhealthy foods in school cafeterias and vending machines, have contributed to the obesity epidemic, particularly among people of lower socioeconomic status.[53]

Special attention must be paid to the role of our culture's frequent consumption of sweets in inducing overeating and obesity. It has been hypothesized that any sweet taste—artificial or not—may cause insulin to be released with resulting increased hunger through lowering the blood sugar level and with resulting increased storage of ingested food as fat.[54] Many experiments have been conducted on this topic, with differing results. In one experiment, when preschool children were offered highly caloric, chocolate milk versus plain milk at lunchtime, twice per week for 16 weeks, they drank much more of the chocolate milk than the plain milk but their intake of lunch foods was the same. Therefore the children consumed far more calories on the chocolate milk days than the plain milk days.[55] Children may have difficulties regulating the amounts of calories that they consume from extremely good-tasting sources. In experiments comparing artificial vs. nonartificial sweeteners, the bulk of the evidence seems to be that people weigh somewhat less when artificial sweeteners or water is substituted for nonartificial ones,[56] although interaction effects between sweeteners and substances such as caffeine deserve further exploration.[57]

As mentioned in Chapter 7, the extensive evidence on the contributions to obesity of sweet foods and drinks, and of food availability, led New York City's then-mayor, Michael Bloomberg, to try to ban nonartificially sweetened drinks of at least 16 ounces from being sold by certain purveyors (e.g., restaurants) starting in 2013. This move elicited a huge amount of controversy, resulting in around a dozen articles just in *The New York Times*. The proposed ban was blocked in the courts, but many people in New York City are still interested in pursuing it, and/or a tax on soda, and these efforts are by no means limited to New York City.

Increased consumption of soda during the past few decades has been seen as one of the primary sources of fuel for the obesity epidemic.[58]

Comparable hypotheses have been posed about the percentage of fat in our foods and overeating. Some people have claimed that we eat more total calories when foods are high in fat than when they're low in fat. Experimenters have investigated this hypothesis by secretly substituting a low-fat version of a food for a high-fat version and then determining how many total calories the experiment's participants ate. These experiments have found that, in such situations, the participants consume fewer total calories.[59]

Consistent with these findings are the great number of experiments now demonstrating that decreasing the energy density of a food (as occurs when its fat content is lowered), including by increasing a food's fiber content, results in our eating fewer calories. For example, substituting mushrooms (which contain fiber but few calories) for meat (which has lots of calories but little fiber), or adding grain fiber to a meal, can increase satiety, decrease calorie consumption, and assist with weight control.[60] (See also Conversation Making Fact #10.)

Conversation making fact #10

One food that has particularly interesting, though not completely understood, effects on how much we eat is soup. When both children and adults are given soup prior to a meal, they eat less of the meal. In fact, their total calorie consumption may decrease that day. It's possible that chunky soup is better at decreasing the amount eaten than is nonchunky soup (perhaps due to the additional fiber in the soup?), although nonchunky tomato soup also seems to be particularly effective at decreasing the amount of food subsequently eaten.[61] It may not surprise you to learn that soup is now usually my choice for a first course when I go out to eat at restaurants. I'm particularly happy when tomato soup is on the menu.

A hot, active, area of research directed at the effects of what you eat on obesity has to do with plate size and portion size. Can varying the size of your plate and/or how much food is on it affect how much you eat and, ultimately, how much you weigh? A great many experiments seem to indicate that they can.[62] For example, Cornell University Professor Brian Wansink and his colleagues casually gave undergraduates either one 400-calorie bag of crackers or four 100-calorie bags to eat while instructing the students to watch a television comedy. Students given the four 100-calorie bags ate 25% fewer calories than did the students given one 400-calorie bag.[63]

177

A final food characteristic that can result in our overeating is whether the food is actually labeled "healthy." There's a tendency to eat more of such foods, thus potentially negating whatever health benefits they might have.[64]

We have been discussing the circumstances under which most people eat more or less depending on the food available. However, not everyone reacts to the food around them in the same way, and not everyone reacts in the same way most of the time. For example, people buy more high-calorie foods at the grocery store when they're hungry.[65] Similarly, an experiment with approximately 100 college women showed that, following exposure to a tempting food cue (the smell of a baking pizza), dieters were more likely to say they wanted to eat and to actually eat more in comparison to nondieters. These results suggest that dieters tend to be more externally responsive than are nondieters.[66] Further, people eat significantly more when they think that they're going to skip a meal, undoubtedly because they've learned through past experience that this will help them make it through the missed meal, similar to the anticipatory eating and drinking described earlier in this book. This may explain why dieters who break their diets may then overeat. They're anticipating future food deprivation, that is, returning to their diets.[67] It has sometimes seemed to me that, when I'm thinking my weight is creeping up and I need to do something about it, I actually eat more. Perhaps this is an example of eating more due to expected future food deprivation.

Some people are strongly affected by food cues in their surroundings—they're externally responsive—and other people aren't. People who are externally responsive generally demonstrate particular physiological responses to food cues. For example, their insulin levels increase. This, in turn, increases their hunger and the likelihood that any food that is eaten will be stored as fat.[68] In other words, externally responsive people are literally turned on by the sight of food. If you add to this the fact that some people are genetically predisposed to store fat in certain locations on their bodies, then the statement "I just look at chocolate cake and it goes to my hips" actually makes some sense. There are externally responsive people at every weight level.[69] Some people who are externally responsive find ways of restraining their eating so that they don't become obese. Unfortunately, we still know very little about what makes some people externally responsive and others not, or the degree to which external responsivity can be modified.

Stressful or stimulating surroundings can affect anyone's eating. Walk into any cocktail party and you'll see the guests eating a great many potato chips, pretzels, and hors d'oeuvres that they would not ordinarily eat. As the conversation flourishes, hands repeatedly dip into the bowls of peanuts and crackers. Laboratory research can help us to understand this behavior. Experiments with rats have shown that the stress of a mild tail pinch increases eating, to the point that the rats gain significant amounts of weight.[70] In addition, rats stressed in this way tend to prefer good-tasting food more than do nonstressed rats.[71] There are similar findings with people. For example, psychologist Debra Zellner and her colleagues showed that when people are stressed they are more likely to choose to eat M&Ms as opposed to grapes.[72] It's even been shown that, on the Mondays following National Football League games, consumption of high-fat, high-calorie food increases in cities whose teams lost the preceding Sunday, decreases in cities whose teams won, and stays the same in cities whose teams didn't play. The effects are particularly marked when the game was won by a narrow margin.[73]

Whether other people are around can also affect how much you eat. For example, evidence suggests that if your friends are obese, then you're more likely to become obese.[74]

In addition, several experiments have shown that people generally eat more when eating with other people than they do alone. However, the effect of other people on the amount that you eat can be more complex than that.[75] Whether you're with someone who professes to be a dieter, or looks as if she or he should be, and whether you're a dieter yourself, influences how much and what you eat. For example, dieters eat more when served snacks by a heavy server, and nondieters eat more when served snacks by a thin server.[76] As another example, psychologist Janet Polivy and her colleagues investigated whether the eating behavior of a woman (the model, whom we'll call Jane) affected the eating behavior of other women (whom we'll call the participants). (See Figure 10.2.) Jane was actually an accomplice of the experimenters, but the participants thought that she was another participant. Jane told half the participants that she was dieting and half the participants that she wasn't. The experimenter instructed Jane and the participants together to eat until they were full. Then Jane ate with each participant individually. Jane ate very little in the presence of half of the participants to whom she'd said that she was and wasn't dieting. She ate a lot in the presence of the other participants. This research design therefore resulted in four groups of participants. The participants to whom Jane had identified herself as dieting generally ate less than the participants to whom Jane had identified herself as not dieting. In addition, there was an overall tendency for all of the participants to eat more when Jane ate more and less when Jane ate less.[77] So Polivy and her colleagues confirmed what you've undoubtedly seen yourself—one member of a group of women refusing dessert only to be followed by each of the other women saying the same thing.

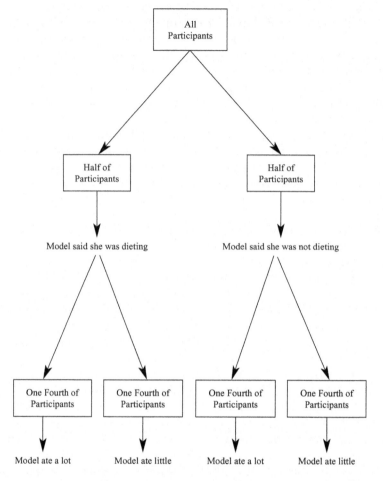

Figure 10.2 Design of Polivy, Herman, Younger, and Erskine's experiment. (Adapted from J. Polivy, C. P. Herman, J. C. Younger, and B. Erskine, "Effects of a Model on Eating Behavior: The Induction of a Restrained Eating Style," *Journal of Personality* 47[1979]: 100–117.)

Special cases

There are several special types of overeating and obesity that are associated with particular behavioral characteristics. One such characteristic that has been extensively investigated is a person's mood. A number of studies have suggested that obese people are more likely to eat when they're experiencing aversive moods such as anxiety or depression than are people who aren't obese.[78] However, other more recent studies have suggested that whether someone is dieting is also important as to whether that person will overeat when depressed. In fact, some researchers believe that depriving yourself of food can lead to overeating, particularly binge eating, no matter what mood someone is in.[79]

The American Psychiatric Association defines binge eating as "Eating, in a discrete period of time (e.g., within any 2-hour period), an amount of food that is definitely larger than what most people would eat in a similar period of time under similar circumstances [and]....A sense of lack of control over eating during the episode (e.g., a feeling that one cannot stop eating or control what or how much one is eating)."[80] The American Psychiatric Association defines binge eating disorder as binge eating accompanied by some other behaviors, such as distress that the binge eating is occurring.[81] In recent years, binge eating and binge eating disorder have come under close scrutiny by researchers and therapists. Approximately 20–40% of adults and children who seek out obesity treatment appear to engage in problematic binge eating, and about 5–8% of all obese people do so.[82] People who engage in binge eating tend to be depressed and to come from families in which there are other impulsiveness disorders such as substance abuse.[83] Further, there appears to be a substantial genetic influence on whether someone develops binge eating disorder.[84]

Possibly related to binge eating disorder is the eating engaged in by people with seasonal affective disorder (SAD). SAD tends to occur among susceptible people during the winter months, when they are exposed to less light. SAD is characterized by depression, a craving for carbohydrates, overeating, and weight gain. However, only a small proportion of obese people suffer from SAD.[85]

Another possibly related eating disorder is night eating syndrome (NES). This syndrome was first described by Albert Stunkard in 1955. However, only in the last decade or two has it received any attention in the research literature. The research has indicated that people with NES are obese and eat over half of their calories at night. They also, on average, eat 600 calories more in a 24-hour period than people who are obese but who don't have NES. People with NES also have great difficulty sleeping. They wake up an average of about 3.5 times per night, as compared with once every other night by people without NES. Further, people with NES eat during about half of their awakenings, but obese people without NES never do. Finally, people with NES tend to be more depressed than obese people without NES, and the mood of those with NES tends to worsen during the evening, something not seen in other obese people.[86]

Various physiological explanations have been proposed for these special cases of overeating and obesity. For example, it has been shown that people with NES don't show the usual rise in blood levels of leptin that is seen in other people. An increase in leptin may decrease appetite and enhance sleep. Therefore people who don't evidence this increase may eat excessively at night and have difficulty sleeping.[87]

The fact that obese people who eat excessively tend to be more depressed than other obese people and also tend to come from families with impulsiveness disorders, has led to another possible physiological explanation for overeating: the level of the neurotransmitter serotonin. A great many studies have shown that serotonin tends to be low in impulsive people, such as people who attempt suicide and in people who are depressed. In addition, high levels of serotonin are associated with decreased motivation to eat.[88] It has therefore been hypothesized that some cases of overeating, such as binging on carbohydrates and seasonal affective disorder, occur because the people with those disorders have low serotonin levels.[89] However, this hypothesis hasn't yet been firmly established.

Get the Fat out: Methods of Decreasing Overeating and Obesity

There are probably more how-to books and Websites on weight loss than on any other do-it-yourself subject. Many of these supposed information sources are ignorant of the research on the origins of overeating and obesity and the methods for decreasing these phenomena. Fortunately, many people with research training have investigated weight-loss techniques. The rest of this chapter provides information about the scientific investigation of methods used to decrease overeating and obesity. Researchers want to determine which treatments work, in both the short run and the long run, and if some treatments are better for some types of obesity than others.

Shake that body: physiological interventions

The most extreme type of physiological intervention consists of several kinds of surgery performed to restrict or bypass parts of the gastrointestinal tract, such as the surgeries undergone by Al Roker of the *Today Show* and New Jersey's Governor, Chris Christie. These operations aim to decrease the amount that someone eats by making them feel full sooner after starting eating and by decreasing the absorption of food from the gastrointestinal tract. The operations are generally safe and very effective, with a majority of patients achieving and maintaining more than half of their targeted weight loss. However, this type of surgery isn't without risk. In addition to the slight risk from the operation itself, there can be side effects such as vomiting. Nevertheless, in general, patients appear to be better adjusted and happier after surgery.[90] This is not surprising given that, as a result of losing large amounts of weight, they're able to engage in physical activities that were previously impossible, they can wear a greater variety of attractive clothes, and they may feel more sexually appealing. The benefits of these sorts of operations make them a viable choice for treating cases of severe obesity. Patients should have BMIs of at least 40 (or at least 35 plus other serious medical problems), and should have attempted (unsuccessfully) to lose weight using other, less drastic means. For other overweight people, those for whom obesity isn't life threatening, the potential dangers and side effects of surgery make it inadvisable.[91]

Various other anatomical manipulations have also been tried. The balloon procedure involves first inserting a deflated balloon into the stomach. The balloon is then inflated and may be left thus in the stomach for many weeks or months. Presumably this device was developed under the assumption that stomach distention will decrease food consumption. However, you should know from Chapter 2 that stomach distention is likely to affect appetite only if the distention is caused by something that has some nutrition to it, a condition that the balloon does not satisfy. It's perhaps not surprising, then, that in an elaborate study in which neither the participants nor the experimenters interacting with them knew who had really had a balloon inserted versus a pretend insertion, those with a real balloon insertion lost no more weight than those who only thought they had a balloon. Due to research results such as these, use of the stomach balloon is no longer recommended except for research purposes.[92]

Liposuction has been tried for years. Unfortunately, it appears not to have a lasting effect. In one experiment, fat removed from the thighs one year previously did not return, but additional fat accumulated on the abdomen, so that patients' total body fat was the same as if they'd never had the liposuction.[93]

Recently, researchers have started examining the decrease in appetite and food craving associated with electrical stimulation of the brain's pre-frontal cortex. However, given that these decreases are temporary and currently involve placing electrodes on the scalp, this method is not a practical one for weight control.[94]

Much better than surgery, much better than anything else that I can think of, would be a little pill that you could take to decrease overeating or facilitate weight loss. I'm not alone in these feelings; huge numbers of people would love to have drugs that prevent overeating and increase weight loss, and the pharmaceutical industry has spent untold amounts of money trying to get us what we want. By this point in the book, you've heard about all kinds of chemicals and physiological processes that occur when you see, smell, taste, eat, and digest food. Every one of those chemicals and physiological processes is a potential target for a drug that would decrease overeating or increase weight loss. As just one of many possible examples, you may remember from Chapter 2 that the chemical cholecystokinin (CCK) is produced during food digestion and may play a role in the termination of feeding. Therefore it's possible that increasing CCK could help with weight control. Unfortunately, ingesting L-Phenylalanine, which is an amino acid that helps the body to release CCK, doesn't seem to decrease food intake in women trying to restrict their intake, and CCK's structure prohibits its being taken orally—it can only be injected, which is not an attractive alternative.[95]

The sad fact is that the history of weight-loss drugs is littered with eliminated choices. From stimulants such as amphetamines (which do decrease food consumption but can have side effects and are addictive); to weight-loss drugs such as fenfluramine, fen-phen (a combination of fenfluramine and phentermine), and Meridia (sibutramine), all withdrawn from FDA approval due to serious side effects;[96] to Alli (which contains the drug orlistat), withdrawn from retail stores by its manufacturer as of March 2014 due to product tampering (see: www.myalli.com/weight-loss-news-press-room/march-25–2014/; Alli can also have side effects); there seem to be no truly viable drug alternatives. It seems that every time the drug industry comes up with a pill to assist your weight loss, serious concerns arise about using that pill. And we haven't even discussed the other problems associated with taking these drugs, such as their not insignificant expense, or the fact that the weight often returns once the drug is stopped. There simply is no magic drug that will solve your weight problems without causing any other problems. Perhaps the act of chewing gum, which can decrease appetite and enhance attention (see Chapters 2 and 8), is a good alternative to a risky obesity drug.

There is, however, a subset of people who overeat or are obese that may be assisted by drug therapy. As you learned earlier in this chapter, there are some types of overeating and obesity that are associated with depression. These include people suffering from binge eating disorder, seasonal affective disorder, and night eating syndrome. Note that in at least some of these cases the overeating is associated with a craving for carbohydrates, and that, as you know from earlier material in this book, some researchers believe that eating carbohydrates can raise serotonin levels and that depression is associated with low serotonin levels. Therefore, some scientists have speculated that some cases of overeating and obesity—those associated with depression and/or carbohydrate craving—may be due to low levels of serotonin.[97] If this is correct, then giving such people drugs to raise their serotonin levels should decrease the overeating as well as alleviate the depression. There has been some success reported in alleviating carbohydrate craving and its associated depression by using drugs that raise serotonin levels. However, this area of research remains quite controversial.[98]

What about diets? Just about every women's magazine at the grocery store checkout counter contains advice about how to lose weight quickly and permanently by using the latest diet. There are low-calorie diets, low-carbohydrate diets, low-fat diets, total fasts, and many others. Why do you think that there are so many? Why are there always new ones? What do you think would happen if there were a diet that truly worked? A diet that allowed you to lose the weight you want without too much suffering, and the weight stayed off permanently?

Well, if there were such a diet, its fame would spread far and wide and there would be no need for any others. So guess what all of this marvelous variety of diets tells us? Diets don't work! Some weight may be lost, but it's usually regained,[99] as seen so publicly in media stars such as Oprah. Even worse, some diets are extremely dangerous. Some can cause severe dehydration, excessive heart rate, or cardiac fibrillation, not to mention the fact that many diets are inadequate nutritionally.[100] Finally, diets are not pleasant. In addition to the constant hunger many of them cause, people on diets show physiological symptoms of stress and have memory difficulties.[101]

So why don't diets result in permanent weight loss? It's important to keep in mind that there's no magic involved in losing weight. Calories from digested food don't disappear unless they're excreted, lost as heat, or used for metabolic or physical work. The only way to truly lose fat as a result of a diet is by eating fewer calories, by using more energy, or both.[102] In addition, as you learned about earlier in this chapter, for an unknown period of time, dieting can decrease metabolic rate, even after the diet has ceased, resulting in difficulty in losing weight and ease of regain once the diet is over. Weight loss may also not last because the person may have an increased appetite due to empty adipose cells, or because the person may simply resume the old food consumption and exercise behaviors that were responsible for the weight gain in the first place.

One method used by many dieters to decrease the number of calories consumed is the substitution of low-calorie foods and drinks for traditional ones. Theoretically, this should decrease the number of calories consumed, as you learned about earlier in this chapter. But only if the low-calorie food is truly a substitution for a high-calorie food that would have otherwise been eaten. In one previous office in which I worked, a popular break for the staff was a trip to the corner store to buy large amounts of Tasti D-Lite. This sweet concoction looks like soft ice cream, but contains almost no fat and relatively few calories. The staff believed that if they ate Tasti D-Lite instead of regular soft ice cream, they would at worst not gain the weight that they would by eating regular soft ice cream, and they might even lose weight. However, in truth, they would not have eaten regular soft ice cream if they had not eaten the Tasti D-Lite, and the Tasti D-Lite was an addition to their regular lunch. Under many types of conditions, it appears that, over extended periods of time, people eating low-calorie foods compensate to at least some degree by eating more total food.[103]

Independent of whether low-calorie foods decrease the total number of calories that you eat and drink, a major problem with these foods is that many just don't taste good. People give the highest taste ratings to foods that are high in sugar and fat.[104] Further, in at least some studies, they expect low-fat foods not to taste good even before they try them, and they rate the taste of full-fat foods as less pleasant if they think they're low in fat.[105] Such judgments may be the result of long experience.[106] The fat in foods contributes significantly to their flavors and textures in the mouth.[107] It's therefore extremely difficult to manufacture low-fat foods that taste as good as high-fat foods. However, fortunately, ice cream manufacturers have been having some success with this very challenging—and important—task.[108]

Nevertheless, as indicated earlier in this chapter, some research has indicated that foods high in fiber and low in calorie density are more satiating than other types of foods. Incorporating such foods into a diet should assist weight loss.[109] It makes me very happy to now be able to buy tasty English muffins constructed so that just one contains one-third of the recommended daily fiber intake. The series of books *Eat This, Not That*, by David Zinczenko, does a good job of illustrating how to choose food wisely in the American food jungle using many of the principles described in this chapter.

Another aspect of the foods and drinks that you consume may be important in successful weight control—the timing and spacing of meals. Experiments with rats and people have suggested that if you eat the same number of calories but divide it up into many small meals instead of eating those calories as one large meal you'll feel more full and will store less of what you eat as fat.[110] But there's a practical problem with this. These results were obtained in laboratories where the total numbers of calories eaten by the participants were strictly controlled. In the world outside of the laboratory, people eating many meals each day as opposed to one meal may eat more total calories, thus negating any beneficial effect of spreading the calories across many meals. It's important that the whole day's calorie intake be managed.[111]

Finally, given that you're more likely to eat easily available and visible food, making food harder to get should decrease eating and, ultimately, body weight. Such strategies can include eating unshelled nuts, having to unwrap individual serving food items, or even just placing a food item out of immediate reach.[112] You can probably think of some ways to adapt such strategies to your own home.

By now I'm sure you've confirmed my prediction and are pretty depressed. All I seem to be saying here is that no weight control techniques work without side effects. But you should know from the material presented at the beginning of this chapter that there's one technique that does work: exercise. (Hence the huge emphasis on exercise in the popular TV show *The Biggest Loser*.) For at least three reasons, exercise can be useful in decreasing obesity, preventing weight gain, and maintaining weight loss. First, exercise, even fidgeting, uses calories. Second, there's some evidence suggesting that, at least under some conditions, exercise can elevate the metabolic rate for several hours following exercise; more total calories are burned than would be burned by the exercise alone. Unfortunately, we as yet know very little about what kind of exercise has this lasting effect on metabolic rate. Third, exercising helps to maintain or build muscle and, pound for pound, muscle burns more calories than fat.[113] At least five other factors add to the attractiveness of exercise as a weight control technique. First, exercise can improve cardiovascular fitness and increase strength. Second, research suggests that exercise can help to improve mood. Third, exercise can help to prevent osteoporosis (abnormally low bone mass). Fourth, exercise can increase people's relative amounts of HDL cholesterol, thus possibly decreasing cardiovascular risk. And last but not least, there's now consistent evidence that exercise can actually improve your cognitive functioning (i.e., it can make you smarter).[114] It's no wonder that many researchers and therapists have promoted exercise as a useful component to any treatment for obesity. The main drawback to using exercise as a treatment for obesity or to prevent weight gain is the difficulty that many people have in adhering to an exercise program.[115]

How much exercise and what kind of exercise are needed to help you lose weight or prevent weight gain? There's been insufficient research on this issue to give a firm answer. However, we can get some ideas by looking at people who are and aren't successful in losing weight or maintaining weight loss and seeing how much they exercise, such as the people who are members of The National Weight Control Registry (members must have lost at least 30 pounds and have kept it off for at least one year; www.nwcronline.com). What such an examination shows is that people who are successful at losing weight or at maintaining weight loss tend to be more physically active than those who aren't. Many pieces of evidence suggest that what is needed is close to 1 hour of exercise per day (including brisk walking).[116]

Data such as these have convinced me to try to exercise at least 1 hour per day, including walking. Living in New York City, even with a busy schedule, this isn't too difficult because I can walk efficiently as a good part of my commuting. I have often walked the 3 miles between my apartment building and my office. In addition, during my work day, I often go to buildings other than the one in which my meeting is located, and that also involves walking. However, at least four times per week, I go to a gym for about 1¼ hours where I do fairly intense aerobic and muscle-building exercises, as well as some stretching. Since I started this regime of at least 1 hour of exercise each day over 10 years ago, it's been far easier to maintain my weight than it has been at any other time in my life. I still need to be careful about what I eat, but I gain much less easily. In addition, when I've had my cardiac fitness level tested, I tested exceedingly well, and my bone strength is good. So I've become a committed exerciser. In fact, perhaps too committed. A couple of years ago my son gave me one of the popular Fitbit devices that tracks such activities as your steps made and stairs climbed. The only problem was, I kept trying to beat my past records, and I was simply spending too much time exercising. I finally stopped wearing the Fitbit after a week in which it said I did 68,426 steps (about 40 miles) and climbed 120 flights of stairs, and that didn't even include the many hours of exercise I did that week on the stationary bike, the elliptical machine, and the weight machines.

Your body and someone else's: interventions involving those around you

You're probably aware that there have been, and continue to be, many attempts to use various forms of psychotherapy or related manipulations of the surroundings to help people lose weight. You can probably guess, from all that you've read so far, that these methods usually aren't too successful. People do often lose weight with the help of therapists and by manipulating aspects of their surroundings. However, that weight is usually regained. Nevertheless, given that these weight control methods are so prevalent, it's important for me to discuss them here.

One approach that has been used in decreasing obesity is to surround the obese person with a supportive group of people, some or all of whom are willing to help the obese person lose weight. These people need not be professionals; they may be trying to lose weight themselves.

One type of weight-loss approach involving a community is weight-loss competitions among people at different work sites, such as workers at different banks. Attrition in this type of competition is very small, as is the number of dollars expended to run these programs.[117] Activity-enhancing programs and other incentives have been provided to try to get whole communities, such as a college or even a city, to lose weight.[118]

More commonly used group methods for decreasing weight are self-help groups. These are groups consisting of people with a similar problem, in this case obesity. They meet online or in person to discuss common experiences, difficulties, and possible solutions. Some groups are entirely run by volunteers, and other groups, such as Weight Watchers, have much more structure. Weight Watchers had its origins about 50 years ago, and states that about one million people attend its meetings each week. It also now has an active presence online (at www.weightwatchers.com).

Using this website, I filled out a "free assessment," and though the results showed that my BMI is in the healthy range, the site urged me to click and pay "to get started today" in losing weight. Weight Watchers also markets its own line of low-calorie foods as part of its weight-loss program. Several recent experiments comparing Weight Watchers to other treatment methods have found significant weight loss with Weight Watchers. However, these results may not be representative of those of typical Weight Watchers participants, because the experiments' participants agreed up front to participate in a year-long experiment, and their Weight Watchers membership was free.[119] Under typical conditions, organizations such as Weight Watchers have high dropout rates, despite the fact that the people who join them are probably fairly motivated to lose weight. Even those who remain lose only moderate amounts of weight. Self-help groups can, however, provide emotional outlets and opportunities for socialization. In addition, participation in such groups usually has a low or moderate financial cost.[120]

In addition to community and self-help groups, many different kinds of psychotherapy are used to try to help people lose weight. One type that has frequently been used is psychodynamic therapy, which usually involves long-term individual psychotherapy. Many psychodynamic therapists believe that weight gain is due to emotional conflicts arising in early childhood. Therefore psychodynamic therapy seeks to treat these emotional conflicts rather than the obesity itself. Because psychodynamic therapists aren't usually researchers as well, there isn't a great deal of objective evidence available regarding the efficacy of psychodynamic therapy. Psychiatrists Colleen S. W. Rand and Albert J. Stunkard conducted a study to try to address this deficiency in the research literature. They mailed invitations to participate to all 572 members of the American Academy of Psychoanalysis. Approximately 104 of these psychodynamic therapists indicated a desire to participate and reported that they were currently treating at least one obese patient. A total of 70 completed more detailed questionnaires that were then sent to them (Questionnaire A), as well as another detailed questionnaire sent 18 months later (Questionnaire B). At the time of Questionnaire A, these therapists' obese patients had already been in treatment for an average of 31 months and had reportedly lost 10 pounds since entering treatment. By the time of Questionnaire B, this amount had reportedly risen to 21 pounds.[121]

A loss of 21 pounds would appear to be validation for the psychodynamic therapists' approach. However, there are some significant problems with this study. To begin with, psychodynamic therapy is extremely expensive, and therefore only the most motivated, as well as the wealthiest, patients would engage in it for years. Second, only a small proportion of the therapists completed questionnaires; therefore it's possible that only those therapists whose patients had been continuously losing weight for a long time chose to participate. Third, it's also possible that the therapists only reported data on the subset of their patients who were losing weight. Fourth, the weight measurements were simply what were reported on the questionnaires; it's impossible to assess their accuracy. Finally, this study assumed that underlying emotional problems are critical in causing obesity and that their treatment is important for long-term weight loss. This assumption is contrary to other information already presented in this book. For example, surgical interventions that result in severely obese patients losing weight are sufficient to improve the psychological well being of the patients. The information on genetic, metabolic, and dietary determinants of obesity also seems to be contrary to the conception that an underlying emotional problem is usually the prime cause of obesity. Clearly, support for the psychodynamic treatment of obesity will have to await further research.

At the other end of the research spectrum are weight-loss methods using behavior therapy or cognitive-behavior therapy. Many behavior therapists see themselves as at least part-time researchers, therapists who are committed to a scientific approach to therapy. Therefore it's not surprising that by far the greatest amount of published research on psychotherapeutic treatments for obesity concerns behavior therapy. Well-known behavioral researchers have acknowledged that even the best executed behavior therapy is unlikely to result in significant long-term weight loss.[122] Yet behavior therapists persist in trying to develop improved ways to help clients lose weight, and the techniques that have been a standard part of the behavioral weight-loss armamentarium are widely touted in the popular weight-loss literature.

For example, a common behavioral weight-loss technique is to make positive consequences such as money or engaging in pleasant activities contingent on appropriate weight-loss behavior. My husband employed this technique with me when we were about to graduate from college and get married in 1974. We decided I should lose about 10 pounds and he told me that he would pay me $5 for every pound that I lost. I was close to destitute at that time, and $50 seemed like a fortune. I lost the weight. However, it returned some years later and is still with me.

Behavior therapists also use techniques in which they teach clients to control the aspects of their surroundings that are likely to lead to overeating. These may include the precommitment devices discussed in Chapter 7, which involve patients learning to avoid situations in which they're likely to be tempted. For example, patients are instructed to make a list before going to the grocery store and stick to it.[123]

An integral part of any behavior therapy weight-loss program is monitoring very carefully the patient's behavior and what's going on in the patient's surroundings. Every attempt is made to obtain reliable, objective data. Teaching self-monitoring of weight, calories consumed, time spent eating, and the like is often part of the process. For example, daily self-weighing has been found to be helpful in weight maintenance.[124] Generally either the therapist or some trusted person other than the patient is responsible for monitoring, as well as delivering, any positive consequences.

Behavior therapy programs for decreasing obesity usually incorporate a variety of techniques, sometimes using drugs, exercise, and nutrition information, in addition to the behavioral techniques already described. This makes it difficult to assess the efficacy of any one particular aspect of treatment. Scientist Martha L. Skender and her colleagues conducted a careful experiment comparing three types of cognitive-behavioral treatment in 127 overweight men and women: treatment including a calorie-reduction diet but no exercise, exercise but no diet, and a combination of diet and exercise. To make sure that there were no differences among the participants before the treatments began, differences that might make it appear that one of the treatments was more or less successful than the others when it really wasn't, participants were assigned at random to one of the three treatments. Registered dieticians worked with the participants in each group every week for 3 months, then every other week for 1½ more months, and then every month for 8 additional months.

At the end of 1 year, the combination group had lost the most weight, an average of 20 pounds, and the exercise only group the least, an average of 6 pounds. However, there was enough variation in weight loss among the members of the three groups that it was possible that these differences in average weight loss were due to chance; the differences among the three groups weren't what scientists call statistically significant. At the end of 2 years, however, there were statistically significant differences among the groups. All three groups had gained weight, such that the diet-only group now weighed 2 pounds more than when they had first started to diet. The exercise-only group and the combination exercise-diet group ended up 6 and 5 pounds below when they had started treatment, respectively. Skender and her colleagues concluded that people lose less weight by exercise than by dieting; however they regain less if they lose weight by exercising as opposed to dieting.[125]

People are apparently faced with a self-control problem: diet and get a quick, large loss that isn't good for you in the long run, or exercise and get an immediate small loss that will stick with you. No wonder it's hard for people to choose exercise rather than dieting for weight loss. One of the best future uses of behavior therapy may be to help people engage in more exercise and other healthy behaviors rather than lose weight per se.[126] Decreasing sedentary activities such as television watching is a good example of what can be encouraged.[127]

191

Many of the techniques suggested in this chapter for changing your environment so as to maintain or decrease your weight are part of Cornell University's Professor Brian Wansink's suggestions for decreasing "mindless eating." Mindless eating (and, especially, overeating) is eating that is influenced by cues in the environment without our awareness of this influence. These influences are omnipresent, but by making sometimes small changes in what surrounds us, we may be able to change our eating behavior.[128]

The Bottom Line

Given all of this research, if you absolutely must lose weight, or if you have trouble preventing weight gain, what should you do? If you're extremely obese, you could qualify for surgical treatment. But what if you're not? Table 10.1 shows my best guess as to how to lose weight successfully and how to keep from gaining. Not all of my suggestions are definitively proven. However, all are at least consistent with the laboratory findings that we have so far. Weight control comes down to making what you eat and how you interact with your surroundings more similar to the conditions that existed when the human species was evolving. Not an easy task, but an achievable one.

A Sense of Proportion: Conclusion

You've read in this chapter about the great many factors that contribute to our overeating and to our becoming, and staying, obese, as well as the

Table 10.1 Research-based suggestions for maintaining current weight or losing relatively small amounts of weight

- Monitor calorie intake carefully.
- Cut back on calories very little, if at all.
- Eat low-fat, low-salt, low-sugar, and high-fiber foods, as well as low glycemic-index-response foods (see Chapter 2).
- Substitute no-calorie beverages for sugar-sweetened beverages.
- Minimize the drinking of alcoholic beverages (see Chapter 11).
- Have soup or another low-calorie-dense food as a first course.
- Consider including chile pepper as part of the meal (see Chapter 15).
- Consider chewing sugarless gum.
- Use small portion and plate sizes.
- Eliminate as many food cues in your surroundings as possible; this may involve obtaining the support of those with whom you live and work.
- Monitor your weight every day
- Exercise aerobically a minimum of 1 hour per day.
- Work out with weights so as to maintain or increase your muscle mass.
- To lose 1 pound in a week, maintain your current level of food intake while increasing your exercise so as to use an additional 3,500 calories per week (e.g., by jogging an additional 6 hours per week or by walking briskly an additional 10 hours per week).

small number of techniques—gastrointestinal surgery and exercise—that seem to result in lasting weight loss. This imbalance isn't really surprising. Our species evolved in surroundings that featured repeated periods of food scarcity.[129] As a result, our bodies are designed to ingest large amounts of calories and to retain those calories.[130] This is a huge problem in the United States and in many other nations, where the prevalence of many different types of very tasty, cheap, and highly advertised food, and of labor-saving devices, is perfect for facilitating obesity.[131]

At the same time, we must deal with the current fashion image, which results in many people, particularly women, who are slightly overweight or even of normal weight, continually trying to diet and lose weight. These dieting efforts involve much time and money, may lead to eating disorders, and may facilitate future weight gain.[132] As pointed out so clearly by Duke University psychologist Kelly D. Brownell and former University of Pennsylvania president Judith Rodin, even when someone's health improves by losing weight, that person is likely to regain the weight, and people whose weights cycle up and down seem to be more at risk for coronary heart disease and other health problems.[133]

For these reasons there has been much controversy over whether many people should even attempt to lose weight. Some physicians and therapists believe that people should try to lose weight only if their weight loss will result in significant health benefits.[134] An editorial in *The New England Journal of Medicine* was even entitled "Losing Weight—An Ill-Fated New Year's Resolution."[135] But life can be hard on people who are overweight, even if they have no health problems. They may suffer from job discrimination and social rejection. They may be perceived as lazy or lacking in will power, despite everything we know about the genetic and physiological determinants of obesity.[136]

Instead of focusing on attempts to help individuals lose weight that they've already accumulated, perhaps we should focus on a potentially more successful goal: restructuring our environment so as to prevent weight gain, so that we all move and eat in a more healthy way and thus curtail the growing obesity epidemic. Food and drink manufacturers' ever-present marketing is designed, not surprisingly, to get us to eat and drink as much of the manufacturers' products as possible. These manufacturers design, place, and advertise their products so as to maximize their impact on us, and we react as expected. We buy and eat the candy placed on the checkout counter at the drugstore, and we buy and drink the 32-ounce sodas (close to 400 calories of pure sugar) advertised on the screen while we wait for the movie to start. However, some people are trying to counter these influences and support healthy eating. In addition to the attempted New York City ban on large sugary drinks described earlier, throughout the United States there are movements to limit fast-food advertisements on television, put healthy foods and drinks at eye level in vending machines, redesign cafeteria lines so that healthy foods are easiest to reach, and prohibit bake sales in schools.[137]

Given everything that the manufacturers do to get us to consume unhealthy foods, and too much food, it surprises me that some people decry these counter-efforts that support healthy eating. Manufacturers can use a panoply of techniques to persuade us—often without our knowledge—to eat more than is good for us, and nothing should be done to stop or even inhibit them? At the height of the NYC soda ban controversy, the cover of the June 6, 2011, *New Yorker* was a drawing of people placed in stocks with such labels on the stocks as "CARBS" and "NYC DEPT. OF MORAL GUIDANCE—NO FEEDING BACKSLIDERS." If it is too controlling to take actions designed to promote healthy eating, why is it okay to allow actions that encourage unhealthy eating? There are profit-making entities that are highly incentivized to get us to eat more, but no profit-making entities that are highly incentivized to get us to eat less, nor will there be. So what recourse do we have to try to counter the efforts of the profit-making entities other than legal and public health mechanisms? And in the meantime, the costs of the obesity epidemic on our health system impact each one of us.

I do not have the answers to all of these questions. However, what I do believe is that, as a society that aims to be healthy and survive for many centuries to come, we need to make sure that we are all fully informed about the influences on our eating and drinking behaviors, and about the consequences of those behaviors. We also need to make sure that aspects of our environment that will increase the probability of healthy eating have at least as much of a shot at doing so as the aspects of our environment that will increase the probability of unhealthy eating. Right now it isn't a fair contest. In the meantime, for myself, I intend to exercise as much as is safe and possible, and to try to structure my surroundings so that they contain limited amounts of high-fat, high-salt, high-sugar, and low-fiber foods.

11

DRINKING YOUR LIFE AWAY
Alcohol Use and Abuse

Among U.S. Army troops stationed in Saudi Arabia in 1991 during the Gulf War, there were only about one-third of the disciplinary problems as compared to troops stationed in other countries. In fact, in the first 6 months of the Gulf War, despite 300,000 troops being stationed in Saudi Arabia, there was a total of only 19 court-martials, fewer than 1 for every 15,000 soldiers.[1] The reason for this low rate of disciplinary problems? Saudi Arabian law, in accordance with the Muslim religion, does not allow any alcohol, and the U.S. Army followed this law while stationed in Saudi Arabia.

Far to the north, in a much different climate than Saudi Arabia—Russia—at current rates, 25% of men will die before the age of 55, with vodka the major cause behind these deaths.[2]

If people behave so much better when they're not under the influence of alcohol, why do so many people abuse the stuff? And if we want these people to stop drinking alcohol, what's the best method? This chapter will tell you what scientific research has found so far for the answers to these questions.

How Much Use and How Much Abuse?

People have made and drunk alcoholic beverages since the beginning of civilization. The archaeological evidence suggests that alcoholic beverages originated in the Near East and then spread to the West. There is evidence of the existence of wine at least 8,000 years ago and of beer at least 6,000 years ago.[3] For most of their existence, wine and beer have had fairly low alcohol contents and were two of the very few safe beverages; regular water supplies have often been contaminated. However, even after the water supply was made safe in most of the United States, and even after techniques were discovered that increased the concentration of alcohol in beverages, large amounts of alcoholic beverages have still been drunk by many people.[4]

Use of alcohol has waxed and waned in the United States. We are currently in one of the lower-use periods.[5] However, by no means is the amount of alcohol drunk by Americans small. Among all American adults, approximately 88% have drunk alcohol at some point in their lives, and 71% in the past year.[6] Among college students, a 2009–2011 national survey showed that 82% had consumed alcohol in the past year, and 62% of underage—younger than 21—students had consumed it in the past 30 days. Even more concerning is the percentage of students who had engaged in binge drinking (at least five drinks in one sitting) in the past two weeks: 44%.[7] Binge drinking is not limited to college students. A 2012 survey indicated that 25% of American adults had participated in binge drinking during the past month.[8]

It's essential in your reading this chapter that you understand the enormous negative impact of all of this drinking. Although there's some evidence that moderate alcohol consumption can decrease coronary heart disease,[9] the cost of excess alcohol consumption—both to individuals and to society in general—is extremely high. Alcohol is one of the leading causes of preventable death in the United States; it's a factor in approximately 80,000 American deaths per year.[10] These deaths occur not only because of the direct effects of alcohol, such as acute alcohol poisoning from the depressant effects of alcohol on the central nervous system, poor nutrition, and cirrhosis of the liver, but also from more indirect effects, such as an increased probability of all types of accidents including car accidents, aggravation of diseases such as bleeding peptic ulcer, a decreased probability of detecting when one is sick or injured, an increased probability of suicide and of being a victim of a homicide, and, in smokers, an increased frequency of smoking.[11] And that's just what can happen to the person who's doing the drinking. People who aren't drinking, but who happen to be near someone who is, are more likely to be the victims of car accidents, homicides, and domestic violence. Further, it's estimated that alcohol consumption costs the United States $224 billion per year due to lost productivity, health care costs, and property damage.[12]

The negative effects of college-student drinking have been extensively studied. Just some of the results are that: alcohol-related blackouts at large campuses result in about half a million dollars in emergency room visits per year, there is far more property damage at colleges with high binge drinking rates, and binge drinking appears to directly lead to risky sex.[13]

But where is the dividing line between alcohol use and alcohol abuse? At what point should you start worrying about someone's alcohol consumption? What, specifically, am I talking about in this chapter when I talk about alcohol abuse and its treatment? The American Psychiatric Association defines alcohol use disorder as "a problematic pattern of alcohol use leading to clinically significant impairment or distress."[14] Note that someone with this disorder does not necessarily have to show tolerance to or withdrawal from alcohol, although these symptoms may be present. Using this definition for alcohol use disorder, approximately 9% of American adults and 5% of 12- to 17-year-olds can be classified as having this disorder during any given 12-month period. Alcohol use disorder is much more common among men than women, and in adults is much less common among Asians than African Americans, whites, and Hispanics. It is highest among Native Americans and Alaska Natives.[15]

Given that almost half of Americans have had a family member with a serious alcohol problem,[16] the costs of alcohol abuse may seem all too familiar. Alcohol abuse is a terrible problem—for the abusers themselves and for those around them. In the meantime, although they may tell you to drink responsibly, alcohol manufacturers and bar owners do what they can to ensure that alcoholic beverages are consumed,[17] making the success of programs seeking to decrease or eliminate drinking all the more difficult. In order to better understand what's helping to maintain drinking, we'll start by taking a close look at the effects of drinking. Then, fortified with that information, we'll be better able to evaluate the myriad of treatments designed to treat alcohol abuse.

Expectations and Realities: The Effects of Drinking Alcohol

Folklore about the effects of drinking alcohol abounds. Consider, for example, the following American, German, and Roman proverbs:

> When drink enters, wisdom departs.[18]

> The drunken mouth reveals the heart's secrets.[19]

> A fellow who argues with a drunk is abusing an absent man.[20]

And note this eloquent quotation from William Shakespeare's *Macbeth*:

> Drink, sir, is a great provoker of three things ... nose-painting, sleep, and urine. Lechery, sir, it provokes, and unprovokes; it provokes the desire, but it takes away the performance.[21]

How accurate are these beliefs? We'll consider both the research concerning the short-term, acute effects of drinking alcohol, and then the long-term effects. However, in order to evaluate this research, I must point out to you a difficulty in trying to figure out the effects of drinking alcohol. Someone's behavior may change after drinking either because of the direct effects of the alcohol or because of the person's expectations of the effects of alcohol. For example, if one person is told that drinking makes you act silly and another person is told that drinking makes you act serious, then, after drinking, the first person might act silly and the second person might act serious. Someone might even use drinking as an excuse to engage in socially unacceptable behavior.[22] Clearly we need to know what effects of alcohol are due to the drug itself and what are due to expectations; the former will be much harder to prevent or change than the latter.

Luckily scientists have figured out a way to tease apart the actual effects of alcohol and the effects of alcohol expectancies using something called the balanced-placebo design, developed by psychologist G. Alan Marlatt and his colleagues.[23] In experiments using this design, half of the participants drink alcohol and half don't, and of each of those two groups, half are led to believe that they've drunk alcohol and half aren't, for a total of four types of participants. In Figure 11.1, how type B participants behave after drinking shows the direct effects of alcohol uncontaminated by expectations, because type B participants drink alcohol but think that they haven't. How type C participants behave after drinking shows the effects of expectations uncontaminated by the direct effects of alcohol, because type C participants don't drink alcohol but think that they have. The experience of type A participants, who drink alcohol and think that they have, is similar to what happens in ordinary life outside of the laboratory. The behavior of type D participants, those who don't drink alcohol and think that they haven't, can be used as a comparison to the behavior of all of the other participant types.

PARTICIPANT EXPECTS TO RECEIVE

		Alcohol	No Alcohol
PARTICIPANT ACTUALLY RECEIVES	Alcohol	A	B
	No Alcohol	C	D

Figure 11.1 Balanced-placebo design. (Adapted from W. H. George and G. A. Marlatt, "Alcoholism: The Evolution of a Behavioral Perspective," in *Recent Developments in Alcoholism*, vol. 1, ed. M. Glanter, New York: Plenum, 1983.)

You're probably wondering how on earth people would think that they were drinking alcohol when they weren't and vice versa. You'll be happy to know that experimenters have become very good at such deceptions. Let's take a participant who's supposed to think that she drank alcohol but that wasn't the case. First the experimenter may ask the participant to rinse out her mouth with mouthwash to inhibit the participant's ability to taste what's to come. Then the experimenter will go to great pains to mix the participant's drink, with the participant watching, from two bottles clearly labeled vodka and tonic water. However, unbeknownst to the participant, all of the liquid in both bottles is tonic water. Finally, the edge of the participant's glass may be swabbed with alcohol to provide the participant with (misleading) odor and taste cues.

One example of what we've learned from experiments using the balanced-placebo design is that alcohol expectancies, and not the direct effects of alcohol, appear to be responsible for people becoming sexually aroused more easily after drinking.[24] However, judging *other* people's sexual arousal is another matter. Psychologist Alan M. Gross and his colleagues, using a balanced-placebo design, had male college students listen to an audiotape of a date rape by a male student of a female student. The results showed that alcohol directly resulted in the experiment's participants being more likely to judge the woman in the tape as being sexually aroused, and waiting until later in the tape before saying that the rapist should cease his sexual advances.[25]

Acute effects

Given the profound changes in the body's physiology after drinking, you'd expect alcohol to have at least some direct effects on behavior. When people drink, alcohol is metabolized in the liver first into acetaldehyde and eventually into carbon dioxide and water. Some of the acetaldehyde in the liver is absorbed into the bloodstream. Acetaldehyde affects most of the tissues in the body.[26] Approximately 50% of Chinese, Japanese, and Koreans lack an enzyme that rids them of small amounts of acetaldehyde. Such people tend not to drink very much, but when they do, they become flushed and can have severe heart palpitations.[27]

Alcohol has many direct physiological effects. In low doses it acts as a stimulant, but in high doses it acts as a depressant.[28] That's why you see people talking a lot at the beginning of a party, and then sitting in a stupor at the end. Relatively large amounts of alcohol and acetaldehyde can cause disruptions in breathing during sleep, a decrease in the amount of restful REM (rapid eye movement) sleep, headaches, and an inhibition of the synthesis of the male hormone testosterone.[29] (See Conversation Making Fact #11.)

Conversation making fact #11

Several different lines of research suggest that moderate drinkers tend to eat more and store more of what they eat as fat when they drink alcohol. For example, scientists Margriet S. Westerterp-Plantenga and Christianne R. T. Verwegen conducted a fascinating experiment in which participants were repeatedly given an apéritif prior to eating as much as they wanted for lunch. On different days the aperitif consisted of wine, beer, fatty fruit juice, protein fruit juice, carbohydrate fruit juice, water, or nothing. All of the aperitifs (except the water) contained the same number of calories. When participants got a wine or beer aperitif, they ate more, faster, and longer, and got full later than when the aperitif didn't contain alcohol. Participants even ate more during the 24 hours following the aperitif if the aperitif contained alcohol.[30] Additional experiments indicate that alcohol directly increases consumption of energy-dense foods, as well as ratings and physiological indicators of appetite.[31] Together, these data suggest avoiding alcohol if you're trying to lose weight.

It has been firmly established that drinking increases aggression.[32] Psychologists have attempted to determine why that might be the case. One theory relates to the concept of self-control discussed in Chapter 7. You'll remember that self-control involves choosing something more delayed that is ultimately of more value over something that is less delayed but is of less value, with impulsiveness being the reverse. Many researchers believe that drinking somehow increases the discounting of delayed events—that it makes people more inclined to choose immediate rewards. Such behavior is called alcohol myopia.[33] If the delayed consequence of a choice is something negative, then alcohol could make someone act as if those negative consequences don't exist. So, for example, someone under the influence might impulsively hit someone, not thinking about the possibility of a jail term. Alcohol myopia might help to explain the greater tendency of intoxicated people to engage in risky behavior, including risky driving.[34]

One of the most investigated areas of alcohol's effects on psychological functioning is the acute effects of alcohol on memory. That alcohol should affect memory won't be a surprise to you. Everyone has heard of cases in which someone drank a lot one evening and then, although never losing consciousness, didn't remember much—or anything—about that evening, a so-called blackout. And it isn't a surprise to physiologists either. Alcohol inhibits the activity of the neurons in the hippocampus, a part of the brain that has been shown to be very important for memory.[35]

But you may be surprised to know that, at least under some conditions, you don't have to drink a large amount of alcohol or have a blackout in order for alcohol to affect your memory. How much disruption of memory there is depends on how much you drink, what you're trying to remember, and what else is going on at the same time.[36] Even just thinking you drank can impair your memory.[37] These alcohol-induced memory problems may be related to the fact that alcohol consumption also increases the tendency of your mind to wander, and makes it less likely that you will notice your mind wandering.[38]

In addition to disrupting memory, alcohol also disrupts other cognitive abilities. For example, although binge drinking does not disrupt college students' performance on a test the following day, it does affect attention and reaction time.[39]

There has also been substantial research on the question of how and under what conditions experienced drinkers show less effects of drinking alcohol. In other words, how and under what conditions does tolerance to alcohol develop? For example, people under the influence may drive better if they've had a lot of experience with driving drunk as opposed to never having attempted this risky behavior. Researchers have tried to figure out whether such changes with experience are due to a diminished physiological effect of the alcohol or to people learning in some way to compensate for alcohol's effects.[40] This is an important question because, to the degree that people enjoy feeling intoxicated, as tolerance develops they may feel compelled to drink larger amounts, resulting in more damage to their bodies. Information about the bases of tolerance may therefore be helpful in figuring out ways to help people cut down on their drinking.

There's substantial evidence indicating that learning is at least partly responsible for developing tolerance to alcohol's effects. Psychologist Bob Remington and his colleagues did an experiment in which some participants got a familiar drink (beer), and the others got an unfamiliar blue, peppermint drink. Both drinks contained exactly the same amount of alcohol, and the participants drank both at the same rate. After drinking, participants performed a hand–eye coordination task in which they searched for words within a grid of jumbled letters. Those participants who drank the unfamiliar blue, peppermint drink rated themselves as being more intoxicated and performed worse on the tasks than the participants who drank beer.[41] Somehow, people who drink a particular alcoholic beverage perform better not just when they have previous experience with any sort of alcohol, but when they have previous experience with that particular beverage. These results are consistent with the findings of apparently less tolerance to the effects of alcohol when it is consumed as part of the relatively unfamiliar energy drink Four Loko.[42]

One possible explanation of these findings is based on the concept of compensatory, opposite physiological reactions.[43] The idea is that any time a drug such as alcohol changes the body's physiology, there are opposite physiological reactions that return the body's state back to normal to maintain homeostasis; these opposite reactions help to keep the body in an optimal, stable state. Now assume that, with experience, these opposite physiological reactions get larger and that, through a learning process, they come to be generated by the aspects of the surroundings that are associated with the drug. Then, if someone repeatedly consumes a specific drug under the same conditions, the opposite physiological reactions will be large and will result in that person exhibiting tolerance to the drug. But if the surroundings or the appearance of the drug change, those opposite reactions won't be as strong and there will be less tolerance. This model has been used to explain why heroin addicts who take their usual doses of heroin in unfamiliar surroundings sometimes overdose. It's thought that in such cases the opposite reactions aren't as large and thus aren't strong enough to counteract the effects of the addicts' usual doses.[44]

Long-term effects

There's no question that, over the long term, the effects of several drinks each day can be extremely damaging to your body. For example, although moderate drinking (1–2 drinks per day), in comparison with abstention, can decrease cardiovascular risk and cognitive decline, drinking larger amounts can result in increased cardiovascular risk and damage to the heart.[45] In addition, the acetaldehyde and excess hydrogen resulting from the metabolism of alcohol can eventually cause cirrhosis and hepatitis. As you already know, repeatedly drinking alcohol can lead to tolerance and physical dependence on alcohol.[46] Physically dependent alcoholics can experience potentially dangerous withdrawal symptoms when they stop drinking.[47] Chapter 13 discusses at length how drinking by a pregnant woman can seriously harm the fetus that she's carrying.

Over time, drinking alcohol can also harm your nutrition. The acetaldehydes from the metabolism of alcohol decrease the effectiveness of vitamins. In addition, alcohol irritates the gastrointestinal tract. Finally, there's evidence that cirrhosis of the liver, which is often present in alcoholics, can cause disturbances in taste and smell, as well as cause decreased appetite. These factors can all combine to cause malnutrition in alcoholics.[48]

Despite what you read in the Conversation Making Fact #11 about moderate drinking contributing to weight gain, drinking very large amounts of alcohol over the long term does not necessarily result in weight gain.

When some people were given 2,200 calories of regular meals each day plus 2,000 calories of alcohol, they showed no consistent weight gain over a 4-week period. However, when other people were given 2,200 calories of regular meals each day plus 2,000 calories of chocolate, on average they gained about 6.5 pounds in 2 weeks. The lack of weight gain when large amounts of alcohol are drunk may be due to excess energy being released in the metabolism of alcohol.[49] Before you get too excited about the lack of any weight gain, however, keep in mind that drinking this amount of alcohol—equivalent to 19 1.5-ounce jiggers of water per day—is extremely damaging to the body in many ways. Cognitive abilities are certainly not immune to the effects of long-term drinking. This would seem inevitable given that with repeated excess drinking, brain density decreases and other types of general brain damage occur.[50] Alcoholics tend to perform worse than nonalcoholics on many types of intellectual tasks, including tasks involving learning, memory, perceptual-motor skills, abstraction, and problem solving. It isn't yet clear how much alcoholics' performance increases after a period of abstinence, but it appears that many improvements will occur if the abstinence occurs for an extended period of time (i.e., years).[51] Wernicke–Korsakoff syndrome, described in Chapter 8, is an example of how long-term excess alcohol consumption can adversely, and permanently, affect memory.

As yet there's no definitive evidence regarding how much drinking and for how long is necessary for cognitive deficits to occur. It's possible that even social drinkers who never consume large amounts of alcohol may have some deficits. More research is needed to settle this issue conclusively.[52] This is all a bit scary if you're a social drinker, as I am. It's hard to read all of the preceding paragraphs and not feel that everyone should be teetotalers. For now, I've decided to limit my drinking to quite small amounts.

Getting to the Bottom of the Bottle: Possible Causes of Drinking

With all of the terrible effects of alcohol, why does anyone drink, particularly large amounts? I'll now attempt to answer that question, beginning with information about the influences of the genes on drinking, and ending with information about the influences of our surroundings on drinking.

The contributions of our genes

There have been multiple theories as to why humans might have evolved so as to be susceptible to alcoholism. One is that, in our evolutionary past, the odor of ethanol was a signal of ripe fruit, and only a signal of ripe fruit, so people who responded positively to that odor were more likely to survive and reproduce.[53] Another theory is that, for much of human history, water sources were contaminated, but were safer when combined with alcohol, so people who could metabolize large amounts of alcohol were more likely to survive and reproduce.[54] Both theories rely on the fact that, similar to the overeating and obesity theories discussed earlier in this book, we no longer live in an environment in which these traits would be adaptive. And in an environment replete with alcohol, at least some of us drink too much, causing harm to ourselves and others. These are hypotheses only, but they can help us to understand the genetic contributions to alcoholism.

It has been known for some time that there are genetic influences on how much someone drinks alcohol. An early, straightforward, approach was to show that breeding together rats or mice with the most preference for alcohol can result in, for example, rats that will drink so much of an alcohol/water mixture as to reach blood alcohol concentrations equivalent to that of a 160-pound man who has drunk approximately eight drinks in 1 hour.[55]

In the ensuing decades many different genes have been shown to contribute to the likelihood of someone abusing alcohol. Certain genes are more common in alcoholics than in their relatives who are not alcoholics. This research has resulted in general agreement that there is no one critical alcoholism gene, but that many genes contribute. These genes may be involved in, for example, how a person metabolizes alcohol, how it affects his or her brain, or how that person responds to stress. Genetically determined abnormalities in the operations of the neurotransmitter dopamine have also been implicated in alcohol abuse, although the results are controversial.[56] An example of the research on the genetic contributions to whether someone becomes an alcoholic, an example that I find particularly fascinating, is the finding that PTC/PROP supertasters (a genetically determined trait—see Chapter 4), taste alcohol as having more burn than do other people, and are less likely to consume alcohol than are other people.[57] I have never liked the taste of alcohol for exactly that reason—to me it burns (as well as being bitter—again, see Chapter 4).

In addition to studies looking for specific genes that contribute to alcoholism, many other types of research demonstrate the influences that genes have on alcoholism. For example, as part of the genetically determined developmental sequence, adolescents are more sensitive than older people to the rewarding, pleasurable, feelings that can come with drinking alcohol, and are less sensitive to the consequences of drinking that would indicate to an older person that enough has been consumed.[58]

Another approach to determining whether genes influence human alcoholism has been to examine people who do and don't have alcoholic relatives to see if there are any physiological traits or genes that tend to distinguish the two groups. Such studies have borne fruit. For example, scientists Marc A. Schuckit and Vidamantas Rayses selected two groups

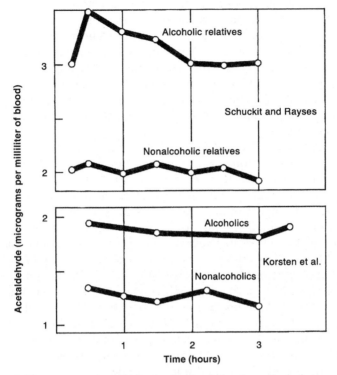

Figure 11.2 Top curve: Acetaldehyde levels following alcohol ingestion by nonalcoholic male participants with and without alcoholic relatives. (Adapted from M. A. Schuckit and V. Rayses, "Ethanol Ingestion: Differences in Blood Acetaldehyde Concentrations in Relatives of Alcoholics and Controls," *Science* 203[1979]: 54–55.) Bottom curve: Acetaldehyde levels following alcohol ingestion by nonalcoholics and alcoholics. (Adapted from M. A. Korsten, S. Matsuzaki, L. Feinman, and C. S. Lieber, "High Blood Acetaldehyde Levels after Ethanol Administration: Difference between Alcoholic and Nonalcoholic Subjects," *The New England Journal of Medicine* 292[8][1975]: 386–389.) Note that the method of alcohol administration in the study by Schuckit and Rayses and the study by Korsten and his colleagues differed so that only the relative, and not the absolute, values obtained in the two studies can be compared.

of young men who were similar in age, race, marital status, and drinking history. However, half of the young men had an alcoholic parent or sibling and the other half didn't. Then Schuckit and Rayses had each of the young men drink the equivalent of approximately two drinks over a 5-minute period and measured their blood acetaldehyde levels.[59] You'll recall that acetaldehyde is a chemical resulting from the metabolism of alcohol, a chemical that affects most of the body's tissues. As Figure 11.2

shows, the participants with alcoholic relatives had much higher levels of acetaldehyde than the participants with nonalcoholic relatives. Because both groups of participants had similar drinking histories, the differences between their acetaldehyde levels couldn't have been due to differences in experience with alcohol. Further, the results were comparable to results obtained by scientist Marc A. Korsten and his colleagues with alcoholics and nonalcoholics.[60] Thus it seems that there may be an inherited tendency for alcoholics and their relatives to metabolize alcohol differently than other people.

Schuckit has also studied hundreds of men who were similar except that only some were sons of alcoholics, from the time when these men were about 20 to when they were about 30. Although both groups of participants had similar drinking histories, Schuckit found that at age 20 the motor performance of the sons of alcoholics tended to be less affected by drinking alcohol. The sons of alcoholics also tended, on average, to report feeling less intoxicated after drinking than the sons of nonalcoholics. Further, 10 years later, those participants in both groups who had shown little reaction to alcohol at age 20 were much more likely to have become alcoholics than were participants who had shown more reaction to alcohol at age 20. Looking just at the sons of alcoholics, 56% of those who had shown little reaction to alcohol at age 20 had, by the age of 30, become alcoholics.[61] This research suggests that in a society in which alcohol is easily available and frequently present, people who show little reaction to it may be likely to drink a great deal.

Another line of research comparing people who do and don't have alcoholic relatives has been conducted by scientists Henri Begleiter and others. This research has shown that, during some visual tasks, men and boys with alcoholic relatives show deficiencies in a particular brain wave called the P3 evoked potential, similar to deficiencies seen in abstinent adult alcoholics. These deficiencies aren't shown by men and boys who do not have alcoholic relatives.[62] Nevertheless, although we know that the size of the P3 evoked potential, which is important in cognitive tasks such as memory, is somehow related to the inheritance of alcoholism, we don't know the nature of that relationship. It's possible, for example, that some genes both directly decrease the size of the P3 evoked potential and make it more likely for someone to become an alcoholic.

Another approach to determining whether there are genetic contributions to alcoholism involves studying twins and adoptees. As explained in Chapters 5 and 10, if there are genetic contributions to alcoholism, then you would expect identical twins to be more similar in terms of alcoholism than fraternal twins, and you would expect adopted children to be more similar in terms of alcoholism to their biological parents than to their adoptive parents. Such studies have repeatedly shown that genes do contribute to whether someone becomes an alcoholic. However, even in identical twins, if one twin is alcoholic, there's only about a 50% chance that the other twin will be alcoholic. Further, most biological children of alcoholics don't themselves become alcoholics.[63] In other words, there's no question that, although genes influence whether someone becomes an alcoholic, other factors are involved.

There are additional, indirect, ways that might provide hints as to whether heredity contributes to alcoholism. If certain personality types or physiological characteristics are associated with alcoholism, and if heredity seems to be involved in those personality types or physiological characteristics, then it's possible (though not certain) that heredity also contributes to alcoholism. Researchers have identified a number of personality traits and physiological characteristics that seem to be associated with alcoholism. These personality traits include impulsiveness (discussed in Chapter 7), anxiety (anxious alcoholics may drink to relieve anxiety), and antisocial personality disorder (defined as "a pervasive pattern of disregard for and violation of the rights of others, occurring since age 15 years").[64] There's evidence that each of these personality characteristics is to some degree influenced by heredity, or at least tends to occur in groups of family members.[65]

The contributions of our surroundings

Many aspects of people's surroundings also seem to affect whether they drink and how much they drink. To take a simple example, what time of day it is and whether other people are present can affect someone's drinking. More specifically, people tend to drink more later in the day and evening, on their days off, and, similar to how much you eat, people tend to drink more when they're with other people.[66] Expanding on that last finding a bit more, when they drink alone, people are more likely to perceive the effects of alcohol as negative, but when they drink with others, people are more likely to perceive the effects of alcohol as positive, reporting, for example, feelings of euphoria.[67]

However, simply being with someone else won't necessarily increase your drinking. It helps if that person drinks heavily. Scientists Donnie W. Watson and Mark B. Sobell conducted an experiment with 64 nonalcoholic men. The men were told that the experiment involved rating art objects and beers. The men were paired with an accomplice of the experimenters whom the men thought was another participant. All of the men rated the beers. In half of the cases, the accomplice also rated the beers and drank a lot. In the other half of the cases, the accomplice rated the art objects and did not drink. The men drank more while making their ratings if they were accompanied by a heavy-drinking accomplice.[68]

Watson and Sobell's experiment is one of many showing how people may drink amounts similar to what they see other people drinking, an effect called modeling. It's for this reason that researchers have thought that modeling could help treat excess drinking.[69] Certainly it appears to make a difference in adolescent excess drinking. Adolescents whose friends drink and who are involved in many social activities with their friends are much more likely to drink excessively than are other adolescents.[70]

Additional information about modeling and other effects of social interactions on alcohol consumption is revealed in the effects of families and roommates on the drinking of young people. If fathers and mothers believe that their children are going to drink a lot, then the children are more likely to do so as they age.[71] And if a college student has a roommate who drinks to excess, then that student's grades will likely be lower, most probably due to drinking more him- or herself.[72]

More indirect effects of other people on our drinking are manifested in the form of advertising. As shown earlier in this book, advertising actually does work, and alcohol manufacturers and purveyors certainly do take advantage of that fact. As one example of how advertising could affect drinking, when University of Missouri students saw pictures of beer cans constructed with their school's colors (what are known in the beer marketing world as "fan cans"), as opposed to ordinary cans, they were less likely to rate beer consumption as dangerous, and also less likely to rate the party scene practices at the University of Missouri as dangerous. These effects of fan cans on their beliefs could encourage students to buy and drink more fan cans than ordinary beer cans.[73]

There are many other examples regarding how aspects of past or current surroundings can affect how much someone drinks. The fact that very early (prior to age 15) exposure to alcohol can by itself increase the probability of later alcohol abuse is one such example.[74] The interpretation of alcohol tolerance as a learned behavior, described previously in this chapter, is another. A further example involving learning comes from experiments with rats showing that they learn to prefer flavors associated with low concentrations of alcohol, even when the alcohol is infused directly into the stomach.[75] Scientists believe that this effect is due to the calories present in alcohol, that the rats associate the taste with the calories and therefore learn to prefer that taste. Similar to sugar, alcohol is an excellent source of energy.[76] This could help to explain why periods of alcohol deprivation appear to result in increased preference for alcohol in both rats and people; perhaps such effects are sometimes due not to alcohol dependence or withdrawal, but instead reflect an increased preference for a source of calories in a situation in which few calories have been forthcoming. Together these findings, and what you read earlier in this book, suggest that perhaps people initially don't like the taste of, say, bourbon, but come to like it after associating it with calories a number of times.

Another way in which researchers have thought that the effects of drinking might affect future drinking has been that some people drink to reduce tension, anxiety, or stress. According to this theory, because alcohol relieves these negative symptoms, people drink more. The only problem is that laboratory investigations have not always shown that drinking relieves these feelings. One possible explanation for the inconsistent findings is that drinking relieves stress in response to situations in which the threat is uncertain as opposed to certain.[77] However, I'm not sure that this modification of the stress-relief theory explains what happens in all situations involving stress and alcohol. When I was about to enter the doctoral program in experimental psychology at Harvard, I tried to waive some first-year graduate courses by taking the exams normally given after the first year of graduate school. There were four 3-hour exams in 1 week, a very grueling schedule, and the last test was on my specialty: learning. Because I was worried about the other exams, which covered subjects that I had covered less as an undergraduate, I didn't study much for the learning exam. It was a lot tougher than I expected, and when I finished it I was very concerned that I had done poorly on that last exam, and that all of my efforts had been in vain (you had to pass every exam in order to waive any first-year course). I wasn't sure that I had failed the last exam, but I feared the worst. On the phone from many miles away, my father strongly urged me to have a drink; that would make me feel better. So I had a few good belts, but instead of no longer being upset, now I felt drunk in addition to upset. That was my first experience with the inaccuracy of the popular belief that drinking can help you to escape your problems. (By the way, I passed all the exams.)

Our surroundings may also affect drinking by interacting with our motivations, as exemplified by the schedule-induced polydipsia (SIP) phenomenon described in Chapter 3. In demonstrations of SIP, rats drink huge amounts of freely available water when they're hungry and when food is delivered at regular intervals. Scientists think that the rats in this situation are motivated to eat, but can't eat whenever they want, and so they drink instead. A number of researchers have thought that SIP might be a good way to study alcohol abuse.[78] These researchers have hypothesized that some instances of excessive drinking may be due to people being unable to satisfy a variety of motivations or drives. Psychologist John L. Falk supported this hypothesis when, using rats, he substituted alcohol solutions for water in a SIP paradigm, and the rats drank enough alcohol to become physically dependent on it and to have continuously high blood alcohol levels.[79]

Another way in which motivation can affect drinking behavior has to do with the effects of money and economics on drinking, similar to the approaches to choice behavior discussed in Chapter 7. How much you drink depends on not only the inherent value of the alcohol, but on how difficult it is to get it and what alternatives are available. To begin with a well-known example, drinking decreased during Prohibition, when alcohol was less available and illegal.[80] Many laboratory experiments have been conducted to determine just what sorts of constraints and contingencies will result in less or more alcohol being drunk.[81] These experiments have shown that, as constraints such as the amount of effort needed to get alcohol increase, the amount of alcohol obtained and consumed decreases. In contrast, as the availability of rewards other than alcohol decreases, drinking of alcohol increases.[82] This last finding raises the possibility that some cases of alcohol abuse may be at least partially due to drinkers perceiving the effects of alcohol as the best part of their lives. This could help explain why people seem to drink more when they live in boring environments (places where there aren't many different activities), and even why fruit flies prefer alcohol more when they've been deprived of sex, as opposed to having recently mated.[83]

This section has described many possible contributors to the development of alcoholism, including factors mostly concerned with people's genes and physiology and factors that are mostly concerned with people's surroundings. It can be confusing trying to sort out what's really responsible for what. There are two basic conclusions that you can draw from all of this information. First, there may be different causes for different cases of alcoholism. This is an important conclusion because it's possible that different treatments may be more or less successful with different cases of alcoholism, depending on the cause of a particular case. Second, each case of alcoholism is likely to be caused by more than one factor. Many scientists now ascribe to a theory of the origins of alcoholism in which there's an inherited tendency to develop it, but alcoholism only occurs if the surroundings that would promote it are also present.[84] In other words, it takes both certain genes and certain surroundings in order for alcoholism to occur.

Taking the Cure

Folklore also abounds about how to "cure" alcoholism, as in this Chinese proverb: "The best cure for drunkenness is while sober to see a drunken man."[85] But is this really the best way to cure alcoholism? Folklore does not always hold up to scientific scrutiny.

The parameters of successful treatment

The first issue of importance to researchers trying to identify successful treatments of alcoholism is whether the treatment has long-lasting effects. Just as with weight control, alcoholism relapses are frequent. Therefore for a treatment to be successful it must have continued success over long follow-up periods.[86] This means that any study purporting to show that an alcoholism treatment works is suspect unless it reports data on the success of the treatment years after it has been completed.

A second issue concerns whether treatment should be on an inpatient or an outpatient basis. A large number of studies have been conducted on this issue. In particular, researchers have focused their attention on the benefits of treatment by for-profit, inpatient, private institutions, many of which are quite expensive, such as the Betty Ford Center. This research indicates that treatment is no more successful when it's inpatient, as opposed to outpatient, or when it's very, as opposed to less, intensive (except perhaps for seriously deteriorated alcoholics). What seems to make the most difference in terms of whether a treatment will be successful is the type of treatment used, not the setting within which the treatment is offered. Thus there seems to be little justification for expending the large number of dollars required for treatment by an expensive, inpatient, private institution, particularly when reimbursement by health care insurers is involved.[87]

Now we come to the most contentious area of all: abstinence versus controlled drinking. Some people, those who view alcoholism as a disease, see the only possible goal of alcoholism treatment as complete abstinence.[88] These people believe that a single sip will often result in a full-blown relapse for a recovered alcoholic. Other people, such as behavior therapists, who see alcoholism as due to a number of factors including aspects of the alcoholic's surroundings, feel that it's possible for some—not all—alcoholics to have as their treatment goal so-called controlled drinking: drinking moderate, safe amounts [89] Complete abstinence has been the approach adopted by the members of Alcoholics Anonymous (AA), as well as by the majority of clinics and alcoholism treatment professionals.[90] This approach is supported by evidence that, for at least some alcoholics, abstinence is essential for full recovery.[91] Nevertheless, evidence has been accumulating over the past 35 years indicating that some alcoholics can successfully achieve controlled drinking.

At this point, many researchers, clinicians, their clients, and their families, accept that at least some alcoholics can successfully engage in controlled drinking.[92] The question has become not if controlled drinking works, but for whom and under what conditions does it work. Two client characteristics that are associated with relatively more success using a treatment goal of controlled drinking are showing few symptoms of alcohol dependence and believing that controlled drinking is possible.[93] There is also evidence that relapses tend to be more severe in clients who have a goal of abstinence as opposed to a goal of controlled drinking. When clients slip and drink more than their treatment goal calls for, the clients with a goal of abstinence drink more than those with a goal of controlled drinking.[94]

Which treatments work?

Dozens of different treatments have been proposed for alcoholism. These treatments vary tremendously and include behavior therapy, medication, and self-help group approaches, among others. For decades researchers have been trying to determine which of these treatments have at least some beneficial effect and which do not. Fortunately, many well-conducted studies have now been done. Scientists can perform statistical tests of the results from large numbers of research participants, including when those participants were actually in different studies. Researchers determine whether, as a whole, the studies indicate that the cessation of alcohol abuse was unlikely to occur by chance, but was instead likely due to the alcoholism treatment.

Psychologist William R. Miller and his colleagues conducted just such an analysis.[95] This analysis found that the most effective treatment is brief intervention. This technique consists of at most three treatment sessions. The content of these sessions may vary, possibly including such elements as assessment of the drinker's problems, advice, or counseling. The clients are usually given printed materials such as self-help manuals to supplement the treatment sessions. Often, the purpose of the sessions is described to the clients as education- rather than treatment-oriented. The sessions and the written materials often focus on using learning theory principles to modify drinking behavior through altering various aspects of the drinker's surroundings, including how other people's behaviors may be encouraging the drinking. Given this context, it's not surprising that the goal of brief interventions is usually to get clients to drink responsibly, rather than to get them to abstain from alcohol. For this reason, brief interventions are usually employed with people whose drinking problems aren't severe and who aren't physically dependent on alcohol. And herein lies the complication with Miller and his colleagues' finding that brief intervention is the most successful treatment. It's possible that brief intervention is the most successful because it's used only with problem drinkers who are in relatively good shape, not because it's the best treatment for alcoholics in general.[96]

Other treatments that Miller and his colleagues found very successful include social skills training (teaching patients how to cope with stressful situations),[97] motivational enhancement (methods of enhancing problem drinkers' motivations to change their drinking behaviors),[98] the community reinforcement approach (which restructures the contingencies in the surroundings so that "sober behavior is more rewarding than drinking behavior"),[99] and behavior contracting (having clients agree to contracts in which specific rewards are given for achieving approximations toward specific goals).[100] However, it's important to remember that, similar to brief intervention, it may be very difficult to use these treatments with seriously debilitated alcoholics. Alcohol abuse can severely limit the cognitive abilities of the abusers, both while they're drinking and when they're sober. These limitations may include problems with planning and with estimating quantities including the quantity of alcohol drunk, and so may inhibit the abilities of some alcoholics to participate in some types of treatments.[101]

Miller and his colleagues' study also seemed to indicate that aversion therapy using nausea has some success. This type of therapy is based on the principles of taste aversion learning discussed in Chapter 6. The basic idea is to follow the taste of alcohol closely by nausea so that an aversion to the alcohol develops. A number of studies have shown this method to be extremely successful at decreasing drinking.[102] Laboratory research on taste aversion learning suggests a number of ways to ensure that nausea-based aversion therapy is as effective as possible. First, in order to obtain the strongest aversion, nausea should closely follow the taste of alcohol, and not precede the taste of alcohol.[103] Second, clinicians should anticipate that an alcoholic, after developing an aversion to one alcoholic beverage, may switch to another alcoholic beverage. In a study of 102 hospitalized alcoholics that I did with two psychology students, K. R. Logue (no relation) and Kerry E. Strauss, approximately 15% of the alcoholics reported taste aversions to alcoholic beverages, even though in many of these cases, prior to the aversions, the participants had had strong preferences for the beverages and had drunk them frequently. However, in very few of these cases did the aversions generalize to anything else, including to any other alcoholic beverages.[104] Thus, although the alcoholics sometimes naturally developed taste aversions to their highly preferred alcoholic beverages, they simply switched to drinking different alcoholic beverages. For aversion therapy to be successful with alcoholics it may be necessary to pair a number of different types of drinks with nausea. A final concern about how to conduct successful aversion therapy is how to induce nausea in a safe and effective manner. Using injected chemicals can be dangerous, and using mechanical methods to induce motion sickness can be messy.[105] A technique called covert sensitization avoids these problems, but is sometimes not as effective at inducing an aversion.[106] In covert sensitization the participants imagine that they feel ill. Unfortunately, with this method it's more difficult to ensure that sufficient illness has been generated.

Perhaps surprisingly, Miller and his colleagues' study shows that treating alcoholics with disulfiram (otherwise known as Antabuse) appears to have very limited effectiveness. Antabuse blocks the normal metabolism of alcohol. If someone has recently taken Antabuse and then drinks alcohol, the acetaldehyde concentration is 5 to 10 times greater than if Antabuse had not been taken,[107] resulting in an extreme physical reaction including "nausea, vomiting...mental confusion...choking, breathing difficulty, and anxiety."[108] This reaction lasts as long as there's alcohol in the blood and can occur even if Antabuse has been consumed as much as 14 days prior to drinking.[109] Thus alcoholics taking Antabuse are exposed to a taste aversion learning situation each time that they drink alcohol. Here the problems with effectiveness may lie with treatment compliance; there can be problems with getting clients to take Antabuse consistently. Scientist George Bigelow and his colleagues required their clients to first deposit a sum of money at a clinic. Each time a client failed to return to the clinic to receive disulfiram, a portion of his or her deposit was sent to charity. The remainder was returned to the client at the end of the study. Using this procedure, Bigelow and his colleagues found significant and consistent decreases in their clients' drinking.[110] Note that Bigelow and his colleagues' procedure is essentially a self-control precommitment technique, as discussed in Chapter 7.

Still another type of treatment approach for which Miller and his colleagues found some support is relapse prevention. This treatment uses a cognitive-behavior therapy approach. Cognitive-behavior therapists have hypothesized that alcoholics relapse because they've previously learned that drinking alcohol is followed by various positive consequences, and that each time a relapse occurs it's an indication that they're not cured, which promotes further drinking. Therefore cognitive-behavior therapists teach their clients how to cope with situations that are likely to lead to relapse, and, if relapses occur, with the relapses themselves.[111]

Miller and his colleagues' study found that self-help manuals, behaviorally oriented marital and family therapy, and cognitive therapy, in which therapists attempt to get alcoholics to change inappropriate thoughts, have also evidenced small but positive effects. In contrast, behavioral self-control training, involving teaching alcoholics how to change their own drinking, has not shown any consistent positive effect. However, the findings from the individual self-control studies examined by Miller and his colleagues were quite mixed, and so behavioral self-control training may be useful under certain conditions.[112] You've already seen that some aspects of behavioral self-control training are integral to other, clearly successful treatments. An experiment conducted by psychologists Reid K. Hester and Harold D. Delaney provided behavioral self-control training via a computer. The participants were nonalcoholic heavy drinkers and the goal of the treatment was moderate, nonproblematic drinking, not abstinence. Participants learned how to monitor their own behaviors, analyze their surroundings to see what might be facilitating drinking, set goals, set up rewards for reaching those goals, and the like. This experiment did find a lasting and positive effect of behavioral self-control training on drinking. Computers and the internet are increasingly being used to good effect in the treatment of alcoholism.[113]

In contrast, Miller and his colleagues' study showed that when controlled studies are conducted, hypnosis, confrontational counseling, and the opportunity to participate in AA have no positive effects whatsoever. The second of these, confrontational counseling, involves such therapist activities as videotaping problem drinkers while they are drunk and then showing the tapes to these people when they are sober.[114] AA is a self-help group that began in 1935 when two alcoholics decided to meet with other alcoholics to promote complete abstention from alcohol. Members are expected to go to meetings regularly and to be available to assist other members who are about to relapse. AA advocates a 12-step approach that begins with participants admitting that they're powerless over alcohol and ends with participants achieving a spiritual awakening. Membership in AA is anonymous and is extremely popular.[115] It's estimated that the total number of AA members in the United States alone is almost 1.3 million.[116]

One experiment by researcher Barbara S. McCrady and her colleagues assessed the effectiveness of AA participation by comparing three types of treatment: behavioral couples therapy, behavioral couples therapy plus relapse prevention, and behavioral couples therapy plus participation in AA.[117] The participants were 90 men who abused or were dependent on alcohol, plus their female partners. The excessive drinking of approximately two-thirds of the men significantly improved; however there was no evidence of greater improvement by the men assigned to the group involving AA participation. In fact, there was some evidence that, on average, the men in the group that involved AA participation did worse than the men in the other two groups. The findings did show that, of the men in the group that included AA participation, those men who regularly attended AA drank less than the other men in that group. However this could just mean that the participants who weren't doing well found ways to avoid the AA sessions; it doesn't mean that AA caused the men who attended to drink less. Despite these and similar findings, like the self-help groups for eating disorders and obesity described in previous chapters, AA may serve an important social and informational function, whether or not it decreases drinking.[118]

An alternative approach to evaluating the success of different treatments has been taken by an ambitious study entitled Project MATCH (Matching Alcoholism Treatments to Client Heterogeneity). This experiment cost $27 million and was conducted with almost 2,000 clients around the country who had either current or previous severe problems with alcohol. The idea was to randomly assign these clients to one of three types of treatment so that the distribution of different types of people in each treatment group would be fairly similar. In addition, the characteristics of each client were to be carefully measured and then correlated with the treatment results. It was hoped that this experiment would show which types of client characteristics resulted in a good outcome with each of the types of treatment. The three types of treatment used were cognitive-behavioral coping skills therapy, motivational enhancement therapy, and 12-step facilitation therapy, modeled after the 12 steps in AA. Each treatment lasted for 12 weeks, and the clients' behaviors were monitored for 1 year after treatment. Contrary to what many people had expected, and contrary to the results of Miller and his colleagues' study, on average the clients in all three groups showed significant improvement, and there were no significant differences in the outcomes of the three types of treatment.[119]

How do we reconcile the results of Project MATCH with those of Miller and his colleagues? Apparently Project MATCH excluded anyone with a drug problem other than alcohol, the participants were all volunteers, and participants all had to have a permanent address and no problems with the law. In the world outside of the laboratory, people who need treatment for alcohol abuse frequently have concurrent problems with other drugs; are compelled to participate in alcohol treatment by the courts, their employers, or by social agencies; are transients; and have legal problems. In other words, the clients in Project MATCH weren't representative of most of the people who need treatment for alcohol abuse, a problem that plagues many studies of alcohol abuse treatment.[120] Further, the 12-step treatment used in Project MATCH wasn't identical to AA because it consisted of individual therapy, as opposed to group sessions. Group AA sessions can involve members being publicly confronted with their problems with alcohol. Some people find such a confrontational approach difficult to endure,[121] which could result in their avoiding participation in AA. However, such confrontations weren't a part of the 12-step facilitation therapy used in Project MATCH. This difference could explain why the 12-step treatment was successful in Project MATCH but not in the studies reviewed by Miller and his colleagues.

You may have noticed that all of the treatment approaches I've discussed are essentially psychological treatments that involve methods of changing drinkers' surroundings in order to change their drinking. For many decades, with the exception of Antabuse, there's been little in the way of effective drugs for alcohol abuse. There have always been drugs that help with the physical symptoms of withdrawal and drugs that can assist alcoholics who feel anxious or depressed,[122] but clearly drugs that block the positive feelings that people have after drinking would also be useful. It is therefore gratifying to report that such drugs have been making their way into clinical use, and that research is showing these drugs to be effective. Two examples are the related drugs naltrexone and nalmefene. Both work by making the body less responsive to the positive effects of alcohol, and they can help decrease the craving for alcohol.[123]

For someone who needs alcohol abuse treatment, the great many alternatives can be somewhat bewildering. I hope that this review of the literature has given you some idea of the range of alternatives as well as of which types of treatments are effective. For an alcoholic who isn't severely deteriorated, who has few symptoms of alcohol dependence, and who believes that controlled drinking is a realistic goal, brief outpatient treatment including assessment of the problem, advice about how to control drinking by modifying surroundings, and self-help manuals, with the aim of getting the alcoholic to drink responsibly, may be a sufficient and successful treatment. However, such a treatment approach will definitely not work for every alcoholic. Other alcoholics may require more extreme manipulations of their surroundings in order to decrease their drinking. For the present at least, psychologists—those who specialize in the origins of behavior and in the methods for changing behavior—have a major role to play in the effective treatment of alcohol abuse.[124]

What you learn at college: alcohol and college students

Before I conclude this chapter, I want to give some special attention to alcohol use and abuse among college students. As I stated at the beginning of this chapter, a recent survey has shown that huge percentages of college students—even those under the age of 21—drink alcohol, and drink it to excess. Specifically, the survey showed that 62% of college students under the age of 21 had consumed alcohol in the past year and 44% of college students had engaged in binge drinking (at least five drinks in one sitting) during the past 2 weeks. Although there is some indication that alcohol consumption has been decreasing over time, with the same survey conducted 3 years earlier showing values of 66% and 46%, respectively, the usage percentages remain extremely large and the pace of decrease extremely slow.[125] And the data indicate that each year almost 2,000 college students die in alcohol-related incidents, another 600,000 are injured, and 97,000 college students are alcohol-related sexual assault or date rape victims.[126]

At the same time, working in higher education as I do, there are dozens, if not hundreds, of articles in professional higher education publications each year regarding how to decrease alcohol consumption among college students. The suggested techniques include changing the goal for students from abstinence to moderate drinking (consistent with research described earlier in this chapter), banning alcohol use in dorms (particularly residential fraternities and sororities, where alcohol use is highest), requiring students to take a course or use an online web tool, informing students that other students don't really drink as much as they think, scheduling more classes on Fridays (so students won't party on Thursday nights), banning alcohol ads in student papers, banning drinking contests, and decreasing drinking opportunities at local bars.[127] One group of presidents has even campaigned to have the legal drinking age decreased to 18 (as it was when I was in college), on the theory that this might help to decrease binge and hidden drinking (what is known as the Amethyst Initiative).[128]

Yet, despite all of these efforts, the drinking goes on and on. In fact, students seem to be constantly developing new methods to ingest large amounts of alcohol, including the game 21 for 21 (drinking 21 drinks as you turn 21 in a bar at midnight, with a convenient vomit bucket provided by the bar nearby), butt chugging (exactly what it sounds like, a way to absorb alcohol very quickly—and dangerously), and the 40-person beer bong, with which 40 students can drink beer continuously from hoses connected to elevated beer kegs.[129]

It's no wonder that college and university presidents have repeatedly described alcohol consumption—not tuition increases, or athletic team scandals, or faculty unrest, or graduation rates—as their biggest problem.[130] It is frankly quite depressing for me, as I have worked on subsequent editions of this book, to see the huge amount of attention paid to the problems of undergraduate-student drinking, along with the huge number of strategies attempted to decrease those problems, but the lack of significant progress, decade after decade. What I can suggest, consistent with the whole approach of this book, is for higher education leaders to redouble their focus on decreasing student drinking using evidence-based practices, including ones in which they themselves have generated evidence. Right now there is inconsistent usage of methods for decreasing college-students' drinking that are based on rigorous research. We need to increase identification of promising strategies, with evaluation using rigorous methods, and increase application and expansion of the demonstratedly successful strategies.

Last Call: Conclusion

We know that despite the many problems associated with drinking alcohol, people still drink. Obviously to some extent this is due to the positive feelings that many people experience when they drink, and people may have little else in their lives that provides them with positive feelings. If there are no good alternatives, alcohol will seem to have great value. Therefore, to decrease excessive drinking, our society will have to provide people who drink with other ways to obtain the rewards that they obtain by drinking. For example, good job opportunities must be provided in areas of the country where they're few and far between and where the associated alcoholism rates are high. Our society can also continue to take the strong steps of maintaining the drinking age and enforcing drunk driving laws.[131] All of these steps are in addition to continuing the development of effective treatments for problem drinking.

However, the alcohol lobby is making it very difficult to decrease problem drinking. This is one of the wealthiest, most effective, and best connected lobbies. Its members frequently host fundraisers for political candidates, events that, of course, include alcohol. There are alcohol lobbyists in virtually every state capital. And there are many other reasons why drinking and its associated problems continue. For example, alcohol ads frequently employ humor or animals that appeal to children under the legal drinking age. Alcoholic beverage manufacturers have also made sure that the possible beneficial effects of moderate drinking on heart disease are widely publicized.[132] All of these factors make decreasing drinking a real challenge, despite the huge economic and health costs of alcohol abuse. My hope is that books such as this one will be weapons in the fight against alcohol abuse.

12

HOW SWEET IT IS

Type 2 Diabetes

Diabetes is a devastating disease in which either the pancreas produces insufficient insulin or the body does not react to the insulin that is produced. As you already know, insulin is a chemical involved in the metabolism of blood sugar, thus ensuring that sugar can be used by the body. With diabetes, blood sugar levels become abnormally high and excess sugar is excreted in the urine.

You're probably wondering why I chose to include a chapter on diabetes. Obviously the integral relationship between diabetes and insulin has something to do with my reasoning. In previous chapters you've learned about the important role that insulin plays in hunger, satiety, and fat storage. In this chapter you'll learn that the origins, effects, and treatment of diabetes are also linked to many other topics in this book, including the preference for sweet, the importance of exercise in obesity, weight maintenance, thirst, and the relationship between food and cognition.

We need to use everything that we know about the psychology of eating and drinking to understand diabetes because of the terribly frequent harm that this disease is inflicting on people in industrialized countries. In the United States, both the number and percentage of people with diabetes is enormous: 25.8 million people (8.3% of the total population) have this disease, and, of those at least 20 years of age, at least 79 million more people are suffering from prediabetes. Although diabetes was formerly seen primarily in older people, it's becoming common at much younger ages; approximately 14.7 million Americans between the ages of 20 and 65 are estimated to have it.[1] So the chances are excellent that either you, or someone very close to you, will at some point suffer from diabetes.

There are striking differences in the frequency of diabetes among different racial and ethnic groups. For example, among American adults, compared to non-Hispanic whites, the percentage of Asians with diabetes is 18% higher, for Hispanics it is 66% higher, and for non-Hispanic blacks it is 77% higher. Among the highest rates are found in Native Americans/ Alaska natives; in these groups 16% of adults have diabetes, though there are large differences depending on geographic region.[2]

For some years now, diabetes has been considered to be a global problem. As countries develop, the prevalence of diabetes among the members of their populations increases. India alone has been estimated to now have 35 million diabetics.[3]

If left untreated, this very common disease has terrible effects on the body. To begin with, blood sugar levels that are too high can cause comas. In addition, over the long term diabetes can damage the walls of the small blood vessels, leading to a host of medical problems including blindness, nerve damage (including impotence in men), kidney disease, circulation problems that can result in amputation of the feet and legs, and cardiovascular diseases. In fact, it's thought that approximately 40% of all cardiovascular diseases in the United States may be due to diabetes.[4] Diabetes is also associated with high levels of harmful fat in the blood and with high blood pressure.[5] Given all of these terrible effects, it's no surprise that in AD 200, the Greek physician Aretaeus provided this description of the experience of those suffering with diabetes: "Life is short, disgusting, and painful."[6]

These terrible effects of diabetes are, of course, accompanied by monetary costs. The yearly health costs for diabetes in the United States are around $174 billion.[7] In addition, worldwide, diabetes decreases worker productivity and therefore can affect economic health and growth.[8]

There are several different types of diabetes. Close to 95% of cases are what is called Type 2 diabetes, and it's on this type that the present chapter will focus. People are on the first rung of the ladder toward Type 2 diabetes when they demonstrate insulin resistance. With insulin resistance, the pancreas releases insulin, but the body's tissues don't react much to its presence. As a result, the pancreas may release increasing amounts of insulin, trying to maintain sugar metabolism. Blood sugar levels will be high—a condition known as impaired glucose tolerance—although not so high as to qualify for a diagnosis of diabetes. Eventually, the pancreas may be unable to keep up with the high blood sugar levels, or may even become unable to secrete much insulin. Then full-blown Type 2 diabetes is present.[9]

"So Sweet Was Ne'er so Fatal"[10]: The Causes of Type 2 Diabetes

As it turns out, Type 2 diabetes, by far the most common kind of diabetes, is intimately tied to eating behavior—both in terms of this affliction's origins and its effects. To understand the relationships between eating and diabetes, it will be helpful first to review a few basic facts from earlier chapters (particularly Chapter 2) about the role of insulin in the eating behavior of the general population.

First recall that your pancreas releases insulin when you come into contact with food or with aspects of your surroundings that have previously been associated with food. For example, in many people, their pancreas releases insulin when they're about to eat a piece of chocolate cake. After it's released, the insulin decreases blood sugar level and increases the probability that whatever is eaten will be stored as fat. Further, the insulin-caused decrease in blood sugar level that occurs when someone detects, but has not yet eaten, food may increase the probability that someone will eat. In other words, this change in blood sugar level may function as a hunger signal. Finally, research has suggested that you release more insulin when you eat foods that are sweet, taste good, or are low in fiber—all of which are consistent with other observations indicating that, when they eat those sorts of foods, people eat more and get fatter.

Now let's build on this information regarding what you eat and insulin levels to explain the origins of diabetes. Recall from Chapter 2 the glycemic index score, a measure of how much glucose different foods add to your blood over a specified period of time. People whose diets naturally contain high proportions of food with high glycemic scores (which are

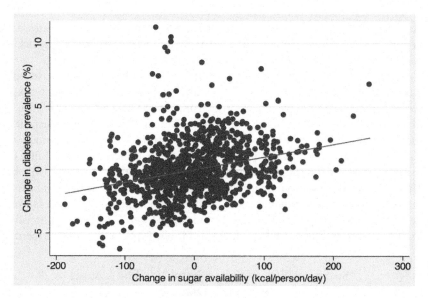

Figure 12.1 The relationship between change in sugar availability (shown as change in the calories of sugar per person per day) with the change in diabetes prevalence (shown as change in the percentage of adults 20–79 years old with diabetes). The diagonal line indicates the overall relationship between change in sugar availability and change in diabetes prevalence. For details on how this line was determined, see the original article. (Reprinted with permission from S. Basu, P. Yoffe, N. Hills, and R. H. Lustig, "The Relationship of Sugar to Population-Level Diabetes Prevalence: An Econometric Analysis of Repeated Cross-Sectional Data," *PLoS ONE* 8[2013]: e57873.)

also the sorts of foods for which more insulin is released) are more likely to develop cardiovascular disease, to be obese, to be insulin resistant, and to develop Type 2 diabetes[11] (see Figure 12.1). Thus there's much circumstantial, if not direct, evidence linking foods with high glycemic scores to the development of Type 2 diabetes.

Add to all of this the fact that the more fat on someone's body—particularly the upper abdomen—the more insulin is produced, and you've a vicious circle: the more insulin, the more fat, and the more fat, the more insulin. All of this is associated with insulin resistance, Type 2 diabetes, and cardiovascular disease. In fact, the relationship between body fat and Type 2 diabetes is so strong that most Type 2 diabetics are obese.[12] This relationship explains why Type 2 diabetes is so common among Americans—obesity is very prevalent and therefore so is diabetes.

Consistent with the research linking body fat to diabetes, much evidence suggests that activity levels are related to insulin levels and the presence of Type 2 diabetes. Studies have shown that men who are physically fit are much less likely to develop Type 2 diabetes later in life.[13] In addition, several studies with particular ethnic populations have shown that when one subset of the population exercises a lot and another subset exercises little, the latter group is much more likely to develop Type 2 diabetes.[14] In fact, decreased exercise, along with an increased percentage of body fat as opposed to muscle, may explain why elderly people tend to be more insulin resistant.[15] You may be getting quite tired by now of my repeated mentions of exercise as an important factor in maintaining lifelong health, but I can assure you that I write only what the data compel me to report!

There's also evidence that your genes play a role in whether you develop Type 2 diabetes. To begin with, it's possible to breed mice that lack a particular gene and, as a result, have increased insulin sensitivity and are less likely to be obese.[16] In people, if one identical twin has Type 2 diabetes, the other twin has a greater than 90% chance of developing it.[17] In recent years, researchers have been able to identify at least 10 different genes that seem to contribute to whether or not someone develops diabetes.[18] Of course, as you already know from the preceding paragraphs, genes by themselves are insufficient to cause Type 2 diabetes. People who exercise a lot, who are thin, and who eat predominantly low glycemic index foods are unlikely to develop diabetes no matter what their genetic makeup. However, unfortunately, Americans who live this way are rare indeed.

You may wonder why on earth it would be advantageous for people to have genes that inclined them toward diabetes in the first place. Why would we have evolved to have such genes? Why would people with such genes have been more likely to survive and reproduce than other people? One explanation is what's known as the thrifty gene hypothesis. According to a version of this theory, having a quick, large insulin response was very useful in surroundings in which food was often scarce.

Insulin, as you'll recall, facilitates the storage of what you eat as fat. When food is scarce, having stored fat helps you to survive. It's thought, for example, that for centuries the Arizona Pima Indians experienced regular periods of famine, so that the only Pimas who survived were those who released much insulin and had high tendencies to store fat. However, when food is plentiful, as it is now for the Pimas, storing lots of fat isn't so good, and much insulin is produced, ultimately leading to insulin resistance and Type 2 diabetes.[19] In fact, among the Arizona Pimas, the frequency of Type 2 diabetes is among the highest of any group in the world.[20] Once again, we see a mismatch between our bodies and our current surroundings, resulting in serious medical concerns.

Sweet and Low: How Type 2 Diabetes Affects Behavior

People and other animals with untreated diabetes behave differently than nondiabetics. Some of these characteristic behaviors are easily observable and can therefore be helpful in diagnosing diabetes. For example, diabetics tend to feel tired. They also drink and urinate frequently.[21] The high levels of blood sugar in diabetics result in unusually high levels of sugar in the urine. This, in turn, causes extra water to be drawn into the urine in order to dilute the unusually high sugar concentration in the urine. Thus there's more volume to the urine, more water is lost from the body, thirst increases, and the diabetic drinks excessively.[22]

Some aspects of diabetics' eating behaviors can help scientists to understand eating behaviors in the general population. Researchers reported some time ago that people eat more when insulin levels are high than when they're low.[23] Based on these results, you would expect diabetics, who have low insulin levels, to eat relatively little, even of the sugary foods on which many people gorge. However, people with diabetes can still eat very large amounts when sugary foods are available. Such observations lead scientists to believe that the eating of large amounts of sugary foods by the general population isn't due to high insulin levels.[24]

Not only amount eaten, but what's eaten, may be affected by diabetes. When a flavor is paired with glucose infused into rats' stomachs, diabetic rats subsequently develop less preference for the flavor than nondiabetic rats. This finding suggests that the release of insulin that normally occurs when glucose is eaten, but does not occur in diabetics, is necessary in order for this type of food preference to develop.[25] How such processes might or might not affect the food preferences of people with diabetes hasn't yet been investigated.

Another possible explanation for why diabetics and nondiabetics might show different food preferences concerns taste sensitivity. In general, diabetics are less sensitive to a variety of tastes, including the taste of glucose, than nondiabetics. The longer that someone has been diabetic, and the more medical complications that someone has had from diabetes, the more likely that person is to have taste deficits. These taste deficits may result from nerve damage due to long-term high blood sugar levels.[26] It's possible that the decreased sweet-taste sensitivity results in diabetics eating sweeter foods so that they'll still be able to taste sweet, but this thereby exacerbates their diabetes. Clearly we need research concerning how diabetics' taste deficits may affect the kinds of foods that they eat.

Given the many physiological effects of diabetes, it will probably not surprise you that diabetics' cognitive functions, such as their abilities to learn a list of symbol–number pairs, are also compromised by this disease. Similarly, declines in cognitive functioning are significantly more likely in elderly people with diabetes.[27] In fact, the high and irregular blood sugar levels associated with diabetes can themselves result in disturbances in cognition. Unfortunately, these cognitive problems can interfere with diabetics' abilities to participate in the diabetes treatments that I'll describe in the next section.[28]

The Sweet Smell of Success: Treatments

As you can see, diabetes is a truly devastating, and all too prevalent, disease. However, there's good news: There are many different, helpful treatments for Type 2 diabetes. (See Conversation Making Fact #12.) Combined, these treatments seem to be making a significant dent in the negative consequences of diabetes. As an example, since 1990 heart attacks in diabetics have declined 68%, as compared to 31% in nondiabetics.[29] Some of the treatments now being used are ones in which a diabetic can engage with minimal medical assistance, or none at all. Others require extensive medical monitoring and support.

Conversation making fact #12

Diabetes, although sometimes difficult to manage, doesn't have to interfere with your life, even if you're very active. Gary Hall, Jr., a world-class Swimmer, has Type 1 diabetes—similar to Type 2 in that there's insufficient insulin, but usually arising at younger ages largely due to genetic causes.[30] Yet despite his disease, Hall won two gold medals, one silver, and one bronze at the 2000 Sydney Olympics. He was diagnosed with diabetes in the years leading up to summer 2000. After his diagnosis, three doctors told him that he could never again compete. However, he found another doctor who worked closely with him and, with the proper care, he was able to triumph.[31]

Given that most patients with Type 2 diabetes are obese,[32] and given that obesity has been thought to be a major cause of Type 2 diabetes, one of the first recommendations that any physician will give a Type 2 diabetic is to lose weight. There's no question that weight loss by itself will very frequently remove the symptoms of Type 2 diabetes. In fact, some researchers believe that a weight loss of as little as 7–10% of body weight may reap significant benefits.[33] But, as described in Chapter 10, losing weight isn't easy, and keeping it off is even harder. Thus, by itself, weight loss is unlikely to serve very many Type 2 diabetics as an effective long-term treatment.

As you've heard so many times in this book, exercise can help us lose weight and then keep the lost weight off, whether we're diabetic or not. However, exercise may have benefits with respect to diabetes that are independent of weight loss. An experiment with middle-aged men showed that 9 weeks of an aerobic exercise program, even with no accompanying weight loss, increased their insulin sensitivity.[34] Another experiment with Type 2 diabetic men and women of varying ages showed that 3 months of a program of aerobic exercise, again even with no weight loss, decreased their need for insulin.[35] A combination of aerobic and resistance training, as opposed to either alone, may be the most effective method for inducing such effects.[36] These effects may be related to changes in the amount of muscle in the experiments' participants. Although the participants' weights didn't change, their bodies may have gained muscle and lost fat. As you know, diabetes is more likely to occur the more body fat you have. Such factors may also be related to the greater tendency of Type 2 diabetes to develop in older people because they tend to have more fat and less muscle. Given this reasoning, it should be possible to help prevent diabetes in elderly people by ensuring that they participate in exercise throughout their lives.[37] Consistent with all of this research, sedentary people are more likely to develop diabetes, and men with Type 2 diabetes are more likely to die if they're physically inactive.[38]

Changing what you eat can also help treat diabetes. As you've already learned in this chapter, the probability of developing diabetes increases if someone eats many foods that have a high glycemic index score—foods that quickly increase blood sugar levels, for example soda, ice cream, and chocolate cake. Thus it shouldn't be surprising that eating in the opposite way, that is, eating foods that don't quickly increase blood sugar levels— high-fiber foods such as beans, whole-wheat bread, and oranges—may help normalize blood sugar levels and control diabetes.[39] In fact, research does indicate that an increase in fiber intake can help diabetics control their blood sugar levels.[40]

When attempts to lose weight, exercise, and change what's eaten are insufficient to control someone's diabetes, the next alternative is drugs. Approximately one-third of Type 2 diabetics use oral medication to help control their diabetes. Many drugs are available for this purpose, and the number and variety of drugs are constantly increasing. For example, some drugs cause the pancreas to release more insulin, some decrease blood sugar levels without affecting insulin levels, and some decrease the rate of carbohydrate digestion.[41] As more is learned about the complex relationships among what's eaten, insulin levels, and diabetes, there are more opportunities for developing new drugs to treat diabetes, drugs that intervene at particular points in these relationships.[42] For instance, consider the experiment with mice described earlier in which mice lacking a certain gene didn't gain weight and remained sensitive to insulin, even when they ate a lot of fat. These findings suggest that it may be possible to treat Type 2 diabetes by blocking the effects of a particular gene.[43]

When other, less interventionist, methods are unsuccessful, insulin injections are used to control Type 2 diabetes. Patients learn to monitor their blood sugar levels very carefully and to inject appropriate amounts of insulin. Approximately one-third of Type 2 diabetics have to do this.[44] Yet even here there's some good news. Diabetics need not repeatedly test their blood and then stick insulin needles into their bodies each day. There are now small insulin pumps combined with continuous blood sugar level sensors that are the size of a pager and can be worn on a waistband. A thin plastic tube carries insulin from the pump to where a needle is inserted into the diabetic's abdomen. Another needle detects blood sugar level. These needles need to be changed only once every few days. This combination device functions as, essentially, an artificial pancreas. Though they can be expensive, insulin pumps are becoming increasingly popular as diabetics and their physicians learn about them and how easy they are to wear.[45] I recently went on a group cycling trip in India, and one member of the group was an extremely impressive young woman, about to graduate high school, who wore an insulin pump on her bike shorts as she adeptly navigated the hills and the herds of wandering cows.

When even insulin injections can't control a diabetic's blood sugar levels, there is one final treatment that is extremely successful for Type 2 diabetics: gastric bypass (and related) surgery (see Chapter 10). Following such surgeries there is often complete remission of the patient's diabetes, independent of weight loss, and continuing for years following the surgery.[46] Why this happens is not yet completely understood, but the positive results are apparently quite robust.

All of these methods for treating Type 2 diabetes involve diabetics performing certain specific behaviors, whether those behaviors consist of eating different foods, exercising, taking medication, or injecting insulin. Often the issue is not whether these treatments work (they do), but is whether diabetics will engage in the appropriate behaviors. Having someone provide professional or even nonprofessional support to the diabetic can be very helpful in this regard, resulting in increased quality of life for the diabetic.[47]

However, there's a sobering note in this story. Although there are many good treatments for diabetes, not everyone hears about them, and not everyone is given advice about what they should do to prevent Type 2 diabetes. These people tend to be poor and less educated. Such people see doctors less often, and even when they do, they are less likely to get the good medical advice that wealthier, more educated people receive.[48] People may not receive the same *quality* of medical care even when they receive the same *quantity* of medical care.

Parting is Such Sweet Sorrow: Conclusion

Diabetes, particularly Type 2 diabetes, is a prevalent disease with extremely serious consequences. What you eat and how you maintain—or don't maintain—your weight have a lot to do with whether you develop Type 2 diabetes, as well as with whether you effectively treat it. Once more we can see that our current surroundings, as opposed to the surroundings in which we evolved, have done us in. In the surroundings in which we evolved, there were few high glycemic index foods, our ancestors had to move around a fair amount in their daily lives, and Type 2 diabetes was extremely rare. Now the incidence of Type 2 diabetes in the United States, and in many other countries, is huge. Yet we should take heart because there are ways to avoid or remove this disease. Medical professionals should work closely with susceptible populations not only to treat, but to prevent diabetes. We all have a responsibility to do what we can to ensure that those around us eat and exercise in ways that promote everyone's health.

13

STRICTLY ABOUT FEMALES

The primary ways in which females reliably differ from males have to do with reproduction. In mammals the female produces an egg that is fertilized and nurtured within her body until the fetus is capable of surviving in the outside world. After birth, for periods ranging from weeks to years, young mammals continue to depend mainly on their mothers' milk for food. This chapter concerns the ways in which female mammalian reproduction affects what's eaten, as well as the ways in which what's eaten affects female mammalian reproduction. I'll focus on the female mammals of greatest concern to most of us: girls and women.

Just because this chapter focuses on females doesn't mean that there's no relationship between eating and male mammalian reproduction. It's possible, for example, that eating too little or the wrong things might affect semen quality. In fact, there's some recent research indicating that this is indeed the case.[1] However, such research is rare. In contrast, research on the relationships between eating and female mammalian reproduction abounds.

It's not surprising that researchers have concentrated on how food and female mammalian reproduction affect each other. The female mammal is the ultimate provider of food to the young both during pregnancy and immediately after birth. This early nutritive relationship is critical to the survival of the offspring. For an infant to survive, the infant's mother must obtain adequate food for herself until the infant is old enough to be weaned.

Thus survival of the woman results in survival of her offspring as well. This means that conception shouldn't occur unless there's a high probability that there will be sufficient food to sustain the woman and her offspring throughout pregnancy and lactation. And this means that women's bodies should have evolved such that their reproductive functions and their eating and drinking behaviors are closely related. For example, given this reasoning you would predict that women should store more fat on their bodies than men, thus enabling women not only to survive but to reproduce during the frequent periods of food scarcity that occurred throughout our evolutionary history. Research supports this prediction: The average percentage of total body weight that consists of fat is 27% for young adult women but is 15% for young adult men.[2]

You'll encounter the evolutionary theme again and again throughout this chapter as we cover menstruation, pregnancy, and lactation. There are many ways in which eating and female reproduction evolved so as to ensure that as many offspring survive as possible.

Curses, Fed Again!

The menstrual cycle, which my friends and I called "the curse" when we were growing up, plays an essential role in human reproduction. There are a number of physical changes that occur during the menstrual cycle, including the release of an egg and the preparation of the uterine lining for the implantation and subsequent growth of an embryo and fetus. However, in addition to ovulation, the menstrual cycle can also involve changes in what and how a woman eats. There can be influence in the other direction as well: What a woman eats can affect her menstrual cycle.

Let's begin with how the menstrual cycle can influence what a woman eats. Many women report cravings for particular foods, notably high-carbohydrate, high-fat, and chocolate foods, in the part of the menstrual cycle just prior to menstruation.[3] If these cravings are regularly accompanied by a number of other symptoms, such as depression, anxiety, and irritability, the woman is said to suffer from premenstrual dysphoric disorder, or, when the symptoms aren't as extensive, premenstrual syndrome (PMS).[4] There has been much discussion about what causes these food cravings.

One possible explanation is based on the fact that basal metabolic rate is significantly higher during the luteal phase of the menstrual cycle,[5] the 2 weeks prior to menstruation. (Figure 13.1 gives a precise definition of the luteal phase.) You learned in previous chapters that people and other animals eat more when they're expending more calories. Therefore it shouldn't surprise you that women eat more calories during the luteal phase.[6] Remember also from previous chapters that people learn to prefer high-calorie foods when they're hungry. Therefore you would also expect that a woman would prefer high-calorie foods (such as chocolate) during the luteal phase.

However, there may be a problem with this explanation. There's evidence that the increased number of calories eaten by women during the luteal phase can be greater than the increased calories that they burn up at that time: Energy expenditure has been found to be 8–20% higher in the luteal phase than prior to ovulation, but energy intake (i.e., calories eaten) has been found to be 10–30% higher during the luteal phase than

DAY   1   2   3   4   5   6   7   8   9   10 11 12 13 14 15 16 17 18 19 20 21 22 23 24 25 26 27 28   1   2   3   4   5

Figure 13.1 A normal menstrual cycle. The first day of menstruation counts as day 1 of a cycle. During the follicular phase, in this example days 6–13, a follicle containing an egg develops in the ovary. At the time of ovulation, here occurring on day 14, the follicle ruptures, thus releasing the mature egg and allowing conception to occur. During the subsequent luteal phase (days 15–28 in this figure), the follicle, which has remained in the ovary, becomes the corpus luteum and secretes several hormones that prepare the uterine lining for implantation of the fertilized egg (should conception occur). If conception does not occur, as in the present example, menstruation and a new cycle begin. (Adapted from M. P. Warren, "Reproductive Endocrinology," in *Handbook of Behavioral Medicine for Women*, eds. E. A. Blechman and K. D. Brownell, New York: Pergamon, 1988.)

prior to ovulation.[7] Therefore, compensating for extra energy expenditure can't be the sole explanation of premenstrual food cravings. Nevertheless, if you think about this situation in the context of our evolving in surroundings with inadequate food supplies, consuming extra calories in the luteal phase might not be such a bad idea. These extra calories would be stored in the woman's body as fat. Then, if conception should occur, there would be an increased chance that the woman and her offspring would survive.

Another explanation of premenstrual food cravings is related to the carbohydrate craving seen in people with seasonal affective disorder (SAD) and in obese carbohydrate cravers, both discussed in Chapter 10. Similar to people with SAD (whose symptoms tend to be worst in the winter) and obese carbohydrate cravers (whose symptoms tend to be worst at certain times of the day), women with PMS experience cyclical symptoms. In addition, people with each of these disorders crave carbohydrates, and these cravings can be suppressed by drugs that increase the level of the neurotransmitter serotonin in the brain. For these reasons psychologists Richard J. Wurtman and Judith J. Wurtman have hypothesized that PMS, as well as SAD and obesity due to carbohydrate craving, are caused or aggravated by insufficient levels of serotonin in the brain. Serotonin levels are affected by the earth's light–dark cycle, thus explaining the periodicity of all three disorders. According to the Wurtmans, when people with these disorders eat carbohydrates, their serotonin levels increase, as do their feelings of well being.[8] Not all scientists avidly adopt this theory, however. More research is needed showing that low serotonin levels are specifically responsible for premenstrual food cravings.

Another approach to explaining premenstrual food cravings involves looking to see if there are any changes in taste or smell sensitivity across the menstrual cycle. Such changes, if they exist, might explain why women's reported cravings change across the menstrual cycle. There hasn't been a great deal of research in this area. One study found no changes in sweet preference as a function of menstrual cycle phase.[9] In contrast, it has been fairly well established that sensitivity to smells increases around the time of ovulation. This may be a side effect of a mechanism designed to increase the probability of conception. Around the time of ovulation, mucus secretions in a woman's body, including those around the cervix and the olfactory epithelium (the tissue up inside your nose that detects odors), become thinner. This may make it easier for the sperm to reach the egg, and it also makes it easier for the woman to detect odors.[10] Perhaps this increased odor sensitivity makes the woman more likely to eat her favorite foods. Again, more research is needed to be sure.

For yet more insights into premenstrual food cravings, let's examine two particular cases: women taking contraceptives and women who have entered menopause. Are their food cravings different from women experiencing normal menstrual cycles? It appears that, in both cases, in comparison to women with normal cycles, cravings either decrease only slightly or don't decrease at all.[11] These findings suggest that, whatever is going on with cravings and the menstrual cycle, the cravings aren't entirely hormonally based.

Now let's consider the flip side of the coin: How might what you eat affect your menstrual cycle? All of the information on this topic flows from the fact that a woman needs approximately 50,000 to 80,000 calories in order to produce a full-term baby.[12] Anything less is likely to result in an underweight, or perhaps even nonviable, baby. From an evolutionary standpoint, producing a substandard offspring would be a waste of the woman's energy, and therefore should be avoided if at all possible. If the woman can't get enough food to produce a healthy infant, then she shouldn't even conceive. Given this reasoning, it's not surprising that inadequate food will disrupt the menstrual cycle and inhibit ovulation.[13] Even simply eating with restraint—eating less than you want—has been associated with menstrual irregularity.[14] This fact was noted in Chapter 9, where I pointed out that anorexics don't menstruate. (Hence the title of the present section: "Curses, Fed Again!") Consistent with these findings, excessive feeding may hasten puberty. Young girls seem to be initiating breast development at earlier ages—an average of 9–10 years, and the explanation may be the increased weight of girls in this age group.[15]

There have been two competing hypotheses as to the mechanism that causes food deprivation to disrupt ovulation.[16] Scientist Rose E. Frisch proposed that what's critical is the woman's percentage of body fat.[17] Women's bodies can't make female hormones such as estrogen and progesterone without fat.[18] Humanity's first artistic expressions seemed to recognize this link between fatness and fertility with such pieces of art as the 22,000-year-old figurine of a very heavy female known as the Venus of Willendorf.[19]

Psychologists Jill E. Schneider and George N. Wade proposed an alternative hypothesis—that what's important for ovulation to occur is the general availability of fuel. Fatty acids metabolized from stored fat are only one component of this available fuel. Also important is the glucose obtained from what's eaten.[20] This hypothesis can help to explain why nonovulating women who have had inadequate food for a long period of time will resume ovulating if given adequate food for a relatively short period.[21]

An interesting question that doesn't yet have a clear answer is how the effects of exercise on menstruation fit into this controversy. Exercise can apparently contribute to menstrual irregularity. Women who exercise a great deal sometimes have lower hormone levels, or even stop menstruating, as well as having fewer premenstrual symptoms.[22] However, we don't know whether exercise is exerting its effect by inducing an energy deficit and decreasing the percentage of body fat, or if exercise is exerting an effect that is independent of the effects of amount of food eaten and percentage of body fat.[23] It's possible that all three factors—amount of food eaten, amount of stored fat, and exercise level—play a role in menstrual regularity.

Even if we assume that all three factors are involved in menstrual regularity, we still don't know what level of any of these three factors is needed before fertility is impaired. Obviously, if a woman eats so little, exercises so much, or becomes so thin that she has no menstrual cycle, reproduction cannot occur. But isn't it possible that eating a bit more, exercising a bit less, or having a bit more body fat might be enough for menstruation to continue, but not enough for ovulation to occur properly? There's laboratory evidence supporting this possibility in hamsters. One experiment gave six hamsters 50% of their usual food intake for 4 days, the length of one estrous cycle (now you know why hamsters can multiply their numbers so quickly). Despite the fact that the hamsters were only partially deprived of food and that this partial deprivation lasted for only 4 days, one of the hamsters didn't ovulate at all and the number of eggs released by each of the other hamsters decreased from an average of 11 to an average of 9.[24]

If it's indeed the case that partial food deprivation inhibits fertility in women, this raises a host of concerns. Some women are chronic dieters, and so may have chronically low metabolic rates, forcing them to eat small amounts even when not dieting in order not to gain weight. Other women will eat very little at breakfast and lunch in order to eat a large dinner at a restaurant in the evening. In addition, some 60% of American women try at least one weight-reduction diet each year, and approximately one-third of American women between the ages of 19 and 39—the prime reproductive years—diet at least once per month.[25] Perhaps all such women are at risk for impaired fertility. Some studies suggest that relatively brief, partial limitations in food at the time of conception can lead to premature birth.[26] And impaired fertility, including menstrual irregularity, isn't the only negative consequence of this behavior. When women diet it's very hard for them to obtain sufficient amounts of essential nutrients such as iron. If it wasn't already abundantly clear from earlier chapters, now you should truly understand that cutting back on calories can have many deleterious effects.

Some additional thoughts before we leave the curse, or rather, after we leave it. How do all of these relationships among eating, hormones, and metabolic rate change after women reach menopause? Let's focus first on metabolic rate. It has only been in the last 25 years that scientists have realized that metabolic rate is higher during the luteal phase of the menstrual cycle. I remember this vividly because I'd suspected for a long time that this was the case; I'd found it easier to lose or maintain my weight in the luteal phase, and wondered if hormonal effects at that time might help to counteract the decreased metabolic rate that often accompanies dieting. I can't tell you how brilliant I felt when researchers confirmed my hypothesis. Now that I've reached that certain age among women, along with many other baby boomers, I'm wondering about menopause. As of yet, no reliable investigations have been done on the metabolic rates of women after menopause. It's possible that, lacking any luteal phases, postmenopausal women may have very low metabolic rates and for that reason be more likely to gain weight. But can regular exercise prevent this from happening? And what does hormonal replacement therapy have to do with metabolic rate, if anything? We just don't know yet. Perhaps, though, by continuing to observe myself I can again obtain information that anticipates the research findings!

Finally, the subject of eating can even help to explain why menopause exists at all. For many years scientists wondered what possible evolutionary advantage there could be to women living long after they could reproduce, what advantage there could be to the many postmenopausal years. Now there's evidence from groups of people living without the trappings of modern civilization indicating that reproductive women who have postmenopausal women (that is, grandmothers) assisting them in obtaining food are more likely to have many healthy children.[27] Having a grandmother can definitely be an advantage.

Eating and Drinking for Two: Pregnancy

A variety of changes take place in a woman's body once conception has occurred. Once again, many of these changes are directed at survival of the fetus: The fetus must get adequate nutrition—either from what the woman eats or from what's stored in her body, or both. However, although what a woman eats or drinks during pregnancy usually has positive effects on the embryo and fetus, some things, when eaten or drunk, can do severe damage. In this section I'll first consider how a woman's food preferences and food aversions may change during pregnancy. Then I'll focus on the relationships between pregnancy and weight gain. Finally, I'll look at how food and drink consumed by the mother may adversely impact her fetus.

Preferences, cravings, and aversions

Who hasn't heard about the food preferences and cravings that pregnant women reputedly evidence? Ice cream, pickles, you name it. Surveys show that some women do indeed develop specific food cravings during pregnancy. The cravings may be for high-calorie foods such as ice cream. However, some food cravings are for low-calorie foods such as fruit or vinegar. Pregnant women may even crave eating such items as clay and earth.[28]

Various explanations have been proposed for all of these sorts of food cravings. When the cravings are for high-calorie foods such as ice cream, it's possible to invoke the energy deficit explanation used to account for the high-calorie food cravings sometimes seen during the luteal phase of the menstrual cycle. As in the luteal phase, metabolic rate is relatively high during pregnancy.[29] The fetus imposes additional caloric requirements on pregnant women. Therefore you would expect pregnant women to show an increased preference for high-calorie foods. Other explanations for the food cravings in pregnancy include the detoxifying properties of clay that may make its consumption advantageous to pregnant women and the increased release of special, natural, narcotic-like chemicals in pregnant women's bodies.[30]

Other changes in women's bodies during pregnancy may also affect what they do and don't want to eat. During pregnancy there are changes in the digestive tract. For example, increased amounts of the small intestine chemical cholecystokinin (CCK), important in digestion, are released, particularly during the first trimester. The increased CCK contributes to the sleepiness felt by women at this time and, because the increased CCK slows the passage of food through the intestinal tract, it also contributes to the nausea and vomiting experienced by over 25% of women during the first trimester,[31] so-called morning sickness. This may explain why some women find high-fat foods aversive at this time. High-fat foods pass more slowly through the digestive tract than low-fat ones.[32] Increased sensitivity to odors has also been hypothesized to contribute to morning sickness.[33]

You might think that morning sickness would be bad for the fetus because the pregnant woman eats less and often vomits. However, some scientists believe that the opposite is actually the case. Scientist Margie Profet hypothesized that morning sickness, with its associated increased odor and food sensitivities and food aversions, increases the survival of the fetus. She proposed that these reactions decrease the amounts that the pregnant woman eats of bitter foods and foods with pungent odors, foods that may be toxic for the fetus even in small amounts. In support of this hypothesis, Profet pointed to the fact that women who vomit during early pregnancy or who feel severely nauseated are less likely to miscarry.[34] However, it's important to remember that such hypotheses, as intriguing and appealing as they may be, are based only on suggestive evidence. There is as yet no evidence showing a causal link between morning sickness and miscarriage.

I hope that this discussion of morning sickness reminds you of what you read about one of the most powerful forms of learning, taste aversion learning, in Chapter 6. You should recall that, with this form of learning, people and other animals can acquire long-lasting aversions to foods whose consumption has been followed only once by nausea. Furthermore, these aversions can form whether the illness was actually caused by the food or not. What if the nausea and vomiting of morning sickness become accidentally paired with specific foods so that taste aversions occur? Women do retrospectively report a significant correlation between when they felt sick during pregnancy and when they developed food aversions. Taste aversion learning may help to explain some of the food aversions of pregnant women. However, we need more detailed study of women during their pregnancies in order to confirm or refute this hypothesis.[35]

You may be very surprised to discover that morning sickness can affect the food preferences of not only the pregnant woman, but also her resulting offspring. Women who experience a great deal of vomiting during their pregnancies are more likely to have offspring who, both as babies and as adults, prefer salt more than the offspring of mothers who experienced little vomiting during their pregnancies. One possible explanation is that the increased salt preference is somehow related to the mothers becoming dehydrated as a result of their vomiting.[36]

Causes and effects of weight gain

Despite their food aversions and relatively high metabolic rates, pregnant women do manage to gain weight. Even in the first trimester women's fat stores increase. This increase can't be due to a greater amount of food eaten during that period. Instead, it's probably another effect of the increased CCK release during the first trimester.[37] Clearly, during human evolution, a tendency for pregnant women to store consumed food as fat, particularly at a time when eating is sometimes inhibited by nausea, would have increased the probability of survival of the mother and her infant. The stored fat is there to help sustain the mother and her fetus if food supplies are inadequate or if the mother becomes ill.

Nevertheless, weight gain is a major concern of many pregnant women. They fear that too much weight will be gained and that not all of that weight will be lost once the baby is born. On average, women gain 33 pounds during pregnancy, of which about 9 pounds consists of stored fat.[38] The Institute of Medicine recommends that a woman gain different amounts during pregnancy depending on how heavy she is for her height—a weight gain of 25–35 pounds for a woman whose weight for her height is average, but more if she's pregnant with twins.[39] Women frequently name pregnancy as contributing to weight gain over their lifetimes.[40] In fact, there is some evidence that pregnant women who gain more than the Institute of Medicine recommends will have an increased weight decades later.[41] However, this research doesn't prove that pregnancy causes subsequent obesity. Perhaps some women are inclined to gain weight throughout their lifetimes—both during pregnancy and after. Again, we need more research to see exactly what is causing what.

Now let's consider how what pregnant women eat and weigh can affect their babies. First, what happens if the woman doesn't eat very much and doesn't gain very much weight? One effect is simply that the resulting infant will weigh too little, which puts such an infant at risk.[42] One study found that teenagers who didn't gain enough during their pregnancies ate about 1,878 calories per day while pregnant, while those who did gain enough weight ate about 2,232 calories per day; and teenagers who didn't gain enough weight were more likely to have low birth weight babies.[43]

There can be additional adverse effects on their offspring when pregnant women gain insufficient amounts of weight. Multiple studies have now shown that severe malnutrition in areas as disparate as the Netherlands (during World War II), Biafra (during the 1967–1970 famine), India (during the famine 100 years ago), and in the current slums of Brazil have resulted in offspring who not only weigh less when they are born, but are more inclined to be obese and develop diabetes as adults. Researchers now believe that the malnutrition during pregnancy actually changes how the offspring's genes are expressed, making the offspring more likely to later gain weight and develop diabetes. Further, these changes are heritable, meaning that grandchildren of the malnourished pregnant woman will also show these effects[44]—more evidence that obesity does not necessarily represent a lapse in self-control on the part of the obese person. Malnutrition during pregnancy is also associated with more daughters than sons being born, and with the offspring having a greater tendency to be schizophrenic.[45] Which is all to say that pregnant women should take care to gain sufficient amounts of weight, and certainly not to pick that period as a time to diet.

What if a woman is very heavy during pregnancy or gains large amounts of weight? Women who have experienced unreliable food sources in the past, and who have been trying to control their weight, are particularly likely to gain much weight during pregnancy.[46] And if a woman gains a lot of weight during pregnancy, and does not already have Type 2 diabetes, such a woman is more likely to develop gestational diabetes, a problem in approximately 2–10% of all pregnancies. Gestational diabetes is similar to Type 2 diabetes (see Chapter 12) and is due to placental hormones interfering with the function of a pregnant woman's insulin. Pregnant women with gestational diabetes have more cravings for sweet foods during the last part of pregnancy. Further, babies born to women with diabetes tend to be very large at birth, so large that their delivery can be difficult or even dangerous for their mothers unless delivery is by caesarean section. In addition, such babies may be born with malformations of the spinal cord or the brain.[47] In fact, such defects are more likely to occur in offspring of overweight pregnant women, even if they don't have diabetes.[48] Clearly it's extremely important for a pregnant woman's blood sugar level, in addition to her weight, to be monitored closely and kept as close to normal limits as possible for the duration of her pregnancy.

When eating or drinking harms or helps

Probably the best known, and certainly one of the most devastating, effects on a fetus of what the mother eats or drinks is fetal alcohol syndrome (FAS). This syndrome consists of a number of specific physiological and behavioral changes that can occur in the offspring of women who drink alcohol while pregnant. First, the facial appearance of a child born with FAS is different from that of a normal child. The head circumference and nose are smaller, the nasal bridge is lower, and the upper lip is thinner than those of a non-FAS infant. The FAS infant also has folds of skin at the inside corners of the eyes that are absent in normal infants. These external physical characteristics remain as the child ages, but may be less prominent. (See Figure 13.2.) The brains of FAS infants and adults are smaller than the brains of non-FAS infants and adults. As FAS infants age, it becomes apparent that their intelligence is significantly below average. FAS infants and adults also tend to be hyperactive, depressed, distractible,

Figure 13.2 Physical appearance of three children with FAS (fetal alcohol syndrome). Copyright 1980 American Association for the Advancement of Science. (Reprinted with permission from A. P. Streissguth, S. Landesman-Dwyer, J. C. Martin, and D. W. Smith, "Teratogenic Effects of Alcohol in Humans and Laboratory Animals," *Science* 209[1980]: 353–361.)

irritable, and impulsive and to show poor coordination, memory, spatial ability, and arithmetic ability.[49]

We don't yet know precisely why maternal drinking during pregnancy has such terrible effects on the offspring, though we do have some clues. The arteries and veins in isolated human umbilical cords have been shown to contract and spasm when exposed to a concentration of alcohol equivalent to that in the blood of a pregnant woman 30 minutes after ingesting one to one and a half drinks of 100-proof whiskey. Such an effect deprives a fetus of essential oxygenated blood.[50] Experiments with fetal rats near term and with very young rat pups have shown that exposure to alcohol can kill millions of brain cells in particular parts of the brain.[51]

So far, most of what I've said about alcohol and pregnancy isn't very controversial. What's controversial is just how much alcohol a pregnant woman has to drink, and when, in order for FAS and other negative consequences to occur. How much is safe? One recent study of women who had at least four drinks per day during pregnancy found negative neurological effects in almost all of the children (e.g., decreased intelligence, language delay, and increased hyperactivity), even though the great majority of the children didn't have the facial features of FAS.[52] In addition, it's now believed that even social drinking causes deleterious effects on the fetus. The more alcohol that is drunk, the worse the effects on the fetus.[53] One study consistently found deleterious effects of alcohol on the offspring of women who drank an average of about one and a half drinks per day before they found out they were pregnant, and an average of about one drink every 2 days after, and another found lower IQs in children of mothers who consumed just one to six drinks per week during pregnancy.[54] Further, it appears that even alcohol drunk in the very earliest part of pregnancy, in the month before the woman realizes she is pregnant, can be harmful to the fetus.[55]

Therefore it now appears that the Surgeon General's and the National Institute on Alcohol Abuse and Alcoholism's recommendations in the 1980s that pregnant women should drink no alcohol, which was controversial at the time, were very likely wise recommendations.[56] In considering these recommendations, it's important to keep in mind that, due to differences between men's and women's bodies, the same amount of alcohol may result in a higher blood alcohol level and more brain damage in a woman than a man, even though the man and the woman are the same height and weight.[57] So, we have progressed from FAS not even being known in 1970 to, beginning in 1989, the government requiring warnings to pregnant women on all alcoholic beverage labels.[58]

This is very serious stuff. Millions of American women have alcohol-related problems, and many, many more don't have problems but don't abstain (see Chapter 11). After learning that they're pregnant, about 10% of women drink at least occasionally, and some much more than that. Many more drink until they find out that they're pregnant. Even with all of the current warnings, in the United States about 1–2 babies out of every 1,000 born have full blown FAS, and many more have less obvious deleterious effects of alcohol.[59]

In addition to alcohol, there have been concerns about many other potentially harmful substances that a pregnant woman consumes. One prime target of such concerns has been caffeine. However, the most recent consensus is consuming moderate amounts of caffeine during pregnancy is not harmful.[60] On the other hand, mental retardation can result in a fetus if the mother consumes fish contaminated with the toxic chemical methylmercury.[61] Pregnant women should eat and drink with caution. Medical consultation and nutritional counseling early in pregnancy are clearly extremely important. If all of the pregnant women in the United States ate and drank properly, the benefits to our society and economy in terms of healthier, better functioning children who became healthier, better functioning adults would be enormous.

Before we leave the inside of the womb, I'd be remiss if I didn't mention what goes on with the fetus's own eating and drinking behaviors. That's right, I'm talking about ingestion by the fetus. You already know that right after a fetus ceases being a fetus, right after she or he is born and is classified as an infant, that infant can taste sweet and shows a preference for it. It turns out that the taste cells of the fetus acquire their final structure at about the fourteenth week of pregnancy. Furthermore, beginning at about the twelfth week of pregnancy, a fetus swallows amniotic fluid. By the end of pregnancy, a fetus may be swallowing over three cups per day. Such behavior may actually be important in keeping the amount of amniotic fluid within a reasonable range. While all of this swallowing is going on, a fetus actually senses chemicals present in the amniotic fluid. Amniotic fluid contains a wide range of chemicals including sugars, fats, and proteins. The relative amounts of these different chemicals can change significantly during the course of a pregnancy, including right after a fetus urinates. (Now you didn't think that the first time a baby ever urinated was right after it was born, did you? A fetus swallows liquids while in the womb and so it also urinates there.) It has been shown that 4-day-old bottle-fed infants prefer the odors of amniotic fluid to the odors of formula or distilled water, suggesting that familiarity with amniotic fluid results in a long-lasting preference for it. Further, we now know that what a pregnant woman eats affects the chemicals present in the amniotic fluid, and thereby can affect the offspring's later food preferences.[62] An experiment with rats demonstrated that if a pregnant rat is infused with alcohol, her pups will consume more alcohol when they are adults.[63]

Before we progress to breastfeeding, there's one last bit of pregnancy-associated eating behavior that I should mention: placentophagy (i.e., a mother eating her placenta after delivery). For reasons that are not yet totally clear, most mammalian species (except people) regularly engage in placentophagy. One possible explanation is that the placenta contains many nutrients that would provide a survival advantage to a female that has just given birth and is starting to lactate. Perhaps such an explanation might also account for why this behavior isn't widespread among people—many women have adequate nutrition such that they don't need the nutrients in the placenta. Nevertheless, some enterprising individuals are promoting postpartum placenta consumption as a way to prevent or cure many psychological ills in newly delivered mothers. However, there is not yet evidence to support most of these claims.[64]

The Essence of Mammalhood: Breast Feeding

Women who choose to breast feed are well aware of the importance of this task for the survival of their infants. As psychologist Peter Wright has stated, "The overriding concern of all mothers, once they have established that their newborn baby is alive and well, is the establishment of a successful feeding relationship."[65] However, breast-feeding mothers may not realize the complexity of the relationship into which they have entered with their infants. There are multiple effects of breast feeding on both the mother and her infant. We'll start by looking at how breast feeding affects the infant, and then look at how it affects the mother.

Breast milk is specifically designed to meet the needs of growing infants. Although it can be contaminated with potential toxins, such as caffeine and other drugs,[66] breast milk, unlike formula, is never mixed at the wrong concentration with unsanitary water. In addition, breast milk contains antibodies, formed in the mother's body, that can help protect the infant from infection.[67] Depending on what the mother eats, breast milk can also contain certain kinds of fatty acids that have been found to raise the breast-fed child's intelligence. (Similar effects are also found with pregnant women.)[68] There can be times when the nutrition of breast-fed infants is inadequate due to inadequate amounts of breast milk or the infant not feeding properly, with resultant damage to the infant including low IQ scores later in life. In general, however, breast feeding is an excellent way to feed an infant.

Breast feeding, and suckling milk in general, have still other positive effects on infants. Drinking milk may help to calm infants by releasing special, natural, narcotic-like substances in the infants' bodies. The result is that the infants make less noise, move around less, and are more tolerant of discomfort. In addition to these effects being appreciated by the mother, they may also be good for the baby, because these behavioral changes help the baby to conserve energy.[69] Remember that one of the overriding themes of the mother–infant relationship, indeed of this whole book, is that we have evolved to behave in ways that would help us to survive in surroundings in which lots of readily available good food isn't present.

Suckling may, in and of itself, have effects similar to infants ingesting milk. The physical act of suckling, whether or not any milk is ingested, triggers the release of chemicals in the infant's intestinal tract that improve digestion and the use of ingested fuel, but it also induces sleepiness, again helping to conserve the infant's energy. These positive effects explain why the use of a pacifier can be advisable, unless parents intend for a child to breast or bottle feed continuously—unlikely in the American culture.[70]

Another effect of breast feeding that has been explored is the connection between breast- versus bottle-fed infants and adulthood obesity. As you can imagine, it's difficult to conduct controlled experiments on relationships of this type. Doing an experiment in which you randomly assign infants to be breast or bottle fed, and then checking to see whether they are obese 30 or 40 years later would be extremely challenging. However, it does appear that infants who are breast fed are less likely to become obese, and that the longer the breast feeding goes on, the less likely the infants are to become obese as adults. This raises the possibility that infants who are breast fed will also be less likely as adults to develop diseases, such as cardiovascular diseases, that are associated with obesity.[71] One explanation for the relationship between breast feeding and later obesity may be that, with a bottle, caregivers are more likely to try to persuade the infant to consume a certain number of ounces of formula even though the infant isn't that hungry.[72] Nevertheless, keep in mind that we don't really know that breast feeding by itself decreases the probability of later obesity. It's possible that mothers who choose to breast feed also tend to have less of other food available for children, are more likely to feed their children healthy food, or exercise more. However, there is evidence that leptin present in breast milk at least contributes to breast-fed infants weighing less later in life.[73] (For more on leptin's role in appetite see Chapter 2.) Nevertheless, even if we assume that adult obesity may be influenced by whether an infant is breast fed, it's important to remember that there are many other influences as well, influences that you read about in earlier chapters, such as individual differences in metabolic rate and whether someone's biological parents are obese.

Now we come to what I think is the most interesting aspect of how breast feeding can influence infants: the effects on infants of the tastes and odors present during breast feeding. There have now been many experiments conducted on this subject. To begin with, we now know that infants live in a much richer gustatory and olfactory world than many people originally supposed. Newborn infants can detect a variety of tastes and smells. Further, in the first few days of life, infants, whether breast fed or not, prefer the odors of lactating breasts. With time, breast-fed infants learn to prefer the odors of their particular mothers' breasts and armpits over those of other breast-feeding women.[74] These preferences would help to keep an infant near his or her own mother, which, particularly in the sort of surroundings in which we evolved, would increase the likelihood of an infant's survival.

Taking this a step further, experiments have now shown that, similar to what happens with amniotic fluid, what a lactating mother eats can affect tastes and odors in her breast milk, and thereby can affect the food preferences of her infant. The majority of this research has been conducted by psychologists Julie A. Mennella and Gary K. Beauchamp and their colleagues at the Monell Chemical Senses Center in Philadelphia.[75] In one such experiment women drank either water or carrot juice while they either were in the last trimester of pregnancy or were lactating. The babies of the carrot-juice-drinking mothers later showed more preference for cereal made with carrot juice (as opposed to water) than the babies of the other women.[76] We also know that infants accidentally fed on a formula deficient in the chemical chloride have an increased preference for salty foods (sodium chloride) when they grow up.[77] Further, infants show a preference for alcohol in breast milk and may learn to like aspects of their surroundings associated with such breast milk.[78] Thus we now have a number of indicators that what a mother eats or drinks can subsequently affect the eating and drinking of her child.

Also yet to be determined are both the short-term and the long-term effects of cigarette smoking on the breast-fed infant. Mennella and

Beauchamp have shown that adults can tell which samples of breast milk come from cigarette smoking women and which do not, and that adults' abilities to identify milk from lactating women who smoke correlates with the concentration of nicotine in the milk. Therefore, in addition to the obvious risks of nicotine in breast milk from smoking mothers, it's possible that infants can detect tastes and odors in breast milk associated with cigarette smoking, and that this experience influences their tendencies to smoke later in life.[79] Once again, we simply don't know the answer to this question; more research is needed. (See Conversation Making Fact #13.)

Conversation making fact #13

It's widely believed in many cultures, including in the United States, that drinking alcohol will improve both the quantity and quality of breast milk. Toward this end, some women, although not drinking much when they're pregnant, will drink once they're lactating. Unfortunately, this appears to be one case in which folklore is contrary to actual fact. Infants actually consume less breast milk when their mothers have drunk alcohol. One possible explanation of this effect might be that infants don't prefer breast milk that has tastes and odors added from the mother's drinking, but this doesn't appear to be what's going on. In fact, the reverse appears to be true—infants whose breast-feeding mothers drink frequently seem to show the most preference for breast milk to which experimenters have added alcohol. Instead, the explanation for why infants get less breast milk when their mothers drink may be that drinking mothers don't produce as much milk.[80] However, once again, more research is needed, especially investigating infants feeding on their mothers' milk when their mothers have and haven't recently been drinking. Perhaps infants whose breast-feeding mothers drank frequently grow up to have a greater preference for alcohol than would have otherwise been the case.

Not only are infants affected by what occurs during or prior to breast feeding, but breast feeding also affects lactating women. For example, breast feeding can have immediate positive effects for women, as well as for their babies. In nursing mothers' bodies, too, special, natural, narcotic-like substances can be released, and perceived stress and depression can decrease.[81]

Another way in which lactating women are affected can be understood best by first remembering that they need even more calories and nutrients than pregnant women, approximately 765 to 980 calories more per day than before they became pregnant.[82] Therefore lactating women should, and do, consume more calories than nonpregnant women.[83] In addition, it's possible that the levels of bodily chemicals important in digestion, such as CCK, change during lactation in order to ensure that lactating women eat more and metabolize well what they eat.[84] You'll recall that metabolic rate is higher in pregnant than nonpregnant women. In lactating women, it's only relatively high after these women eat; at other times, the metabolic rate of lactating women is similar to that of women who have given birth but aren't lactating;[85] this helps lactating women to avoid being depleted by the caloric demands of lactation.

Many women see the lactation period as a time to lose the extra fat accumulated during pregnancy. Overweight breast-feeding women who diet and exercise to lose, on average, 1 pound per week have infants who grow normally;[86] thus losing weight while lactating doesn't appear to be harmful to the baby. And, indeed, lactating women are better able to lose weight from their hips and abdomen, where weight is deposited during pregnancy and places from which it's traditionally difficult to lose weight. However, suckling an infant seems to decrease the heat generated by the muscles and to increase energy storage in certain parts of the lactating woman's body. It also makes the woman sleepy. This sleepiness, and the consequently decreased activity level, may be useful for the survival of the infant in that these effects tend to keep the mother nearby.[87] Shakespeare, the consummate observer of our behavior, alluded to such effects when he had Cleopatra say: "Does thou not see my baby at my breast, that sucks the nurse asleep?"[88] All of these suckling effects decrease the woman's energy usage, thus lessening the effects of the caloric drain of the production of milk.[89] This could help to explain the fact that most women who have given birth—at least for the first time—don't lose sufficient weight to return to their prepregnancy weight.

"A Woman is a Dish for the Gods"[90]: Conclusion

Eating, drinking, and female reproduction are inextricably intertwined. Many aspects of eating behavior help to ensure that healthy children are produced and that their mothers are healthy enough to continue to produce. This chapter demonstrates clearly, perhaps more than any other chapter, how the psychology of eating and drinking is tied to our bodies' and our genes' survival. We can't survive, and we can't reproduce, unless we eat and drink properly. Therefore natural selection has resulted in a variety of mechanisms to ensure that appropriate eating and drinking behaviors will meet the unusual nutritional requirements of conception, pregnancy, and lactation. However, natural selection has not provided for every modern-day adverse contingency. We did not evolve in surroundings in which toxins such as caffeine or alcohol were common. Further, some of the adaptations that are present, such as the tendency of pregnant and lactating women to store fat, although useful in the surroundings in which we evolved, aren't as necessary now, and can even cause weight problems in a society in which having sufficient food isn't a problem for most people. As research continues, the resulting information will make it even easier for parents and their physicians to ensure the health of mothers and their offspring.

14

WHEN AND WHY SMOKING
AFFECTS YOUR WEIGHT

Approximately 18% of the adults in the United States currently smoke cigarettes—approximately 42 million people, and another approximately 50 million are ex-smokers. These huge numbers are tragic because smoking is responsible for more disease and death than any other preventable behavior. Almost 500,000 deaths per year in the United States are attributed to smoking. Smoking increases the risk of heart diseases, respiratory diseases, stroke, and cancer, to name a few. In addition, cigarette smoking is responsible for millions of dollars being spent on cigarettes that could be spent on something else, for days lost from work, and for increases in health care insurance costs. Many people who quit smoking take several attempts before they're finally able to quit, and most of those who attempt to quit experience withdrawal from their addiction to nicotine. The withdrawal symptoms include irritability, anxiety, difficulty concentrating, and, most importantly for this book, increased appetite.[1] Nicotine exposure during pregnancy and breast feeding can also have a number of negative effects, including (if during pregnancy) increasing salt preference in the offspring, and (if during lactation) interfering with infants' sleep.[2]

Given all of these terrible consequences, why do people start smoking, and if they do smoke, why do they not all quit? There are many good answers that can be given to this question, most of which are beyond the scope of this book. However, there's one answer that is within the scope of this book: body weight.

Several different studies have shown that a great many people believe that smoking helps control weight. For example, in one study, approximately 10% of male smokers and 5% of female smokers started smoking because they thought that it would help them to lose weight. In another study, 47% of men and 59% of women continued to smoke because they feared that they would gain weight if they stopped. In fact, some of the study's participants—most often women—after stopping smoking had restarted because they feared that stopping caused them to gain weight.

A 1997 survey of men by *Psychology Today* found that 30% stated that they smoke to control their weight. Finally, in another study, among children 9–14 years of age, those who reported that they were thinking of starting to smoke were also those who tended to be worried about their weight.[3]

Consider this quote from Asne Seierstad's work of nonfiction, *The Bookseller of Kabul*:

> This time desire takes over: [Bibi Gul, who is overweight] stretches out her hand and whispers, "Can I have one?" Silence descends. Is Grandmother starting to smoke? "Mummy," Leila cries and tears the cigarette out of her hand. Mansur gives her another one and Leila leaves the room in protest. Bibi Gul sits happily puffing away, laughing quietly. She even stops the rocking to and fro and holds the cigarette up in the air, inhaling deeply. "I'll eat less," Bibi Gul explains.[4]

There certainly are a lot of people who believe that cigarette smoking helps you lose or maintain your weight, and that stopping smoking makes you gain weight. How accurate are these beliefs? If smoking does affect

---

Conversation making fact #14

Smoking marijuana cigarettes has vastly different effects on appetite and eating than smoking tobacco cigarettes. People who say that smoking marijuana gives them the munchies are basically correct. Scientists Richard W. Foltin, Marian W. Fischman, and Maryanne F. Byrne investigated these effects in an extremely difficult experiment in which six men (in two groups of three men each) lived in a residential laboratory for 13 days. The participants had no direct contact with anyone else, and their eating behaviors were continuously monitored. Each day of the experiment, the participants smoked either four marijuana cigarettes or four placebo cigarettes. The amounts of food eaten at meals did not differ significantly on marijuana and placebo days. However, on marijuana days, the participants greatly increased the amounts of certain types of food that they ate (sweet solid snacks such as candy bars) so that in total on these days the participants' caloric intakes increased by a whopping 40 percent. Not surprisingly, participants gained significant amounts of weight on the marijuana days.[6] So, in addition to many other reasons, if you want to control your weight, don't smoke marijuana!

---

weight, by what mechanisms do such effects occur? Once we know the facts concerning smoking and body weight, we can develop strategies for ensuring that, when someone is deciding whether or not to smoke, that person won't be worrying about his or her weight.[5]

As has been the case in prior chapters, answering questions about eating behavior in this chapter will frequently require consideration of results from experiments conducted with rats. Conducting experiments with rats allows researchers to control various aspects of the experiments to a degree that would not be possible if the experiments were conducted with people. I'll first present the research about weight and starting or continuing smoking, and then about weight and stopping smoking. All comments in this chapter refer only to the smoking of tobacco cigarettes. (For information about smoking marijuana see Conversation Making Fact #14.)

You're *Smoking,* But How About Your Metabolic Rate?

Let's begin at the beginning. What happens to body weight when people start or continue smoking, and why does it happen? People who begin smoking cigarettes do, on average, lose weight; in addition, on average, smokers weigh less than nonsmokers. (See Figure 14.1.) An exception to this generalization appears to be black women, among whom obesity rates are relatively high whether or not they're smokers.[7]

Rats exposed to nicotine show effects similar to those shown by people. Psychologist Neil E. Grunberg and his colleagues Kathryn A. Popp and Suzan E. Winders gave rats regular ground laboratory chow plus ground Oreo cookies, ground potato chips, and water—a food selection guaranteed to get the rats to pig out, so to speak. Sometimes the rats were infused with nicotine, and other times they were infused with saline (salty water that has no physiological effects). When the rats were receiving infusions of nicotine, they ate fewer Oreo cookies and weighed less than when they were receiving saline infusions.[8]

All of these results show that smoking tobacco or exposure to nicotine by themselves constrain body weight. The question then becomes: What's responsible for this constraint on weight? Therefore, next I'll consider the evidence for and against three explanations: the possible effects of smoking on the total number of calories eaten, on the amount of sweet foods eaten, and on energy expenditure.

The first possible explanation for the lower body weights associated with smoking is that smoking decreases the total number of calories eaten. In people this decrease in calories eaten could, in turn, be due to a decrease in appetite, changes in the ways we use our hands (picking

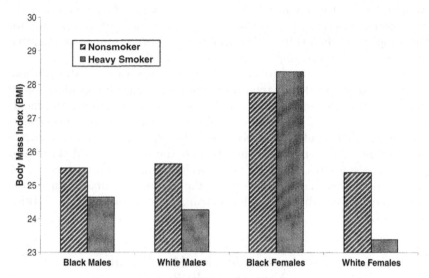

Figure 14.1 BMI (body mass index) for male and female, white and black, nonsmokers and heavy smokers. (Adapted from R. C. Klesges, M. DeBon, and A. Meyers, "Obesity in African American Women: Epidemiology, Determinants, and Treatment Issues," in *Body Image, Eating Disorders, and Obesity: An Integrative Guide for Assessment and Treatment*, ed. J. K. Thompson, Washington, DC: American Psychological Association, 1996.)

up a cigarette instead of food), changes in the ways we use our mouths (putting a cigarette in the mouth instead of food), and so on.[9] You might think that the fact that rats, just like people, eat less and weigh less when infused with nicotine indicates that changes in hand or oral activity can't explain the effects of smoking on people's eating and weight. Rats are usually exposed to nicotine by means of a needle, not a cigarette, so it's not possible to explain any nicotine-related decreases in rats' eating as due to changes in hand activity or oral activity. However, keep in mind that, in rats as well as in people, more than one mechanism could be responsible for any decrease in eating resulting from smoking or nicotine exposure. Therefore, even though changes in hand or oral activity can't explain the effects seen in rats, such mechanisms could still be at work in people.

There have now been several experiments exploring the relationships between smoking and the amount eaten. One study, conducted by psychologist Joan B. Beckwith using 766 women aged 20–30 years, found that the degree to which these women felt compelled to eat wasn't significantly correlated with their levels of smoking.[10] Consistent with this finding, an experiment conducted by scientist Kenneth A. Perkins and his colleagues found no differences in hunger or amount eaten among men and women smokers who, after abstaining from smoking overnight, were exposed to different amounts of nicotine. Some participants were given an unlit cigarette, some smoked only a very low nicotine cigarette, and some smoked their usual cigarette.[11] These two experiments seem to indicate that, at least in people, a decrease in appetite and the amount of calories eaten does not appear to explain the lower weights among smokers. Nevertheless, in another experiment, nicotine exposure significantly decreased the rate at which food passed through people's gastrointestinal tracts, and as you'll probably remember from Chapter 2, such delayed emptying is associated with a decrease in appetite.[12]

Consistent with the evidence on gastrointestinal emptying, evidence collected with rats suggests that the lower weights associated with smoking are indeed due to a decrease in the total amount of food eaten. Rats given injections of nicotine, as well as rats given long-term exposure to smoke, decrease the amount of food that they eat, to the point of having a suppressed growth rate. In addition, exposure to smoke or nicotine raises these rats' blood sugar levels, thus, perhaps, making them less hungry and less likely to eat.[13] Further, recent research with rats and mice has shown that nicotine affects appetite through its specific effects in the hypothalamus.[14] (You'll remember that the hypothalamus is critical in the control of appetite.)

Let's consider a second explanation for the lower body weights of smokers. Perhaps smoking and exposure to nicotine decrease the amount of sweet foods that someone eats.[15] According to this explanation, when someone starts smoking, the total number of calories eaten doesn't change, but the proportion of calories that comes from sweet foods decreases. You should remember from Chapter 10 that some researchers believe that eating good-tasting foods, such as sweet foods, can lead to obesity; the taste of sweet may lead to increased storage of what's eaten as fat.

Psychologist Neal E. Grunberg and his colleague David E. Morse investigated this hypothesis by using a rather large sample: the behavior of all the people in the United States. These researchers examined the average number of cigarettes smoked per person as a function of the average amount each person ate of 41 different foods over the years 1964–1977. There were substantial differences in the numbers of cigarettes smoked per person in some of these years. As it turned out, in years when the number of cigarettes per person was relatively high, the number of pounds of sugar eaten was relatively low and vice versa.[16] However, it's important to note that Grunberg and Morse's data, although very suggestive, consist entirely of correlations between the numbers of cigarettes smoked and the pounds of sugar eaten. (See Figure 14.2.) This means that variation in one of these variables might not necessarily cause the variation in the other variable; instead, some third variable—say, for

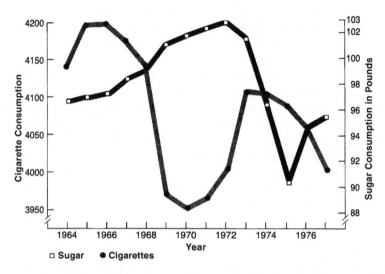

Figure 14.2 Number of cigarettes consumed per person and number of pounds of sugar consumed per person during the years 1964–1977. (Adapted from N. E. Grunberg and D. E. Morse, "Cigarette Smoking and Food Consumption in the United States," *Journal of Applied Social Psychology* 14[1984]: 310–317.)

example, the amount of alcohol drunk—could cause the variation in both the number of cigarettes smoked and the pounds of sugar eaten.

Looking at the behavior of individuals, we find data that more directly support the hypothesis that smoking decreases the eating of sweet foods. Results from laboratory experiments, including the experiment by Grunberg, Popp, and Winders described earlier in this chapter, show that when people or rats smoke or are exposed to nicotine they eat fewer sweet foods while not changing how much they eat of other foods.[17]

One possible explanation for the decrease in the amount of sweet foods eaten by smokers is a decreased preference for the taste of sweet. We know that people are less sensitive to some odors when they smoke,[18] so perhaps they're also less sensitive to some tastes and thus prefer those tastes less. In fact, women smokers have more difficulty detecting low concentrations of sugar than do women nonsmokers.[19] This could result in these smokers consuming fewer sweet foods than nonsmokers.

Another possible explanation for the decrease in the amounts of sweet foods eaten by smokers comes from work on preferences for different brands of cigarettes. A smoker's rated pleasantness of a particular brand or rated satisfaction provided by a particular brand is highly correlated with the smoker's reported perception of the sweetness of that brand.[20] Perhaps smokers eat fewer sweet foods because their desire for the taste of sweet is satisfied by the cigarettes themselves. It's beyond me how cigarettes could seem sweet, but I'm not a smoker. In any case, as far as I'm aware, there has been no research investigating the possibility that cigarettes help to satisfy smokers' desire for the taste of sweet.

At last we come to the third explanation of the lower weights among smokers: Perhaps smoking increases the number of calories expended by increasing metabolic rate.[21] If this were so, and if smokers ate the same total amount as nonsmokers—something that we have already established—then smokers would weigh less than nonsmokers.

There is indeed evidence supporting this hypothesis.[22] For example, one experiment found that smokers' metabolic rates were 10% higher during a 24-hour period when they smoked than during a 24-hour period when they abstained from smoking.[23] However, there's a difficulty in interpreting these results. Because chronic smokers were used, we don't know if the metabolic rates observed in the smokers when they were smoking, which were greater than when they weren't smoking, were also greater than before they started smoking. It's possible that starting smoking doesn't change metabolic rate, but that stopping smoking decreases it.

In summary, there's at least some evidence supporting all three hypotheses—that smokers consume less total calories, that they decrease the total amount of sweet foods they eat, and that their metabolic rates are increased. All of these hypotheses deserve additional research.

The Enlarging Effects of Quitting

Many people who stop smoking gain weight. One study measured the weights of over 5,000 African American and European American men and women when they quit smoking. On average, those of European descent gained 9.3 pounds, and those of African descent gained 14.6 pounds.[24] People who manage to remain abstinent for a long period of time are more likely to gain weight than people who remain abstinent for only a short period of time.[25] Thus successful quitting often comes with an unwelcome consequence: noticeable weight gain.

However, this picture may not be as bad as it seems. For one thing, it's possible that the weight gained by quitting is no more than the weight that wasn't gained or that was lost because the person smoked in the first place. In addition, there are individual differences in whether someone gains weight after quitting; some people don't gain any weight at all. By examining what types of people do and don't gain weight when they stop smoking, and under what conditions there's a weight gain, it may be possible to obtain clues as to what causes these weight gains to occur. Even more importantly, it may be possible to develop strategies for preventing a weight gain when someone quits smoking. Researchers have examined the possible effects of a number of factors on quitting-related weight gain.

Some of these factors are closely related to ones that I discussed in the previous section of this chapter as possibly responsible for the lower weights associated with starting or continuing smoking. Such factors include the amount eaten (hypothesized to increase when someone quits), the percentage of sweet foods eaten (also hypothesized to increase when someone quits), and metabolic rate (hypothesized to decrease when someone quits). There are data to support each of these hypotheses, and so researchers have looked even deeper, trying to determine exactly why each of these factors might increase weight after quitting. For example, researchers have examined the possibility that the amount eaten after quitting increases because people are coping with stress, because pleasant odors (such as those of food) help to decrease the urge to smoke, because nicotine withdrawal disrupts insulin levels, or because of the need to continue to satisfy a high oral drive.[26] When my father, a long-time four-pack-a-day smoker, quit he took to sucking constantly on hard candies, a significant problem for his teeth for the short period that he continued to have any. In the case of the increased preference for sweet following quitting, perhaps quitters try to substitute for the sweetness provided by their now-absent cigarettes.[27] The lower metabolic rate that occurs when people quit smoking may be due to the effects of nicotine on certain parts of the nervous system,[28] thus helping to explain the lower weight gain of ex-smokers who use nicotine gum, and the fact that ex-smokers who engage in relatively more aerobic exercise are less likely to gain weight.[29] As you learned earlier in Chapter 10, exercise can raise metabolic rate. Exercise appears to be a useful strategy for weight control, even in ex-smokers.

There's been additional work investigating the relationship between removal of the chemical nicotine and the weight gain seen in ex-smokers. Heavier smokers are more likely to gain weight when they quit than are moderate or light smokers.[30] In addition, when people quit, the more they chew nicotine gum, or the greater the concentration of nicotine in their gum, the less likely they are to gain weight.[31] Finally, when rats used to receiving nicotine injections instead receive saline injections, they eat significantly greater amounts of Oreos and gain significantly more weight than other rats.[32] Thus, there's indeed a clear relationship between removal of nicotine and weight gain. However, these experiments by themselves don't tell us why nicotine removal tends to cause weight gain. It may be that nicotine removal affects metabolic rate as suggested in the previous paragraph. But nicotine removal may also affect appetite, food preferences, and activity level.

One study speaks to some of these possibilities. Scientists Janet Gross, Maxine L. Stitzer, and Janelle Maldonado found that ex-smokers who chewed nicotine gum reported smaller increases in hunger and amounts of food eaten following quitting than ex-smokers who chewed placebo gum (gum that the participants thought contained nicotine but didn't).[33]

A number of experiments with rats and people have implicated the neurotransmitter dopamine in what determines how much weight someone gains after quitting (you previously read about dopamine in Chapter 2). Having certain genes that influence the concentration of dopamine in the brain also seems to influence the size of the post-quitting weight gain.[34] Such results open up the possibility that, someday, individual smokers could have individual treatments tailored to help them control their weight after quitting.

Unfortunately, data on the possible ways that nicotine removal may affect weight gain are still rather limited. It would be particularly interesting to find out if the effects of nicotine skin patches are similar to those of nicotine gum, or if the act of chewing the gum, and not just the nicotine in the gum, is somehow important in the appetite decreases seen in nicotine gum chewers. You'll recall that Chapter 10 pointed out that gum chewing seems to help control appetite. We do know that nicotine withdrawal symptoms are decreased about the same amount with the gum as with the patches,[35] but we don't yet know if these two nicotine-replacement methods are also similar in their effects on appetite and weight gain.

A final factor hypothesized to be responsible for the weight gain following quitting smoking is an ex-smoker's personality. There are suggestions in the research literature that some personality traits may be correlated with how much weight smokers gain after quitting. It has been shown that women with histories of serious depression are more likely to gain weight after quitting than women who don't have histories of serious depression. The reverse appears to be true for men; men with histories of depression gain less after quitting.[36] In addition, the sorts of people who tend to continue to eat excessively once they know that they have broken their diet, people whose eating can become what's called disinhibited, also tend to gain relatively more weight after quitting smoking.[37] These studies are intriguing, but much remains to be done to tie down just what sorts of personality traits are consistently associated with weight gain after quitting smoking.

The close relationship between quitting smoking and weight gain has led psychologist Bonnie Spring and her colleagues to develop combined treatments for smoking cessation and weight control. Their research has shown that such combined treatment is not harmful, and may even be beneficial to smokers who want to be ex-smokers. Further, women smokers who are particularly concerned about gaining weight if they quit are less likely to have negative moods after quitting if they exercise as part of the combined smoking cessation-weight control treatment.[38]

In summary, some people gain weight when they stop smoking, and in some cases this may be due to their eating more food, particularly more sweet food. However, a decrease in metabolic rate that occurs following

Table 14.1 Research-based suggestions for minimizing weight gain after quitting smoking

---

- Chew nicotine gum and/or use nicotine skin patches.
- If you're a woman and you've a history of depression, it would probably be helpful to ensure that the depression is well under control when quitting smoking, possibly by the combined use of cognitive behavior therapy and antidepressant medication.[39]
- It may be helpful not to quit during a stressful period.
- Engage in regular aerobic exercise.
- Consider following some or all of the suggestions listed in Table 10. 1.

---

quitting probably also causes weight gain in some people. It's not yet clear precisely what role nicotine plays in the weight gain that can occur following quitting. Table 14.1 puts together the research-based suggestions for minimizing weight gain after quitting that have been discussed in this section. Future research will undoubtedly continue to pursue all of these issues.

The Butt Stops Here: Conclusion

The widespread opinion that smokers weigh less than nonsmokers and that ex-smokers risk weight gain is an accurate one. These unfortunate consequences may encourage people to begin this dangerous habit and, once they have started, contribute to making it difficult to quit. This is particularly the case because the weight changes occur relatively close in time to the smoking. In contrast, the negative health consequences of smoking are often very delayed. Therefore, similar to some of the other choices that we analyzed earlier in this book, even though the negative health consequences of the weight gained from stopping smoking aren't as severe as the ultimate negative health consequences of continuing to smoke, some people have difficulty seeing the greater advantage of quitting than of continuing to smoke. Medication that helps to delay or prevent the weight gain associated with quitting may help keep quitters from relapsing. People probably also believe—incorrectly—that every person who stops smoking will gain large numbers of pounds. Not only are there individual differences in weight gain that seem to be related to people's specific characteristics, but particular actions such as the use of nicotine gum and aerobic exercise may help to prevent a weight gain— assuming such a gain isn't desired.

Researchers are beginning to understand the many complex factors responsible for these findings, such as types of foods eaten, metabolic rate, and stress. Ultimately, these research results can be used to help free smokers from feeling that they must keep smoking, or resume smoking, in order not to gain excess weight.

Finally, I should emphasize that a great deal of the research described in this chapter has concerned nicotine by itself, not nicotine as an ingredient of tobacco. This means that this research on nicotine applies, not just to traditional cigarettes, cigars, pipes, and chewing tobacco, but also to nicotine gum, nicotine patches, and to e-cigarettes (electronic devices resembling a cigarette that deliver nicotine in a vapour without any tobacco smoke). Some people use e-cigarettes, as they use nicotine patches and nicotine gum, to help themselves quit. However, some people use e-cigarettes as a means of continuing to receive nicotine without inhaling tobacco smoke. By using e-cigarettes you may indeed avoid some of the cancer-causing toxins in cigarette smoke, but you will still be exposed to addictive nicotine and all of its effects, including its effects on body weight.

15

WE DO NOT LIVE BY
BREAD ALONE

Cuisine, Beer, and Wine

> I believe that how you eat and how you choose your food is
> an act that combines the political—your place in the world
> of other people—with the most intensely personal—the
> way you use your mind and your senses, together, for the
> gratification of your soul.
>
> Alice Waters (1994)[1]

Thus wrote Alice Waters, founder in 1971 of Berkeley's famed Chez
Panisse restaurant which, along with master chef Julia Child's early 1960s
television show, helped to inspire an American cuisine that went beyond
the postwar period's canned vegetables, pot roast, fruit cocktail, and TV
dinners.[2] If you're over the age of 50 you probably remember those days
when adventuresome eating was an occasional pizza or Chinese food,
and salad often contained Jell-O.

Now American TV has a whole network devoted to food, and there
are countless gourmet cooking shows on that network and others. There
are many thousands of outstanding American chefs and home cooks cre-
ating new flavor and texture combinations using traditional American
foods such as tomatoes, corn, and chocolate. Many restaurants feature
local ingredients, as well as American wines and beers.[3]

But what makes American cuisine *American*? In fact, what makes any
cuisine a *cuisine*? What factors are responsible for the particular characteristics of a given cuisine? This chapter will provide you with answers to
these questions, as well as with some information about beer and wine
tasting. Research described in previous chapters concerning how and why
people choose certain foods and drinks comes together in this chapter to
help you understand how people end up consuming certain combinations
or patterns of specific foods and drinks. Here you'll gain a sense of how
scientific investigations—with rats as well as people—can give you both
a better understanding of, and better enjoyment of, the food and drink
that you consume. You'll see how your genes, your experiences, and

evolutionary processes all contribute to what you do when you actually sit down to dinner. This chapter is about love and war and their interactions with the pleasures of the palate. As Julia Child would have said, "Bon appétit!"

Cooking with Gas: Cuisine

Our understanding of what makes a cuisine a cuisine begins with Elisabeth Rozin, cookbook writer and culinary historian. When I was in graduate school, one of the Harvard faculty told me about Rozin's first cookbook, *The Flavor-Principle Cookbook*, first published in 1973 but now out of print and never widely circulated. This book held what amounted to cult status among psychologists at that time. It quickly became my favorite cookbook because not only did it contain fascinating, easy-to-make recipes from many different cuisines, but it explained some of the psychological principles behind cuisine, principles that I'd never previously contemplated and found absolutely absorbing. For example, from this cookbook I learned that it was possible, in principle, to create a Chinese hamburger. For a budding experimental psychologist who loved to eat but who had a slew of food aversions, this was a safe way into the food world using scientific analysis.

In her fascinating writings Rozin elucidated for all of us the primary elements of cuisine. These elements consist of the foods used, the techniques employed to modify those foods, the flavorings added to those foods, and cultural constraints that restrict what types of food may be eaten or how the foods may be prepared.[4] Put all of this together and, voilà, you have a cuisine. (See Figure 15.1.) Although the behaviors of animals other than people may demonstrate certain elements of cuisine, such as the salting of sweet potatoes by monkeys described in Chapter 1, true cuisine with all of its characteristics appears to be a uniquely human enterprise. In this section you'll be treated first to a thorough description of the elements of cuisine, then to examples of various cuisines and information about two of the most famous, and most desired, flavor principles—chile pepper and chocolate—and finally to two examples of cultural constraints—the sacred cow and cannibalism.

The building blocks of cuisine

The elements of cuisine begin with the foods around you. Particular foods can be a part of your cuisine only if they're present in your surroundings. However, those foods, and thus the nature of a given cuisine, can change as people move to new locations and bring their old foods with them or

Figure 15.1 The result of scientific study of cuisine. (Drawing by E. Stein reprinted from *The Chronicle of Higher Education* [December 1, 1993]: B3. Reprinted with permission from E. Stein.)

bring foods back from other locations. Although many people dispute whether Columbus's first visit to the Americas was of positive historical significance, no one can dispute the resulting enormous changes in many of the world's cuisines. You may not realize that tomatoes, chile peppers, and chocolate are all native to the Americas and thus weren't part of non-American cuisines until well after 1492.[5] Just try to imagine Italian cuisine without tomatoes, Szechuan cooking without chile peppers, and Swiss dessert without chocolate. But the fact is that those foods have only been a part of those cuisines for the last several hundred years.

Nevertheless, not all of the foods that are available will become part of a given cuisine. Among the most powerful factors determining whether they do is whether the foods are inherently pleasurable to the senses of sight, smell, and taste. As you've learned in previous chapters, people find certain tastes more pleasurable than others. Among the highly preferred tastes are those that are sweet or salty, or that have been associated with lots of calories. Thus, for example, people learn to like foods that are very high in fat. (See Conversation Making Fact #15.) When psychologist Luna Abdallah and her colleagues asked 102 normal-weight men to rate 39 biscuits and cakes that differed in terms of their fat and sugar contents, the ones that were rated the most pleasant had (big surprise) the highest sugar and fat contents.[6]

Conversation making fact #15

Given what you know about food preferences, it shouldn't surprise you to learn that some well-known chefs have reported that their secret ingredient is, you guessed it, fat. When restaurant patrons wonder why food in a restaurant tastes so much better than at home, it may be because the restaurant uses far more fat than any home cook ever would. One famous New York restaurant's menu included a poached halibut with Swiss chard, which sounds low in calories. But the restaurant poached the halibut by immersing it in a quart of hot goose fat for 13 minutes.[7] So all of you fish eaters out there who feel so virtuous when you order poached fish, beware! You may be taking in more fat than I am when I eat my nice lean beef fillet.

There are also cases in which people learn to like foods that are inherently aversive—such as chile peppers and coffee—and those foods become part of a cuisine. I'll discuss how this happens with chile peppers in a later section. Earlier you learned how associating coffee with sugar, milk, or caffeine might result in people coming to like this initially aversive beverage.

Whether an available food becomes part of a cuisine may also depend on the ability of people to digest or metabolize that food. For example, when we discussed genetic contributions to food preferences, you learned that many adults are lactose intolerant. If most of the people in a cultural group are lactose intolerant, then milk isn't likely to be a part of that group's cuisine. As another example, although fava beans are toxic for some people, they may increase resistance to malaria. Therefore, in populations in which resistance to malaria is more useful than the toxicity of fava beans is damaging—which occurs in various Mediterranean populations—fava beans should be, and are, a part of that population's cuisine.[8]

The technology—including food preparation techniques—available to a particular group of people is also an important determinant of that group's cuisine. Until fermentation was discovered, no cuisine could contain alcoholic beverages. The advent of cooking and, much more recently, refrigerators, are two more examples in which technological developments caused huge changes in what people ate.[9]

In fact, such developments can affect more than what people eat. Harvard anthropologist Richard Wrangham has argued that when our ancestors started cooking almost 2 million years ago, that enabled them to net more energy from their food, which in turn enabled the evolution of our relatively large brains, and thus our ability to demonstrate all kinds of particularly human behaviors. However, this is a hypothesis, and a controversial one. Not all researchers agree that our ancestors' cooking is linked to our big brains in this way.[10]

In recent decades, the lines between chefs and chemists and engineers are blurring, as food lovers use science to help them create delicious, innovative dishes, taking cuisine to new levels. There is now a whole field entitled molecular gastronomy, dedicated to the study and application of the chemical reactions that occur during cooking.[11] There is even a general education course at Harvard entitled "Science and Cooking: From Haute Cuisine to Soft Matter Science," taught by faculty from Harvard's School of Engineering and Applied Sciences, with weekly guest lectures by chefs. Topics covered include such matters as spherification.[12] I myself have been the beneficiary of such scientific knowledge. Using agar-agar and a pipette from a kit entitled "Cuisine R-Evolution" that I bought at the American Museum of Natural History, I have made balsamic vinegar "pearls," which look like large caviar and are absolutely delicious served on crisp greens.

Another important factor in determining the constituents of any cuisine is the nutrition provided by the cuisine. The only cultures that will survive are obviously those that obtain and consume foods that are nutritionally balanced. There are many different ways of doing this. One way is by combining the foods eaten. In the northeastern United States a typical, nutritionally complete meal might consist of a piece of chicken, salad, and a baked potato. But in Mexico, a nutritionally complete meal might consist of corn tortillas, beans, and tomatoes. Another way to ensure a nutritionally complete cuisine is by treating particular foods. Native Americans developed a method of treating corn with an alkali solution that significantly enhances the nutritional value of the corn.[13]

Another factor influencing which foods are part of a cuisine has to do with cost. By this I don't just mean how much money a food costs, which is certainly important, but also the amount of energy required to prepare a food. If a group of 10 people living at subsistence level must walk 50 miles through a desert in order to obtain grain and then spend several days working to make a single loaf of bread from that grain, bread won't be a part of that group's cuisine.

Other people's food preferences and practices—what we might call food cultural beliefs—can also affect a cuisine, as you learned when we discussed the contributions of our surroundings to food preferences. This can involve such relatively simple matters as what people like to eat for breakfast and dinner; North Americans prefer "breakfast" foods such as scrambled eggs and "dinner" foods such as green beans at the meals that they have learned are appropriate for these foods.[14] Cultural beliefs can also involve what kinds of substances are even considered food.

As another example, the laws of *kashrut*, which determine the kosher food practices of Jews, are passed from generation to generation. The cultural traditions of *kashrut* are so strong that they can affect the consumption of foods that appear not to be kosher, but actually are. You've already learned that people have trouble eating things that aren't forbidden foods but look like them.[15] In 1985 my sister married the son of an Orthodox rabbi. There wasn't much money for this event, so she and I made all of the food. Jews who observe *kashrut*, such as my sister's future father-in-law, won't eat both meat and dairy products as part of the same meal, so meals have to contain either meat and no dairy or vice versa. We chose to make a dairy meal for the wedding reception, which included a mushroom pâté. It looked just like a regular meat pâté, but it was made entirely of vegetable and dairy products. I'll never forget how my sister's brand new father-in-law looked at it. "What's that?" he asked suspiciously. "Mushroom pâté," we replied. After much persuasion, he finally ate it, but he didn't look happy about it.

Cultural beliefs about which foods are appropriate to eat may or may not help to ensure that people eat foods that are good for them. In Kenya, among the Mbeere people, pregnant women were traditionally not allowed to consume bitter substances such as certain medicinal juices, a practice that, as described in Chapter 13, may have helped to protect these women's fetuses. However, in western Kenya, women in some ethnic groups have traditionally not been allowed to eat eggs, even when there were a great many eggs available.[16] Perhaps originally there was some health benefit to this prohibition, but any such benefit isn't clear now. Similarly, the practice of keeping kosher, in which Jews eat only certain foods or combinations of foods, results in food consumption that may have ensured health in ancient times but may not be relevant now.[17]

Perhaps one of the best examples of how food cultural beliefs affect a cuisine occurs when a person moves from one culture to another. It can be extremely challenging for immigrants to find foods that they enjoy, and immigrants can feel compelled to consume their new culture's foods in order to demonstrate that they are a part of that culture.[18] By looking at how cuisines spread or die out, one may see which cultures are dominating others. As noted by Anthelme Brillat-Savarin, a famous French gastronome who lived at the turn of the 19th century, "Tell me what you eat and I will tell you who you are."[19]

The final factor influencing cuisines that I'll discuss is neophobia—the fear of new foods—which you learned about when we discussed the contributions of our experiences to food preference. This fear of new foods is probably responsible for the fact that most cuisines revolve around a number of flavor principles, or characteristic flavorings. The flavor principles identify dishes as belonging to a particular tradition.[20] They make the food seem familiar and safe. People add these flavorings to many of the dishes in a given cuisine. Thus you can take hamburger, a food not present in Asian cuisines, add soy sauce, rice wine, and ginger root to it, and end up with a hamburger that tastes "Chinese." Someone who usually eats Chinese food would be much more likely to try hamburger when it's imbued with these characteristic Chinese flavorings than otherwise.[21] This same preference for familiar foods results in cuisines often containing foods from people's childhoods and causes people far from home to miss their usual foods.

The craving for familiar foods hit me personally when I spent 3 weeks in Japan in the early 1990s. Remember that I'm very low on the trait of sensation seeking and I eat no fish. Japanese food often uses ingredients or cooking techniques unfamiliar to Americans and often contains fish or fish sauce. The result was that in Japan at that time I simply couldn't find satisfying food. Everything seemed strange or impossible to eat, and I could never get full. Even a dessert such as chocolate cake in what was billed as a Western-style restaurant seemed too light and airy, not at all satisfying (it was probably just low in fat). In desperation, one dinnertime I persuaded my husband to go to Denny's, someplace we would never go in the United States. I ordered what was described on the menu as a hamburger, but what I got was a ground meat patty that tasted very different from American hamburger meat, no bun, and the patty was drowning in gravy. Even with this disappointment, I thought I'd have no problem when I ordered vanilla ice cream for dessert. But it came sprinkled with ground-up frosted corn flakes cereal. I ate it, but it was very strange. Now truly desperate, I took my 5-year-old son on a lengthy trip on public transportation to Tokyo Disneyland. Surely there we would find familiar, satisfying food. While walking around we saw a sign for pizza. In ecstasy I approached the restaurant selling it only to find that they had just two kinds of pizza—with pineapple or shrimp topping. The shrimp was definitely out and at that time I'd never heard of putting fruit on pizza, so we left the restaurant without getting any food. My trip to Japan was the only trip I've ever been on during which I really lost weight. When I came back I couldn't stop stuffing myself with typical high-fat, high-sugar American food and I quickly gained back all of the weight that I'd lost.

Taking the concept of flavor principles a step farther, scientists have begun using new techniques to determine how flavor principles interact during a meal. In one approach, the flavor compounds present in hundreds of cooking ingredients were examined to determine how much overlap there was among the different ingredients. In Western, but not Asian, cuisines, ingredients that have some flavor compounds in common turn out to pair well as part of a meal. In another approach, pairs of astringent and fatty foods were examined to show how they complimented each other. Alternating consumption of an astringent and a fatty food prevented the taste of the former from becoming too—unpleasantly—astringent, and the taste of the latter from becoming too—unpleasantly—fatty. It is therefore not surprising that many cuisines pair astringent (such as red wine) and fatty (such as red meat) elements.[22]

Eating by example: some cuisines and flavor principles

Elisabeth Rozin has provided extensive listings of the flavor principles of different cuisines.[23] Table 15.1 shows examples of the flavor principles that Rozin believes are the most important factors in identifying many ethnic cuisines. Note that cultures that are in close geographical proximity tend to have overlapping flavor principles. For instance, soy sauce is common to Japanese, Chinese, and Korean cuisines, and olive oil is common to many Mediterranean cuisines. Cuisines can be influenced by immigrant groups as well. South African Cape Malay cuisine shows the influence

Table 15.1 Flavor principles in different cuisines

Cuisine	Flavor Principles
China	Soy sauce, rice wine, and ginger root:
Peking	+ miso and/or garlic and/or sesame
Szechuan	+ sweet-sour-hot
Canton	+ black bean-garlic
Japan	Soy sauce, sake, and sugar
Korea	Soy sauce, brown sugar, sesame, and chile
India	Curry:
Northern India	cumin, ginger, garlic + variations
Southern India	mustard seed, coconut, tamarind, chile + variations
Central Asia	Cinnamon, fruit, nut
Middle East	Lemon, parsley
West Africa	Tomato, peanut, chile
Northeastern Africa	Garlic, cumin, mint
Morocco	Cumin, coriander, cinnamon, ginger + onion and/or tomato and/or fruit
Greece	Olive oil, lemon, oregano
Southern Italy and Southern France	Olive oil, garlic, parsley, and/or anchovy
Italy, France	Olive oil, garlic, basil
Provence	Olive oil, thyme, rosemary, marjoram, sage
Spain	Olive oil, onion, pepper, tomato
Northern and Eastern Europe	Sour cream, dill or paprika or allspice or caraway
Normandy	Apple, cider, calvados
Northern Italy	Wine vinegar, garlic
Mexico	Tomato, chile

Source: Adapted from E. Rozin, *Ethnic Cuisine: The Flavor Principle Cookbook*, Brattleboro, VT: The Stephen Greene Press, 1983.

of South African Dutch, French, Indian, and Indonesian immigrants, as well as of the indigenous cuisine; and Vietnamese cuisine blends the flavors of China, France, India, Thailand, Laos, and Cambodia.[24]

For a detailed example of the influences that shape a particular cuisine, I'd like to tell you about Cajun cuisine, a cuisine that I find particularly fascinating. The Cajuns are a group of people who live in an area of Louisiana close to New Orleans. The word *Cajun* comes from the word *Acadian*; Cajuns were originally from Nova Scotia (Acadia) in French Canada. They were transported involuntarily to Louisiana by British soldiers in the 18th century.[25] The area where they arrived has also been inhabited by, among others, the French, Native Americans, and Africans brought there as slaves.

The Cajuns's new location, the bayou, was near the Gulf of Mexico and filled with swamps, lakes, and islands. Seafood was plentiful, particularly oysters, crawfish (a larger variety of the crayfish), and crab. Chile peppers also grew well in the area. Okra was also a popular food among the Africans, and a popular seasoning among the Native Americans was a powder made from sassafras leaves.

The various groups of people in the area had their own unique cooking techniques. Both the Cajuns and the French were familiar with *roux*, a sauce base that's made by combining melted butter and flour. The Africans used a slow-tempered cooking fire along with a heavy iron pot.

The combination of all of these ingredients and techniques resulted in the now-famous Cajun dish called gumbo. This particular dish, more than any other, is identified with Cajun cooking because it represents the unique mixture of cultures that is Cajun cooking. Cajun cuisine is quite different from Creole cuisine in nearby New Orleans; Creole cuisine is almost identical to French except that local ingredients are used instead of traditional French ingredients.[26]

One of the most perplexing and intriguing flavor principles is chile pepper, and its burn- and pain-inducing ingredient, capsaicin. Most people initially find eating chile pepper unpleasant. The physical effects of chile pepper in the mouth are similar to the effects of being burned—there's a sensation of pain as well as burn.[27] As a result, chile pepper has been sold as a powder for hikers and skiers to apply to their feet to keep them warm in cold weather. It's been used on fences to keep elephants away from crops, as a spray to deter attackers of both the human and the grizzly bear variety, and as an ingredient in early 20th century wallpaper paste in Appalachia to keep rats from eating wallpaper.[28] Yet, amazingly, this New World plant has been cultivated for at least 6,000 years, and is now grown and eaten around the globe. Chile peppers are an integral part of cuisines as diverse as Mexican, Szechuan, and Hungarian.[29] There's even a Chile Pepper Institute at New Mexico State University that disseminates and preserves information about chile peppers. The institute's Web site, www.chilepepperinstitute.org, can tell you the hotness of different kinds of chile peppers (the hottest is called Trinidad Moruga Scorpion). Because chile pepper seems such an unlikely popular food, by examining how people come to like it, we can perhaps elucidate some of the many ways in which flavors come to be frequently used flavor principles.

Let's start by looking at who does and doesn't like to eat chile pepper. Rats exposed to chile pepper won't eat it, but they can learn to prefer it if they're exposed to other rats that have eaten it.[30] Similarly, chimpanzees exposed to chile peppers through contact with people can acquire a preference for it.[31] Nevertheless, we're the only omnivores that regularly eat chile pepper; preference for chile pepper is one of the few differences between the real-world food preferences of people and other animals. But it's important to keep in mind that there are significant individual differences in how much different people like chile pepper. Some people prefer large amounts, and some people don't like it at all.

Now let's consider some of the reasons that some people may come to prefer chile pepper while others don't. First, there may be genetic differences in how much pain someone feels upon eating chile pepper, with people who feel less pain preferring chile pepper more. Scientists have been able to construct transgenic mice that lack the receptor cells that detect the burn of chile pepper.[32] These mice—as well as perhaps some people—may prefer large amounts of chile pepper because, for genetic reasons, they don't detect the chile pepper burn. In contrast, PTC/PROP (phenylthiocarbamide and 6-N-propylthiouracil) supertasters, whose unusually sensitive taste trait is genetically based, as described in Chapter 4, tend to perceive more burn from chile pepper, probably because they tend to have more cells in their mouths that are specialized for pain detection.[33] Given the greater burn that they feel, PTC/PROP supertasters may prefer chile pepper less than other people.

But even granted that there may be genetic factors responsible for some of the differences in chile pepper preference among people, it's still very unusual for a child to prefer chile pepper the first time that the child eats it. Only after a number of exposures to chile pepper does preference for it increase, with a great many adults coming to prefer it.[34] Therefore our experiences, and not just our genes, contribute to our liking chile pepper.

Initially, people may sample chile pepper because of social pressure. Later, they may come to like it because of the large amounts of vitamins A and C that it contains; the increase in salivation and gastric movement that it engenders, which assists in the digestion of starchy foods; or the zest that it adds to a meal. Other possible explanations are that it masks the odors and tastes of spoiled food and that it causes sweating and thus body cooling, which is useful in hot climates. However, as of yet we have little or no direct evidence supporting any of these possible explanations. Another possibility is that the pain that accompanies eating chile pepper is enjoyed because it seems dangerous but is actually safe—a manifestation of the sensation-seeking trait.[35] There's also evidence that, although repeated bites of chile pepper in the same meal greatly increase the burn, repeated meals of chile pepper over periods of days greatly decrease the burn, thus suggesting another way in which experience could increase the preference for chile pepper.[36] However, it's been argued that the decrease in chile pepper burn (the pain) that comes from daily exposure to chile pepper is too small to explain the accompanying increase in chile preference.[37] Still another possible explanation is that the negative physiological reaction on first tasting chile pepper—that is, the pain— may, with experience, come to be counteracted or even overwhelmed by an opposite, positive, physiological reaction.[38] This hypothesis has received some support in experiments with another widely consumed but initially aversive substance, coffee.[39]

Evidence has confirmed what has long been suspected, that chile pepper kills food bacteria and therefore may be particularly useful in warm climates where food can spoil more quickly. Scientist Paul W. Sherman and his colleagues have shown that chile pepper can inhibit a whopping 80% of bacterial growth in food, and that cookbooks from warm climates are more likely to contain recipes that use chile pepper.[40] Yet as intriguing as these results may be, they can't explain why people in cold climates also often like chile pepper. It's possible that there are many ways by which different people may come to prefer chile pepper.

There's one other attribute of chile pepper eating that's particularly relevant to this book. Recent evidence indicates that, when capsaicin is part of a meal, people tend to eat less and feel more full. In addition, people eating chile pepper consume relatively more carbohydrates, and less fat. Chile pepper consumption has therefore been suggested as a useful part of a weight management strategy.[41]

The other flavor principle that I'd like to cover is chocolate. Chocolate is every bit as, if not more, fascinating than chile pepper. Similar to chile pepper, chocolate is popular all over the world. However, again like chile pepper, it originated in the New World and has only been available to most of the world for the past several hundred years. In fact, it was only after chocolate was brought to Europe that it was manufactured with sugar and milk into the form of chocolate with which we are most familiar today: milk chocolate. Prior to that time, for at least 2,500 years, Mesoamerican communities used chocolate in various unsweetened forms.[42] Today, similar to chile pepper, chocolate is big business, with worldwide sales topping $90 billion per year.[43]

But here is where any similarities between chile pepper and chocolate stop. Chocolate isn't aversive the first time someone tastes it. Even though some people get migraine headaches about 24 hours after eating chocolate,[44] most people love it the first time, and every time, they eat it. Studies have found that chocolate is one of the most frequently craved foods. For example, close to 50% of American women crave it.[45] One sample of self-described chocoholics, 92% of whom were women, reported eating, on average, 12 2-ounce bars of chocolate per week.[46]

Love of chocolate is everywhere. A restaurant in Philadelphia that I visited a few years ago had this aphorism on the wall: "Forget love, I would rather fall in chocolate." When I was traveling in Germany some years ago I stumbled upon the Imhoff Chocolate Museum in Köln. This museum covers everything you would ever want to know about chocolate, from how the cacao tree's seeds are processed to make chocolate, to images of chocolate in art—and, oh yes, there are plenty of free samples. My favorite was the sugar wafers that had been dipped in a huge fountain of liquid chocolate. I wasn't alone in loving this museum; it was extremely crowded with people of all ages and types. Chocolate obsession even frequents the Internet. Table 15.2 lists chocolate "rules" that I received in an e-mail from Sarah Wahlert, whose father, John Wahlert, is a biology professor who worked with me and who will do (almost) anything as long as you give him chocolate.

The past decade has seen an explosion of research on psychology and chocolate, with at least two dozen articles published in the journal *Appetite* alone. This research provides information on how chocolate affects our behavior, as well as what factor or factors are responsible for the incredible liking for chocolate, and how to modify that liking. We now know that chocolate contains substantial amounts of chemicals that are extremely helpful in preventing cardiovascular and other diseases.[47]

Table 15.2 Chocolate rules

1 Put "eat chocolate" at the top of your list of things to do today. That way, at least you'll get one thing done.
2 If you've got melted chocolate all over your hands, you're eating it too slowly.
3 Chocolate covered raisins, cherries, orange slices, and strawberries all count as fruit, so eat as many as you want!
4 The problem: How to get 2 pounds of chocolate home from the store in a hot car. The solution: Eat it in the parking lot.
5 Diet tip: Eat a chocolate bar before each meal. It'll take the edge off your appetite and you'll eat less.
6 Chocolate has many preservatives. Preservatives make you look younger.
7 Q: Why is there no such organization as Chocoholics Anonymous? A: Because no one wants to quit.
8 A nice box of chocolates can provide your total daily intake of calories in one place … isn't that handy?
9 If you can't eat all your chocolate, it will keep in the freezer. But if you can't eat all your chocolate, what's wrong with you?

In addition, recent experiments suggest that consumption of chocolate can improve mood. It can also improve cognitive functioning in older people, including those suffering from mild cognitive impairments.[48] Such effects probably occur too long after instances of chocolate eating for our ancestors to have eaten chocolate in order to obtain those medicinal benefits. But there are several factors that undoubtedly do contribute to our eating so much chocolate. One is that the chocolate that we eat is usually mixed with sugar, thus tapping into our largely innate preference for sweet tastes and arousing strong sensual and pleasurable sensations.[49] Another reason is that chocolate is high in fat. You'll remember from our discussion of the contributions of our experiences to food preferences that we learn to prefer foods that are high in calories, and that fat contains more calories per ounce than carbohydrates or protein. One ounce of milk chocolate contains about 150 calories, as well as significant amounts of calcium, potassium, magnesium, vitamin A, and vitamin B_3, all essential nutrients.[50] Chocolate also contains caffeine, which has an unusual flavor by itself. One ounce of bittersweet chocolate contains about one-third the amount of caffeine as a cup of tea. Chapter 8 discussed the fact that caffeine is a stimulant. So it's possible that some people who eat very large amounts of chocolate find its stimulating effects to be rewarding, as do rats.[51] Chocolate also has a smooth, pleasant texture and melts at body temperature, thus adding to its appeal.

This brings us to love (remember I promised that this chapter would cover love, as well as war; the war part is later). Soon after it was brought to Europe, chocolate was touted as an aphrodisiac.[52] Both the 2001 film and the originating book *Chocolat* link chocolate with love. And of course you're all familiar with the strong association of chocolate with Valentine's Day. Doesn't this all seem to be a bit too much of a coincidence? Why is it that chocolate, throughout its history, has been continually associated with love and sex? One reason may have to do with chocolate's chemical effects on the brain. However, so far, there's been no scientific proof of this scintillating possibility.

Chocolate may have other chemical effects on the body that people find pleasurable or rewarding. For example, it's been shown that there are chemicals in chocolate that may have effects on the brain similar to marijuana.[53] In addition, there's discussion by scientists that people who crave chocolate tend, on average, to be more depressed than are noncravers, and that such people claim that eating chocolate makes them less depressed. In support of these claims, there's evidence that a particular kind of antidepressant medication also eliminates chocolate craving, and that chocolate contains relatively large amounts of tryptophan (the serotonin precursor; see Figure 8.1)—you'll recall that low levels of serotonin are associated with depression.[54]

Chocolate craving can cause negative effects. In addition to its resulting in overconsumption of chocolate and all that that entails, it is apparently distracting, and thus can impede certain types of memory.[55] There have therefore been many attempts to figure out the best methods for decreasing chocolate craving. Strategies such as training the skill of disidentification ("the ability to separate oneself from thoughts about cravings," an example of a mindfulness skill) and taking a brisk walk are examples of what has been found to be helpful.[56]

Way before many researchers were interested in chocolate, I was fortunate to be among some of the few who were. You may remember from earlier chapters the informal Cuisine Group to which I used to belong. We met once a month to discuss various topics concerning food. Each meeting had a theme. I'll never forget the day we did chocolate. It was right before Easter and Barbara Kirshenblatt-Gimblett, the New York University professor in whose New York City loft we met, had bought us huge chocolate bunnies and other chocolate items made by hand in a candy store in Queens. We had chocolate for lunch, listened to lectures about chocolate in the afternoon, and went to a restaurant that served a dessert entitled "Death by Chocolate" in the evening. We discussed such matters as which part of the chocolate bunny you eat first and why, how difficult it is to manufacture artificial chocolate flavor, and the possible connections of chocolate with sexual behavior. Total heaven.

Thou shalt not eat: examples of forbidden eating, the sacred cow, cannibalism, and vegetarianism

In this section I'll discuss three examples of cultural constraints on cuisine that have received particular attention: the sacred cow in India, cannibalism, and vegetarianism. All three examples concern situations in which a readily available food could be part of a cuisine but, for cultural reasons, is not. In both cases, research evidence discussed in earlier chapters can be brought to bear to understand why these cultural constraints may or may not exist.

In India, Hindus have a prohibition against eating cows, which are considered sacred. Hindu pilgrims will even touch their foreheads to a cow's tail for purification purposes. Given that so many people in India don't have enough food, and that the cows in India may be causing harm to the environment by overgrazing, treating cows as sacred seems counterproductive. However, using the sorts of food choice analyses described earlier in this book, scientist Marvin Harris and others have contended that treating cows in India as sacred is actually greatly beneficial to India's economy.

According to Harris, oxen (castrated male cattle) are essential to the Indian agricultural system, providing the power necessary to till the soil.

It's difficult for farmers to share oxen because, as a result of the monsoon rains, all of the crops tend to become ready for harvesting at the same time. Therefore most farmers need to have their own oxen. Oxen also provide transportation. And in order to get oxen, cows are necessary. During droughts, cows may become infertile. However, if they're not kept alive, there won't be any cows to produce oxen.

Cattle are allowed to wander along the roads. Although it may appear that the cattle are permitted to wander freely because they're "sacred," they're actually eating the grass along the road so that their owners don't have to feed them. When wandering cows end up in downtown, religiously conservative New Delhi, where they may cause traffic accidents and die from eating plastic bags, municipal cow catchers gently capture the cows and take them to a suburban location where they can comfortably live for the rest of their lives.

If a farmer has to make a choice between feeding his cows or his oxen, the oxen are usually fed, thus protecting the farmer's immediate survival, though perhaps sacrificing future survival. Further, in general, the food that's given to cattle consists mostly of the parts of plants that people can't eat.

Cattle also provide dung, which is very important in India both as cooking fuel and as fertilizer. In some parts of India virtually 100% of the dung is used for these purposes. On a recent visit to India, I saw women shaping dung patties for later burning (as Americans would shape hamburger patties), and then making elaborate geometrical piles of them.

Finally, statistics on the relative number of cows versus oxen show that there are far more oxen than cows, perhaps because of differential amounts of neglect. In any case, when a cow does die, it can be touched only by a member of the lowest Indian caste, the Untouchables. A member of this caste will take the carcass and use the hide to make leather and leather products, which can be sold. This provides a sort of welfare system for some of India's poorest people.

For all of these reasons Harris and others believe that the treatment of cows in India as sacred is actually beneficial to the Indian economy. Through the centuries, those Indians who treated cows as sacred may have been more likely to survive than people who didn't. Thus a cultural trait concerning food choice that appears to be based in religion may actually be a result of a complex array of economic, ecological, and political factors.[57] Given that people evolved in surroundings in which the food supplies were often inadequate, it's not surprising that cuisines, as well as other aspects of culture, often reflect optimal solutions for maximizing survival.[58]

The prohibition against eating the flesh of your own species seems less difficult to figure out. After all, if we regularly ate other people then the human species would be less likely to survive. Nevertheless, eating each other has fueled our imaginations on Broadway in the show *Sweeney Todd: The Demon Barber of Fleet Street* and at the movie theaters in the films *Hannibal* and *Silence of the Lambs*.

However cannibalism has rarely been a part of our species' reality, except when people were facing situations of absolute starvation, situations that have been perceived as regrettable acts or antisocial behavior, rather than as accepted practice.[59] A true story of such a situation was recounted in the book and film *Alive*, in which survivors of a plane crash in the Andes run out of food and then eat the bodies of people killed in the crash. Similar to what occurs among rats, eating other people was facilitated by being very hungry. Seeing other people do it, a possible instance of the observational learning seen in many species, also helped,[60] as did covering up the bodies to minimize the cues that the meat was coming from a person.

But are we so sure that cannibalism has never been a regular practice? Or is that just what we'd like to believe? After all, as discussed in Chapter 1, one of our closest relatives, chimpanzees, will hunt and kill some of their closest relatives, monkeys. For decades researchers have argued over whether there have been human societies in which cannibalism was a regular occurrence. Some researchers have felt that, prior to 1900, there may have been societies that engaged in regular cannibalism, but accurate, complete records from that time have been difficult to obtain.[61] Research in Spain has found human bones dating back approximately 750,000 years that were arrayed in a way consistent with butchering processes. Remains of Neanderthals in France from approximately 100,000 years ago provide similar evidence. Other researchers have claimed that there's much evidence for cannibalism around AD 1000 by the Anasazi Indians in the American Southwest.[62] Yet there have always been ways to explain away what was found. For example, the sorts of remains found could have been due to ritual executions.[63]

However, one set of findings seemed to indicate that cannibalism did take place, at least on one occasion, among the Anasazi Indians (ancestors of today's Hopi and Zuni tribes). This research took advantage of the field of biogeochemistry, which permits scientists to analyze the body parts of living and dead animals to determine what foods they ate, allowing scientists to put a new twist on an old slogan, "You are what you eat."[64]

A few years ago pathologist Richard A. Marlar and his colleagues published an article in *Nature* demonstrating an instance of what appeared to be Anasazi cannibalism. These scientists investigated an archaeological site near the Four Corners area of the American Southwest. This particular site contained several pit houses that were suddenly abandoned around AD 1150. Two of the pit houses contained the remains of seven people—males and females of varying ages. The bodies had been taken apart, defleshed, and burned in a manner consistent with butchering and cooking. Butchering tools with blood residue were found near the bodies, as was a cooking pot containing a type of human protein. However, these items can be explained as something other than cannibalism; by itself, none of this evidence proves definitively that the seven people were killed on purpose or that they were eaten. The key evidence was in the third pit house. In that dwelling were the remains of a hearth, and in that hearth was a human coprolite (fossil fecal remains) that wasn't burned and so had been deposited after the last fire there. Analyses showed that the coprolite had resulted from a meal that consisted of almost entirely meat, and that it contained protein found only in nonintestinal human cells. Thus, this coprolite resulted from a human eating human flesh.

Apparently this happened at a time of severe drought in the Four Corners area, resulting in great stress among the tribes there. Some scientists believe that one group of Anasazi attacked another, killed them, ate them, and defecated in their hearth as a parting gesture of contempt. (This is the part of the chapter on war that I promised you.) Others have pointed out that at other times of stress in the food supply, the Anasazi definitely didn't resort to cannibalism, so whatever happened with that coprolite is an anomaly.[65] Undoubtedly scientists will continue analyzing coprolites to see just how anomalous a finding this was.

The prohibition against eating members of your own species can extend to species closely associated with your own. Rats are unlikely to eat mice if the rat has been raised with a mouse.[66] People generally don't eat the members of other species with which they live and which they consider to possess human traits. In the United States and other Western countries, such species include cats and dogs.

Before we leave the fascinating topic of eating members of our own or related species, I'd like to make a few comments about vegetarianism. Vegetarianism and its variants—avoiding all flesh foods, avoiding all flesh foods except fish, and avoiding all flesh foods except fish and fowl—are fairly common in Western countries. You learned in Chapter 9 that semivegetarianism is often associated with eating disorders. People also avoid meat for reasons of health—the additives or fat that meat contains. However, another reason that people avoid meat is because of their concerns about the ethics of how animals are raised for food or because of their disgust at eating meat.[67] Given these findings and the material in the preceding paragraphs, one wonders if some of these cases of meat avoidance are generalizations or expansions of the prohibition against eating human meat. The flesh foods that are generally the most acceptable—fish and fowl—are also those that are most dissimilar to human meat.

Another example of how people's close associations with other species can affect vegetarianism is that people who don't themselves eat meat for ethical reasons are uncomfortable with their pets eating meat. Which is more of a problem than you might think because people who don't eat meat for ethical reasons also tend to have more pets than do other people. Which all results in what is known as the vegetarian's dilemma—vegetarian pet owners may feel that a meat-containing diet is best for their pet, and yet feel uncomfortable feeding them such a diet because of harm to other animals.[68]

Pleasures of the Palate With a Kick: Beer and Wine Tasting

When my husband and I were in graduate school, and when we came to New York for our first jobs, money was scarce. But we wanted to have interesting parties so, on several occasions, we had beer-tasting parties (they're a lot cheaper than wine-tasting parties). At these parties we distributed the beer in small, clear plastic cups without any identifying information and asked everyone attending to rate their preferences for the different beers. We awarded prizes to those people who gave the highest rankings to the most expensive beers and to those people who gave the highest rankings to the cheapest beers. Interestingly, partygoers who really liked beer tended to give high rankings to the more expensive beers, and those who didn't like beer (such as me) tended to give high rankings to the less expensive beers. This apparently happened because the more expensive beers also tended to be the strongest tasting. Many years later, we now know that PTC/PROP super-tasters (such as me), discussed in detail in Chapters 4 and 5, tend to perceive beer, among other items, as more bitter than nontasters. So if you don't like beer, the next time someone makes fun of you for turning up your nose at some expensive microbrewed ale, you can explain that it's because you possess a taste sensitivity that the ale lover does not, and it's the ale lover who's really obtuse.

Much more common than beer tasting is wine tasting, a great vehicle for demonstrating how the varied scientific approaches that underlie the psychology of eating and drinking can come together to help us understand particular eating and drinking behaviors. An examination of the wine-tasting process can help us understand not only how wines are evaluated, but how any food or drink is evaluated, as well as the factors that affect those evaluations.

Given that many of you have probably never engaged in formal wine tasting, it will be helpful if I begin by briefly describing the wine-tasting procedure. The first step is simply to look at the wine. Then it's swirled in the glass to increase its aroma and bouquet, which are smelled in the next step. Finally the wine is tasted in small sips. It's rolled over the tongue and bits of bread or cheese may be taken between sips. Some wine tasters spit out the sips of wine without swallowing them. This prevents the possible adverse effects of alcohol on sensory sensitivity.[69]

Each of these steps is performed separately, quietly, and with as little distraction as possible. As you learned in Chapter 4, this separation and isolation in the wine-tasting process permit more attention to be focused on each of the steps. People are more likely to report detecting low levels of specific tastes or odors under these conditions. Another way to help increase people's reported sensitivity to tastes and odors during wine tasting is to offer rewards for accurate judgments or to set up a competition among the wine tasters. A factor that affects everyone's odor sensitivity no matter how motivated they are is the temperature of the wine. When wine is very cold it's harder to smell. Most people who taste wine without distractions, and when the wine is at the appropriate temperature, can become skilled at discriminating among various types of wine.

To judge the odor of a wine, wine tasters pay attention to both the wine's aroma, which consists of the odors arising from the type of grape used in making the wine, and the wine's bouquet, which consists of the odors derived from fermentation, processing, or aging. Calling the various odors by specific names may help in their identification. For example, many people describe the aroma of the Sauvignon Blanc grape as spicy. The shape of the wine glass influences how these odors are perceived. In judging the taste of the wine, the wine is rolled around on the tongue so that all of the taste receptors are stimulated.[70] Carbonation, as is found in champagne as well as beer, is tasted by means of stimulation of the tongue's taste receptors for sour.[71]

In addition to smell and taste, the senses of vision and touch are critical to wine tasting. The visual judgment of a wine includes judging both the wine's color and its appearance; for example, whether it's cloudy.[72] If the color of a wine is unusual for its type, this may affect the wine taster's judgment of other aspects of the wine, such as the wine's taste. Certain tastes are associated with certain colors, and it's harder to detect a taste if its usually associated color isn't present.[73] If the wine is cloudy, a taster may be more likely to judge the wine's taste as below par. This probably happens because, in the past, that taster has encountered cloudy wine and it did not taste good. However, given that appearance and taste aren't always correlated, it's important to try to prevent such interactive effects. One solution is to drink the wine out of a glass painted black, so that it's impossible to see the wine. Then the merits of the wine's taste can be judged by themselves.

To assess the touch of the wine, a wine taster notes any astringency on the tongue, as well as whether the wine feels full or thin. The wine feels thin when there's a low alcohol content and full when there's a high alcohol content.[74] Beer has also been studied with regard to touch. How thirst quenching a beer is turns out to depend on the degree to which it's carbonated and the density of bubbles in the beer—the more bubbles, the more thirst quenching.[75]

There are several psychological processes that you have to watch out for when wine tasting because they can interfere with your making good judgments. One of these is that when sensory cells, such as those for taste and smell, are repeatedly stimulated during a wine-tasting session, they tire out and are less likely to respond than at the beginning of the wine tasting. This is why wine tasters may take bites of bread between sips and why they taste slowly. They're trying to keep their sensory cells at maximum sensitivity.

Another problem has to do with the words used to describe what's seen, smelled, tasted, and felt. Terms such as *fruity, pale yellow,* and *woody* are used frequently. However, there's no guarantee that the same word used by two different people has the same meaning for both of them. In addition, over time the use of certain words may change.[76]

Memory is also very important in wine tasting. A taster needs to compare wines to absolute standards developed from previous tastings. In addition, if too large a series of wines is tasted during one session, those tasted in the middle are likely to suffer in terms of the taster's memory of them. People tend to remember the beginning and end of a long series of tasted wines better than they do the middle.[77] Completing a rating form can help a taster to remember what has been tasted.[78]

Still another issue is the influence of people's expectations on their actual sensory experience of the wine. Being told something positive or negative about a wine prior to tasting it can change someone's ratings of that wine.[79] In fact, being told that a wine's price is relatively high not only increases someone's ratings of its taste, but also increases activity in the parts of the brain that are thought to be responsible for our experiencing pleasure.[80] As another example of how context can affect wine consumption, when a British supermarket played German Bierkeller music, customers were more likely to buy German wine, and when the supermarket played French accordion music, customers were more likely to buy French wine.[81] Given all of these sorts of effects, it's not surprising that some unscrupulous people have been able to dupe some other people into buying wine that is worth much less than its (sometimes falsified) label, bottle, and contents would justify.[82]

Restaurants

And now a few words about restaurants. Much of what you've learned in this book so far has relevance for the eating and drinking that goes on in restaurants—when, what, and how you eat and drink in these establishments. But there's even more psychology involved in what you consume in restaurants than you might think. For example, smelling a fruity odor can make you more likely to choose a fruit dessert in a buffet; presenting a dish artfully on a plate (where the presentation is in accordance with your culture's standards) can result in your rating a food as tasting better, while eating in the dark can result in your rating a food lower and eating more than usual; and different kinds of music can increase or decrease your perceived pleasantness of a dish, while hearing drinking songs in a bar can make you stay there longer.[83] And then there are menus.... Although there isn't yet much in the way of rigorous research on menu construction, there is plenty of lore about how to get customers to eat certain dishes (usually expensive ones), and more of them.[84]

As we discussed earlier in this book, purveyors (in this case, restaurant owners, managers, and servers) have the goal of getting you to spend more (which usually also means eating and drinking more), and they will use all kinds of strategies to achieve that. You, on the other hand, are probably unaware (at least until now) that this kind of influence is going on. In addition, your own goal may not be the same as the restaurant's—you may want to have a satisfying meal at a reasonable price, a meal that does not result in your gaining weight or eating more salt, sugar, or fat than is good for you. The purveyors seem to have many tools available for achieving their goals, but customers seem to often be in the dark and influenced to engage in behaviors incompatible with their own goals.

Public health officials are devoting much effort to addressing this imbalance. It is for this reason that former New York City mayor, Michael Bloomberg, made much news by requiring some New York City restaurants to post the calorie counts of their dishes.[85] More broadly, in New York City and across the United States, groups of people as seemingly disparate as chefs, elected officials, and parents are banding together to spread information and change the environment in ways that will promote healthy, affordable, eating and drinking—in restaurants and elsewhere. The strategies being used have previously proved successful in other arenas, and so there is reason for optimism regarding the current efforts.[86] Going to restaurants is a wonderful way to socialize and to have new experiences—to explore new tastes and new cultures. Having confidence in the healthfulness of what is consumed there will only make the experience that much more enjoyable.

Parting is so Sweet and Sour

This chapter's coverage of cuisine and beer and wine tasting provides excellent examples of the advantages of taking an interdisciplinary, scientific approach to the psychology of eating and drinking. Our enjoyment of food and drink will continue to be enhanced by this type of approach, which takes into account all of our senses, past experiences, genes, and current surroundings, including our companions.

I'd like to end this final chapter with two quotations that illustrate the eternal value of food and drink.

Kissing don't last: cookery do!
George Meredith, 19th century English novelist and poet[87]

We may live without poetry, music and art;
We may live without conscience, and live without heart;
We may live without friends; we may live without books;
But civilized man cannot live without cooks.
He may live without books,—what is knowledge but grieving?
He may live without hope,—what is hope but deceiving?
He may live without love,—what is passion but pining?
But where is the man that can live without dining?

Edward Robert Bulwer Lytton,
19th century English statesman and poet[88]

REFERENCES

1 INTRODUCTION

1 W. Shakespeare, *Twelfth Night* in *The Complete Works of William Shakespeare*, ed. W. A. Wright, Garden City, NY: Garden City Books, 1623/1936, p. 707.

2 S. Sotomayor, *My Beloved World*, New York: Alfred A. Knopf, 2013, p. 105.

3 H. Gleitman, *Psychology*, New York: W. W. Norton, 1981, p. 1.

4 W. J. Davis, "Motivation and Learning: Neurophysiological Mechanisms in a 'Model' System," *Learning and Motivation* 15(1984): 377–393.

5 E. M. Blass and M. H. Teicher, "Suckling," *Science* 210(1980): 15–22.

6 C. Thorne, "Feeding Behavior of Domestic Dogs and the Role of Experience," in *The Domestic Dog: Its Evolution, Behaviour, and Interactions with People*, ed. J. Serpell, New York: Cambridge University Press, 1995.

7 R. J. Herrnstein and E. G. Boring, *A Source Book in the History of Behavior*, Cambridge, MA: Harvard University Press, 1965.

8 M. Bearzi and C. Stanford, "A Bigger, Better Brain," *American Scientist* 98(2010): 402–409.

9 H. Van Lawick-Goodall, *In the Shadow of Man*, New York: Dell, 1971.

10 M. Kawai, "Newly-Acquired Pre-Cultural Behavior of the Natural Troop of Japanese Monkeys on Koshima Islet," *Primates* 6(1965): 1–30.

11 C. B. Stanford, "Chimpanzee Hunting Behavior and Human Evolution," *American Scientist* (May/June 1995): 256–261.

12 S. A. Barnett, *The Rat: A Study in Behavior*, Chicago: Aldine, 1963.

13 J. J. Wurtman and R. J. Wurtman, "Sucrose Consumption Early in Life Fails to Modify the Appetite of Adult Rats for Sweet Foods," *Science* 205(1979): 321–322.

14 Barnett, *The Rat*.

15 H. R. Kissileff, J. L. Guss, and L. J. Nolan, "What Animal Research Tells Us about Human Eating," in *Food Choice, Acceptance and Consumption*, eds. H. L. Meiselman and H. J. H. MacFie, New York: Blackie Academic & Professional, 1996.

2 DOWN THE HATCH

1 J. Z. Young, "Influence of the Mouth on the Evolution of the Brain," in *Biology of the Brain*, ed. P. Person, Washington, DC: American Association for the Advancement of Science, 1968, p. 21.

2 S. J. Cooper, "From Claude Bernard to Walter Cannon. Emergence of the Concept of Homeostasis," *Appetite* 51(2008): 419–427.

3 J. Maurer, D. L. Taren, P. J. Teixeira, C. A. Thomson, T. G. Lohman, S. B. Going, and L. B. Houtkooper, "The Psychosocial and Behavioral Characteristics Related to Energy Misreporting," *Nutrition Reviews* 64(2006): 53–66.

4 W. B. Cannon and A. L. Washburn, "An Explanation of Hunger," *The American Journal of Physiology* 29(1912): 441–454.

5 W. B. Cannon, "Hunger and Thirst," in *The Foundations of Experimental Psychology*, ed. C. Murchison, Worcester, MA: Clark University Press, 1929.

6 E. Stellar, "The Physiology of Motivation," *Psychological Review* 61(1954): 5–22.

  A. J. Stunkard and S. Fox, "The Relationship of Gastric Motility and Hunger: A Summary of the Evidence," *Psychosomatic Medicine* 33(1971): 123–134.

7 Ibid.

8 M. L. Power and J. Schulkin, "Anticipatory Physiological Regulation in Feeding Biology: Cephalic Phase Responses," *Appetite* 50(2008): 194–206.

9 G. M. Finch, J. E. L. Day, Razak, D. A. Welch, and P. J. Rogers, "Appetite Changes under Free-Living Conditions during Ramadan Fasting," *Appetite* 31(1998): 159–170.

10 J. R. Brobeck, "Food Intake as a Mechanism of Temperature Regulation," *Journal of Biology and Medicine* 20(1948): 545–552.

11 E. S. Kraly and E. M. Blass, "Increased Feeding in Rats in a Low Ambient Temperature," in *Hunger: Basic Mechanisms and Clinical Implications*, eds. D. Novin, W. Wyrwicka, and G. A. Bray, New York: Raven Press, 1976.

  J. Le Magnen, *Neurobiology of Feeding and Nutrition*. New York: Academic Press, 1992.

12 H. D. Janowitz and M. I. Grossman, "Some Factors Affecting the Food Intake of Normal Dogs and Dogs with Esophagostomy and Gastric Fistula," *American Journal of Physiology* 159(1949): 143–148.

13 G. P. Smith, "Pregastric and Gastric Satiety," in *Satiation: From Gut to Brain*, ed. G. P. Smith, New York: Oxford University Press, 1998.

14 M. M. Hetherington and E. Boyland, "Short-Term Effects of Chewing Gum on Snack Intake and Appetite," *Appetite* 48(2007): 397–401.

  S. Higgs and A. Jones, "Prolonged Chewing at Lunch Decreases Later Snack Intake," *Appetite* 62(2013): 91–95.

15 P. J. Rogers and H. G. Schutz, "Influence of Palatability on Subsequent Hunger and Food Intake: A Retrospective Replication," *Appetite* 19(1992): 155–156.

  M. G. Tordoff and M. I. Friedman, "Drinking Saccharin Increases Food Intake and Preference IV. Cephalic Phase and Metabolic Factors," *Appetite* 12(1989): 37–56.

  "Saccharin Consumption Increases Food Consumption in Rats," *Nutrition Reviews* 48(1990): 163–165.

16 D. G. Mook and M. C. Votaw, "How Important Is Hedonism? Reasons Given by College Students for Ending a Meal," *Appetite* 18(1992): 69–75.

17 Janowitz and Grossman, "Some Factors Affecting the Food Intake of Normal Dogs and Dogs with Esophagostomy and Gastric Fistula."

  H. D. Janowitz and F. Hollander, "Effect of Prolonged Intragastric Feeding on Oral Ingestion," *Federation Proceedings* 12(1953): 72.

  I. Share and E. Martyniuk, "Effect of Prolonged Intragastric Feeding on Oral Food Intake in Dogs," *American Journal of Physiology* 169(1952): 229–235.

18 M. Clegg and A. Shafat, "Energy and Macronutrient Composition of Breakfast Affect Gastric Emptying of Lunch and Subsequent Food Intake, Satiety and Satiation," *Appetite* 54(2010): 517–523.

M. Yao and S. B. Roberts, "Dietary Energy Density and Weight Regulation," *Nutrition Reviews* 59(2001): 247–258.

19 B. J. Rolls, E. A. Bell, and M. L. Thorwart, "Water Incorporated into a Food but Not Served with a Food Decreases Energy Intake in Lean Women," *American Journal of Clinical Nutrition* 70(1999): 448–455.

B. J. Rolls, V. H. Castellanos, J. C. Halford, A. Kilara, D. Panyam, C. L. Pelkman, G. P. Smith, and M. L. Thorwart, "Volume of Food Consumed Affects Satiety in Men," *American Journal of Clinical Nutrition* 67(1998): 1170–1177.

20 D. Greenberg, "Intestinal Satiety," in *Satiation: From Gut to Brain*, ed. G. P. Smith, New York: Oxford University Press, 1998.

Smith, "Pregastric and Gastric Satiety."

21 J. Mayer, "The Glucostatic Theory of Regulation of Food Intake and the Problem of Obesity," *Bulletin of the New England Medical Center* 14(1952): 43–49.

22 Ibid.

23 G. C. Kennedy, "The Role of Depot Fat in the Hypothalamic Control of Food Intake in the Rat," *Proceedings of the Royal Society of London*, 140B(1953): 578–592.

Mayer, "The Glucostatic Theory of Regulation of Food, Intake and the Problem of Obesity."

J. Mayer, "Regulation of Energy Intake and the Body Weight: The Glucostatic Theory and the Lipostatic Hypothesis," *Annals New York Academy of Sciences* 63(1955): 15–43.

24 R. B. S. Harris, "Is Leptin the Parabiotic "Satiety" Factor? Past and Present Interpretations," *Appetite* 61(2013): 111–118.

25 S. Ritter, "Glucoprivation and the Glucoprivic Control of Food Intake," in *Feeding Behavior: Neural and Humoral Controls*, eds. R. C. Ritter, S. Ritter, and C. D. Barnes, New York: Academic Press, 1986.

26 K. L. Morris and M. B. Zemel, "Glycemic Index, Cardiovascular Disease, and Obesity," *Nutrition Reviews* 57(1999): 273–276.

27 S. Holt, J. Brand, C. Soveny, and J. Hansky, "Relationship of Satiety to Postprandial Glycaemic, Insulin, and Choecystokinin Responses," *Appetite* 18(1992): 129–141.

28 Morris and Zemel, "Glycemic Index, Cardiovascular Disease, and Obesity."

29 S. Ibrügger, M. Kristensen, M. S. Mikkelsen, and A. Astrup, "Flaxseed Dietary Fiber Supplements for Suppression of Appetite and Food Intake," *Appetite* 58(2012): 490–495.

L. S. Roe, J. S. Meengs, and B. J. Rolls, "Salad and Satiety. The Effect of Timing of Salad Consumption on Meal Energy Intake," *Appetite* 58(2012): 242–248.

30 J. H. Lavin and N. W. Read, "The Effect on Hunger and Satiety of Slowing the Absorption of Glucose: Relationship with Gastric Emptying and Postprandial Blood Glucose and Insulin responses," *Appetite* 25(1995): 89–96.

31 D. A. Vanderweele, "Insulin as a Satiating Signal," in *Satiation: From Gut to Brain*, ed. G. P. Smith, New York: Oxford University Press, 1998.

32 G. P. Smith and J. Gibbs, "The Satiating Effects of Cholecystokinin and Bombesin-Like Peptides," in *Satiation: From Gut to Brain*, ed. G. P. Smith, New York: Oxford University Press, 1998.

33 A. Weller, G. P. Smith, and J. Gibbs, "Endogenous Cholecystokinin Reduces Feeding in Young Rats," *Science* 247(1990): 1589–1591.

34 N. Geary, "Glucagon and the Control of Meal Size," in *Satiation: From Gut to Brain*, ed. G. P. Smith, New York: Oxford University Press, 1998.

35 C. De Graaf and T. Hulshof, "Effects of Weight and Energy Content of Preloads on Subsequent Appetite and Food Intake," *Appetite* 26(1996): 139–151.

36 S. D. Poppitt and A. M. Prentice, "Energy Density and Its Role in the Control of Food Intake: Evidence from Metabolic and Community Studies," *Appetite* 26(1996): 153–174.

37 A. Furchner-Evanson, Y. Petrisko, L. Howarth, T. Nemoseck, and M. Kern, "Type of Snack Influences Satiety Responses in Adult Women," *Appetite* 54(2010): 564–569.

   J. D. Latner and M. Schwartz, "The Effects of a High-Carbohydrate, High-Protein or Balanced Lunch upon Later Food Intake and Hunger Ratings" *Appetite* 33(1999):119–128.

   M. Porrini, R. Crovetti, G. Testolin, and S. Silva, "Evaluation of Satiety Sensations and Food Intake after Different Preloads," *Appetite* 25(1995): 17–30.

   B. J. Rolls, I. C. Fedoroff, J. F. Guthrie, and L. J. Laster, "Foods with Different Satiating Effects in Humans," *Appetite* 15(1990): 115–126.

   A. Tournier and J. Louis-Sylvestre, "Effect of the Physical State of a Food on Subsequent Intake in Human Subjects," *Appetite* 16(1991): 17–24.

38 H. Bruch, "The Frölich Syndrome: Report of the Original Case," *American Journal of Diseases of Children* 58(1939): 1282, 1283, 1285.

39 A. W. Hetherington and S. W. Ranson, "Hypothalamic Lesions and Adiposity in the Rat," *Anatomical Record* 78(1940): 149–172.

40 B. G. Hoebel and P. Teitelbaum, "Hypothalamic Control of Feeding and Self-Stimulation," *Science* 135(1962): 375–377.

41 J. Mayer and N. B. Marshall, "Specificity of Gold Thioglucose for Ventromedial Hypothalamic Lesions and Hyperphagia," *Nature* 178(1956): 1399–1400.

42 B. K. Anand and J. R. Brobeck, "Localization of a 'Feeding Center' in the Hypothalamus of the Rat," *Proceedings of the Society for Experimental Biology and Medicine* 77(1951): 323–324.

43 Hoebel and Teitelbaum, "Hypothalamic Control of Feeding and Self-Stimulation."

44 Stellar, "The Physiology of Motivation."

45 W. Wyrwicka, *Brain and Feeding Behavior*, Springfield, IL: Charles C. Thomas, 1988.

46 J. R. Stellar and E. Stellar, *The Neurobiology of Motivation and Reward*, New York: Springer-Verlag, 1985.

47 H. J. Grill and J. M. Kaplan, "Caudal Brainstem Participates in the Distributed Neural Control of Feeding," in *Handbook of Behavioral Neurobiology: Vol. 10. Neurobiology of Food and Fluid Intake*, ed. E. M. Stricker, New York: Plenum, 1990.

   A. J. W. Scheurink, "Neuroscience of Energy Substrate Homeostasis," in *Food Intake and Energy Expenditure*, eds. M. S. Westerterp-Plantenga, E. W. H. M. Fredrix, and A. B. Steffens, Boca Raton, FL: CRC Press, 1994.

   P. Winn, "The Lateral Hypothalamus and Motivated Behavior: An Old Syndrome Reassessed and a New Perspective Gained," Current Directions in Psychological Science 4(1995): 182–187.

48 Winn, "The Lateral Hypothalamus and Motivated Behavior."

49 O. Grimm, M. J. Jacob, N. B. Kroemer, L. Krebs, S. Vollstädt-Klein, A. Kobiella, U. Wolfensteller, and M. N. Smolka, "The Personality Trait Self-Directedness

Predicts the Amygdala's Reaction to Appetizing Cues in fMRI," *Appetite* 58(2012): 1023–1029.

J. H. Jennings, G. Rizzi, A. M. Stamatakis, R. L. Ung, and G. D. Stuber, "The Inhibitory Circuit Architecture of the Lateral Hypothalamus Orchestrates Feeding," *Science* 341(2013): 1517–1521.

50 R. D. Myers and M. L. McCaleb, "Feeding: Satiety Signal from Intestine Triggers Brain's Noradrenergic Mechanism," *Science* 209(1980): 1035–1037.

51 Stellar and Stellar, *The Neurobiology of Motivation and Reward.*

52 S. E. Leibowitz, "Hypothalamic Neurotransmitters in Relation to Normal and Disturbed Eating Patterns," in *Human Obesity*, eds. R. J. Wurtman and J. J. Wurtman, New York: New York Academy of Sciences, 1987.

K. J. Simansky, "Serotonin and the Structure of Satiation," in *Satiation: From Gut to Brain*, ed. G. P. Smith, New York: Oxford University Press, 1998.

53 M. M. Leguid, A. Laviano, and F. Rossi-Fanelli, "Food Intake Equals Meal Size Times Mean Number," *Appetite* 31(1998): 404.

54 B. G. Stanley and E. R. Gillard, "Hypothalamic Neuropeptide Y and the Regulation of Eating Behavior and Body Weight," *Psychological Science* 3(1994): 9–15.

55 A. H. Merrill, Jr., "Apo A-IV: A New Satiety Signal," *Nutrition Reviews* 51(1993): 273–275.

56 L. A. Campfield, "Metabolic and Hormonal Controls of Food Intake: Highlights of the Last 25 Years," *Appetite* 29(1997): 135–152.

S. C. Woods, "The Insulin Story: A 25-Year Perspective," *Appetite* 28(1997): 281–282.

57 T. Gura, "Obesity Sheds Its Secrets," *Science* 275(1997): 751–753.

S. C. Woods, R. J. Seeley, D. Porte, and M. W. Schwartz, "Signals that Regulate Food Intake and Energy Homeostasis," *Science* 280(1998): 1378–1383.

58 Campfield, "Metabolic and Hormonal Controls of Food Intake."

T. H. Moran and E. E. Ladenheim, "Identification of Receptor Populations Mediating the Satiating Actions of Brain and Gut Peptides," in *Satiation: From Gut to Brain*, ed. G. P. Smith, New York: Oxford University Press, 1998.

59 J. A. Hogan, "Homeostasis and Behaviour," in *Analysis of Motivational Processes*, eds. E. M. Toates and T. R. Halliday, London: Academic Press, 1980.

60 S. Higgs, "Memory for Recent Eating and Its Influences on Subsequent Food Intake," *Appetite* 39(2002): 159–166.

61 P. Rozin, S. Dow, M. Moscovitch, and S. Rajaram, "What Causes Humans to Begin and End a Meal? A Role for Memory for What Has Been Eaten, as Evidenced by a Study of Multiple Meal Eating in Amnesic Patients," *Psychological Science* 9(1998): 392–396.

62 S. Higgs and J. E. Donohoe, "Focusing on Food during Lunch Enhances Lunch Memory and Decreases Later Snack Intake," *Appetite* 57(2011): 202–206.

63 D. S. Ramsay, R. J. Seeley, R. C. Bolles, and S. C. Woods, "Ingestive Homeostasis: The Primacy of Learning," in *Why We Eat What We Eat: The Psychology of Eating*, ed. E. D. Capaldi, Washington, DC: American Psychological Association, 1996.

64 E. L. Gibson and D. D. Booth, "Food-Conditioned Odour Rejection in the Late Stages of the Meal, Mediating Learnt Control of Meal Volume by Aftereffects of Food Consumption," *Appetite* 34(2000): 295–303.

65 L. L. Birch, L. McPhee, S. Sullivan, and S. Johnson, "Conditioned Meal Initiation in Young Children," *Appetite* 13(1989): 105–113.

66 H. Bruch, *Eating Disorders*, New York: Basic Books, 1973.

67 Ibid.

68 D. A. Booth, "The Behavioral and Neural Sciences of Ingestion," in *Handbook of Behavioral Neurobiology: Vol. 10. Neurobiology of Food and Fluid Intake*, ed. E. M. Stricker, New York: Plenum, 1990.

　H. R. Kissileff, J. L. Guss, and L. J. Nolan, "What Animal Research Tells Us about Human Eating," in *Food Choice, Acceptance and Consumption*, eds. H. L. Meiselman and H. J. H. MacFie, New York: Blackie Academic & Professional, 1996.

　E. Stellar, "Brain and Behavior," in *Handbook of Behavioral Neurobiology: Vol. 10. Neurobiology of Food and Fluid Intake*, ed. E. M. Stricker, New York: Plenum, 1990.

　E. M. Stricker, "Homeostatic Origins of Ingestive Behavior," in *Handbook of Behavioral Neurobiology: Vol. 10. Neurobiology of Food and Fluid Intake*, ed. E. M. Stricker, New York: Plenum, 1990.

3 "YOU NEVER MISS THE WATER TILL THE WELL RUNS DRY"

1 P. Rosenzweig, *The Book of Proverbs*, New York: Philosophical Library, 1965, p. 3.

2 F. Herbert, *Dune*, New York: Ace Books, 1965, p. 36.

3 F. Manz and A. Wentz, "The Importance of Good Hydration for the Prevention of Chronic Diseases," *Nutrition Reviews* 63(2005): S2–S5.
　S. M. Shirreffs, "The Importance of Good Hydration for Work and Exercise Performance," *Nutrition Reviews* 63(2005): S14–S21.

4 H. A. Guthrie, *Introductory Nutrition*, Saint Louis, MO: Mosby, 1975.

5 J. T. Fitzsimons, "Thirst and Sodium Appetite," in *Handbook of Behavioral Neurobiology: Vol. 10. Neurobiology of Food and Fluid Intake*, ed. E. M. Stricker, New York, Plenum, 1990.

6 E. F. Adolph, "Water Metabolism," *Annual Review of Physiology* 9(1947): 381–408.
　N. Kleitman, "The Effect of Starvation on the Daily Consumption of Water by the Dog," *American Journal of Physiology* 81(1927): 336–340.

7 D. Engell, "Interdependency of Food and Water Intake in Humans," *Appetite* 10(1988): 133–141.
　S. Lepkovsky, R. Lyman, D. Fleming, M. Nagumo, and M. M. Dimick, "Gastrointestinal Regulation of Water and Its Effect on Food Intake and Rate of Digestion," *American Journal of Physiology* 188(1957): 327–331.

8 Lepkovsky et al., "Gastrointestinal Regulation of Water and Its Effect on Food Intake and Rate of Digestion. "

9 E. M. Stricker and J. G. Verbalis, "Hormones and Behavior: The Biology of Thirst and Sodium Appetite," *American Scientist* 76(3)(1988): 261–267.
　J. G. Verbalis, "Clinical Aspects of Body Fluid Homeostasis in Humans, " in *Handbook of Behavioral Neurobiology: Vol. 10. Neurobiology of Food and Fluid Intake*, ed. E. M. Stricker, New York, Plenum, 1990.

10 B. J. Rolls and E. T. Rolls, *Thirst*, Cambridge, UK: Cambridge University Press, 1982.

11 Fitzsimons, "Thirst and Sodium Appetite."

12 Rolls and Rolls, *Thirst*.

13 Fitzsimons, "Thirst and Sodium Appetite."

E. M. Stricker, "Homeostatic Origins of Ingestive Behavior," in *Handbook of Behavioral Neurobiology: Vol. 10. Neurobiology of Food and Fluid Intake*, ed. E. M. Stricker, New York, Plenum, 1990.

14 Rolls and Rolls, *Thirst*.

15 J. E. Brody, *Jane Brody's The New York Times Guide to Personal Health*, New York: Avon Books, 1982.

16 K. Oatley, "Dissociation of the Circadian Drinking Pattern from Eating," *Nature* 229(1971): 494–496

17 Engell, "Interdependency of Food and Water Intake in Humans."

18 Rolls and Rolls, *Thirst*.

19 Rosenzweig, *The Book of Proverbs*, p. 73.

20 R. S. Weisinger, "Conditioned and Pseudoconditioned Thirst and Sodium Appetite," in *Control Mechanisms of Drinking*, eds. G. Peters, J. T. Fitzsimons, and L. Peters-Haefeli, Berlin: Springer-Verlag, 1975.

21 J. L. Falk, "The Nature and Determinants of Adjunctive Behavior," *Physiology and Behavior* 6(1971): 577–588.

22 T. F. Doyle and H. H. Samson, "Schedule-Induced Drinking in Humans: A Potential Factor in Excessive Alcohol Use," *Drug and Alcohol Dependence* 16(1985): 117–132.

23 W. B. Cannon, "The Physiological Basis of Thirst," *Proceedings of the Royal Society, London* 90(1917–1918): 283–301.

W. B. Cannon, "Hunger and Thirst," in *The Foundations of Experimental Psychology*, ed. C. Murchison, Worcester, MA: Clark University Press, 1929.

24 E. F. Adolph, *Physiology of Man in the Desert*, New York: Hafner, 1969.

25 Rolls and Rolls, *Thirst*.

26 N. E. Miller, R. I. Sampliner, and P. Woodrow, "Thirst-Reducing Effects of Water by Stomach Fistula vs. Water by Mouth Measured by Both a Consummatory and an Instrumental Response," *Journal of Comparative and Physiological Psychology* 50(1957): 1–5.

27 K. Schmidt-Nielsen, "How Are Control Systems Controlled?" *American Scientist* 82(1994): 38–44.

28 Rolls and Rolls, *Thirst*.

29 R. T. Bellows, "Time Factors in Water Drinking in Dogs," *American Journal of Physiology* 125(1939): 87–97.

30 M. F. Montgomery, "The Role of the Salivary Glands in the Thirst Mechanism," *American Journal of Physiology* 96(1931): 221–227.

F. R. Steggerda, "Observations on the Water Intake in an Adult Man with Dysfunctioning Salivary Glands," *American Journal of Physiology* 132(1941): 517–521.

31 S. C. Wooley and O. W. Wooley, "Salivation to the Sight and Thought of Food: A New Measure of Appetite," *Psychosomatic Medicine* 35(1973): 136–142.

32 J. M. Brunstrom and A. W. Macrae, "Effects of Temperature and Volume on Measures of Mouth Dryness, Thirst and Stomach Fullness in Males and Females," *Appetite* 29(1997): 21–42.

33 Fitzsimons, "Thirst and Sodium Appetite."
Rolls and Rolls, *Thirst*.

34 E. M. Stricker and M. L. Hoffmann, "Control of Thirst and Salt Appetite in Rats: Early Inhibition of Water and NaCl Ingestion," *Appetite* 46(2006): 234–237.

35 B. Andersson, "Polydipsia Caused by Intrahypothalamic Injections of Hypertonic NaCl-Solutions," *Experientia* 8(1952): 157–158.

36 B. Andersson and S. M. McCann, "Drinking, Antidiuresis and Milk Ejection from Electrical Stimulation within the Hypothalamus of the Goat," *Acta Physiologica Scandinavica* 35(1955): 191–201.

37 P. Teitelbaum, "Disturbances in Feeding and Drinking Behavior after Hypothalamic Lesions," in *Nebraska Symposium on Motivation,* ed. M. R. Jones, Lincoln: University of Nebraska Press, 1961.

P. Teitelbaum and A. N. Epstein, "The Lateral Hypothalamic Syndrome: Recovery of Feeding and Drinking after Lateral Hypothalamic Lesions," *Psychological Review* 69(1962): 74–90.

38 Rolls and Rolls, *Thirst.*

39 Fitzsimons, "Thirst and Sodium Appetite."

40 A. C. Guyton, "Blood Pressure Control—Special Role of the Kidneys and Body Fluids," *Science* 252(1991): 1813–1816.

41 B. G. Hoebel, "Neuroscience and Appetitive Behavior Research: 25 Years," *Appetite* 29(1997): 119–133.

42 Rolls and Rolls, *Thirst.*

P. J. Russell, A. E. Abdelaal, and G. J. Mogenson, "Graded Levels of Hemorrhage: Thirst and Angiotensin II in the Rat," *Physiology and Behavior* 15(1975): 117–119.

43 Fitzsimons, "Thirst and Sodium Appetite."

Rolls and Rolls, *Thirst.*

44 I. Kupfermann, "Hypothalamus and Limbic System II: Motivation," in *Principles of Neural Science,* 2nd ed., eds. E. R. Kandel and J. H. Schwartz, New York: Elsevier, 1985.

45 Stricker and Verbalis, "Hormones and Behavior."

46 Falk, "The Nature and Determinants of Adjunctive Behavior."

47 E. S. Kraly, "Physiology of Drinking Elicited by Eating," *Psychological Review* 91(1984): 478–490.

E. S. Kraly, "Histamine: A Role in Normal Drinking," *Appetite* 6(1985): 153–158.

48 M. Jijande, P. Lopez-Sela, J. I. Brime, R. Bernardo, F. Diaz, M. Costales, and B. Marin, "Insulin Stimulation of Water Intake in Humans," *Appetite* 15(1990): 81–87.

49 Weisinger, "Conditioned and Pseudoconditioned Thirst and Sodium Appetite."

50 F. M. Toates, "Homeostasis and Drinking," *The Behavioural and Brain Sciences* 2(1979): 95–139.

51 B. J. Rolls and P. A. Phillips, "Aging and Disturbances of Thirst and Fluid Balance," *Nutrition Reviews* 48(1990): 137–144.

A. J. Triana, V. Apanius, C. Richmond, and V. H. Castellanos, "Restricting Fluid Intake during a Single Meal Did Not Affect Food Intake in Older Adults," *Appetite* 41(2003): 79–86.

52 R. Chernoff, "Thirst and Fluid Requirements," *Nutrition Reviews* 52(1994): S3–S5.

53 Rolls and Phillips, "Aging and Disturbances of Thirst and Fluid Balance."

4 THE NOSE KNOWS
(AND SO DOES THE TONGUE)

1 L. Bartoshuk, "Separate Worlds of Taste," *Psychology Today* 14(1980): 48–49, 51, 54–56, 63.

2 The Fragrance Foundation, *New York* (November 13, 1995): 133.

3 F. A. Geldard, *The Human Senses,* 2nd ed., New York: Wiley, 1972.

4 T. Engen, *The Perception of Odors,* New York: Academic Press, 1982.

5 V. B. Duffy and L. M. Bartoshuk, "Sensory Factors in Feeding," in *Why We Eat What We Eat: The Psychology of Eating*, ed. E. D. Capaldi, Washington, DC: American Psychological Association, 1996.

6 M. Pollan, *The Omnivore's Dilemma: A Natural History of Four Meals*, New York: Penguin Books, 2006.

7 J. M. Auel, *The Clan of the Cave Bear*, Toronto: Bantam, 1980, p. 37.

8 J. Garcia, E. R. Ervin, and R. A. Koelling, "Learning with Prolonged Delay of Reinforcement," *Psychonomic Science* 5(1966): 121–122.

9 C. Pfaffmann, M. Frank, and R. Norgren, "Neural Mechanisms and Behavioral Aspects of Taste," *Annual Review of Psychology* 3(1979): 283–325.

10 M. I. Friedman and R. D. Mattes, "Chemical Senses and Nutrition," in *Smell and Taste in Health and Disease*, eds. T. V. Getchell, L. M. Bartoshuk, R. L. Doty, and J. B. Snow, New York: Raven Press, 1991.

11 J. E. Steiner, "Facial Expressions of the Neonate Infant Indicating the Hedonics of Food-Related Chemical Stimuli," in *Taste and Development*, ed. J. M. Weiffenbach, Bethesda, MD: U.S. Department of Health, Education, and Welfare, 1977.

12 J. Bohannon, "A Taste for Controversy," *Science* 328(2010): 1471–1473.

13 L. M. Bartoshuk, "Taste," in *Stevens' Handbook of Experimental Psychology*, 2nd ed., vol. 1, eds. R. C. Atkinson, R. J. Herrnstein, G. Lindzey, and R. D. Luce, New York: Wiley, 1988.

    Geldard, *The Human Senses*.

14 Ibid.

15 Bartoshuk, "Separate Worlds of Taste."

16 C. Pfaffmann, "Gustatory Nerve Impulses in Rat, Cat and Rabbit," *Journal of Neurophysiology* 18(1955): 429–440.

17 K. Arvidson and U. Friberg, "Human Taste: Response and Taste Bud Number in Fungiform Papillae," *Science* 209(1980): 807–808.

18 I. J. Miller and L. M. Bartoshuk, "Taste Perception, Taste Bud Distribution, and Spatial Relationships," in *Smell and Taste in Health and Disease*, eds. T. V. Getchell, L. M. Bartoshuk, R. L. Doty, and J. B. Snow, New York: Raven Press, 1991.

19 Pfaffmann et al., "Neural Mechanisms and Behavioral Aspects of Taste."

20 S. McLaughlin and R. F. Margolskee, "The Sense of Taste," *American Scientist* 82(1994): 538–545.

21 G. Miller, "Sweet Here, Salty There: Evidence for a Taste Map in the Mammalian Brain," *Science* 333(2011): 1213.

22 Bartoshuk, "Separate Worlds of Taste."

    L. M. Bartoshuk, G. P. Dateo, D. J. Vandenbelt, R. L. Buttrick, and L. Long, "Effects of Gymnema Sylvestre and Synsepalum Dulcificum on Taste in Man," in *Olfaction and Taste: Proceedings of the Third International Symposium*, ed. C. Pfaffman, New York: Rockefeller University Press, 1969.

    K. Kurihara, Y. Kurihara, and L. M. Beidler, "Isolation and Mechanism of Taste Modifiers: Taste-Modifying Protein and Gymnemic Acids," in *Olfaction and Taste: Proceedings of the Third International Symposium*, ed. C. Pfaffman, New York: Rockefeller University Press, 1969.

23 G. Borg, H. Diamant, B. Oakley, L. Strom, and Y. Zotterman, "A Comparative Study of Neural and Psychophysical Responses to Gustatory Stimuli," in *Olfaction and Taste II*, ed. T. Hayashi, Oxford, UK: Pergamon, 1963.

24 Bartoshuk, "Separate Worlds of Taste."

    Bartoshuk et al., "Effects of Gymnema Sylvestre and Synsepalum Dulcificum on Taste in Man."

G. J. Henning, J. N. Brouwer, H. van der Well, and A. Francke, "Miracle, the Sweetness—lnducing Principle from Miracle Fruit," in *Olfaction and Taste: Proceedings of the Third International Symposium*, ed. C. Pfaffman, New York: Rockefeller University Press, 1969.

Kurihara et al., "Isolation and Mechanism of Taste Modifiers."

25 Bartoshuk, "Taste."

26 A. Caicedo and S. D. Roper, "Taste Receptor Cells that Discriminate between Bitter Stimuli," *Science* 291(2001): 1557–1560.

J. Chandrashekar, K. L. Mueller, M. A. Hoon, E. Adler, L. Feng, W. Guo, and C. S. Zuker, "T2Rs Function as Bitter Taste Receptors," *Cell* 100(2000): 703–711.

27 A. Sclafani, "The Sixth Taste?" *Appetite* 43(2004): 1–3.

D. V. Smith and R. F. Margolskee, "Making Sense of Taste," *Scientific American* (March 2001): 32–39.

28 T. A. Gilbertson, L. Liu, D. A. York, and G. A. Bray, "Dietary Fat Preferences Are Inversely Correlated with Peripheral Gustatory Fatty Acid Sensitivity," in *Olfaction and Taste XII: An International Symposium*, ed. C. Murphy, New York: New York Academy of Sciences, 1998.

S. S. Schiffman, B. G. Graham, E. A. Sattely-Miller, and Z.S. Warwick, "Orosensory Perception of Dietary Fat," *Current Directions in Psychological Science* 7(1998): 137–143.

29 J. E. Amoore, "Specific Anosmias," in *Smell and Taste in Health and Disease*, eds. T. V. Getchell, L. M. Bartoshuk, R. L. Doty, and J. B. Snow, New York: Raven Press, 1991.

30 M. L. Pelchat, C. Bykowski, F. F. Duke, and D. R. Reed," Excretion and Perception of a Characteristic Odor in Urine after Asparagus Ingestion: A Psychophysical and Genetic Study," *Chemical Senses* 36(2011): 9–17.

31 L. B. Buck, "Olfactory Receptors and Odor Coding in Mammals," *Nutrition Reviews* 62(2004): S184–S188.

32 R. Axel, "The Molecular Logic of Smell," *Scientific American* (October 1995): 154–159.

33 W. S. Cain, "Olfaction," in *Stevens' Handbook of Experimental Psychology*, 2nd ed., vol. 1, eds. R. C. Atkinson, R. J. Herrnstein, G. Lindzey, and R. D. Luce, New York: Wiley, 1988.

34 Axel, "The Molecular Logic of Smell."

B. D. Rubin and L. C. Katz, "Optical Imaging of Odorant Representations in the Mammalian Olfactory Bulb," *Neuron* 23(1999): 499–511.

35 American Chemical Society, "New 'Artificial Nose' Device Can Speed Diagnosis of Sepsis," *Science Daily* (published online September 9, 2013): www.sciencedailycom/releases/2013/09/130909092338.htm.

M. S. Freund and N. S. Lewis, "A Chemically Diverse Conducting Polymer-Based 'Electronic Nose,' "*Proceedings of the National Academy of Sciences* 92(1995): 2652–2656.

36 G. Miller, "Axel, Buck Share Award for Deciphering How the Nose Knows," *Science* 306(2004): 207.

37 R. Rajan, J. P. Clement, and U. S. Bhalla, "Rats Smell in Stereo," *Science* 311(2006): 666–670.

Z. Zou and L. B. Buck, "Combinatorial Effects of Odorant Mixes in Olfactory Cortex," *Science* 311(2006): 1477–1481.

38 G. K. Beauchamp and J. R. Mason, "Comparative Hedonics of Taste," in *The Hedonics of Taste*, ed. R. C. Bolles, Hillsdale, NJ: Lawrence Erlbaum Associates, 1991.

39 M. Ditzen, M. Pellegrino, and L. B. Vosshall, "Insect Odorant Receptors are Molecular Targets of the Insect Repellent DEET," *Science* 319(2008): 1838–1842.

40 C. J. Wysocki, J. D. Pierce, and A. N. Gilbert, "Geographic, Cross-Cultural, and Individual Variation in Human Olfaction," in *Smell and Taste in Health and Disease*, eds. T. V. Getchell, L. M. Bartoshuk, R. L. Doty, and J. B. Snow, New York: Raven Press, 1991.

41 R. C. van der Wal and L. F. van Dillen, "Leaving a Flat Taste in Your Mouth: Task Load Reduces Taste Perception," *Psychological Science* (published online May 30, 2013). DOI: 10.1177/0956797612471953.

42 L. Haase, E. Green, and C. Murphy, "Males and Females Show Differential Brain Activation to Taste When Hungry and Sated in Gustatory and Reward Areas," *Science* 57(2011): 421–434.

43 L. M. Bartoshuk, "Bitter Taste of Saccharin Related to the Genetic Ability to Taste the Bitter Substance 6-N-Propylthiouracil," *Science* 205(1979): 934–935.

Bartoshuk, "Taste."

A. Drewnowski, S. A. Henderson, and A. B. Shore, "Taste Responses to Naringin, a Flavonoid, and the Acceptance of Grapefruit Juice Are Related to Genetic Sensitivity to 6-N-Propylthiouracil," *American Journal of Clinical Nutrition* 66(1997): 391–397.

A. Drewnowski, S. A. Henderson, A. B. Shore, and A. Barratt-Fornell, "Sensory Responses to 6-N-Propylthiouracil (PROP), or Sucrose Solutions and Food Preferences in Young Women," in *Olfaction and Taste XII: An International Symposium*, ed. C. Murphy, New York: New York Academy of Sciences, 1998.

H. Kalmus, "Inherited Sense Defects," *Scientific American* 186(5)(1952): 64–70.

K. L. Keller, L. Steinmann, R. J. Nurse, and B. J. Tepper, "Genetic Taste Sensitivity to 6-N-Propylthiouracil Influences Food Preference and Reported Intake in Preschool Children," *Appetite* 38(2002): 3–12.

44 L. M. Bartoshuk and V. B. Duffy, "Supertasting and Earaches: Genetics and Pathology Alter Our Taste Worlds," *Appetite* 23(1994): 292–293.

U. Kim, E. Jorgenson, H. Coon, M. Leppert, N. Risch, and D. Drayna, "Positional Cloning of the Human Quantitative Trait Locus Underlying Taste Sensitivity to Phenylthiocarbamide," *Science* 299(2003): 1221–1225.

45 Kalmus, "Inherited Sense Defects."

46 S.-W. Guo, F.-M. Shen, Y.-D. Wang, and C.-J. Zheng, "Threshold Distributions of Phenylthiocarbamide (PTC) in the Chinese Population," in *Olfaction and Taste XII: An International Symposium*, ed. C. Murphy, New York: New York Academy of Sciences, 1998.

47 Bartoshuk and Duffy, "Supertasting and Earaches."

48 M. Proust, *Swann's Way*, New York: Vintage Books, 1970, p. 36.

49 W. S. Cain, "To Know with the Nose: Keys to Odor Identification," *Science* 203(1979): 467–470.

M. D. Rabin and W. S. Cain, "Odor Recognition: Familiarity, Identifiability, and Encoding Consistency," *Journal of Experimental Psychology: Learning, Memory, and Cognition* 10(1984): 316–325.

50 M. D. Kass, M. C. Rosenthal, J. Pottackal, and J. P. McGann, "Fear Learning Enhances Neural Responses to Threat-Predictive Sensory Stimuli," *Science* 342(2013): 1389–1392.

51 P. Pliner and C. Steverango, "Effect of Induced Mood on Memory for Flavors," *Appetite* 22(1994): 135–148.

52 R. L. Doty, L. M. Bartoshuk, and J. B. Snow, "Causes of Olfactory and Gustatory Disorders," in *Smell and Taste in Health and Disease*, eds. T. V. Getchell, L. M. Bartoshuk, R. L. Doty, and J. B. Snow, New York: Raven Press, 1991.

53 J. C. Stevens, W. S. Cain, A. Demarque, and A. M. Ruthruff, "On the Discrimination of Missing Ingredients: Aging and Salt Flavor," *Appetite* 16(1991): 129–140.

54 M. L. Pelchat, "You Can Teach an Old Dog New Tricks: Olfaction and Responses to Novel Foods by the Elderly," *Appetite* 35(2000): 153–160.

55 T. Engen, *Odor Sensation and Memory*, New York: Praeger, 1991.

   H. J. Hoffman, E. K. Ishii, and R. H. Macturk, "Age-Related Changes in the Prevalence of Smell-Taste Problems among the United States Adult Population," in *Olfaction and Taste XII: An International Symposium*, ed. C. Murphy, New York: New York Academy of Sciences, 1998.

   J. M. Weiffenbach, "Chemical Senses in Aging," in *Smell and Taste in Health and Disease*, eds. T. V. Getchell, L. M. Bartoshuk, R. L. Doty, and J. B. Snow, New York: Raven Press, 1991.

56 Weiffenbach, "Chemical Senses in Aging."

57 M. E. Briley, "Food Preferences of the Elderly," *Nutrition Reviews* 52(1994): S21–S23.

   Friedman and Mattes, "Chemical Senses and Nutrition."

58 R. L. Doty, P. Shaman, S. L. Applebaum, R. Giberson, L. Siksorski, and L. Rosenberg, "Smell Identification Ability: Changes with Age" *Science* 226(1984): 1441–1443.

59 R. L. Best and K. M. Appleton, "Comparable Increases in Energy, Protein and Fat Intake Following the Addition of Seasonings and Sauces to an Older Person's Meal," *Appetite* 56(2011): 179–182.

60 Stevens et al., "On the Discrimination of Missing Ingredients."

61 T. Hummel, C. Rothbauer, S. Barz, K. Grosser, E. Pauli, and G. Kobal, "Olfactory Function in Acute Rhinitis," in *Olfaction and Taste XII: An International Symposium*, ed. C. Murphy, New York: New York Academy of Sciences, 1998.

62 R. D. Fowler, "A Matter of Taste," *APA Monitor* (May 1997): 3.

63 T. R. Scott, "The Role of Taste in Feeding," *Appetite* 37(2001): 111–113.

5 GENES RULE—OR DO THEY?

1 R. Estruch, E. Ros, J. Salas-Salvadó, M.-I. Covas, D. Corella, F. Aros, et al., "Primary Prevention of Cardiovascular Disease with a Mediterranean Diet," *The New England Journal of Medicine* 368(2013): 1279–1290.

2 J. Money and A. A. Ehrhardt, *Man and Woman, Boy and Girl*, Baltimore: Johns Hopkins University Press, 1972.

3 C. Pfaffmann, "Biological and Behavioral Substrates of the Sweet Tooth," in *Taste and Development*, ed. J. M. Weiffenbach, Bethesda, MD: U.S. Department of Health, Education, and Welfare, 1977.

4 J. Brody, *Jane Brody's Nutrition Book*, New York: Norton, 1981.

   K. K. Kiple and K. C. Omelas, eds., *The Cambridge World History of Food*, Cambridge, UK: Cambridge University Press, 2000.

   Pfaffmann, "Biological and Behavioral Substrates of the Sweet Tooth."

5 P. Rozin, "Human Food Selection: The Interaction of Biology, Culture and Individual Experience," in *The Psychobiology of Human Food Selection*, ed. L. M. Barker, Westport, CT: AVI Publishing, 1982.

6 S. D. Anton, C. K. Martin, H. Han, S. Coulon, W. T. Cefalu, P. Geiselman, and
D. A. Williamson, "Effects of Stevia, Aspartame, and Sucrose on Food Intake,
Satiety, and Postprandial Glucose and Insulin Levels," *Appetite* 55(2010):
37–43.

Q. Yang, Z. Zheng, E. Gregg, W. D. Flanders, R. Merritt, and F. B. Hu,
"Added Sugar Intake and Cardiovascular Diseases Mortality among US
Adults," *JAMA Internal Medicine* (published online February 3, 2014). DOI:
10.1001/jamainternmed.2013.13563.

7 T. R. Maone, R. D. Mattes, J. C. Bernbaum, and G. K. Beauchamp, "A New
Method for Delivering a Taste without Fluids to Preterm and Term Infants,"
Developmental Psychobiology 23(1990): 179–191.

8 J. E. Steiner, "Facial Expressions of the Neonate Infant Indicating the
Hedonics of Food-Related Chemical Stimuli," in *Taste and Development*, ed.
J. M. Weiffenbach, Bethesda, MD: U.S. Department of Health, Education, and
Welfare, 1977, pp. 174–175.

9 H. J. Grill and R. Norgren, "Chronically Decerebrate Rats Demonstrate
Satiation but Not Bait Shyness," *Science* 201(1978): 267–269.

10 N. W. Jerome, "Taste Experience and the Development of a Dietary Preference
for Sweet in Humans: Ethnic and Cultural Variations in Early Taste
Experience," in *Taste and Development*, ed. J. M. Weiffenbach, Bethesda,
MD: U.S. Department of Health, Education, and Welfare, 1977.

11 R. R. Bell, H. H. Draper, and J. G. Bergan, "Sucrose, Lactose, and Glucose
Tolerance in Northern Alaskan Eskimos," *The American Journal of Clinical
Nutrition* 26(1973): 1185–1190.

12 Jerome, "Taste Experience and the Development of a Dietary Preference for
Sweet in Humans."

13 G. K. Beauchamp and M. Moran, "Dietary Experience and Sweet Taste
Preference in Human Infants," *Appetite* 3(1982): 139–152.

14 J. J. Wurtman and R. J. Wurtman, "Sucrose Consumption Early in Life Fails to
Modify the Appetite of Adult Rats for Sweet Foods," *Science* 205(1979): 321–322.

15 J. A. Desor and G. K. Beauchamp, "Longitudinal Changes in Sweet Preferences
in Humans," *Physiology and Behavior* 39(1987): 639–641.

J. A. Desor, L. S. Greene, and O. Maller, "Preferences for Sweet and Salty in
9- to 15-Year Old and Adult Humans," *Science* 190(1975): 686–687.

A. W. Logue and M. E. Smith, "Predictors of Food Preferences in Humans,"
Appetite 7(1986): 109–125.

Wurtman and Wurtman, "Sucrose Consumption Early in Life Fails to
Modify the Appetite of Adult Rats for Sweet Foods."

16 Desor et al., "Preferences for Sweet and Salty in 9- to 15-Year Old and Adult
Humans."

17 M. T. Conner and D. A. Booth, "Preferred Sweetness of a Lime Drink and
Preference for Sweet over Non-Sweet Foods, Related to Sex and Reported Age
and Body Weight," *Appetite* 10(1988): 25–35.

Logue and Smith, "Predictors of Food Preferences in Humans."

S. Parker, N. Kamel, and D. Zellner, "Food Craving Patterns in Egypt:
Comparisons with North America and Spain," *Appetite* 40(2003):
193–195.

H. Tuorila-Ollikainen and S. Mahlamaki-Kultanen, "The Relationship of
Attitudes and Experiences of Finnish Youths to Their Hedonic Responses to
Sweetness in Soft Drinks," *Appetite* 6(1985): 115–124.

18 S. Damak, M. Rong, K. Yasumatsu, Z. Kokrashvili, V. Varadarajan,
S. Zou, P. Jiang, Y. Ninomiya, and R. F. Margolskee, "Detection of Sweet and

Umami Taste in the Absence of Taste Receptor T1r3," *Science* 301(2003): 850–853.

M. Frank, "The Distinctiveness of Responses to Sweet in the Chorda Tympani Nerve," in *Taste and Development,* ed. J. M. Weiffenbach, Bethesda, MD: U.S. Department of Health, Education, and Welfare, 1977.

19 R. Coopersmith and M. Leon, "Enhanced Neural Response to Familiar Olfactory Cues," *Science* 225(1984): 849–851.

20 www.hfiinfo.proboards.com.

Medline Plus, "Hereditary Fructose Intolerance." Available online at: www.nlm.nih.gov/medlineplus/ency/article/000359.htm.

21 M. Nachman, "The Inheritance of Saccharin Preference," *Journal of Comparative and Physiological Psychology* 52(1959): 451–457.

22 L. S. Greene, J. A. Desor, and O. Maller, "Heredity and Experience: Their Relative Importance in the Development of Taste Preference in Man," *Journal of Comparative and Physiological Psychology* 89(1975): 279–284.

M. Krondl, P. Coleman, J. Wade, and J. Milner, "A Twin Study Examining the Genetic Influence on Food Selection," *Human Nutrition: Applied Nutrition* 37A(1983): 189–198.

23 Greene et al., "Heredity and Experience."

24 K. M. Eny, T. M. S. Wolever, B. Fontaine-Bisson, and A. El-Sohemy, "Genetic Variant in the Glucose Transporter Type 2 is Associated with Higher Intakes of Sugars in Two Distinct Populations," *Physiological Genomics* 33(2008): 355–360.

A. Fushan, C. T. Simons, J. P. Slack, A. Manichaikul, and D. Drayna, "Allelic Polymorphism within the TAS1R3 Promoter Is Associated with Human Taste Sensitivity to Sucrose," *Current Biology* 19(2009): 1288–1293.

25 L. L. Birch, "Children's Food Preferences: Developmental Patterns and Environmental Influences," in *Annals of Child Development*, vol. 4, ed. R. Vasta, Greenwich, CT: JAI Press, 1987.

B. G. Galef, "Mechanisms for the Transmission of Acquired Patterns of Feeding from Adult to Weanling Rats," in *Taste and Development,* ed. J. M. Weiffenbach, Bethesda, MD: U.S. Department of Health, Education, and Welfare, 1977.

B. G. Galef, "Communication of Information Concerning Distant Diets in a Social, Central -Place Foraging Species: *Rattus Norvegicus,*" in *Social Learning: Psychological and Biological Perspectives*, eds. T. R. Zentall and B. G. Galef, Hillsdale, NJ: Lawrence Erlbaum Associates, 1988.

26 J. Yudkin, "Patterns and Trends in Carbohydrate Consumption and Their Relation to Disease," *Nutrition Society Proceedings* 23(1964): 149–16227.

27 G. K. Beauchamp and B. J. Cowart, "Congenital and Experiential Factors in the Development of Human Flavor Preferences," *Appetite* 6(1985): 357–372.

28 D. Denton, *The Hunger for Salt*, New York: Springer-Verlag, 1982.

J. Schulkin, *Sodium Hunger: The Search for a Salty Taste*, New York: Cambridge University Press, 1991.

29 L. M. Bartoshuk and G. K. Beauchamp, "Chemical Senses," *Annual Review of Psychology* 45(1994): 419–449.

30 M. R. Bloch, "The Social Influence of Salt," in *Human Nutrition*, San Francisco: W. H. Freeman, 1978.

Denton, *The Hunger for Salt.*

31 Bloch, "The Social Influence of Salt."

32 Denton, *The Hunger for Salt.*

33 A. N. Epstein, "Prospectus: Thirst and Salt Appetite," in *Handbook of Behavioral Neurobiology: Vol. 10. Neurobiology of Food and Fluid Intake*, ed. E. M. Stricker, New York: Plenum, 1990.

N. E. Rowland, "Sodium Appetite, " in *Taste, Experience, and Feeding*, eds. E. D. Capaldi and T. L. Powley, Washington, DC: American Psychological Association, 1990.

34 A. N. Epstein, "Hormonal Synergy as the Cause of Salt Appetite," in *The Physiology of Thirst and Sodium Appetite*, eds. G. de Caro, A. N. Epstein, and M. Massi, New York: Plenum, 1986.

M. Massi and A. N. Epstein, "Angiotensin/Aldosterone Synergy Governs the Salt Appetite of the Pigeon," *Appetite* 14(1990): 181–192.

35 U. Roze, "How to Select, Climb, and Eat a Tree," *Natural History* (May 1985): 63–69.

36 R. J. Contreras and M. Frank, "Sodium Deprivation Alters Neural Responses to Gustatory Stimuli," *The Journal of General Physiology* 73(1979): 569–594.

37 T. R. Scott and B. K. Giza, "Coding Channels in the Taste System of the Rat," *Science* 249(1990): 1585–1587.

38 L. Wilkins and C. P. Richter, "A Great Craving for Salt by a Child with Cortico-Adrenal Insufficiency," *JAMA* 114(1940): 866–868.

39 Desor et al., "Preferences for Sweet and Salty in 9-to 15-Year Old and Adult Humans."

40 M. Leshem, A. Saadi, N. Alem, and K. Hendi, "Enhanced Salt Appetite, Diet and Drinking in Traditional Bedouin Women in the Negev," *Appetite* 50(2008): 71–82.

41 M. Leshem, A. Abutbul, and R. Eilon, "Exercise Increases the Preference for Salt in Humans," *Appetite* 32(1999): 251–260.

42 D. H. Passe, J. R. Stofan, C. L. Rowe, C. A. Horswill, and R. Murray, "Exercise Condition Affects Hedonic Responses to Sodium in a Sport Drink," *Appetite* 52(2009): 561–567.

43 Epstein, "Prospectus."

44 J. A. DeSimone, G. K. Beauchamp, A. Drewnowski, and G. H. Johnson, "Sodium in the Food Supply: Challenges and Opportunities," *Nutrition Reviews* 71(2013): 52–59.

45 B. G. Galef, "Social Interaction Modifies Learned Aversions, Sodium Appetite, and Both Palatability and Handling-Time Induced Dietary Preference in Rats (*Rattus Norvegicus*)," *Journal of Comparative Psychology* 100(1986): 432–439.

46 G. K. Beauchamp, "The Human Preference for Excess Salt," *American Scientist* 75(1)(1987): 27–33.

47 R. L. Huggins, R. Di Nicolantonio, and T. O. Morgan, "Preferred Salt Levels and Salt Taste Acuity in Human Subjects after Ingestion of Untasted Salt," *Appetite* 18(1992): 111–119.

48 N. Ayya and G. K. Beauchamp, "Short-Term Effects of Diet on Salt Taste Preference," *Appetite* 18(1992): 77–82.

49 J. Quilez and J. Salas-Salvado, "Salt in Bread in Europe: Potential Benefits of Reduction," *Nutrition Reviews* 70(2012): 666–678.

50 DeSimone et al., "Sodium in the Food Supply."

51 NIH Consensus Development Conference: Lactose Intolerance and Health. Final Panel Statement. Available online at: http://consensus.nih.gov/2010/lactosestatement.htm.

52 N. Kretchmer, "Lactose and Lactase," in *Human Nutrition*, San Francisco: W. H. Freeman, 1978.

53 Ibid.

F. J. Simoons, "Geography and Genetics as Factors in the Psychobiology of Human Food Selection," in *The Psychobiology of Human Food Selection*, ed. L. M. Barker, Westport, CT: AVI Publishing, 1982.

54 Kretchmer, "Lactose and Lactase."

55 S. A. Tishkoff, F. A. Reed, A. Ranciaro, B. F. Voight, C. C. Babbitt, J. S. Lilverman, et al., "Convergent Adaptation of Human Lactate Persistence in Africa and Europe," *Nature Genetics* 39(2007): 31–40.

O. Arjamaa and T. Vuorisalo, "Gene-Culture Coevolution and Human Diet," American Scientist (March–April 2010): 140, 142–147.

56 Arjamaa and Vuorisalo, "Gene-Culture Evolution and Human Diet."

M. Balter, "In a Cold Snap, Farmers Turned to Milk," *Science* 329(2010): 1465.

57 "Season, Latitude, and Ability of Sunlight to Promote Synthesis of Vitamin D3 in Skin," *Nutrition Reviews* 47(1989): 252–253.

58 Simoons, "Geography and Genetics as Factors in the Psychobiology of Human Food Selection."

59 M. A. Sandell and P. A. S. Breslin, "Variability in a Taste-Receptor Gene Determines Whether We Taste Toxins in Food," *Current Biology* 16(2006): R792–R794.

60 J. E. Hayes, B. S. Sullivan, and V. B. Duffy, "Explaining Variability in Sodium Intake through Oral Sensory Phenotype, Salt Sensation and Liking," *Physiology and Behavior* 100(2010): 369–210.

61 Steiner, "Facial Expressions of the Neonate Infant Indicating the Hedonics of Food-Related Chemical Stimuli," p. 175.

62 Ibid.

63 Grill and Norgren, "Chronically Decerebrate Rats Demonstrate Satiation but Not Bait Shyness."

64 F. A. Geldard, *The Human Senses*, 2nd ed., New York: Wiley, 1972.

E. V. Glanville and A. R. Kaplan, "Food Preference and Sensitivity of Taste for Bitter Compounds," *Nature* 205(1965): 851–853.

Rozin, "Human Food Selection."

65 O. Tornwäll, K. Silventoinen, K. Keskitalo-Vuokko, M. Perola, J. Kaprio, and H. Tuorila, "Genetic Contribution to Sour Taste Preference," *Appetite* 58(2012): 687–694.

66 D. G. Liem, R. P. Bogers, P. S. Dagnelie, and C. de Graff, "Fruit Consumption of Boys (8–11 years) Is Related to Preferences for Sour Taste," *Appetite* 46(2006): 93–96.

67 M. Zuckerman, *Sensation Seeking: Beyond the Optimal Level of Arousal*, Hillsdale, NJ: Lawrence Erlbaum Associates, 1979.

68 Logue and Smith, "Predictors of Food Preferences in Humans."

69 M. Zuckerman, ed., *Biological Bases of Sensation Seeking, Impulsivity, and Anxiety*, Hillsdale, NJ: Lawrence Erlbaum Associates, 1983.

70 C. Byrd-Bredbenner, M. Johnson, V. M. Quick, J. Walsh, G. W. Greene, S. Hoerr, et al., "Sweet and Salty. An Assessment of the Snacks and Beverages Sold in Vending Machines on US Post-Secondary Institution Campuses," *Appetite* 58(2012): 1143–1151.

6 ONE PERSON'S MEAT IS ANOTHER PERSON'S POISON

1 S. W. Mintz, *Tasting Food, Tasting Freedom: Excursions into Eating, Culture, and the Past*, Boston: Beacon Press, 1996, p. 8.

2 G. Vogel, "For More Protein, Filet of Cricket," *Science* 327(2010): 811.

3 "Eating Bugs Could Save the World," *Science* 340(2013): 794.

4 www.fda.gov/ICECI/ComplianceManuals/CompliancePolicyGuidanceManual/ucm074596.htm.

5 P. D. Balsam, J. D. Deich, and R. Hirose, "The Roles of Experience in the Transition from Dependent to Independent Feeding in Ring Doves," in *Developmental Psychobiology*, ed. G. Turkewitz, New York: New York Academy of Sciences, 1992.

   B. G. Galef, "Weaning from Mother's Milk to Solid Foods: The Developmental Psychobiology of Self-Selection of Foods by Rats," in *Developmental Psychobiology*, ed. G. Turkewitz, New York: New York Academy of Sciences, 1992.

   J. A. Mennella and G. K. Beauchamp, "Early Flavor Experiences: Research Update," *Nutrition Reviews* 56(1998): 205–211.

6 P. Rozin, "The Selection of Foods by Rats, Humans, and Other Animals," in *Advances in the Study of Behavior*, vol. 6, eds. J. S. Rosenblatt, R. A. Hinde, E. Shaw, and C. Beer, New York: Academic Press, 1976.

7 C. P. Richter, "Total Self Regulatory Functions in Animals and Human Beings," *The Harvey Lecturers* 38(1942–1943): 63–103.

8 C. M. Davis, "Self Selection of Diet by Newly Weaned Infants," *American Journal of Disease of Children* 36(1928): 651–679.

   C. M. Davis, "Can Babies Choose Their Food?" *The Parents' Magazine* (January 1930): 22, 23, 42, 43.

   C. M. Davis, "Results of the Self-Selection of Diets by Young Children," *The Canadian Medical Association Journal* (September 1939): 257–261.

9 W. F. Hill, "Effects of Mere Exposure on Preferences in Nonhuman Animals," *Psychological Bulletin* 85(1978): 1177–1198.

10 Ibid.

   R. B. Zajonc, "Attitudinal Effects of Mere Exposure," *Journal of Personality and Social Psychology* (Monograph Supplement 9) (No. 2, Part 2)(1968): 1–27.

11 B. Raudenbush and R. A. Frank, "Assessing Food Neophobia: The Role of Stimulus Familiarity," *Appetite* 32(1999): 261–271.

   H. Tuorila and S. Mustonen, "Reluctant Trying of an Unfamiliar Food Induces Negative Affection for the Food." *Appetite* 54(2010): 418–421.

12 L. J. Cooke, C. M. A. Haworth, and J. Wardle, "Genetic and Environmental Influences on Children's Food Neophobia," *American Journal of Clinical Nutrition*, 86(2007): 428–433.

   S. Nicklaus, V. Boggio, C. Chabanet, and S. Issanchou, "A Prospective Study of Food Variety Seeking in Childhood, Adolescence and Early Adult Live," *Appetite* 44(2005): 289–297.

13 P. Pliner, "The Effects of Mere Exposure on Liking for Edible Substances," *Appetite* 2(1982): 283–290.

14 L. L. Birch, L. McPhee, B. C. Shoba, E. Pirok, and L. Steinberg, "What Kind of Exposure Reduces Children's Food Neophobia," *Appetite* 9(1987): 171–178.

15 L. L. Birch and M. Deysher, "Caloric Compensation and Sensory Specific Satiety: Evidence for Self Regulation of Food Intake by Young Children," *Appetite* 7(1986): 323–331.

   Hill, "Effects of Mere Exposure on Preferences in Nonhuman Animals."

   L. J. Nolan and M. M. Hetherington, "The Effects of Sham Feeding-Induced Sensory Specific Satiation and Food Variety on Subsequent Food Intake in Humans," *Appetite* 52(2009): 720–725.

16 D. J. Stang, "When Familiarity Breeds Contempt, Absence Makes the Heart Grow Fonder: Effects of Exposure and Delay on Taste Pleasantness Ratings," *Bulletin of the Psychonomic Society* 6(1975): 273–275.

17 B. J. Rolls, E. T. Rolls, and E. A. Rowe, "The Influence of Variety on Human Food Selection and Intake," in *The Psychobiology of Human Food Selection*, ed. L. M. Barker, Westport, CT: AVI Publishing, 1982.

18 B. J. Rolls, "Experimental Analyses of the Effects of Variety in a Meal on Human Feeding," *The American Journal of Clinical Nutrition* 42(1985): 932–939.

19 E. D. Capaldi and G. J. Privitera, "Flavor-Nutrient Learning Independent of Flavor-Taste Learning with College Students," *Appetite* 49(2007): 712–715.

D. Mayntz, D. Raubenheimer, M. Salomon, S. Toft, and S. J. Simpson, "Nutrient-Specific Foraging in Invertebrate Predators," *Science* 307(2005): 111–113.

20 P. Rozin, "Specific Aversions as a Component of Specific Hungers," in *Biological Boundaries of Learning*, eds. M. E. P. Seligman and J. L. Hager, New York: Appleton-Century-Crofts, 1972.

21 American Psychiatric Association, *Diagnostic and Statistical Manual of Mental Disorders,* 5th ed., Washington, DC: APA, 2013.

M. Cooper, *Pica*, Springfield, IL: Charles C. Thomas, 1957.

22 Rozin, "The Selection of Foods by Rats, Humans, and Other Animals."

23 Rozin, "Specific Aversions as a Component of Specific Hungers."

24 E. D. Capaldi, "Conditioned Food Preferences," in *Why We Eat What We Eat: The Psychology of Eating*, ed. E. D. Capaldi, Washington, DC: American Psychological Association, 1996.

A. Sclafani, "Learned Controls of Ingestive Behaviour," *Appetite* 29(1997): 153–158.

25 Rozin, "The Selection of Foods by Rats, Humans, and Other Animals."

26 D. I. Lozano, S. L. Crites, and S. N. Aikman, "Changes in Food Attitudes as a Function of Hunger," *Appetite* 32(1999): 207–218.

G. D. Mower, R. G. Mair, and T. Engen, "Influence of Internal Factors on the Perceived Intensity and Pleasantness of Gustatory and Olfactory Stimuli," in *The Chemical Senses and Nutrition*, eds. M. R. Kare and O. Maller, New York: Academic Press, 1977.

27 E. L. Gibson and J. Wardle, "Energy Density Predicts Preferences for Fruit and Vegetables in 4-Year-Old Children," *Appetite* 41(2003): 97–98.

28 E. H. Zandstra and W. El-Deredy, "Effects of Energy Conditioning on Food Preferences and Choice," *Appetite* 57(2011): 45–49.

29 D. A. Booth, P. Mather, and J. Fuller, "Starch Content of Ordinary Foods Associatively Conditions Human Appetite and Satiation, Indexed by Intake and Eating Pleasantness of Starch-Paired Flavours," *Appetite* 3(1982): 163–184.

30 L. L. Birch and M. Deysher, "Conditioned and Unconditioned Caloric Compensation: Evidence for Self Regulation of Food Intake in Young Children," *Learning and Motivation* 16(1985): 341–355.

31 U.S. Department of Agriculture and U.S. Department of Health and Human Services. *Dietary Guidelines for Americans*, 2010. Available online at: www.health.gov/dietaryguidelines/dga2010/DietaryGuidelines2010.pdf.

32 A. W. Logue, I. Ophir, and K. E. Strauss, "The Acquisition of Taste Aversions in Humans," *Behaviour Research and Therapy* 19(1981): 319–333.

33 A. W. Logue, "Taste Aversion and the Generality of the Laws of Learning," *Psychological Bulletin* 86(1979): 276–296.

M. L. Pelchat and P. Rozin, "The Special Role of Nausea in the Acquisition of Food Dislikes by Humans," *Appetite* 3(1982): 341–351.

Rozin, "The Selection of Foods by Rats, Humans, and Other Animals."

34 S. A. Barnett, *The Rat: A Study in Behavior*, Chicago: Aldine, 1963.

35 M. E. P. Seligman and J. L. Hager, eds., *Biological Boundaries of Learning*, New York: Appleton-Century-Crofts, 1972.

36 J. Garcia, D. J. Kimeldorf, and R. A. Koelling, "Conditioned Aversion to Saccharin Resulting from Exposure to Gamma Radiation," *Science* 122(1955): 157–158.

37 M. Nachman and J. H. Ashe, "Learned Taste Aversions in Rats as a Function of Dosage, Concentration, and Route of Administration of LiCl," *Physiology and Behavior* 10(1973): 73–78.

38 S. Lamon, G. T. Wilson, and R. C. Leaf, "Human Classical Aversion Conditioning: Nausea versus Electric Shock in the Reduction of Target Beverage Consumption," *Behaviour Research and Therapy* 15(1977): 313–320.

39 J. Garcia and R. A. Koelling, "Relation of Cue to Consequence in Avoidance Learning," *Psychonomic Science* 4(1966): 123–124.

40 B. M. Slotnick, F. Westbrook, and F. M. C. Darling, "What the Rat's Nose Tells the Rat's Mouth: Long Delay Aversion Conditioning with Aqueous Odors and Potentiation of Taste by Odors," *Animal Learning and Behavior* 25(1997): 357–369.

41 F. Etscorn and R. Stephens, "Establishment of Conditioned Taste Aversions with a 24-Hour CS–US Interval," *Physiological Psychology* 1(1973): 251–253.

42 J. Garcia, B. K. McGowan, and K. F. Green, "Biological Constraints on Conditioning," in *Biological Boundaries of Learning*, eds. M. E. P. Seligman and J. L. Hager, New York: Appleton-Century-Crofts, 1972.

H. Hoffmann, P. Hunt, and N. E. Spear, "Ontogenetic Differences in CS Palatability Following Conditioned Taste Aversion Training," *Learning and Motivation* 22(1991): 329–352.

43 J. Garcia and A. R. Gustavson, "Carl R. Gustavson (1946–1996) Pioneering Wildlife Psychologist," *APS Observer* (January 1997): 34–35.

C. R. Gustavson, "Comparative and Field Aspects of Learned Food Aversions," in *Learning Mechanisms in Food Selection*, eds. L. M. Barker, M. R. Best, and M. Domjan, Waco, TX: Baylor University Press, 1977.

C. R. Gustavson, L. P. Brett, J. Garcia, and D. J. Kelly, "A Working Model and Experimental Solutions to the Control of Predatory Behavior," in *Behavior of Captive Wild Animals*, eds. H. Markowitz and V. J. Stevens, Chicago: Nelson-Hall, 1978.

44 F. Baeyens, P. Eelen, O. Van den Bergh, and G. Crombez, "Flavor–Flavor and Color–Flavor Conditioning in Humans," *Learning and Motivation* 21(1990): 434–455.

M. S. Fanselow and J. Birk, "Flavor–Flavor Associations Induce Hedonic Shifts in Taste Preference," *Animal Learning and Behavior* 10(1982): 223–228.

45 D. A. Zellner, P. Rozin, M. Aron, and C. Kulish, "Conditioned Enhancement of Human's Liking for Flavor by Pairing with Sweetness," *Learning and Motivation* 14(1983): 338–350.

46 K. Ackroff and A. Sclafani, "Flavor Preferences Conditioned by Sugars: Rats Learn to Prefer Glucose Over Fructose," *Physiology and Behavior* 50(1991): 815–824.

47 L. L. Birch, D. Birch, D. W. Marlin, and L. Kramer, "Effects of Instrumental Consumption on Children's Food Preference," *Appetite* 3(1982): 125–134.

48 L. L. Birch, S. I. Zimmerman, and H. Hind, "The Influence of Social-Affective Context on the Formation of Children's Food Preferences," *Child Development* 51(1980): 856–861.

49 L. J. Cooke, L. C. Chambers, E. V. Añez, and J. Wardle, "Facilitating or undermining? The Effect of Reward on Food Acceptance. A Narrative Review," *Appetite* 57(2011): 493–497.
   A. Grubliauskiene, M. Verhoeven, and S. Dewitte, "The Joint Effect of Tangible and Non-Tangible Rewards on Healthy Food Choices in Children," *Appetite* 59(2012): 403–408.

50 B. Wansink, K. van Ittersum, and C. Werle, "How Negative Experiences Shape Long-Term Food Preferences. Fifty Years from the World War II Combat Front," *Appetite* 52(2009): 750–752.

51 J. O. Fisher and L. L. Birch, "Restricting Access to Palatable Foods Affects Children's Behavioral Response, Food Selection, and Intake," *American Journal of Clinical Nutrition* 69(1999): 1264–1272.

52 A. T. Galloway, L. M. Fiorito, L. A. Francis, and L. L. Birch, "'Finish Your Soup': Counterproductive Effects of Pressuring Children to Eat on Intake and Affect," *Appetite* 46(2006): 318–323.

53 S. K. Escalona, "Feeding Disturbances in Very Young Children," *American Journal of Orthopsychiatry* 15(1945): 76–80.

54 Ibid., p. 78.

55 J. E. Steiner, "Facial Expressions of the Neonate Infant Indicating the Hedonics of Food-Related Chemical Stimuli," in *Taste and Development*, ed. J. M. Weiffenbach, Bethesda, MD: U.S. Department of Health, Education, and Welfare, 1977.

56 T. M. Field, R. Woodson, R. Greenberg, and D. Cohen, "Discrimination and Imitation of Facial Expressions by Neonates," *Science* 218(1982): 179–181.

57 F. Baeyens, D. Vansteenwegen, J. De Houwer, and G. Crombez, "Observational Conditioning of Food Valence in Humans," *Appetite* 27(1996): 235–250.
   L. Barthomeuf, S. Rousset, and S. Droit-Volet, "Emotion and Food. Do the Emotions Expressed on Other People's Faces Affect the Desire to Eat Liked and Disliked Food Products? *Appetite* 52(2009): 27–33.

58 L. L. Birch, "Generalization of a Modified Food Preference," *Child Development* 52(1981): 755–758.
   L. L. Birch, "Children's Food Preferences: Developmental Patterns and Environmental Influences," in *Annals of Child Development*, vol. 4, ed. R. Vasta, Greenwich, CT: JAI Press, 1987.

59 J. Greenhalgh, A. J. Dewey, P. J. Horne, C. F. Lowe, J. H. Griffiths, and C. J. Whitaker, "Positive- and Negative Peer Modelling Effects on Young Children's Consumption of Novel Blue Foods," *Appetite* 52(2009): 646–653.

60 E. Addessi, A. T. Galloway, E. Visalberghi, and L. L. Birch, "Specific Social Influences on the Acceptance of Novel Foods in 2–5-Year-Old Children," *Appetite* 45(2005): 264–271.

61 K. Hobden and P. Pliner, "Effects of a Model on Food Neophobia in Humans," *Appetite* 25(1995): 101–114.

62 B. G. Galef, "Mechanisms for the Social Transmission of Acquired Food Preferences from Adult to Weanling Rats," in *Learning Mechanisms in Food Selection*, eds. L. M. Barker, M. R. Best, and M. Domjan, Waco, TX: Baylor University Press, 1977.

63 B. G. Galef and E. E. Whiskin, "Socially Transmitted Food Preferences Can Be Used to Study Long-Term Memory in Rats," *Animal Learning and Behavior* 31(2003): 160–164.

64 E. van de Waal, C. Borgeaud, and A. Whiten, "Potent Social Learning and Conformity Shape a Wild Primate's Foraging Decisions," *Science* 340(2013): 483–485.

65 M. J. Lavin, B. Freise, and S. Coombes, "Transferred Flavor Aversions in Adult Rats," *Behavioral and Neural Biology* 28(1980): 15–33.

S. Revusky, S. Coombes, and R. W. Pohl, "US Preexposure: Effects on Flavor Aversions Produced by Pairing a Poisoned Partner with Ingestion," *Animal Learning and Behavior* 10(1980): 83–90.

66 W. Gantz, N. Schwartz, J. R. Angelini, and V. Rideout, "Food for Thought: Television Food Advertising to Children in the United States," The Henry J. Kaiser Family Foundation (2007). Available online at: http://kff.org/other/food-for-thought-television-food-advertising-to/.

67 G. Cairns, D. Angus, G. Hastings, and M. Caraher, "Systematic Reviews of the Evidence on the Nature, Extent and Effects of Food Marketing to Children," *Appetite* 62(2013): 209–215.

M. E. Goldberg, G. J. Gorn, and W. Gibson, "TV Messages for Snack and Breakfast Foods: Do They Influence Children's Preferences?" *Journal of Consumer Research* 5(1978): 73–81.

R. Koordeman, D. J. Anschutz, R. B. van Baaren, and R. C. M. E. Engels, "Exposure to Soda Commercials Affects Sugar-Sweetened Soda Consumption in Young Women. An Observational Experimental Study," *Appetite* 54(2010): 619–622.

68 C. Radnitz, S. Byrne, R. Goldman, M. Sparks, M. Gantshar, and K. Tung, "Food Cues in Children's Television Programs," *Appetite* 52(2009): 230–233.

69 F. M. Kramer, K. Rock, and D. Engell, "Effects of Time of Day and Appropriateness on Food Intake and Hedonic Ratings at Morning and Midday," *Appetite* 18(1992): 1–13.

R. I. Stein and C. J. Nemeroff, "Moral Overtones of Food: Judgments of Others Based on What They Eat," *Personality and Social Psychology Bulletin* 21(1995): 480–490.

H. Tuorila, "Selection of Milks with Varying Fat Contents and Related Overall Liking, Attitudes, Norms and Intentions," *Appetite* 8(1987): 1–14.

D. A. Zellner, W. F. Stewart, P. Rozin, and J. M. Brown, "Effect of Temperature and Expectations on Liking for Beverages," *Physiology and Behavior* 44(1988): 61–68.

70 E. van Herpen and H. C. M. Trijp, "Front-of-Pack Nutrition Labels. Their Effect on Attention and Choices When Consumers Have Varying Goals and Time Constraints," *Appetite* 57(2011): 148–160.

71 P. Rozin and A. Fallon, "The Psychological Categorization of Foods and Non-Foods: A Preliminary Taxonomy of Food Rejections," *Appetite* 1(1980): 193–201.

72 S. Anzman-Grasca, J. S. Savage, M. E. Marini, J. O. Fisher, and L. L. Birch, "Repeated Exposure and Associative Conditioning Promote Preschool Children's Liking of Vegetables," *Appetite* 58(2012): 543–553.

E. D. Capaldi and G. J. Privitera, "Decreasing Dislike for Sour and Bitter in Children and Adults," *Appetite* 50(2008): 139–145.

S. M. de Droog, M. Buijzen, and P. M. Valkenburg, "Enhancing Children's Vegetable Consumption Using Vegetable-Promoting Picture Books. The Impact of Interactive Shared Reading and Character-Product Congruence," *Appetite* 73(2014): 73–80.

A. Lakkakula, J. P. Geaghan, W.-P. Wong, M. Zanovec, S. H. Pierce, and G. Tuuri, "A Cafeteria-Based Testing Program Increased Liking of Fruits and

Vegetables by Lower, Middle and Upper Elementary School-Age Children," *Appetite* 57(2011): 299–302.

A. Lakkakula, J. Geaghan, M. Zanovec, S. Pierce, and G. Tuuri, "Repeated Taste Exposure Increases Liking for Vegetables by Low-Income Elementary School Children," *Appetite* 55(2010): 226–231.

73 L. L. Birch, "Effects of Peer Models' Food Choices and Eating Behaviors on Preschoolers' Food Preferences," *Child Development* 51(1980): 489–496.

74 Rozin and Fallon, "The Psychological Categorization of Foods and Non-Food."

75 P. Rozin and A. E. Fallon, "A Perspective on Disgust," *Psychological Review* 94(1987): 23–41.

76 "No Seconds," *Time* (May 23, 1994): 14.

7 THIS OR THAT

1 S. R. X. Dall, I. C. Cuthill, N. Cook, and M. Morphet, "Learning about Food: Starlings, Skinner Boxes, and Earthworms," *Journal of the Experimental Analysis of Behavior* 67(1997): 181–192.

F. D. Provenza and R. P. Cincotta, "Foraging as a Self-Organizational Learning Process: Accepting Adaptability at the Expense of Predictability," in *Diet Selection: An Interdisciplinary Approach to Foraging Behaviour*, ed. R. N. Hughes, Oxford: Blackwell Scientific, 1993.

2 M. L. Platt, E. M. Brannon, T. L. Briese, and J. A. French, "Differences in Feeding Ecology Predict Differences in Performance between Golden Lion Tamarins (*Leontopithecus rosalia*) and Wied's Marmosets (*Callithrix kuhli*) on Spatial and Visual Memory Tasks," *Animal Learning and Behavior* 24(1996): 384–393.

3 K. Milton, "Diet and Primate Evolution," *Scientific American* (August 1993): 86.

4 Ibid., pp. 86–93.

5 B. Heinrich and J. Marzluff, "Why Ravens Share," *American Scientist* 83(1995): 342–349.

6 G. S. Wilkinson, "Food Sharing in Vampire Bats," *Scientific American* (February 1990): 76–82.

7 W. M. Baum, "On Two Types of Deviation from the Matching Law: Bias and Undermatching," *Journal of the Experimental Analysis of Behavior* 22(1974): 231–242.

R. J. Herrnstein, "On the Law of Effect," *Journal or the Experimental Analysis of Behavior* 13(1970): 243–266.

8 P. de Villiers, "Choice in Concurrent Schedules and a Quantitative Formulation of the Law of Effect," in *Handbook of Operant Behavior*, eds. W. K. Honig and J. E. R. Staddon, Englewood Cliffs, NJ: Prentice Hall, 1977.

T. M. Foster, W. Temple, B. Robertson, V. Nair, and A. Poling, "Concurrent-Schedule Performance in Dairy Cows: Persistent Undermatching," *Journal of the Experimental Analysis of Behavior* 65(1996): 57–80.

9 W. M. Baum, "Choice in Free-Ranging Wild Pigeons," *Science* 185(1974): 78–79.

10 E. W. Menzel and E. J. Wyers, "Cognitive Aspects of Foraging Behavior," in *Foraging Behavior: Ecological, Ethological, and Psychological Approaches*, eds. A. C. Kamil and T. D. Sargent, New York: Garland, 1981, p. 355.

11 Ibid.

12 A. C. Kamil and T. D. Sargent, "Introduction," in *Foraging Behavior: Ecological, Ethological, and Psychological Approaches*, eds. A. C. Kamil and T. D. Sargent, New York: Garland, 1981.

13 S. R. Hursh, "Economic Concepts for the Analysis of Behavior," *Journal of the Experimental Analysis of Behavior* 34(1980): 219–238.

S. E. G. Lea, "The Psychology and Economics of Demand," *Psychological Bulletin* 85(1978): 441–466.

14 A. Drewnowski, "Obesity, Diets, and Social Inequalities," *Nutrition Reviews* 67(2009): S36–S39.

A. Drewnowski, "Healthier Foods Cost More," *Nutrition Reviews* 68(2010): 184–185.

V. Inglis, K. Ball, and D. Crawford, "Does Modifying the Household Food Budget Predict Changes in the Healthfulness of Purchasing Choices among Low- and High-Income Women? *Appetite* 52(2009): 273–279.

D. M. Dave and I. R. Kelly, "How Does the Business Cycle Affect Eating Habits," *Social Science and Medicine* 74(2012): 254–262.

15 J. E. R. Staddon, *Adaptive Behavior and Learning*, New York: Cambridge University Press, 1983.

16 G. H. Pyke, "Honeyeater Foraging: A Test of Optimal Foraging Theory," *Animal Behaviour* 29(1981): 878–888.

G. H. Pyke, "Optimal Foraging in Hummingbirds: Rule of Movement between Inflorescences," *Animal Behaviour* 29(1981): 889–896.

G. H. Pyke, "Why Hummingbirds Hover and Honeyeaters Perch," *Animal Behaviour* 29(1981): 861–867.

17 S. H. Mitchell and J. Brener, "Energetic and Motor Responses to Increasing Force Requirements," *Journal of Experimental Psychology: Animal Behavior Processes* 17(1991): 174–185.

18 S. E. G. Lea, "The Analysis of Need," in *Animal Cognition and Behavior*, ed. R. L. Mellgren, New York: North-Holland, 1983.

J. G. Goode, K. Curtis, and J. Theophano, "Group Shared Food Patterns as a Unit of Analysis," in *Nutrition and Behavior*, ed. S. A. Miller, Philadelphia: Franklin Institute, 1981.

19 S. M. Cantor and M. B. Cantor, "Socioeconomic Factors in Fat and Sugar Consumption," in *The Chemical Senses and Nutrition*, eds. M. R. Kare and O. Maller, New York: Academic Press, 1977.

M. Krondl and D. Lau, "Social Determinants in Human Food Selection," in *The Psychobiology of Human Food Selection*, ed. L. M. Barker, Westport, CT: AVI Publishing, 1982.

N. S. Scrimshaw and L. Taylor, "Food," *Scientific American* (September 1980): 78–88.

J. Yudkin, "Patterns and Trends in Carbohydrate Consumption and Their Relation to Disease," *Nutrition Society Proceedings* 23(1964): 149–162.

20 E. A. Smith, "Optimization Theory in Anthropology: Applications and Critiques," in *The Latest on the Best: Essays on Evolution and Optimality*, ed. J. Dupre, Cambridge, MA: MIT Press, 1987.

B. Winterhalder, "The Analysis of Hunter-Gatherer Diets: Stalking an Optimal Foraging Model," in *Food and Evolution: Toward a Theory of Human Food Habits*, eds. M. Harris and E. B. Ross, Philadelphia: Temple University Press, 1987.

21 K. Hill and A. M. Hurtado, "Hunter-Gatherers of the New World," *American Scientist* (September/October 1989): 436–443.

22 M. R. Berenbaum, *Bugs in the System: Insects and Their Impact on Human Affairs*, Reading, MA: Addison-Wesley, 1995.

23 G. W. Ainslie, "Impulse Control in Pigeons," *Journal of the Experimental Analysis of Behavior* 21(1974): 485–489.

A. W. Logue, *Self-Control: Waiting until Tomorrow for What You Want Today*, Englewood Cliffs, NJ: Prentice Hall, 1995.

H. Rachlin and L. Green, "Commitment, Choice and Self Control," *Journal of the Experimental Analysis of Behavior* 17(1972): 15–22.

24 B. F. Skinner, *Notebooks*, Englewood Cliffs, NJ: Prentice Hall, 1980, p. 59.

25 Logue, *Self-Control*.

26 E. Fantino, "The Future Is Uncertain: Eat Dessert First," *Behavioral and Brain Sciences* 18(1995): 125–126.

27 L. B. Forzano and A. W. Logue, "Predictors of Adult Humans' Self-Control and Impulsiveness for Food Reinforcers," *Appetite* 19(1992): 33–47.

J. M. Kirk and A. W. Logue, "Effects of Deprivation Level on Humans' Self-Control for Food Reinforcers," *Appetite* 28(1997): 215–226.

28 *Annie* (October 20, 1981). Manuscript in the Theatre Collection in the New York Public Library for the Performing Arts, New York, NY.

29 I. C. Gilby and R. W. Wrangham, "Risk-Prone Hunting by Chimpanzees (*Pan troglodytes schweinfurthii*) Increases During Periods of High Diet Quality," *Behavioral Ecology and Sociobiology* 61(2007): 1771–1779.

30 M. A. Wogar, C. M. Bradshaw, and E. Szabadi, "Effect of Lesions of the Ascending 5-Hydroxytryptaminergic Pathways on Choice between Delayed Reinforcers," *Psychopharmacology* 111(1993): 239–243.

31 A. R. Damasio, "On Some Functions of the Human Prefrontal Cortex," in *Structure and Functions of the Human Prefrontal Cortex*, eds. J. Grafman, K. J. Holyoak, and F. Boller, New York: New York Academy of Sciences, 1995.

32 T. A. Hare, C. F. Camerer, and A. Rangel, "Self-Control in Decision Making Involves Modulation of the vmPFC Valuation System," *Science* 324(2009): 646–648.

N. Kolling, T. E. J. Behrens, R. B. Mars, and M. F. S. Rushworth, "Neural Mechanisms of Foraging," *Science* 336(2012): 95–98.

33 G. W. Ainslie, "Specious Reward: A Behavioral Theory of Impulsiveness and Impulse Control," *Psychological Bulletin* 82(1975): 463–496.

H. Rachlin, "Self-Control," *Behaviorism* 2(1974): 94–107.

34 J. E. Mazur and A. W. Logue, "Choice in a Self Control Paradigm: Effects of a Fading Procedure," *Journal of the Experimental Analysis of Behavior* 30(1978): 11–17.

J. B. Schweitzer and B. Sulzer-Azaroff, "Self-Control: Teaching Tolerance for Delay in Impulsive Children," *Journal of the Experimental Analysis of Behavior* 50(1988): 173–186.

35 W. Mischel, Y. Shoda, and M. L. Rodriguez, "Delay of Gratification in Children," *Science* 244(1989): 933–938.

36 J. Grosch and A. Neuringer, "Self-Control in Pigeons under the Mischel Paradigm," *Journal of the Experimental Analysis of Behavior* 35(1981): 3–21.

A. W. Logue and T. E. Peña-Correal, "Responding during Reinforcement Delay in a Self-Control Paradigm," *Journal of the Experimental Analysis of Behavior* 41(1984): 267–277.

37 A. W. Logue and J. E. Mazur, "Maintenance of Self-Control Acquired through a Fading Procedure: Follow-Up on Mazur and Logue (1978)," *Behavior Analysis Letters* 1(1981): 131–137.

38 L. B. Forzano and R. J. Corry, "Self-Control and Impulsiveness in Adult Human Females," *Learning and Motivation* 29(1998): 184–199.

Grosch and Neuringer, "Self-Control in Pigeons under the Mischel Paradigm."

39 B. F. Skinner, *Walden Two*, New York: Macmillan, 1948, pp. 107–108.

40 A. M. Smith, *Blue Shoes and Happiness*, New York: Pantheon Books, 2006, p. 181.

41 K. Le Billon, "No Chicken tenders, S'il Vous Plait: How a Couple of Young Foodophobes Learned to Eat like the French," *The New York Times Magazine* (March 18, 2012): 98.

42 L. B. Forzano and A. W. Logue, "Self-Control in Adult Humans: Comparison of Qualitatively Different Reinforcers," *Learning and Motivation* 25(1994): 65–82.

K. Jackson and T. D. Hackenberg, "Token Reinforcement, Choice, and Self-Control in Pigeons," *Journal of the Experimental Analysis of Behavior* 66(1996): 29–49.

43 R. F. Baumeister, K. D. Vohs, and D. M. Tice, "The Strength Model of Self-Control," *Current Directions in Psychological Science* 16(2007): 351–355.

F. Lange and F. Eggert, "Sweet Delusion: Glucose Drinks Fail to Counteract Ego Depletion," *Appetite* 75(2014): 54–63.

M. A. Sanders, S. D. Shirk, C. J. Burgin, and L. L. Martin, "The Gargle Effect: Rinsing the Mouth with Glucose Enhances Self-Control," *Psychological Science* 23(2012): 1470–1472.

X. T. Wang and R. D. Dvorak, "Sweet Future: Fluctuating Blood Glucose Levels Affect Future Discounting," *Psychological Science* 21(2010): 183–188.

44 Logue, *Self-Control*.

A. W. Logue, M. L. Rodriguez, T. E. Peña-Correal, and B. C. Mauro, "Choice in a Self-Control Paradigm: Quantification of Experience-Based Differences," *Journal of the Experimental Analysis of Behavior* 41(1984): 53–67.

45 R. H. Thaler and C. R. Sunstein, *Nudge: Improving Decisions about Health, Wealth, and Happiness*. New York: Penguin, 2009.

46 L. H. Epstein, K. K. Dearing, L. G. Roba, and E. Finkelstein, "The Influence of Taxes and Subsidies on Energy Purchased In an Experimental Purchasing Study," *Psychological Science*, 21(2010): 406–414.

T. M. Marteau, G. J. Hollands, and P. C. Fletcher, "Changing Human Behavior to Prevent Disease: the Importance of Targeting Automatic Processes," *Science* 337(2012): 1492–1495.

C. Nederkoorn, R. C. Havermans, J. C. A. H. Giesen, and A. Jansen, "High Tax on High Energy Dense Goods and Its Effects on the Purchase of Calories in a Supermarket. An Experiment. *Appetite* 56(2011): 760–765.

47 H. L. Meiselman, D. Hedderley, S. L. Staddon, B. J. Pierson, and C. R. Symonds, "Effect of Effort on Meal Selection and Meal Acceptability in a Student Cafeteria," *Appetite* 23(1994): 43–55.

48 M. C. Grynbaum, "Fighting Soda Rule, Industry Focuses on Personal Choice," *The New York Times* (July 2, 2012): A10–A12.

V. Yee, "Weight-Loss Leaders Back Bloomberg Soda Plan," *The New York Times* (September 5, 2012): A25.

49 M. Schulte-Mecklenbeck, M. Sohn, E. de Bellis, N. Martin, and R. Hertwig, "A Lack of Appetite for Information and Computation. Simple Heuristics in Food Choice," *Appetite* 71(2013): 242–251.

50 J. E. R. Staddon and J. M. Hinson, "Optimization: A Result or a Mechanism?" *Science* 221(1983): 976–977.

M. D. Zeiler, "On Optimal Choice Strategies," *Journal of Experimental Psychology: Animal Behavior Processes* 13(1987): 31–39.

8 YOU ARE WHAT YOU EAT AND DRINK

1 W. Shakespeare, *Julius Caesar* in *The Complete Works of William Shakespeare*, ed. W. A. Wright, Garden City, NY: Garden City Books, 1599/1936, p. 634.

2 L. Carroll, *The Annotated Alice*, New York: Bramhall House, 1960, p. 57.
3 C. M. Hasler, "Functional Foods: The Western Perspective," *Nutrition Reviews* 53(1996): S6–S10.

W. Weng and J. Chen, "The Eastern Perspective on Functional Foods Based on Traditional Chinese Medicine," *Nutrition Reviews* 54(1996): S11–S16.
4 C. de Jager, L. Dye, E. A. de Bruin, L. Butler, J. Fletcher, D. J. Lamport, et al., "Criteria for Validation and Selection of Cognitive Tests for Investigating the Effects of Foods and Nutrients," *Nutrition Reviews* 72(2014): 162–179.

J. A. J. Schmitt, "Nutrition and Cognition: Meeting the Challenge to Obtain Credible and Evidence-Based Facts," *Nutrition Reviews* 68(2010): S2–S5.
5 A. R. Lecours, M. Mandujano, and G. Romero, "Ontogeny of Brain and Cognition: Relevance to Nutrition Research," *Nutrition Reviews* 59(2001): S7–S12.

E. Pollitt, "Timing and Vulnerability in Research on Malnutrition and Cognition," *Nutrition Reviews*, 54(1996): S49–S55.

M. Sigman, "Nutrition and Child Development: More Food for Thought," *Directions in Psychological Science* 4(1995): 52–55.
6 J. L. Brown and E. Pollitt, "Malnutrition, Poverty and Intellectual Development," *Scientific American* (February 1996): 38–43.
7 H. N. Ricciuti, "Nutrition and Mental Development," *Psychological Science* 2(1993): 43–46.
8 J. Blumberg, "Nutrient Requirements of the Healthy Elderly—Should There Be Specific RDAs?" *Nutrition Reviews* 52(1994): S15–S18.

J. E. Morley, "Nutritional Modulation of Behavior and Immunocompetence," *Nutrition Reviews* 52(1994): S6–S8.
9 D. Benton and P. Y. Parker, "Breakfast, Blood Glucose, and Cognition," *American Journal of Clinical Nutrition* 67(1998): 772S–778S.

E. Pollitt, E. Jacoby, and S. Cueto, "School Breakfast and Cognition among Nutritionally At-Risk Children in the Peruvian Andes," *Nutrition Reviews* 54(1996): S22–S26.
10 A. Smith, A. Ralph, and G. McNeill, "Influences of Meal Size on Post-Lunch Changes in Performance Efficiency, Mood, and Cardiovascular Function," *Appetite* 16(1991): 85–91.
11 L. Aarøe and M. B. Petersen, "Hunger Games: Fluctuations in Blood Glucose Levels Influence Support for Social Welfare," *Psychological Science* 24(2013): 2550–2556.
12 J. Bryan, S. Osendarp, D. Hughes, E. Calvaresi, K. Baghurst, and J.-W. van Klinken, "Nutrients for Cognitive Development in School-Aged Children," *Nutrition Reviews* 62(2004): 295–306.

D. K. Dror and L. H. Allen, "Effect of Vitamin B_{12} Deficiency on Neurodevelopment in Infants: Current Knowledge and Possible Mechanisms," *Nutrition Reviews* 66(2008): 250–255.

S. J. M. Osendarp, L. E. Murray-Kolb, and M. M. Black, "Case Study on Iron in Mental Development—In Memory of John Beard (1947–2009)," *Nutrition Reviews* 68(2010): S48–S52.
13 B. A. Golomb, "Cholesterol and Violence: Is There a Connection?" *Annals of Internal Medicine* 128(1998): 478–487.

J. R. Kaplan, M. F. Muldoon, S. B. Manuck, and J. J. Mann, "Assessing the Observed Relationship between Low Cholesterol and Violence-Related Mortality: Implications for Suicide Risk." *Annals of the New York Academy of Sciences* 836(1997): 57–80.

14 L. Pauling, "Orthomolecular Psychiatry," *Science* 160(1968): 265–271.

15 American Psychiatric Association, *Diagnostic and Statistical Manual of Mental Disorders* (Rev. ed.), 3rd ed., Washington, DC: APA, 1987.

S. C. Bowden, "Separating Cognitive Impairment in Neurologically Asymptomatic Alcoholism from Wernicke–Korsakoff Syndrome: Is the Neurological Distinction Justified?" *Psychological Bulletin* 107(1990): 355–366.

P. M. Dreyfus, "The Nutritional Management of Neurological Disease," in *Nutrition and Behavior*, ed. S. A. Miller, Philadelphia: Franklin Institute, 1981.

16 T. A. Ban, "Megavitamin Therapy in Schizophrenia," in *Nutrition and Behavior*, ed. S. A. Miller, Philadelphia: Franklin Institute, 1981.

M. Barinaga, "Vitamin C Gets a Little Respect," *Science* 254(1991): 374–376.

Pauling, "Orthomolecular Psychiatry."

17 K. Leutwyler, "Suicide Prevention," *Scientific American* (March 1997): 18, 20.

P. I. Markowitz and E. F. Coccaro, "Biological Studies of Impulsivity, Aggression, and Suicidal Behavior," in *Impulsivity and Aggression*, eds. E. Hollander and D. J. Stein, New York: Wiley, 1995.

J. B. Richards and H. de Wit, "Effects of Serotonin Depletion in Rats on Three Models of Impulsive Behavior," *Pharmacology, Biochemistry and Behavior* 57(1997): 620.

18 Golomb, "Cholesterol and Violence."

19 B. Spring, "Effects of Foods and Nutrients on the Behavior of Normal Individuals," in *Nutrition and the Brain*, vol. 7, eds. R. J. Wurtman and J. J. Wurtman, New York: Raven Press, 1986.

H. M. van Praag and C. Lemus, "Monoamine Precursors in the Treatment of Psychiatric Disorders," in *Nutrition and the Brain*, vol. 7, eds. R. J. Wurtman and J. J. Wurtman, New York: Raven Press, 1986.

20 J. D. Fernstrom, "Nutrition, Brain Function and Behavior," in *Nutrition and Behavior*, ed. S. A. Miller, Philadelphia: Franklin Institute, 1981.

R. J. Wurtman and J. J. Wurtman, "Nutrients, Neurotransmitter Synthesis, and the Control of Food Intake," in *Eating and Its Disorders*, eds. A. J. Stunkard and E. Stellar, New York: Raven Press, 1984.

21 S. N. Young, "The Clinical Psychopharmacology of Tryptophan," in *Nutrition and the Brain*, vol. 7, eds. R. J. Wurtman and J. J. Wurtman, New York: Raven Press, 1986.

22 C. R. Markus, G. Panhuysen, A. Tuiten, H. Koppeschaar, D. Fekkes, and M. L. Peters, "Does Carbohydrate-Rich, Protein-Poor Food Prevent a Deterioration of Mood and Cognitive Performance of Stress-Prone Subjects When Subjected to a Stressful Task?" *Appetite* 31(1998): 49–65.

23 Carroll, *The Annotated Alice*, p. 73.

24 H. M. Lloyd, P. J. Rogers, D. I. Hedderley, and A. F. Walker, "Acute Effects on Mood and Cognitive Performance of Breakfasts Differing in Fat and Carbohydrate Content," *Appetite* 27(1996): 151–164.

W. H. Meck and R. M. Church, "Nutrients That Modify the Speed of Internal Clock and Memory Storage Processes," *Behavioral Neuroscience* 101(1987): 467–475.

Spring, "Effects of Foods and Nutrients on the Behavior of Normal Individuals."

25 J. Ingwersen, M. A. Defeyter, D. O. Kennedy, K. A. Wesnes, and A. B. Scholey, "A Low Glycaemic Index Breakfast Cereal Preferentially Prevents Children's

Cognitive Performance from Declining Throughout the Morning," *Appetite* 49(2007): 240–244.

P. Lattimore, J. Walton, S. Bartlett, A. Hackett, and L. Stevenson, "Regular Consumption of a Cereal Breakfast. Effects on Mood and Body Image," *Appetite* 55(2010): 512–521.

K. A. Wesnes, C. Pincock, and A. Scholey, "Breakfast is Associated with Enhanced Cognitive Function in Schoolchildren," *Appetite* 59(2012): 646–649.

26 H. Francis and R. Stevenson, "The Longer-Term Impacts of Western Diet on Human Cognition and the Brain," *Appetite* 63(2013): 119–128.

P. Valladolid, P. Stucchi, V. Cano, M. S. Fernández-Alfonso, B. Merino, M. Gil-Ortega, et al., "High-Fat Diets Impair Spatial Learning in the Radial-Arm Maze in Mice," *Neurobiology of Learning and Memory* 95(2011): 80–85.

27 A. Meule, A. K. Skirde, R. Freund, C. Vögele, and A. Kübler, "High-Calorie Food-Cues Impair Working Memory Performance in High and Low Food Cravers," *Appetite* 59(2012): 264–269.

C.-B. Zhong and S. E. DeVoe, "You Are How You Eat: Fast Food and Impatience," *Psychological Science* 21(2010): 619–622.

28 B. Spring, J. Chiodo, M. Harden, M. J. Bourgeois, J. D. Mason, and L. Lutherer, "Psychobiological Effects of Carbohydrates," *Journal of Clinical Psychiatry* 50(Supplement)(1980): 27–33.

29 E. Hartman, "Effects of L-Tryptophan on Sleepiness and on Sleep," *Journal of Psychiatric Research* 17(1982/83): 107–113.

P. D. Leathwood and P. Pollet, "Diet-Induced Mood Changes in Normal Populations," *Journal of Psychiatric Research* 17(1982/83): 147–154.

B. Spring, J. Chiodo, and D. J. Bowen, "Carbohydrates, Tryptophan, and Behavior: A Methodological Review," *Psychological Bulletin* 102(1987): 234–256.

M. W. Yogman, S. H. Zeisel, and C. Roberts, "Assessing Effects of Serotonin Precursors on Newborn Behavior," *Journal of Psychiatric Research* 17(1982/83): 123–133.

30 B. Spring, O. Maller, J. Wurtman, L. Digman, and L. Cozolino, "Effects of Protein and Carbohydrate Meals on Mood and Performance: Interactions with Sex and Age," *Journal of Psychiatric Research* 17(1982/83): 155–167.

31 M. L. Wolraich, D. B. Wilson, and J. W. White, "The Effect of Sugar on Behavior or Cognition in Children: A Meta-Analysis," *JAMA* 274(1995): 1617–1621.

32 A. Scholey, L. A. Downey, J. Ciorciari, A. Pipingas, K. Nolidin, M. Finn, et al., "Acute Neurocognitive Effects of Epigallocatechin Gallate (EGCG)," *Appetite* 58(2012): 767–770.

33 C. J. Edmonds, R. Crombie, H. Ballieux, M. R. Gardner, and L. Dawkins, "Water Consumption, not Expectancies about Water Consumption, Affects Cognitive Performance in Adults," *Appetite* 60(2012): 148–153.

R. Fadda, G. Rapinett, D. Grathwohl, M. Parisi, R. Fanari, C. M. Caló, et al., "Effects of Drinking Supplementary Water at School on Cognitive Performance in Children," *Appetite* 59(2012): 730–737.

P. Ritz and G. Berrut, "The Importance of Good Hydration for Day-to-Day Health," *Nutrition Reviews* 63(2005): S6–S13.

34 J. Prescott and J. Wilkie, "Pain Tolerance Selectively Increased by a Sweet-Smelling Odor," *Psychological Science* 18(2007): 308–311.

35 R. A. Baron and M. I. Bronfen, "A Whiff of Reality: Empirical Evidence Concerning the Effects of Pleasant Fragrances on Work-Related Behavior," *Journal of Applied Social Psychology* 24(1994): 1179–1203.

36 L. D. Dickey, *Clinical Ecology*, Springfield, IL: Charles C. Thomas, 1976.
   M. Barinaga, "Better Data Needed on Sensitivity Syndrome," *Science* 251(1991): 1558.

37 G. Guroff, "Inborn Errors of Amino Acid Metabolism in Relation to Diet," in *Nutrition and Behavior*, ed. S. A. Miller, Philadelphia: Franklin Institute, 1981.

38 "The Maternal Phenylketonuria Collaborative Study: A Status Report," *Nutrition Reviews* 52(1994): 390–393.

39 D. S. King, "Food and Chemical Sensibilities Can Produce Cognitive-Emotional Symptoms," in *Nutrition and Behavior*, ed. S. A. Miller, Philadelphia: Franklin Institute, 1981.

40 L. R. Caporael, "Ergotism: The Satan Loosed in Salem," *Science* 192(1976): 21–26.
   M. K. Matossian, "Ergot and the Salem Witchcraft Affair," *American Scientist* 70(July/August 1982): 355–357.

41 W. N. Arnold, "Absinthe," *Scientific American* 260(June 1989): 112–117.

42 American Psychiatric Association, *Diagnostic and Statistical Manual of Mental Disorders*, 5th ed., Arlington, VA: American Psychiatric Association, 2013.

43 E. Childs and H. de Wit, "Subjective, Behavioral, and Physiological Effects of Acute Caffeine in Light, Nonindependent Caffeine Users," *Psychopharmacology* 185(2006): 514–523.
   L. Dawkins, F.-Z. Shahzad, S. S. Ahmed, and C. J. Edmonds, "Expectation of Having Consumed Caffeine Can Improve Performance and Mood," *Appetite* 57(2011): 597–600.
   E. A. De Bruin, M. J. Rowson, L. Van Buren, J. A. Rycroft, and G. N. Owen, "Black Tea Improves Attention and Self-Reported Alertness," *Appetite* 56(2011): 235–240.

44 S. H. Mitchell, H. de Wit, and J. P. Zacny, "Caffeine Withdrawal Symptoms and Self-Administration Following Caffeine Deprivation," *Pharmacology Biochemistry and Behavior* 51(1995): 941–945.

45 N. J. Richardson, P. J. Rogers, and N. A. Elliman, "Conditioned Flavour Preferences Reinforced by Caffeine Consumed after Lunch," *Physiology and Behavior* 60(1996): 257–263.

46 J. E. Brody, "Breaking, or at Least Taming, the Caffeine Habit," *The New York Times* (September 13, 1995): C9.

47 A. Astrup, S. Toubro, S. Cannon, P. Hein, L. Breum, and J. Madsen, "Caffeine: A Double-Blind, Placebo-Controlled Study of Its Thermogenic, Metabolic, and Cardiovascular Effects in Healthy Volunteers," *American Journal of Clinical Nutrition* 51(1990): 759–767.
   J. E. Brody, "The Latest on Coffee? Don't Worry. Drink Up," *The New York Times* (September 13, 1995): C1, C6.

48 American Psychiatric Association, *Diagnostic and Statistical Manual of Mental Disorders*, 5th ed., pp. 503–504.

49 B. J. Brockel and D. A. Cory-Slechta, "Lead-Induced Decrements in Waiting Behavior: Involvement of D2-Like Dopamine Receptors," *Pharmacology, Biochemistry and Behavior* 63(1999): 423–434.

50 S. M. Koger, "Environmental toxicants and developmental disabilities," *American Psychologist* 60(2005): 243–255.
   H. L. Needleman, S. K. Geiger, and R. Frank, "Lead and IQ Scores: A Reanalysis," *Science* 227(1985): 701–702, 704.
   H. L. Needleman, J. A. Riess, M. J. Tobin, G. E. Biesecker, and J. B. Greenhouse, "Bone Lead Levels and Delinquent Behavior," *JAMA* 275(1996): 363–369.

51 J. Eisinger, "Sweet Poison," *Natural History* (July 1996): 48–53.
52 "Was the Ill-Fated Franklin Expedition a Victim of Lead Poisoning," *Nutrition Reviews* 47(1989): 322–323.
53 S. Klitzman, T. D. Matte, and D. E. Kass, "The Urban Physical Environment and Its Effects on Health," in *Cities and the Health of the Public*, eds. N. Freudenberg, S. Galea, and D. Vlahov, Nashville, TN: Vanderbilt University Press, 2006.
54 I. Chen, "Lead's Buried Legacy," *Scientific American* (September 2013): 28–30.
55 American Psychiatric Association, *Diagnostic and Statistical Manual of Mental Disorders*, 5th ed., pp. 59–61.
56 J. L. Rapoport, M. S. Buchsbaum, T. P. Zahn, H. Weingartner, C. Ludlow, and E. J. Mikkelsen, "Dextroamphetamine: Cognitive and Behavioral Effects in Normal Prepubertal Boys," *Science* 199(1978): 560–563.
   M. A. Stewart, "Hyperactive Children," *Scientific American* 222(April 1970): 94–99.
57 H. D. Posavac, S. M. Sheridan, and S. S. Posavac, "A Cueing Procedure to Control Impulsivity in Children with Attention Deficit Hyperactivity Disorder," *Behavior Modification* 23(1999): 234–253.
58 L. J. Stevens, T. Kuczek, and L. E. Arnold, "Solving the Puzzle of Attention Deficit Hyperactivity Disorder," *Nutrition Reviews* 69(2011): 383–384.
59 Koger, "Environmental toxicants and developmental disabilities."
60 B. E. Feingold, "Dietary Management of Behavior and Learning Disabilities," in *Nutrition and Behavior*, ed. S. A. Miller, Philadelphia: Franklin Institute, 1981.
61 R. B. Kanarek, "Artificial Food Dyes and Attention Deficit Hyperactivity Disorder," *Nutrition Reviews* 69(2011): 385–391.
   www.nimh.nih.gov/health/publications/attention-deficit-hyperactivity-disorder/index.shtml?utm_source=REFERENCES_R7.
   Stevens et al., "Solving the Puzzle of Attention Deficit Hyperactivity Disorder."
62 Stevens et al., "Solving the Puzzle of Attention Deficit Hyperactivity Disorder."
63 A. P. Allen and A. P. Smith, "Demand Characteristics, Pre-Test Attitudes and Time-On-Task Trends in the Effects of Chewing Gum on Attention and Reported Mood in Healthy Volunteers," *Appetite* 59(2012): 349–356.
   A. Scholey, "Chewing Gum and Cognitive Performance: A Case of a Functional Food with Function but No Food?" *Appetite* 43(2004): 215–216.
64 S. V. Onyper, T. L. Carr, J. S. Farrar, and B. R. Floyd, "Cognitive Advantages of Chewing Gum. Now You See Them, Now You Don't," *Appetite* 57(2011): 321–328.
65 Ibid.
   L. Tucha and W. Simpson, "The Role of Time on Task Performance in Modifying the Effects of Gum Chewing on Attention," *Appetite* 56(2011): 299–301.
66 B. Brecht, *Galileo*, trans. C. Laughton, New York: Grove, 1966, p. 61.

9 "HUNGER TALKS A MOST PERSUASIVE LANGUAGE"

1 P. Rosenzweig, *The Book of Proverbs*, New York: Philosophical Library, 1965, p. 89.
2 M. S. Exton, "Infection-Induced Anorexia: Active Host Defence Strategy," *Appetite* 29(1997): 369–383.

L. M. Hecker and D. P. Kotler, "Malnutrition in Patients with AIDS," *Nutrition Reviews* 48(1990): 393–401.

S. Rivière, S. Gillette-Guyonnet, F. Nourhashemi, and B. Vellas, "Nutrition and Alzheimer's Disease," *Nutrition Reviews* 57(1999): 363–367.

S. B. Roberts, "Energy Regulation and Aging: Recent Findings and Their Implications," *Nutrition Reviews* 58(2000): 91–97.

H. P. Weingarten, "Mechanisms of Food Intake Suppression Induced by Inflammation of the Intestines," Paper presented at the Columbia University Seminar on Appetitive Behavior, New York, May 14, 1992.

3 J. E. Blundell, "Psychopharmacology of Centrally Acting Anorectic Agents," in *Psychopharmacology and Food*, eds. M. Sandler and T. Silverstone, New York: Oxford University Press, 1985.

4 D. H. Baucom and P. A. Aiken, "Effect of Depressed Mood on Eating among Obese and Nonobese Dieting and Nondieting Persons," *Journal of Personality and Social Psychology* 41(1981): 577–585.

J. Polivy and C. P. Herman, "Clinical Depression and Weight Change: A Complex Relation," *Journal of Abnormal Psychology* 85(1976): 338–340.

5 R. J. Colman, R. M. Anderson, S. C. Johnson, E. K. Kastman, K. J. Kosmatka, T. M. Beasley, et al., "Caloric Restriction Delays Disease Onset and Mortality in Rhesus Monkeys," *Science* 325(2009): 201–204.

A. V. Witte, M. Fobker, R. Gellner, S. Knecht, and A. Flöel, "Caloric Restriction Improves Memory in Elderly Humans," *Proceedings of the National Academy of Sciences* 106(2009): 1255–1260.

6 C. W. Levenson and N. J. Rich, "Eat Less, Live Longer? New Insights into the Role of Caloric Restriction in the Brain," *Nutrition Reviews* 65(2007): 412–415.

A. Taguchi, L. M. Wartschow, and M. F. White, "Brain Irs2 Signaling Coordinates Life Span and Nutrient Homeostasis," *Science* 317(2007): 369–372.

G. Wolf, "Calorie Restriction Increases Life Span: A molecular Mechanism," *Nutrition Reviews* 64(2006): 89–92.

7 J. Dibbell, "The Fast Supper," *New York* (October 30, 2006): 44–49, 130.

8 R. F. Kushner, "Body Weight and Mortality," *Nutrition Reviews* 51(1993): 127–136.

L. Lissner, P. M. Odell, R. B. D'Agostino, J. Stokes, B. E. Kreger, A. J. Belanger, and K. D. Brownell, "Variability of Body Weight and Health Outcomes in the Framingham Population," *The New England Journal of Medicine* 324(1991): 1839–1844.

9 J. A. Mattison, G. S. Roth, T. M. Beasley, E. M. Tilmont, A. M. Handy, R. L. Herbert, et al., "Impact of Caloric Restriction on Health and Survival in Rhesus Monkeys from the NIA Study," *Nature* 489(2012): 318–321.

10 K. F. Adams, A. Schatzkin, T. B. Harris, V. Kipnis, T. Mouw, R. Ballard-Barbash, et al., "Overweight, Obesity, and Mortality in a Large Prospective Cohort of Persons 50 to 71 Years Old," *The New England Journal of Medicine* 355(2006): 763–778.

K. M. Flegal, B. K. Kit, H. Orpana, and B. I. Graubard, "Association of All-Cause Mortality with Overweight and Obesity Using Standard Body Mass Index Categories," *JAMA* 309(2013): 71–82.

S. H. Jee, J. W. Sull, J. Park, S.-Y. Lee, H. Ohrr, E. Guallar, and J. M. Samet, "Body-Mass Index and Mortality in Korean Men and Women," *The New England Journal of Medicine* 355(2006): 779–787.

11 Exton, "Infection-Induced Anorexia."

310

12 D. Grady, "Unusual Molecule Could Be Key to Cancer Patients' Weight Loss," *The New York Times* (March 12, 1996): C3.

B. E. Meyerowitz, T. G. Burish, and S. M. Levy, *Cancer, Nutrition, and Eating Behavior: Introduction and Overview*, in *Cancer, Nutrition, and Eating Behavior*, eds. T. G. Burish, S. M. Levy, and B. E. Meyerowitz, Hillsdale, NJ: Lawrence Erlbaum Associates, 1985.

13 I. L. Bernstein and C. M. Treneer, "Learned Food Aversions and Tumor Anorexia," in *Cancer, Nutrition, and Eating Behavior*, eds. T. G. Burish, S. M. Levy, and B. E. Meyerowitz, Hillsdale, NJ: Lawrence Erlbaum Associates, 1985.

T. B. Comeau, J. B. Epstein, and C. Migas, "Taste and Smell Dysfunction in Patients Receiving Chemotherapy: A Review of Current Knowledge," *Support Care Cancer* 9(2001): 575–580.

S. K. Das, S. Eder, S. Schauer, C. Diwoky, H. Temmel, B. Guertl, et al., "Adipose Triglyceride Lipase Contributes to Cancer-Associated Cachexia," *Science* 333(2011): 233–238.

P. Todorov, P. Cariuk, T. McDevitt, B. Coles, K. Fearon, and M. Tisdale, "Characterization of a Cancer Cachectic Factor," *Nature* 379(1996): 739–742.

14 I. L. Bernstein and M. M. Webster, "Learned Food Aversions: A Consequence of Cancer Chemotherapy," in *Cancer, Nutrition, and Eating Behavior*, eds. T. G. Burish, S. M. Levy, and B. E. Meyerowitz, Hillsdale, NJ: Lawrence Erlbaum Associates, 1985.

15 D. J. Broberg and I. L. Bernstein, "Candy as a Scapegoat in the Prevention of Food Aversions in Children Receiving Chemotherapy," *Cancer* 60(1987): 2344–2347.

16 R. A. Boakes, N. Tarrier, B. W. Barnes, and M. H. N. Tattersall, "Prevalence of Anticipatory Nausea and Other Side-Effects in Cancer Patients Receiving Chemotherapy," *European Journal of Cancer* 29A(1993): 866–870.

17 G. R. Morrow and P. L. Dobkin, "Anticipatory Nausea and Vomiting in Cancer Patients Undergoing Chemotherapy Treatment: Prevalence, Etiology, and Behavioral Interventions," *Clinical Psychology Review* 8(1988): 517–556.

18 Rosenzweig, *The Book of Proverbs*, p. 18.

19 H. Bruch, *The Golden Cage*, Cambridge, MA: Harvard University Press, 1978, p. 62.

20 R. L. Palmer, *Anorexia Nervosa*, New York: Penguin, 1980, p. 20.

21 Bruch, *The Golden Cage*, p. 61.

22 American Psychiatric Association, *Diagnostic and Statistical Manual of Mental Disorders*, 5th ed., Washington, DC: APA, 2013, pp. 338–339.

23 Ibid.

24 Ibid., p. 339.

25 Ibid.

N. Chisuwa and J. A. O'Dea, "Body Image and Eating Disorders amongst Japanese Adolescents. A Review of the Literature," *Appetite* 54(2010): 5–15.

26 Bruch, *The Golden Cage*, p. 3.

27 K. D. Brownell, "Dieting and the Search for the Perfect Body: Where Physiology and Culture Collide," *Behavior Therapy* 22(1991): 1–12.

28 Y. Simon, F. Bellisle, M.-O. Monneuse, B. Samuel-Lajeunesse, and A. Drewnowski, "Taste Responsiveness in Anorexia Nervosa," *British Journal of Psychiatry* 162(1993): 244–246.

29 C. A. Forestell, A. M. Spaeth, and S. A. Kane, "To Eat or Not to Eat Red Meat. A Closer Look at the Relationship between Restrained Eating and Vegetarianism in College Females," *Appetite* 58(2012): 319–325.

C. A. Timko, J. M. Hormes, and J. Chubski, "Will the Real Vegetarian Please Stand Up? An Investigation of Dietary Restraint and Eating Disorder Symptoms in Vegetarians Versus Non-Vegetarians," *Appetite* 58(2012): 982–990.

30 K. A. Halmi and S. R. Sunday, "Temporal Patterns of Hunger and Fullness Ratings and Related Cognitions in Anorexia and Bulimia," *Appetite* 16(1991): 219–237.

G. Milos, C. Kuenzli, C. M. Soelch, S. Schumacher, H. Moergeli, and C. Mueller-Pfeiffer, "How Much Should I Eat? Estimation of Meal Portions in Anorexia Nervosa," *Appetite* 63(2013): 42–47.

31 Halmi and Sunday, "Temporal Patterns of Hunger and Fullness Ratings and Related Cognitions in Anorexia and Bulimia."

S. R. Sunday and K. A. Halmi, "Micro- and Macroanalyses of Patterns within a Meal in Anorexia and Bulimia Nervosa," *Appetite* 26(1996): 21–36.

K. A. Tappe, S. E. Gerberg, D. J. Shide, B. J. Rolls, and A. E. Anderson, "Videotape Assessment of Changes in Aberrant Meal-Time Behaviors in Anorexia Nervosa after Treatment," *Appetite* 30(1998): 171–184.

32 E. Stice, "Risk and Maintenance Factors for Eating Pathology: A Meta-Analytic Review," *Psychological Bulletin* 128(2002): 825–848.

33 S. Grabe, L. M. Ward, and J. S. Hyde, "The Role of the Media in Body Image Concerns among Women: A Meta-Analysis of Experimental and Correlational Studies," *Psychological Bulletin* 134(2008): 460–476.

34 S. Grabe and J. S. Hyde, "Ethnicity and Body Dissatisfaction among Women in the United States: A Meta-analysis," *Psychological Bulletin* 132(2006): 622–640.

35 W. Grimes, "Isabelle Caro, Anorexic Model, Dies at 28," *The New York Times* (published online December 31, 2010): www.nytimes.com/2010/12/31/world/europe/31caro.html?_r=0#.

R. Johnson, "Walking a Thin Line," *Vogue* (April 2007): 380–385, 403.

36 J. J. Brumberg, *The Body Project: An Intimate History of American Girls*, New York: Vintage, 1997.

37 J. L. Wilson, R. Peebles, and K. K. Hardy, "Surfing for Thinness: A Pilot Study of Pro-Eating Disorder Web Site Usage in Adolescents with Eating Disorders," *Pediatrics* 118(2006): e1635.

38 A. Feingold and R. Mazzella, "Gender Differences in Body Image Are Increasing," *Psychological Science* 9(1998): 190–195.

39 J. Alleva, A. Jansen, C. Martijn, J. Schepers, and C. Nederkoorn, "Get Your Own Mirror. Investigating How Strict Eating Disordered Women Are in Judging the Bodies of Other Eating Disordered Women," *Appetite* 68(2013): 98–104.

40 C. Davis, J. V. G. A. Durnin, M. Gurevich, A. Le Maire, and M. Dionne, "Body Composition Correlates of Weight Dissatisfaction and Dietary Restraint in Young Women," *Appetite* 20(1993): 197–207.

41 A. E. Fallon and P. Rozin, "Sex Differences in Perceptions of Desirable Body Shape," *Journal of Abnormal Psychology* 94(1985): 102–105.

42 K. D. Brownell, "Eating Disorders in Athletes," in *Eating Disorders and Obesity: A Comprehensive Handbook*, eds. K. D. Brownell and C. G. Fairburn, New York: The Guilford Press, 1995.

J. Polivy and L. Thomsen, "Dieting and Other Eating Disorders," in *Handbook of Behavioral Medicine for Women,* eds. E. A. Blechman and K. D. Brownell, New York: Pergamon, 1988.

43 L. A. Klos and J. Sobal, "Weight and Weddings. Engaged men's body weight ideals and wedding weight management behaviors. *Appetite* 60(2012): 133–139.

L. A. Neighbors and J. Sobal, "Weight and Weddings: Women's Weight Ideals and Weight Management Behaviors for Their Wedding Day," *Appetite* 50(2008): 550–554.

A. Williams, "Before Spring Break, the Anorexic Challenge," *The New York Times* (April 2, 2006): 1–6.

44 H. Brubach, "The Athletic Esthetic," *The New York Times Magazine* (June 23, 1996): 48–51.

J. Longman, "Female Athletes Embrace Size, Spurring a Debate Over Weight," *The New York Times* (February 8, 2007): D1, D4.

45 American Psychiatric Association, *Diagnostic and Statistical Manual of Mental Disorders*, 5th ed., p. 243.

46 H. G. Pope, A. J. Gruber, P. Choi, R. Olivardia, and K. A. Phillips, "Muscle Dysmorphia: An Unrecognized Form of Body Dysmorphic Disorder," *Psychosomatics* 38(1997): 548–557.

47 J. O. Fisher and L. L. Birch, "Restricting Access to Foods and Children's Eating," *Appetite* 32(1999): 405–419.

M. Tiggemann and J. Lowes, "Predictors of Maternal Control over Children's Eating Behaviour," *Appetite* 39(2002): 1–7.

48 E. Stice, W. S. Agras, and L. D. Hammer, "Risk Factors for the Emergence of Childhood Eating Disturbances: A Five-Year Prospective Study," *International Journal of Eating Disorders* 25(1999): 375–387.

49 M. Kostanski and E. Gullone, "Dieting and Body Image in the Child's World: Conceptualization and Behavior," *Journal of Genetic Psychology* 160(1999): 488–496.

50 L. Smolak, M. P. Levine, and F. Schermer, "Parental Input and Weight Concerns among Elementary School Children," *International Journal of Eating Disorders* 25(1999): 263–271.

51 P. J. Lattimore and M. Butterworth, "A Test of the Structural Model of Initiation of Dieting among Adolescent Girls," *Journal of Psychosomatic Research* 46(1999): 295–299.

52 H. Bruch, *Eating Disorders*, New York: Basic Books, 1973.

53 W. D. Pierce and W. F. Epling, "Activity Anorexia: An Interplay between Basic and Applied Behavior Analysis," *The Behavior Analyst* 17(1994): 7–23.

J. L. Weed, M. A. Lane, G. S. Roth, D. L. Speer, and D. K. Ingram, "Activity Measures in Rhesus Monkeys on Long-Term Calorie Restriction," *Physiology and Behavior* 62(1997): 97–103.

54 C. G. Fairburn, "Physiology of Anorexia Nervosa," in *Eating Disorders and Obesity: A Comprehensive Handbook*," eds. K. D. Brownell and C. G. Fairburn, New York: The Guilford Press, 1995.

D. S. Goldbloom and S. H. Kennedy, "Medical Complications of Anorexia Nervosa," in *Eating Disorders and Obesity: A Comprehensive Handbook*, eds. K. D. Brownell and C. G. Fairburn, New York: The Guilford Press, 1995.

W. H. Kaye, "Neurotransmitters and Anorexia Nervosa," in *Eating Disorders and Obesity: A Comprehensive Handbook*, eds. K. D. Brownell and C. G. Fairburn, New York: The Guilford Press, 1995.

55 R. H. Striegel-Moore and C. M. Bulik, "Risk Factors for Eating Disorders," *American Psychologist* 62(2007): 181–198.

56 S. S. Van Buskirk, "A Two-Phase Perspective on the Treatment of Anorexia Nervosa," *Psychological Bulletin* 84(1977): 529–538.

57 W. S. Agras and H. C. Kraemer, "The Treatment of Anorexia Nervosa: Do Different Treatments Have Different Outcomes?" in *Eating and Its Disorders*, eds. A. J. Stunkard and E. Stellar, New York: Raven Press, 1984.

P. E. Garfinkel and D. M. Garner, *Anorexia Nervosa*, New York: Brunner/ Mazel, 1982.

58 Agras and Kraemer, "The Treatment of Anorexia Nervosa."

G. R. Leon, *Treating Eating Disorders*, Brattleboro, VT: Lewis Publishing, 1983.

Van Buskirk, "A Two-Phase Perspective on the Treatment of Anorexia Nervosa."

59 W. H. Kaye, "Neurotransmitters and Anorexia Nevosa."

B. T. Walsh, "Pharmacotherapy of Eating Disorders," in *Eating Disorders and Obesity: A Comprehensive Handbook*, eds. K. D. Brownell and C. G. Fairburn, New York: The Guilford Press, 1995.

G. T. Wilson, C. M. Grilo, and K. M. Vitousek, "Psychological Treatment of Eating Disorders," *American Psychologist* 62(2007): 199–216.

60 Garfinkel and Garner, *Anorexia Nervosa*.

61 K. M. Pike, K. Loeb, and K. Vitousek, "Cognitive-Behavioral Therapy for Anorexia Nervosa and Bulimia Nervosa," in *Body Image, Eating Disorders, and Obesity: An Integrative Guide for Assessment and Treatment*, ed. J. K. Thompson, Washington, DC: American Psychological Association, 1996.

J. K. Thompson, L. J. Heinberg, and A. J. Clarke, "Treatment of Body Image Disturbance in Eating Disorders," in *Body Image, Eating Disorders, and Obesity: An Integrative Guide for Assessment and Treatment*, ed. J. K. Thompson, Washington, DC: American Psychological Association, 1996.

Wilson, Grilo, and Vitousek, "Psychological Treatment of Eating Disorders."

62 Wilson, Grilo, and Vitousek, "Psychological Treatment of Eating Disorders."

63 B. T. Walsh, "The Future of Research on Eating Disorders," *Appetite* 42(2004): 5.

64 Ibid., p. 9.

65 American Psychiatric Association, *Diagnostic and Statistical Manual of Mental Disorders*, 5th ed., p. 589.

66 Ibid.

67 Ibid.

B. T. Walsh and M. J. Devlin, "Eating Disorders: Progress and Problems," *Science* 280(1998): 1387–1390.

68 Garfinkel and Garner, *Anorexia Nervosa*, p. 5.

69 E. Stice, R. P. Cameron, J. D. Killen, C. Hayward, and C. B. Taylor, "Naturalistic Weight-Reduction Efforts Prospectively Predict Growth in Relative Weight and Onset of Obesity among Female Adolescents," *Journal of Consulting and Clinical Psychology* 67(1999): 967–974.

70 K. Taylor, "Council Speaker Recounts Her Struggles with Bulimia and Alcoholism," *The New York Times* (May 14, 2013): A18, A20.

71 J. E. Mitchell, "Medical Complications of Bulimia Nervosa," in *Eating Disorders and Obesity: A Comprehensive Handbook*, eds. K. D. Brownell and C. G. Fairburn, New York: The Guilford Press, 1995.

G. E. Romanos, F. Javed, E. B. Romanos, and R. C. Williams, "Oro-Facial Manifestations in Patients with Eating Disorders," *Appetite* 59(2012): 499–504.

72 G. Russell, "Bulimia Nervosa: An Ominous Variant of Anorexia Nervosa," *Psychological Medicine* 9(1979): 429–448.

73 A. W. Logue, "Taste Aversion and the Generality of the Laws of Learning." *Psychological Bulletin* 86(1979): 276–296.
A. W. Logue, K. R. Logue, and K. E. Strauss, "The Acquisition of Taste Aversions in Humans with Eating and Drinking Disorders," *Behaviour Research and Therapy* 21(1983): 275–289.

74 "Energy Expenditure and the Control of Body Weight," *Nutrition Reviews* 47(1989): 249–252.
H. E. Gwirtsman, W. H. Kaye, E. Obarzanek, D. T. George, D. C. Jimerson, and M. H. Ebert, "Decreased Caloric Intake in Normal-Weight Patients with Bulimia: Comparison with Female Volunteers," *American Journal of Clinical Nutrition* 49(1989): 86–92.
T. Léonard, C. Foulon, and B. Samuel-Lajeunesse, "High Resting Energy Expenditure in Normal-Weight Bulimics and Its Normalization with Control of Eating Behavior," *Appetite* 27(1996): 223–233.

75 "Influence of Altered Body Weight on Energy Expenditure," *Nutrition Reviews* 53(1995): 265–268.

76 C. M. Hadigan, B. T. Walsh, M. J. Devlin, J. L. LaChaussée, and H. R. Kissileff, "Behavioral Assessment of Satiety in Bulimia Nervosa," *Appetite* 18(1992): 233–241.
B. J. Rolls, "The Role of Sensory-Specific Satiety in Food Intake and Food Selection," in *Taste, Experience, and Feeding*, eds. E. D. Capaldi and T. L. Powley, Washington, DC: American Psychological Association, 1990.
Sunday and Halmi, "Micro- and Macroanalyses of Patterns within a Meal in Anorexia and Bulimia Nervosa."

77 Striegel-Moore and Bulik, "Risk Factors for Eating Disorders.

78 K. A. Halmi, "Eating Disorder Research in the Past Decade, "in *Women and Mental Health*, eds. J. A. Sechzer, S. M. Pfafflin, F. L. Denmark, A. Griffin, and S. J. Blumenthal, New York: New York Academy of Sciences, 1996.
Walsh and Devlin, "Eating Disorders."

79 Leon, *Treating Eating Disorders.*
Russell, "Bulimia Nervosa."

80 A. J. Stunkard and T. A. Wadden, "Restrained Eating and Human Obesity," *Nutrition Reviews* 48(1990): 78–86.
R. J. Tuschl, "From Dietary Restraint to Binge Eating: Some Theoretical Considerations," *Appetite* 14(1990): 105–109.

81 M. R. Lowe and K. L. Eldredge, "The Role of Impulsiveness in Normal and Disordered Eating," in *The Impulsive Client*, eds. W. G. McCown, J. L. Johnson, and M. B. Shure, Washington, DC: American Psychological Association, 1993.
S. L. McElroy, H. G. J. Pope, P. E. J. Keck, and J. I. Hudson, "Disorders of Impulse Control," in *Impulsivity and Aggression*, eds E. Hollander and D. J. Stein, New York: Wiley, 1995.

82 W. H. Kaye, G. K. Frank, C. C. Meltzer, J. P. Price, C. W. McConaha, P. J. Crossan, K. L. Klump, and L. Rhodes, "Altered Serotonin 2A Receptor Activity in Women Who Have Recovered from Bulimia Nervosa," *The American Journal of Psychiatry* 158(2001): 1152–1155.

83 E. Stice and W. S. Agras, "Subtyping Bulimic Women along Dietary Restraint and Negative Affect Dimensions," *Journal of Consulting and Clinical Psychology* 67(1999): 460–469.
Walsh and Devlin, "Eating Disorders."

84 C. Bohon and E. Stice, "Negative Affect and Neural Response to Palatable Food Intake in Bulimia," *Appetite* 58(2012): 964–970.

K. Presnell, E. Stice, and J. Tristan, "Experimental Investigation of the Effects of Naturalistic Dieting on Bulimic Symptoms: Moderating Effects of Depressive Symptoms." *Appetite* 50(2008): 91–101.

85 K. M. Pirke, "Physiology of Bulimia Nervosa," in *Eating Disorders and Obesity: A Comprehensive Handbook*, eds. K. D. Brownell and C. G. Fairburn, New York: The Guilford Press, 1995.

T. E. Weltzin, M. H. Fernstrom, and W. H. Kaye, "Serotonin and Bulimia Nervosa," *Nutrition Reviews* 52(1994): 399–408.

86 Wilson, Grilo, and Vitousek, "Psychological Treatment of Eating Disorders."

87 Ibid.

88 Walsh and Devlin, "Eating Disorders."

89 Wilson, Grilo, and Vitousek, "Psychological Treatment of Eating Disorders."

90 A. Winzelberg, "The Analysis of an Electronic Support Group for Individuals with Eating Disorders," *Computers in Human Behavior* 13(1997): 393–407.

10 THE BATTLE WITH THE BULGE

1 B. M. King, "The Modern Obesity Epidemic, Ancestral Hunter-Gatherers, and the Sensory/Reward Control of Food Intake," *American Psychologist* 68(2013): 88–96.

2 C. P. F. Marinangeli and A. N. Kassis, "Use of Dual X-Ray Absorptiometry to Measure Body Mass During Short- to Medium-Term Trials of Nutrition and Exercise Interventions," *Nutrition Reviews* 71(2013): 332–342.

3 R. S. Ahima and M. A. Lazar, "The Health Risk of Obesity—Better Metrics Imperative," *Science* 341(2013): 856–858.

4 J. K. Larsen, M. Ouwens, R. C. M. E. Engels, R. Eisinga, and T. van Strien, "Validity of Self-Reported Weight and Height and Predictors of Weight Bias in Female College Students," *Appetite* 50(2008): 386–389.

5 L. Bartoshuk, "The 'Obesity Epidemic': An Interview with Katherine Flegal," *Observer*, 23(1)(2010): 3, 48–49.

6 C. L. Ogden, M. D. Carroll, B. K. Kit, and K. M. Flegal, "Prevalence of Childhood and Adult Obesity in the United States," *JAMA* 311(2014): 806–814.

7 www.cdc.gov/obesity/data/adult.html.

8 Ogden, Carroll, Kit, and Flegal, "Prevalence of Childhood and Adult Obesity in the United States."

9 www.petobesityprevention.com/2012-national-pet-obesity-survey-results/.

10 B. M. Popkin, L. S. Adair, and S. W. Ng, "Global Nutrition Transition and the Pandemic of Obesity in Developing Countries," *Nutrition Reviews* 70(2012): 3–21.

11 Ahima and Lazar, "The Health Risk of Obesity."

J. R. Erion, M. Wosiski-Kuhn, A. Dey, S. Hao, C. L. Davis, N. K. Pollock, and A. M. Stranahan, "Obesity Elicits Interleukin 1-Mediated Deficits in Hippocampal Synaptic Plasticity," *The Journal of Neuroscience* 34(2014): 2618–2631.

12 Ahima and Lazar, "The Health Risk of Obesity."

13 M. -P. St-Onge and S. B. Heymsfield, "Overweight and Obesity Are Linked to Lower Life Expectancy," *Nutrition Reviews* 61(2003): 313–316.

14 C. L. Hoyt, J. L. Burnette, L. Auster-Gussman, "'Obesity Is a Disease,' Examining the Self-Regulatory Impact of This Public-Health Message," *Psychological Science* (published online January 24, 2014). DOI: 10.1177/0956797613516981.

15 K. D. Brownell, "Dieting and the Search for the Perfect Body: Where Physiology and Culture Collide," *Behavior Therapy* 22(1991): 1–12.

A. S. Bruce, W. R. Black, J. M. Bruce, M. Daldalian, L. E. Martin, and A. M. Davis, "Ability to Delay Gratification and BMI in Preadolescence," *Obesity*, 19(2011): 1101–1102.

R. Pingitore, B. L. Dugoni, R. S. Tindale, and B. Spring, "Bias against Overweight Job Applicants in a Simulated Employment Interview," *Journal of Applied Psychology* 79(1994): 909–917.

S.-J. Salvy, J. C. Bowker, L. A. Nitecki, M. A. Kluczynski, L. J. Germeroth, and J. N. Roemmich, "Impact of Simulated Ostracism on Overweight and Normal-Weight Youths' Motivation to Eat and Food Intake," *Appetite* 56(2011): 39–45.

16 M. Zavodny, "Does Weight Affect Children's Test Scores and Teacher Assessments Differently?" *Economics of Education Review* 34(2013): 135–145.

17 T. M. Cutting, J. O. Fisher, K. Grimm-Thomas, and L. L. Birch, "Like Mother, Like Daughter: Familial Patterns of Overweight Are Mediated by Mothers' Dietary Disinhibition," *American Journal of Clinical Nutrition* 69(1999): 608–613.

T. T. Foch and G. E. McClearn, "Genetics, Body Weight, and Obesity," in *Obesity*, ed. A. J. Stunkard, Philadelphia: W. B. Saunders, 1980.

J. O. Hill and E. L. Melanson, "Overview of the Determinants of Overweight and Obesity: Current Evidence and Research Issues," *Medicine and Science in Sports and Exercise* 31(1999): S515–S521.

18 R. Gurney, "The Hereditary Factor in Obesity," *Archives of Internal Medicine* 57(1936): 557–561.

19 A. J. Stunkard, T. T. Foch, and Z. Hrubec, "A Twin Study of Human Obesity," *The JAMA* 256(1986): 51–54.

20 A. J. Stunkard, T. I. Sorensen, C. Hanis, T. W. Teasdale, R. Chakraborty, W. J. Schull, and F. Schulsinger, "An Adoption Study of Human Obesity," *The New England Journal of Medicine* 314(1986): 193–198.

21 S. Carnell and J. Wardle, "Appetitive Traits in Children. New Evidence for Associations with Weight and a Common, Obesity-Associated Genetic Variant," *Appetite* 53(2009): 260–263.

22 C. Bouchard, A. Tremblay, J.-P. Després, A. Nadeau, P. J. Lupien, G. Thériault, J. Dussault, S. Moorjani, S. Pinault, and G. Fournier, "The Response to Long-Term Overfeeding in Identical Twins," *The New England Journal of Medicine* 322(1990): 1477–1482.

23 A. W. Ferrante, "Improving Metabolism by Throwing Out All the JNK," *Science* 339(2013): 147–148.

D. Y. Oh and J. M. Olefsky, "Wnt Fans the Flames in Obesity," *Science* 329(2010): 397–398.

24 M. Asai, S. Ramachandrappa, M. Joachim, Y. Shen, R. Zhang, N. Nuthalapati, et al., "Loss of Function of the Melanocortin 2 Receptor Accessory Protein 2 Is Associated with Mammalian Obesity," *Science* 341(2013): 275–278.

25 C. E. Smith and J. M. Ordovás, "Update on Perilipin Polymorphisms and Obesity," *Nutrition Reviews* 70(2012): 611–621.

26 A. Herbert, N. P. Gerry, M. B. McQueen, I. M. Heid, A. Pfeufer, T. Illig, et al., "A Common Genetic Variant Is Associated with Adult and Childhood Obesity," *Science* 312(2006): 279–283.

27 L. Sjöström, "The Contribution of Fat Cells to the Determination of Body Weight," in *Symposium on Obesity: Basic Mechanisms and Treatment*, ed. A. J. Stunkard, Philadelphia: W. B. Saunders, 1978.

L. Sjöström, "Fat Cells and Body Weight," in *Obesity*, ed. A. J. Stunkard, Philadelphia: W. B. Saunders, 1980.

28 Ibid.

29 J. Marx, "Cellular Warriors at the Battle of the Bulge," *Science* 299(2003): 846–849.

D. A. Williamson, E. Ravussin, M.-L. Wong, A. Wagner, A. DiPaoli, S. Caglayan, et al., "Microanalysis of Eating Behavior of Three Leptin Deficient Adults Treated with Leptin Therapy," *Appetite* 45(2005): 75–80.

30 B. P. Barnett, Y. Hwang, M. S. Taylor, H. Kirchner, P. T. Pfluger, V. Bernard, et al., "Glucose and Weight Control in Mice with a Designed Ghrelin O-Acyltransferase Inhibitor," *Science* 330(2010): 1689–1692.

J. Buss, P. J. Havel, E. Epel, J. Lin, E. Blackburn, and J. Daubenmier, "Associations of Ghrelin with Eating Behaviors, Stress, Metabolic Factors, and Telomere Length among Overweight and Obese Women: Preliminary Evidence of Attentuated Ghrelin Effects in Obesity? *Appetite* 76(2014): 84–94.

J. A. King, L. K. Wasse, D. J. Stensel, and M. A. Nimmo, "Exercise and Ghrelin. A Narrative Overview of Research," *Appetite* 68(2013): 83–91.

31 V. K. Ridaura, J. J. Faith, F. E. Rey, J. Cheng, A. E. Duncan, A. L. Kau, et al., "Gut Microbiota From Twins Discordant for Obesity Modulate Metabolism in Mice," *Science* 341(2013): 1079.

32 R. A. Hegele, "Lessons from Genetic Studies in Native Canadian Populations," *Nutrition Reviews* 57(1999): S43–S50.

33 E. Jéquier, "Energy Utilization in Human Obesity," in *Human Obesity*, eds. R. J. Wurtman and J. J. Wurtman, New York: New York Academy of Sciences, 1987.

E. Ravussin and E. Danforth, "Beyond Sloth—Physical Activity and Weight Gain," *Science* 283(1999): 184–185.

34 Jéquier, "Energy Utilization in Human Obesity."

35 D. L. Elliot, L. Goldberg, K. S. Kuehl, and W. M. Bennett, "Sustained Depression of the Resting Metabolic Rate after Massive Weight Loss," *American Journal of Clinical Nutrition* 49(1989): 93–96.

R. E. Keesey and S. W. Corbett, "Metabolic Defense of the Body Weight Set-Point," in *Eating and Its Disorders*, eds. A. J. Stunkard and E. Stellar, New York: Raven Press, 1984.

N. Steen, R. A. Oppliger, and K. D. Brownell, "Metabolic Effects of Repeated Weight Loss and Regain in Adolescent Wrestlers," *JAMA* 260(1988): 1–50.

36 H. T. Edwards, A. Thorndike, and D. B. Dill, "The Energy Requirements in Strenuous Muscular Exercise," *The New England Journal at Medicine* 213(1935): 532–535.

A. M. Knab, R. Shanely, R. Andrew, and K. D. Corbin, "A 45-Minute Vigorous Exercise Bout Increases Metabolic Rate for 14 Hours," *Medicine and Science in Sports and Exercise* 43(2011): 1643–1648.

37 C. Bouchard, A. Tremblay, J.-P. Després, G. Thériault, A. Nadeau, P. J. Lupien, S. Moorjani, D. Prudhomme, and G. Fournier, "The Response to Exercise with Constant Energy Intake in Identical Twins," *Obesity Research* 2(1994): 400–410.

38 J. Rocha, J. Paxman, C. Dalton, E. Winter, and D. Broom, "Effects of an Acute Bout of Aerobic Exercise on Immediate and Subsequent Three-Day Food Intake and Energy Expenditure in Active and Inactive Men," *Appetite* 71(2013): 369–378.

M. M. Schubert, B. Desbrow, S. Sabapathy, and M. Leveritt, "Acute Exercise and Subsequent Energy Intake," *Appetite* 63(2013): 92–104.

39 R. E. Andersen, C. J. Crespo, S. J. Bartlett, L. J. Cheskin, and M. Pratt, "Relationship of Physical Activity and Television Watching with Body Weight and Level of Fatness among Children: Results from the Third National Health and Nutrition Examination Survey," *JAMA* 279(1998): 938–942.

C. S. Berkey, H. R. H. Rockett, A. E. Field, M. W. Gillman, A. L. Frazier, C. A. Camargo, and G. A. Colditz, "Activity, Dietary Intake, and Weight Changes in the Longitudinal Study of Preadolescent and Adolescent Boys and Girls," *Pediatrics* 105(2000): 854–862.

40 W. H. Dietz, "Childhood Obesity," in *Human Obesity*, eds. R. J. Wurtman and J. J. Wurtman, New York: New York Academy of Sciences, 1987.

R. C. Klesges, M. L. Shelton, and L. M. Klesges, "Effects of Television on Metabolic Rate: Potential Implications for Childhood Obesity," *Pediatrics* 91(1993): 281–286.

S. Marsh, C. Ni Mhurchu, and R. Maddison, "The Non-Advertising Effects of Screen-Based Sedentary Activities on Acute Eating Behaviours in Children, Adolescents, and Young Adults. A Systematic Review," *Appetite* 71(2013): 259–273.

41 R. R. Mellecker, L. Lanningham-Foster, J. A. Levine, and A. M. McManus, "Energy Intake During Activity Enhanced Video Game Play," *Appetite* 55(2010): 343–347.

42 A. D. Calvin, R. E. Carter, T. Adachi, P. G. Macedo, F. N. Albuquerque, C. van der Walt, et al., "Effects of Experimental Sleep Restriction on Caloric Intake and Activity Energy Expenditure," *Chest* 144(2013): 79–86.

C. N. Hart, M. A. Carskadon, R. V. Considine, J. L. Fava, J. Lawton, H. A. Raynor, et al., "Changes in Children's Sleep Duration on Food Intake, Weight, and Leptin," *Pediatrics* 132(2013): e1473–e1480.

43 Jéquier, "Energy Utilization in Human Obesity."

J. A. Westrate, T. Dopheide, L. Robroch, P. Deurenberg, and J. G. Hautvast, "Does Variation in Palatability Affect the Postprandial Response in Energy Expenditure?" *Appetite* 15(1990): 209–219.

44 Keesey and Corbett, "Metabolic Defense of the Body Weight Set-Point."

45 J. A. Levine, N. L. Eberhardt, and M. D. Jensen, "Role of Nonexercise Activity Thermogenesis in Resistance to Fat Gain in Humans," *Science* 283(1999): 212–214.

46 Ravussin and Danforth, "Beyond Sloth."

47 L. Spitzer and J. Rodin, "Human Eating Behavior: A Critical Review of Studies in Normal Weight and Overweight Individuals," *Appetite* 2(1981): 293–329.

48 R. G. Laessle, S. Lehrke, and S. Duckers, "Laboratory Eating Behavior in Obesity," *Appetite* 49(2007): 399–404.

S. Tanihara, T. Imatoh, M. Miyazaki, A. Babazono, Y. Momose, M. Baba, et al., "Retrospective Longitudinal Study on the Relationship between 8-Year Weight Change and Current Eating Speed," *Appetite* 57(2011): 179–183.

B. Wansink and C. R. Payne, "Eating Behavior and Obesity at Chinese Buffets," *Obesity* 16(2008): 1957–1960.

49 A. H. Lichtenstein, "Dietary Fat: A History," *Nutrition Reviews* 57(1999): 11–14.

50 H. A. Jordan and T. A. Spiegel, "Palatability and Oral Factors and Their Role in Obesity," in *The Chemical Senses and Nutrition*, eds. M. R. Kare and O. Maller, New York: Academic Press, 1977.

A. Sclafani and D. Springer, "Dietary Obesity in Adult Rats: Similarities to Hypothalamic and Human Obesity Syndromes," *Physiology and Behavior* 17(1976): 461–471.

51 N. C. Howarth, E. Satzman, and S. B. Roberts, "Dietary Fiber and Weight Regulation," *Nutrition Reviews* 59(2001): 129–139.

S. B. Roberts, "High-Glycemic Index Foods, Hunger, and Obesity: Is There a Connection?" *Nutrition Reviews* 58(2000): 163–169.

52 L. H. Epstein, K. D. Fletcher, J. O'Neill, J. N. Roemmich, H. Raynor, and M. E. Bouton, "Food Characteristics, Long-Term Habituation and Energy Intake. Laboratory and Field Studies," *Appetite* 60(2012): 40–50.

H. A. Raynor and L. H. Epstein, "Dietary Variety, Energy Regulation, and Obesity," *Psychological Bulletin* 127(2001): 325–341.

53 L. Macdonald, S. Cummins, and S. Macintyre, "Neighbourhood fast food environment and area deprivation—substitution or concentration? *Appetite* 49(2007): 251–254.

D. A. Williamson, H. Han, W. D. Johnson, C. K. Martin, and R. L. Newton, "Modification of the School Cafeteria Environment Can Impact Childhood Nutrition. Results From the Wise Mind and LA Health Studies," *Appetite* 61(2013): 77–84.

54 M. G. Tordoff and M. l. Friedman, "Drinking Saccharin Increases Food Intake and Preference—IV. Cephalic Phase and Metabolic Factors," *Appetite* 12(1989): 37–56.

J. R.Vasselli, "Carbohydrate Ingestion, Hypoglycemia, and Obesity," *Appetite* 6(1985): 53–59.

55 J. F. Wilson, "Preschool Children Maintain Intake of Other Foods at a Meal Including Sugared Chocolate Milk," *Appetite* 16(1991): 61–67.

56 M. C. Daniels and B. M. Popkin, "Impact of Water Intake on Energy Intake and Weight Status: A Systematic Review," *Nutrition Reviews* 68(2010): 505–521.

M. A. Pereira, "Diet Beverages and the Risk of Obesity, Diabetes, and Cardiovascular Disease: A Review of the Evidence," *Nutrition Reviews* 71(2013): 433–440.

57 S. E. Swithers, A. A. Martin, K. M. Clark, A. F. Laboy, and T. L. Davidson, "Body Weight Gain in Rats Consuming Sweetened Liquids," *Appetite* 55(2010): 528–533.

58 M. Bittman, "Viva México!" *The New York Times* (December 1, 2013): 1.

A. Conkle, "Eating Into the Nation's Obesity Epidemic," *Observer* 19(8) (2006): 39, 45.

E. C. Gogolak, "Another State Court Rejects Limits on Sugary Drinks," *The New York Times* (July 31, 2013): A17.

59 J. Fricker, D. Chapelot, P. Pasquet, R. Rozen, and M. Apfelbaum, "Effect of a Covert Fat Dilution on the Spontaneous Food Intake by Lean and Obese Subjects," *Appetite* 24(1995): 121–138.

T. V. E. Kral, L. S. Roe, and B. J. Rolls, "Does Nutrition Information about the Energy Density of Meals Affect Food Intake in Normal-Weight Women?" *Appetite* 39(2002): 137–145.

J. Louis-Sylvestre, A. Tournier, D. Chapelot, and M. Chabert, "Effect of a Fat-Reduced Dish in a Meal on 24-H Energy and Macronutrient Intake," *Appetite* 22(1994): 165–172.

B. J. Rolls, E. A. Bell, V. H. Castellanos, M. Chow, C. L. Pelkman, and M. L. Thorwart, "Energy Density but Not Fat Content of Foods Affected Energy Intake in Lean and Obese Women," *American Journal of Clinical Nutrition* 69(1999): 863–871.

M. Yao and S. B. Roberts, "Dietary Energy Density and Weight Regulation," *Nutrition Reviews* 59(2001): 247–258.

60 L. J. Cheskin, L. M. Davis, L. M. Lipsky, A. H. Mitola, T. Lycan, V. Mitchell, et al., "Lack of Energy Compensation Over 4 Days When White Button Mushrooms Are Substituted for Beef," *Appetite* 51(2008): 50–57.

L. Cloetens, M. Ulmius, A. Johansson-Persson, B. Åkesson, and G. Önning, "Role of Dietary Beta-Glucans in the Prevention of Metabolic Syndrome," *Appetite* 70(2012): 444–458.

S. Pentikäinen, L. Karhunen, L. Flander, K. Katina, A. Meynier, P. Aymard, et al., "Enrichment of Biscuits and Juice with Oat ⊠-glucan enhances post-prandial satiety," *Appetite* 75(2014): 150–156.

K. H. Poddar, M. Ames, C. Hsin-Jen, M. J. Feeney, Y. Wang, and L. J. Cheskin, "Positive Effect of Mushrooms Substituted for Meat on Body Weight, Body Composition, and Health Parameters. A 1-Year Randomized Clinical Trial," *Appetite* 71(2013): 379–387.

61 A. Himaya and J. Louis-Sylvestre, "The Effect of Soup on Satiation," *Appetite* 30(1998): 199–210.

H. A. Jordan, "The Satiating Efficiency of Foods," *Physiology and Behavior* 32(1984): 319–332.

J. Rolls, I. C. Fedoroff, J. F. Guthrie, and L. J. Laster, "Foods with Different Satiating Effects in Humans," *Appetite* 15(1990): 115–126.

M. K. Spill, L. L. Birch, L. S. Roe, and B. J. Rolls, "Serving Large Portions of Vegetable Soup at the Start of A Meal Affected Children's Energy and Vegetable Intake," *Appetite* 57(2011): 213–219.

62 A. B. Geier, P. Rozin, and G. Doros, "Unit Bias: A New Heuristic That Helps Explain the Effect of Portion Size on Food Intake," *Psychological Science* 17(2006): 521–525.

J. Koh and P. Pliner, "The Effects of Degree of Acquaintance, Plate Size, and Sharing on Food Intake," *Appetite* 52(2009): 595–602.

B. J. Rolls, L. S. Roe, T. V. E. Kral, J. S. Meengs, and D. E. Wall, "Increasing the Portion Size of a Packaged Snack Increases Energy Intake in Men and Women," *Appetite* 42(2004): 63–69.

B. Wansink, "From Mindless Eating to Mindlessly Eating Better," *Physiology and Behavior* 100(2010): 454–463.

63 B. Wansink, C. R. Payne, and M. Shimizu, "The 100-Calorie Semi-Solution: Sub-Packaging Most Reduces Intake among the Heaviest," *Obesity* 19(2011): 1098–1100.

64 M. T. McCann, J. M. W. Wallace, P. J. Robson, K. L. Rennie, T. A. McCaffrey, R. W. Welch, and M. B. E. Livingstone, "Influence of Nutrition Labelling on Food Portion Size Consumption," *Appetite* 65(2013): 153–158.

V. Provencher, J. Polivy, and C. P. Herman, "Perceived Healthiness of Food. If It's Healthy, You Can Eat More!" *Appetite* 52(2009): 340–344.

65 A. Tal and B. Wansink, "Fattening Fasting: Hungry Grocery Shoppers Buy More Calories, Not More Food," *JAMA Internal Medicine* 173(2013): 1146–1148.

66 I. C. Federoff, J. Polivy, and C. P. Herman, "The Effect of Pre-Exposure to Food Cues on the Eating Behavior of Restrained and Unrestrained Eaters," *Appetite* 28(1997): 33–47.

67 M. G. Lowe, "The Role of Anticipated Deprivation in Overeating," *Addictive Behaviors* 7(1982): 103–112.

68 J. Rodin, "Current Status of the Internal-External Hypothesis for Obesity," *American Psychologist* 36(1981): 361–372.

69 Ibid.

70 N. E. Rowland and S. M. Antelman, "Stress Induced Hyperphagia and Obesity in Rats: A Possible Model for Understanding Human Obesity," *Science* 191(1976): 310–312.

71 S. M. Antelman and A. R. Caggiula, "Tails of Stress Related Behavior: A Neuropharmacological Model," in *Animal Models in Psychiatry and Neurology*, eds. I. Hanin and E. Usdin, New York: Pergamon, 1977.

 D. M. Marques, A. E. Fisher, M. S. Okrutny, and N. E. Rowland, "Tail Pinch Induced Fluid Ingestion: Interactions of Taste and Deprivation," *Physiology and Behavior* 22(1979): 37–41.

72 D. A. Zellner, S. Loaiza, Z. Gonzalez, J. Pita, J. Morales, D. Pecora, and A. Wolf, "Food Selection Changes Under Stress," *Physiology and Behavior* 87(2006): 789–793.

73 Y. Cornil and P. Chandon, "From Fan to Fat? Vicarious Losing Increases Unhealthy Eating, but Self-Affirmation is an Effective Remedy," *Psychological Science* (published online August 7, 2013). DOI: 10.1177/0956797613481232.

74 N. A. Christakis and J. H. Fowler, "The Spread of Obesity in a Large Social Network Over 32 Years," *The New England Journal of Medicine* 357(2007): 370–379.

75 C. P. Herman, D. A. Roth, and J. Polivy, "Effects of the Presence of Others on Food Intake: A Normative Interpretation," *Psychological Bulletin* 129(2003): 873–886.

76 B. McFerran, D. W. Dahl, G. J. Fitzsimons, and A. C. Morales, "Might an Overweight Waitress Make You Eat More? How the Body Type of Others Is Sufficient to Alter Our Food Consumption," *Journal of Consumer Psychology* 20(2010): 146–151.

77 J. Polivy, C. P. Herman, J. C. Younger, and B. Erskine, "Effects of a Model on Eating Behavior: The Induction of a Restrained Eating Style," *Journal of Personality* 47(1979): 100–117.

78 M. Macht and G. Saelens, "Emotions and Eating in Everyday Life," *Appetite* 35(2000): 65–71.

 R. Plutchik, "Emotions and Attitudes Related to Being Overweight," *Journal of Clinical Psychology* 32(1976): 21–24.

79 A. J. Stunkard and T. A. Wadden, "Restrained Eating and Human Obesity," *Nutrition Reviews* 48(1990): 78–86.

 R. J. Tuschl, "From Dietary Restraint to Binge Eating: Some Theoretical Considerations," *Appetite* 14(1990): 105–109.

 M. R. Yeomans and E. Coughlan, "Mood-Induced Eating. Interactive Effects of Restraint and Tendency to Overeat," *Appetite* 52(2009): 290–298.

80 American Psychiatric Association, *Diagnostic and Statistical Manual of Mental Disorders,* 5th ed., Washington, DC: APA, 2013, p. 350.

81 Ibid.

82 B. H. Lourenço, T. Arthur, M. D. B. Rodrigues, I. Guazzelli, E. Frazzatto, S. Deram, et al., "Binge Eating Symptoms, Diet Composition and Metabolic Characteristics of Obese Children and Adolescents," *Appetite* 50(2008): 223–230.

 M. D. Marcus, "Binge Eating and Obesity," in *Eating Disorders and Obesity: A Comprehensive Handbook*, eds. K. D. Brownell and C. G. Fairburn, New York: The Guilford Press, 1995.

83 M. R. Lowe and K. L. Eldredge, "The Role of Impulsiveness in Normal and Disordered Eating," in *The Impulsive Client*, eds. W. G. McCown,

J. L. Johnson, and M. B. Shure, Washington, DC: American Psychological Association, 1993.

B. T. Walsh and M. J. Devlin, "Eating Disorders: Progress and Problems," *Science* 280(1998): 1387–1390.

84 R. H. Striegel-Moore and C. M. Bulik, "Risk Factors for Eating Disorders," *American Psychologist* 62(2007): 181–198.

85 R. J. Wurtman and J. J. Wurtman, "Carbohydrates and Depression," *Scientific American* 260(January 1989): 68–75.

86 G. S. Birketvedt, J. Florholmen, J. Sundsfjord, B. Østerud, D. Dinges, W. Bilker, and A. Stunkard, "Behavioral and Neuroendocrine Characteristics of the Night-Eating Syndrome," *JAMA* 282(1999): 657–663.

A. Stunkard, "Two Eating Disorders: Binge Eating Disorder and the Night Eating Syndrome," *Appetite* 34(2000): 333–334.

87 Ibid.

88 P. M. Whitaker-Azmitia and S. J. Peroutka, eds., *The Neuropharmacology of Serotonin*, New York: New York Academy of Sciences, 1990.

89 S. L. McElroy, H. G. J. Pope, P. E. J. Keck, and J. I. Hudson, "Disorders of Impulse Control," in *Impulsivity and Aggression*, eds. E. Hollander and D. J. Stein, New York: Wiley, 1995.

Wurtman and Wurtman, "Carbohydrates and Depression."

90 M. M. Furtado, S. A. Shikora, and E. Saltzman, "Long-Term Outcomes and Complications of Obesity Surgery: An Overview," *Nutrition in Clinical Care* 7(2004): 31–36.

J. J. Kim, M. E. Tarnoff, and S. A. Shikora, "Surgical Approaches to Weight Loss," *Nutrition in Clinical Care* 7(2004): 12–18.

L. H. Powell, J. E. Calvin III, and J. E. Calvin, Jr., "Effective Obesity Treatments," *American Psychologist* 62(2007): 234–246.

91 Powell et al., "Effective Obesity Treatments."

92 R. B. Hogan, J. H. Johnston, B. W. Long, J. Q. Sones, L. A. Hinton, J. Burge, and S. A. Corrigan, "A Double-Blind, Randomized, Sham-Controlled Trial of the Gastric Bubble for Obesity," *Gastrointestinal Endoscopy* 35(1989): 381–385.

93 T. L. Hernandez, J. M. Kittelson, C. K. Law, L. L. Ketch, N. R. Stob, R. C. Lindstrom, et al., "Fat Redistribution Following Suction Lipectomy: Defense of Body Fat and Patterns of Restoration," *Obesity (Silver Spring)* 19(2011): 1388–1395.

94 R. L. Goldman, J. J. Borckardt, H. A. Frohman, P. M. O'Neil, A. Madan, and L. K. Campbell, "Prefrontal Cortex Transcranial Direct Current Stimulation (tDCS) Temporarily Reduces Food Cravings and Increases the Self-Reported Ability to Resist Food in Adults with Frequent Food Craving," *Appetite* 56(2011): 741–746.

95 "Brain, Food," *Scientific American* (November 1991): 124.

R. J. Pohl-Krauza, J. L. Navia, E. Y. M. Madore, J. E. Nyrop, and C. L. Pelkman, "Effects of L-Phenylalanine on Energy Intake in Overweight and Obese Women," *Appetite* 51(2008): 111–119.

96 R. W. Foltin, T. H. Kelly, and M. W. Fischman, "The Effects of D-Amphetamine on Food Intake of Humans Living in a Residential Laboratory," *Appetite* 15(1990): 33–45.

S. Heshka and S. B. Heymsfield, "Pharmacological Treatment of Obesity," in *Eating Disorders and Obesity: A Comprehensive Handbook*, eds. K. D. Brownell and C. G. Fairburn, New York: The Guilford Press, 1995.

G. Kolata, "How Fen-Phen, a Diet 'Miracle,' Rose and Fell," *The New York Times* (September 23, 1997): F1, F6.

A. Pollack, "F.D.A. Panel Backs Drug to Treat Obesity," *The New York Times* (December 8, 2010): B1, B2.

Powell, Calvin III, and Calvin Jr., "Effective Obesity Treatments."

97 P. J. Rogers, "Food Choice, Mood and Mental Performance: Some Examples and Some Mechanisms," in *Food Choice, Acceptance and Consumption*, eds. H. L. Meiselman and H. J. H. MacFie, London: Blackie Academic & Professional, 1996.

98 Wurtman and Wurtman, "Carbohydrates and Depression."

G. T. Wilson, C. M. Grilo, and K. M. Vitousek, "Psychological Treatment of Eating Disorders," *American Psychologist* 62(2007): 199–216.

99 T. Mann, A. J. Tomiyama, E. Wrestling, A.-M. Lew, B. Samuels, and J. Chatman, "Medicare's Search for Effective Obesity Treatments," *American Psychologist* 62(2007): 220–233.

100 J. Dwyer, "Sixteen Popular Diets: Brief Nutritional Analyses," in *Obesity*, ed. A. J. Stunkard, Philadelphia: W. B. Saunders, 1980.

J. Eisenstein, S. B. Roberts, G. Dallal, and E. Saltzman, "High-Protein Weight-Loss Diets: Are They Safe and Do They Work? A Review of the Experimental and Epidemiologic Data," *Nutrition Reviews* 60(2002): 189–200.

101 D. A. Anderson, J. R. Shapiro, J. D. Lundgren, L. E. Spataro, and C. A. Frye, "Self-Reported Dietary Restraint Is Associated with Elevated Levels of Salivary Cortisol," *Appetite* 38(2002): 13–17.

K. E. D'Anci, K. L. Watts, R. B. Kanarek, and H. A. Taylor, "Low-Carbohydrate Weight-Loss Diets. Effects on Cognition and Mood," *Appetite* 52(2009): 96–103.

102 H. A. Guthrie, *Introductory Nutrition*, St. Louis, MO: Mosby, 1975.

103 C. De Graaf, J. J. M. M. Drijvers, N. J. H. Zimmermanns, K. H. Van het Hof, J. A. Westrate, H. Van den Berg, E. J. M. Velthuis-te Wierik, K. R. Westerterp, W. P. H. G. Verboeket-van de Venne, and M. S. Westerterp-Plantenga, "Energy and Fat Compensation during Long Term Consumption of Reduced Fat Products," *Appetite* 29(1997): 305–323.

R. W. Foltin, M. W. Fischman, C. S. Emurian, and J. J. Rachlinski, "Compensation for Caloric Dilution in Humans Given Unrestricted Access to Food in a Residential Laboratory," *Appetite* 10(1988): 13–24.

104 L. Abadallah, M. Chabert, B. Le Roux, and J. Louis-Sylvestre, "Is Pleasantness of Biscuits and Cakes Related to Their Actual or to Their Perceived Sugar and Fat Contents?" *Appetite* 30(1998): 309–324.

105 P. Kähkönen and H. Tuorila, "Effect of Reduced-Fat Information on Expected and Actual Hedonic and Sensory Ratings of Sausages," *Appetite* 30(1998): 13–23.

A. Westcombe and J. Wardle, "Influence of Relative Fat Content Information on Responses to Three Foods," *Appetite* 28(1997): 49–62.

106 A. Drewnowski, "Sensory Properties of Fats and Fat Replacements," *Nutrition Reviews* 50(1992): 17–20.

107 A. Drewnowski, "The New Fat Replacements: A Strategy for Reducing Fat Consumption," *Postgraduate Medicine* 87(1990): 111–114, 117–118, 121.

108 J. Moskin, "Creamy, Healthier Ice Cream? What's the Catch?" *The New York Times* (published online July 26, 2006): www.nytimes.com/2006/07/26/dining/26cream.html?pagewanted=all&_r=0.

109 W. J. Pasman, W. H. M. Saris, M. A. J. Wauters, and M. S. Westerterp-Plantenga, "Effect of One Week of Fibre Supplementation on Hunger and Satiety Ratings and Energy Intake," *Appetite* 29(1997): 77–87.

B. Rolls and R. A. Barnett, *Volumetrics: Feel Full on Fewer Calories*, New York: HarperCollins, 2000.

110 G. A. Leveille, "Adipose Tissue Metabolism: Influence of Periodicity of Eating and Diet Composition," *Federation Proceedings* 29(1970): 1294–1301.

D. P. Speechly and R. Buffenstein, "Greater Appetite Control Associated with an Increased Frequency of Eating in Lean Males," *Appetite* 33(1999): 285–297.

111 D. A. Booth and A. Nouwen, "Satiety. No Way to Slim," *Appetite*, 55(2010): 718–721.

112 T. A. Brunner, "It Takes Some Effort. How Minimal Physical Effort Reduces Consumption Volume," *Appetite* 71(2013): 89–94.

K. Kennedy-Hagan, J. E. Painter, C. Honselman, A. Halvorson, K. Rhodes, and K. Skwir, "The Effect of Pistachio Shells as a Visual Cue in Reducing Caloric Consumption," *Appetite* 57(2011): 418–420.

G. J. Privitera and F. M. Zuraikat, "Proximity of Foods in a Competitive Food Environment Influences Consumption of a Low Calorie and a High Calorie Food," *Appetite* 76(2014): 175–179.

113 K. D. Brownell, "Exercise in the Treatment of Obesity," in *Eating Disorders and Obesity: A Comprehensive Handbook*, eds. K. D. Brownell and C. G. Fairburn, New York: The Guilford Press, 1995.

114 S. S. Bassuk, T. S. Church, and J. E. Manson, "Why Exercise Works Magic," *Scientific American* (August 2013): 74–79.

L. Bherer, K. I. Erickson, and T. Liu-Ambrose, "A Review of the Effects of Physical Activity and Exercise on Cognitive and Brain Functions in Older Adults," *Journal of Aging Research* 2013(2013): 1–8.

G. Mammen and G. Faulkner, "Physical Activity and the Prevention of Depression," *American Journal of Preventive Medicine* 45(2013): 649–657.

A. Singh, L. Uijtdewilligen, J. W. R. Twisk, W. van Mechelen, and M. J. M. Chinapaw, "Physical Activity and Performance at School," *Archives of Pediatrics and Adolescent Medicine* 166(2012): 49–55.

115 K. D. Brownell and A. J. Stunkard, "Physical Activity in the Development and Control of Obesity," in *Obesity*, ed. A. J. Stunkard, Philadelphia: W. B. Saunders, 1980.

J. S. Stern, "Is Obesity a Disease of Inactivity?" in *Eating and Its Disorders*, eds. A. J. Stunkard and E. Stellar, New York: Raven Press, 1984.

116 J. E. Brody, "Panel Urges Hour of Exercise a Day; Sets Diet Guidelines," *The New York Times* (September 6, 2002): A1, A18.

J. M. Jakicic, B. H. Marcus, K. I. Gallagher, M. Napolitano, and W. Lang, "Effect of Exercise Duration and Intensity on Weight Loss in Overweight, Sedentary Women," *JAMA* 290(2003): 1323–1330.

M. L. Klem, R. R. Wing, M. T. McGuire, H. M. Seagle, and J. O. Hill, "A Descriptive Study of Individuals Successful at Long-Term Maintenance of Substantial Weight Loss," *American Journal of Clinical Nutrition* 66(1997): 239–246.

117 K. D. Brownell, R. Y. Cohen, A. J. Stunkard, M. R. J. Felix, and N. B. Cooley, "Weight Loss Competitions at the Work Site: Impact on Weight, Morale and Cost Effectiveness," *American Journal of Public Health* 74(1984): 1283–1285.

118 "Stephens College Meets Weight Loss Goal," *Inside Higher Ed* (published online January 3, 2011): www.insidehighered.com/quicktakes/2011/01/03/stephens-college-meets-weight-loss-goal.

S. Strom, "A City Tries to Slim Down," *The New York Times* (June 14, 2011): B1, B4.

119 S. A. Jebb, A. L. Ahern, A. D. Olson, L. M. Aston, C. Holzapfel, J. Stoll, et al., "Primary Care Referral to a Commercial Provider for Weight Loss Treatment Versus Standard Care: A Randomised Controlled Trial," *The Lancet* 378(2011): 1485–1492.

A. M. Pinto, J. L. Fava, D. A. Hoffmann, and R. R. Wing, "Combining Behavioral Weight Loss Treatment and a Commercial Program: A Randomized Clinical Trial," *Obesity* 21(2013): 673–680.

120 J. D. Latner, G. T. Wilson, A. J. Stunkard, and M. L. Jackson, "Self-Help and Long-Term Behavior Therapy for Obesity," *Behaviour Research and Therapy* 40(2002): 805–812.

A. Stunkard, H. Levine, and S. Fox, "The Management of Obesity: Patient Self-Help and Medical Treatment," *Archives of Internal Medicine* 125(1970): 1067–1072.

R. B. Stuart and C. Mitchell, "Self-Help Groups in the Control of Body Weight," in *Obesity*, ed. A. J. Stunkard, Philadelphia: W. B. Saunders, 1980.

121 C. S. W. Rand, "Treatment of Obese Patients in Psychoanalysis," in *Symposium on Obesity: Basic Mechanisms and Treatment*, ed. A. J. Stunkard, Philadelphia: W. B. Saunders, 1978.

A. J. Stunkard, "Psychoanalysis and Psychotherapy," in *Obesity*, ed. A. J. Stunkard, Philadelphia: W. B. Saunders, 1980.

122 G. T. Wilson, "Behavioral Approaches to the Treatment of Obesity," in *Eating Disorders and Obesity: A Comprehensive Handbook*, eds. K. D. Brownell and C. G. Fairburn, New York: The Guilford Press, 1995.

123 M. P. Poelman, E. de Vet, E. Velema, J. C. Seidell, and I. H. Steenhuis, "Behavioural Strategies to Control the Amount of Food Selected and Consumed," *Appetite* 72(2013): 156–165.

124 R. R. Wing, D. F. Tate, A. A. Gorin, H. A. Raynor, J. L. Fava, and J. Machan, "'STOP Regain': Are There Negative Effects of Daily Weighing?" *Journal of Consulting and Clinical Psychology* 75(2007): 652–656.

125 M. L. Skender, G. K. Goodrick, D. J. Del Junco, R. S. Reeves, L. Darnell, A. M. Gotto, and J. P. Foreyt, "Comparison of 2-Year Weight Loss Trends in Behavioral Treatments of Obesity: Diet, Exercise, and Combination Interventions," *Journal of the American Dietetic Association* 96(1996): 342–346.

126 Wilson, "Behavioral Approaches to the Treatment of Obesity."

127 L. H. Epstein, B. E. Saelens, M. D. Myers, and D. Vito, "Effects of Decreasing Sedentary Behaviors on Activity Choice in Obese Children," *Health Psychology* 16(1997): 107–113.

J. J. Otten, K. E. Jones, B. Littenberg, and J. Harvey-Berino, "Effects of Television Viewing Reducation on Energy Intake and Expenditure in Overweight and Obese Adults," *Archives of Internal Medicine* 169(2009): 2109–2115.

T. N. Robinson, "Reducing Children's Television Viewing to Prevent Obesity," *JAMA* 282(1991): 1561–1567.

128 B. Wansink, *Mindless Eating: Why We Eat More Than We Think*, New York: Bantam, 2006.

B. Wansink, "From Mindless Eating to Mindlessly Eating Better," *Physiology and Behavior* 100(2010): 453–463.

129 S. M. Garn and W. R. Leonard, "What Did Our Ancestors Eat?" *Nutrition Reviews* 47(1989): 337–345.

130 M. Konner, "What Our Ancestors Ate," *The New York Times Magazine* (June 5, 1988): 54–55.

131 K. D. Brownell and K. B. Horgen, *Food Fight: The Inside Story of the Food Industry, America's Obesity Crisis, and What We Can Do about It,* Chicago: Contemporary Books, 2004.

"Filling the World's Belly," *The Economist* (December 13, 2003): 3–6.

S. K. McCrady-Spitzer and J. A. Levine, "Nonexercise Activity Thermogenesis: A Way Forward to Treat the Worldwide Obesity Epidemic," *Surgery for Obesity and Related Diseases* 8(2012): 501–506.

M. Nestle, *Food Politics: How the Food Industry Influences Nutrition and Health,* 10th ed., Berkeley: University of California Press, 2013.

132 K. D. Brownell and J. Rodin, "The Dieting Maelstrom: Is It Possible and Advisable to Lose Weight?" *American Psychologist* 49(1994): 781–791.

A. K. Lindeman, "Quest for Ideal Weight: Costs and Consequences," *Medicine and Science in Sports and Exercise* 31(1999): 1135–1140.

D. D. Stallone, "The Influence of Obesity and Its Treatment on the Immune System," *Nutrition Reviews* 52(1994): 37–50.

S. C. Wooley, "Maelstrom Revisited," *American Psychologist* 50(1995): 943–944.

133 K. D. Brownell and J. Rodin, "Medical, Metabolic, and Psychological Effects of Weight Cycling," *Archives of Internal Medicine* 154(1994): 1325–1330.

134 Brownell and Rodin, "The Dieting Maelstrom."

Wooley, "Maelstrom Revisited."

135 J. P. Kassirer and M. Angell, "Losing Weight—An Ill-Fated New Year's Resolution," *The New England Journal of Medicine* 338(1998): 52–54.

136 K. D. Brownell, "Dieting and the Search for the Perfect Body: Where Physiology and Culture Collide," *Behavior Therapy* 22(1991): 1–12.

137 S.-Y. Chou, I. Rashad, and M. Grossman, "Fast-Food Restaurant Advertising on Television and Its Influence on Childhood Obesity," *Journal of Law and Economics* 51(2008): 599–618.

J. Couzin-Frankel, "Tackling America's Eating Habits, One Store at a Time," *Science* 337(2012): 1473–1475.

J. Medina, "New Policy Outlaws Bake Sales in Schools," *The New York Times* (October 3, 2009): A17, A20.

B. Wansink, D. R. Just, and J. McKendry, "Lunch Line Redesign," *The New York Times* (October 22, 2010): A35.

11 DRINKING YOUR LIFE AWAY

1 "Good Soldiers," *The New York Times* (February 16, 1991): 9.

2 D. Zaridze, S. Lewington, A. Boroda, G. Scélo, R. Karpov, A. Lazarev, and I. Konobeevskaya, "Alcohol and Mortality in Russia: Prospective Observational Study of 151,000 Adults," *The Lancet* (published online January 21, 2014). DOI: 10.1016/S0140-6736(13)62247-3.

3 M. Dayagi-Mendels, *Drink and Be Merry: Wine and Beer in Ancient Times,* Jerusalem: The Jewish Museum, 1999.

4 B. L. Vallee, "Alcohol in the Western World," *Scientific American* (June 1998): 80–85.

5 D. F. Musto, "Alcohol in American History," *Scientific American* (April 1996): 78–83.

6 www.niaaa.nih.gov/alcohol-health/overview-alcohol-consumption/alcohol-facts-and-statistics.

7 http://core.siu.edu/results/index.html.
8 www.niaaa.nih.gov/alcohol-health/overview-alcohol-consumption/alcohol-facts-and-statistics.
9 A. L. Klatsky, "Drink to Your Health?" *Scientific American* (February 2003): 75–81.
10 www.niaaa.nih.gov/alcohol-health/overview-alcohol-consumption/alcohol-facts-and-statistics.
11 P. Hudson, "The Medical Examiner Looks at Drinking," in *Drinking: Alcohol in American Society—Issues and Current Research*, eds. J. A. Ewing and B. A. Rouse, Chicago: Nelson-Hall, 1978.
   S. H. Mitchell, H. de Wit, and J. P. Zacny, "Effect of Varying Ethanol Dose on Cigarette Consumption in Healthy Normal Volunteers," *Behavioural Pharmacology* 6(1995): 339–365.
   Vallee, "Alcohol in the Western World."
12 www.niaaa.nih.gov/alcohol-health/overview-alcohol-consumption/alcohol-facts-and-statistics.
13 J. S. DeSimone, "Binge Drinking and Risky Sex among College Students," *NBER Working Paper No. 15953* (April 2010).
   M. P. Mundt and L. I. Zakletskaia, "Prevention for College Students Who Suffer Alcohol-Induced Blackouts Could Deter High-Cost Emergency Department Visits," *Health Affairs* 31(2012): 1–8.
   H. Wechsler and T. F. Nelson, "What We Have Learned From the Harvard School of Public Health College Alcohol Study: Focusing Attention on College Student Alcohol Consumption and the Environmental Conditions That Promote It," *Journal of Studies on Alcohol and Drugs* (July 2008): 1–8.
14 American Psychiatric Association, *Diagnostic and Statistical Manual of Mental Disorders*, 5th ed., Washington, DC: APA, 2013, p. 490.
15 Ibid.
16 Vallee, "Alcohol in the Western World."
17 Y. M. Ibrahim, "Guinness and Grand Met in $22 Billion Deal," *The New York Times* (May 13, 1997): D1, D10.
   R. P. Keeling, "Drinking in College: The Politics of Research and Prevention," *Journal of American College Health* 47(1998): 51–55.
18 P. Rosenzweig, *The Book of Proverbs*, New York: Philosophical Library, 1965, p. 15.
19 Ibid., p. 47.
20 R. Williams, *Latin Quips at Your Fingertips: Witty Sayings by Wise Romans*, New York: Barnes & Noble Books, 2000, p. L.
21 W. Shakespeare, *Macbeth* in *The Complete Works of William Shakespeare*, ed. W. A. Wright, Garden City, NY: Garden City Books, 1623/1936, p. 1035.
22 B. Critchlow, "The Powers of John Barleycorn: Beliefs about the Effects of Alcohol on Social Behavior," *American Psychologist* 41(1986): 751–764.
23 W. H. George and G. A. Marlatt, "Alcoholism: The Evolution of a Behavioral Perspective," in *Recent Developments in Alcoholism*, vol. 1, ed. M. Galanter, New York: Plenum, 1983.
   G. A. Marlatt, B. Demming, and J. B. Reid, "Loss of Control Drinking in Alcoholics: An Experimental Analogue," *Journal of Abnormal Psychology* 81(1973): 233–241.
24 J. G. Hull and C. F. Bond, "Social and Behavioral Consequences of Alcohol Consumption and Expectancy: A Meta-Analysis," *Psychological Bulletin* 99(1986): 347–360.

25 A. M. Gross, T. Bennett, L. Sloan, B. P. Marx, and J. Juergens, "The Impact of Alcohol and Alcohol Expectancies on Male Perception of Female Sexual Arousal in a Date Rape Analog," *Experimental and Clinical Psychopharmacology* 9(2001): 380–388.

26 C. S. Lieber, "The Metabolism of Alcohol," *Scientific American* 234(March 1976): 25–33.

27 American Psychiatric Association, *Diagnostic and Statistical Manual of Mental Disorders.*

   M. McGue, "The Behavioral Genetics of Alcoholism," *Current Directions in Psychological Science* 8(1999): 109–115.

28 N. K. Mello, "Some Aspects of the Behavioral Pharmacology of Alcohol," in *Psychopharmacology: A Review of Progress, 1957–1967,* ed. D. H. Efron, Washington, DC: U.S. Government Printing Office, 1968.

29 D. Goldberg, "Red Head," *The Lancet* 1(May 2, 1981): 1003.

   D. E. Johnston, Y.-B. Chiao, J. S. Gavaler, and D. H. Van Thiel, "Inhibition of Testosterone Synthesis by Ethanol and Acetaldehyde," *Biochemical Pharmacology* 30(1981): 1827–1831.

   J. B. Knowles, S. G. Laverty, and H. A. Kuechler, "Effects of Alcohol on REM Sleep," *Quarterly Journal of Studies on Alcohol* 29(1968): 342–349.

   V. C. Taasan, A. J. Block, P. G. Boyson, J. W. Wynne, C. White, and S. Lindsey, "Alcohol Increases Sleep Apnea and Oxygen Desaturation in Asymptomatic Men," *The American Journal of Medicine* 71(1981): 240–245.

30 M. S. Westerterp-Plantenga and C. R. T. Verwegen, "The Appetizing Effect of an Apéritif in Overweight and Normal-Weight Humans," *American Journal of Clinical Nutrition* 69(1999): 205–212.

31 M. M. Joosten, C. de Graaf, A. Rietman, R. F. Witkamp, and H. F. J. Hendriks, "Short-Term Oral Exposure to White Wine Transiently Lowers Serum Free Fatty Acids," *Appetite* 55(2010): 124–129.

   P. M. Suter, E. Häsler, and W. Vetter, "Effects of Alcohol on Energy Metabolism and Body Weight Regulation: Is Alcohol a Risk Factor for Obesity?" *Nutrition Reviews* 55(1997): 157–171.

   M. R. Yeomans, "Short Term Effects of Alcohol on Appetite in Humans. Effects of Context and Restrained Eating," *Appetite* 55(2010): 565–573.

32 B. J. Bushman and H. M. Cooper, "Effects of Alcohol on Human Aggression: An Integrative Research Review," *Psychological Bulletin* 107(1990): 341–354.

33 C. M. Steele and R. A. Josephs, "Alcohol Myopia: Its Prized and Dangerous Effects," *Psychological Bulletin* 45(1990): 921–933.

34 S. E. Burian, A. Liguori, and J. H. Robinson, "Effects of Alcohol on Risk-Taking during Simulated Driving," *Human Psychopharmacology* 17(2002): 141–150.

   K. Fromme, E. Katz, and E. D'Amico, "Effects of Alcohol Intoxication on the Perceived Consequences of Risk Taking," *Experimental and Clinical Psychopharmacology* 5(1997): 14–23.

35 D. M. Lovinger, G. White, and F. F. Weight, "Ethanol Inhibits NMDA-Activated Ion Current in Hippocampal Neurons," *Science* 243(1989): 1721–1724.

36 H. Moskowitz and J. T. Murray, "Decrease of Iconic Memory after Alcohol," *Journal of Studies on Alcohol* 37(1976): 278–283.

   R. S. Ryback, "The Continuum and Specificity of the Effects of Alcohol on Memory," *Quarterly Journal of Studies on Alcohol* 32(1971): 995–1016.

37 S. L. Assefi and M. Garry, "Absolut®Memory Distortions: Alcohol Placebos Influence the Misinformation Effect," *Psychological Science* 14(2003): 77–80.

38 M. A. Sayette, E. D. Reichle, and J. W. Schooler, "Lost in the Sauce: The Effects of Alcohol on Mind Wandering," *Psychological Science* 20(2009): 747–752.

39 J. Howland, D. J. Rohsenow, J. A. Greece, C. A. Littlefield, A. Almeida, T. Heeren, et al., "The Effects of Binge Drinking on College Students' Next-Day Academic Test-Taking Performance and Mood State," *Addiction* 105(2010): 655–665.

40 J. R. Wenger, T. M. Tiffany, C. Bombarier, K. Nicholls, and S. C. Woods, "Ethanol Tolerance in the Rat Is Learned," *Science* 213(1981): 575–577.

41 B. Remington, P. Roberts, and S. Glautier, "The Effect of Drink Familiarity on Tolerance to Alcohol," *Addictive Behaviors* 22(1996): 45–53.

42 S. Siegel, "The Four-Loko Effect," *Perspectives on Psychological Science* 6(2011): 357–362.

43 S. E. Taylor, "Asymmetrical Effects of Positive and Negative Events: The Mobilization–Minimization Hypothesis," *Psychological Bulletin* 110(1991): 67–85.

44 S. Siegel, R. E. Hinson, M. D. Krank, and J. McCully, "Heroin 'Overdose' Death: Contribution of Drug-Associated Environmental Cues," *Science* 216(1982): 436–437.

45 R. E. LaPorte, J. A. Cauley, L. H. Kuller, K. Flegal, J. S. Gavaler, and D. Van Thiel, "Alcohol, Coronary Heart Disease, and Total Mortality," in *Recent Developments in Alcoholism*, vol. 3, ed. M. Galanter, New York: Plenum, 1985.

    M. J. Stampfer, J. H. Kang, J. Chen, R. Cherry, and F. Grodstein, "Effects of Moderate Alcohol Consumption on Cognitive Function in Women," *The New England Journal of Medicine* 352(2005): 245–253.

    D. H. Van Thiel and J. S. Gavaler, "Myocardial Effects of Alcohol Abuse: Clinical and Physiologic Consequences," in *Recent Developments in Alcoholism*, vol. 3, ed. M. Galanter, New York: Plenum, 1985.

    D. H. Van Thiel, J. S. Gavaler, and D. C. Lehotay, "Biochemical Mechanisms Responsible for Alcohol-Associated Myocardiopathy," in *Recent Developments in Alcoholism*, vol. 3, ed. M. Galanter, New York: Plenum, 1985.

46 Lieber, "The Metabolism of Alcohol."

47 S. Siegel, "Morphine Analgesic Tolerance: Its Situation Specificity Supports a Pavlovian Conditioning," *Science* 193(1976): 323–325.

    Siegel et al., "Heroin 'Overdose' Death."

48 R. O. Deems, M. I. Friedman, L. S. Friedman, S. J. Munoz, and W. C. Maddrey, "Chemosensory Function, Food Preferences and Appetite in Human Liver Disease," *Appetite* 20(1993): 209–216.

    C. S. Lieber, "The Influence of Alcohol on Nutritional Status," *Nutrition Reviews* 46(1988): 241–254.

    Lieber, "The Metabolism of Alcohol."

49 Lieber, "The Metabolism of Alcohol."

50 G. Freund, "Neurobiological Relationships between Aging and Alcohol Abuse," in *Recent Developments in Alcoholism*, vol. 2, ed. M. Galanter, New York: Plenum, 1984.

    C. J. Golden, B. Graber, I. Blose, R. Berg, J. Coffman, and S. Bloch, "Difference in Brain Densities between Chronic Alcoholic and Normal Control Patients," *Science* 211(1981): 508–510.

R. E. Tarter and C. M. Ryan, "Neuropsychology of Alcoholism: Etiology, Phenomenology, Process, and Outcome," in *Recent Developments in Alcoholism*, vol. 1, ed. M. Galanter, New York: Plenum, 1983.

51 S. J. Nixon, "Neurocognitive Performance in Alcoholics: Is Polysubstance Abuse Important? *Psychological Science* 10(1999): 181–185.

A. A. Patkar, C. A. Marsden, P. C. Naik, D. A. Kendall, R. Gopalakrishnan, M. J. Vergare, and S. P. Weinstein, "Differences in Peripheral Noradrenergic Function among Actively Drinking and Abstienent Alcohol-Dependent Individuals," *American Journal on Addictions* 13(2004): 225–235.

M. J. Rosenbloom, A. Pfefferbaum, and E. V. Sullivan, "Recovery of Short-Term Memory and Psychomotor Speed but Not Postural Stability with Long-Term Sobriety in Alcoholic Women," *Neuropsychology* 18(2004): 589–597.

S. Zinn, R. Stein, and H. S. Swartzwelder, "Executive Functioning Early in Abstinence From Alcohol," *Alcoholism: Clinical and Experimental Research* 28(2004): 1338–1346.

52 S. Y. Hill and C. Ryan, "Brain Damage in Social Drinkers? Reasons for Caution," in *Recent Developments in Alcoholism*, vol. 3, ed. M. Galanter, New York: Plenum, 1985.

53 D. Stephens and R. Dudley, "The Drunken Monkey Hypothesis," *Natural History* (December 2004–January 2005): 40–44.

54 S. Johnson, *The Ghost Map: The Story of London's Most Terrifying Epidemic—and How It Changed Science, Cities, and the Modern World.* New York: Riverhead Books, 2006.

55 J. A. Ewing and B. A. Rouse, "Drinks, Drinkers, and Drinking," in *Drinking: Alcohol in American Society—Issues and Current Research*, eds. J. A. Ewing and B. A. Rouse, Chicago: Nelson-Hall, 1978.

56 J. I. Nurnberger and L. J. Bierut, "Seeking the Connections: Alcoholism and Our Genes," *Scientific American* (April 2007): 46–53.

57 V. B. Duffy, J. M. Peterson, and L. M. Bartoshuk, "Associations between Taste Genetics, Oral Sensation and Alcohol Intake," *Physiology and Behavior* 82(2004): 435–445.

58 L. Spear, "The Teenage Brain: Adolescents and Alcohol," *Current Directions in Psychological Science* 22(2013): 52–57.

59 M. A. Schuckit and V. Rayses, "Ethanol Ingestion: Differences in Blood Acetaldehyde Concentrations in Relatives of Alcoholics and Controls," *Science* 203(1979): 54–55.

60 M. A. Korsten, S. Matsuzaki, L. Feinman, and C. S. Lieber, "High Blood Acetaldehyde Levels after Ethanol Administration: Difference between Alcoholic and Nonalcoholic Subjects," *The New England Journal of Medicine* 292(8)(1975): 386–389.

61 M. A. Schuckit, "Low Levels of Response to Alcohol as a Predictor of Future Alcoholism," *American Journal of Psychiatry* 151(1994): 184–189.

62 H. Begleiter, B. Porjesz, B. Bihari, and B. Kissin, "Event-Related Brain Potentials in Boys at Risk for Alcoholism," Science 225(1984): 1493–1496.

J. Polich, V. E. Pollock, and F. E. Bloom, "Meta-Analysis of P300 Amplitude from Males at Risk for Alcoholism," *Psychological Bulletin* 115(1994): 55–73.

63 C. R. Cloninger, M. Bohman, S. Sigvardsson, and A.-L. Von Knorring, "Psychopathology in Adopted-Out Children of Alcoholics: The Stockholm Adoption Study," in *Recent Developments in Alcoholism*, vol. 3, ed. M. Galanter, New York: Plenum, 1985.

K. S. Kendler, C. A. Prescott, M. C. Neale, and N. L. Pedersen, "Temperance Board Registration for Alcohol Abuse in a National Sample of Swedish Male Twins," *Archives of General Psychiatry* 54(1997): 178–184.

McGue, "The Behavioral Genetics of Alcoholism."

64 American Psychiatric Association, *Diagnostic and Statistical Manual of Mental Disorders*, p. 659.

65 Ibid.

66 J. M. De Castro, "Social, Circadian, Nutritional, and Subjective Correlates of the Spontaneous Pattern of Moderate Alcohol Intake of Normal Humans," *Pharmacology, Biochemistry and Behavior* 35(1990): 923–931.

P. Doty and and H. de Wit, "Effect of Setting on the Reinforcing and Subjective Effects of Ethanol in Social Drinkers," *Psychopharmacology* 118(1995): 19–27.

M. Lennernäs, L. Hambraeus, and T. Åkerstedt, "Shift Related Dietary Intake in Day and Shift Workers," *Appetite* 25(1995): 253–265.

67 Doty and de Wit, "Effect of Setting on the Reinforcing and Subjective Effects of Ethanol in Social Drinkers."

68 D. W. Watson and M. B. Sobell, "Social Influences on Alcohol Consumption by Black and White Males," *Addictive Behaviors* 7(1982): 87–91.

69 R. L. Collins and G. A. Marlatt, "Social Modeling as a Determinant of Drinking Behavior: Implications for Prevention and Treatment," *Addictive Behaviors* 6(1981): 233–239.

R. L. Collins and G. A. Marlatt, "Psychological Correlates and Explanations of Alcohol Use and Abuse," in *Medical and Social Aspects of Alcohol Abuse*, eds. B. Tabakoff, P. B. Sutker, and C. I. Randall, New York: Plenum, 1983.

70 G. N. Braucht, "How Environments and Persons Combine to Influence Problem Drinking: Current Research Issues," in *Recent Developments in Alcoholism*, vol. 1, ed. M. Galanter, New York: Plenum, 1983.

T. C. Harford, "Drinking Patterns among Black and Nonblack Adolescents: Results of a National Survey," in *Alcohol and Culture: Comparative Perspectives from Europe and America*, ed. T. F. Babor, New York: New York Academy of Sciences, 1986.

71 S. Madon, M. Guyll, R. Spoth, and J. Willard, "Self-Fulfilling Prophecies: The Synergistic Accumulative Effect of Parents' Beliefs on Children's Drinking Behavior, *Psychological Science* 15(2004): 837–845.

72 M. Kremer and D. Levy, "Peer Effects and Alcohol Use among College Students," *Journal of Economic Perspectives* 22(2008): 189–206.

73 C. Loersch and B. D. Bartholow, "The Color of Safety: Ingroup-Associated Colors Make Beer Safer," *Journal of Experimental Social Psychology* 47(2011): 190–194.

74 C. L. Odgers, A. Caspi, D. S. Nagin, A. R. Piquero, W. S. Sluske, B. J. Milne, et al., "Is It Important to Prevent Early Exposure to Drugs and Alcohol among Adolescents? *Psychological Science* 19(2008): 1037–1044.

75 K. Ackroff and A. Sclafani, "Flavor Preferences Conditioned by Intragastric Infusion of Ethanol in Rats," *Pharmacology, Biochemistry and Behavior* 68(2002): 327–338.

R. Mehiel and R. C. Bolles, "Learned Flavor Preferences Based on Caloric Outcome," *Animal Learning and Behavior* 12(1984): 421–427.

J. Sherman, K. W. Rusiniak, and J. Garcia, "Alcohol Ingestive Habits: The Role of Flavor and Effect," in *Recent Developments in Alcoholism*, vol. 2, ed. M. Galanter, New York: Plenum, 1984.

76 W. J. Darby, "The Nutrient Contributions of Fermented Beverages," in *Fermented Food Beverages in Nutrition*, eds. C. F. Gastineau, W. J. Darby, and T. B. Turner, New York: Academic Press, 1979.

R. Passmore, "The Energy Value of Alcohol," in *Fermented Food Beverages in Nutrition*, eds. C. F. Gastineau, W. J. Darby, and T. B. Turner, New York: Academic Press, 1979.

77 D. E. Bradford, B. L. Shapiro, and J. J. Curtin, "How Bad Could It Be? Alcohol Dampens Stress Responses to Threat of Uncertain Intensity," *Psychological Science* (published online October 21, 2013). DOI: 10.1177/0956797613499923.

78 T. F. Doyle and H. H. Samson, "Schedule-Induced Drinking in Humans: A Potential Factor in Excessive Alcohol Use," *Drug and Alcohol Dependence* 16(1985): 117–132.

A. L. Riley and C. W. Wetherington, "Schedule-Induced Polydipsia: Is the Rat a Small Furry Human? (An Analysis of an Animal Model of Human Alcoholism)," in *Contemporary Learning Theories: Instrumental Conditioning Theory and the Impact of Biological Constraints on Learning*, eds. S. B. Klein and R. R. Mowrer, Hillsdale, NJ: Lawrence Erlbaum Associates, 1989.

79 J. L. Falk and H. H. Samson, "Schedule-Induced Physical Dependence on Ethanol," *Pharmacological Reviews* 27(1976): 449–464.

J. L. Falk and M. Tang, "Animal Model of Alcoholism: Critique and Progress," in *Alcohol Intoxication and Withdrawal*, vol. 38, ed. M. M. Gross, New York: Plenum, 1977.

80 S. I. Ornstein and D. Levy, "Price and Income Elasticities of Demand for Alcoholic Beverages," in *Recent Developments in Alcoholism*, vol. 1, ed. M. Galanter, New York: Plenum, 1983.

J. Rabow and R. K. Watts, "The Role of Alcohol Availability in Alcohol Consumption and Alcohol Problems," in *Recent Developments in Alcoholism*, vol. 1 ed. M. Galanter, New York: Plenum, 1983.

81 D. L. Brito and C. K. Strain, "A Model of the Consumption of Alcohol," in *Advances in Behavioral Economics: Vol. 3. Substance Use and Abuse*, eds. L. Green and J. H. Kagel, Norwood, NJ: Ablex Publishing Corporation, 1996.

G. M. Heyman, "Elasticity of Demand for Alcohol in Humans and Rats," in *Advances in Behavioral Economics: Vol. 3. Substance Use and Abuse*, eds. L. Green and J. H. Kagel, Norwood, NJ: Ablex Publishing Corporation, 1996.

82 R. E. Vuchinich and J. A. Tucker, "Contributions from Behavioral Theories of Choice to an Analysis of Alcohol Abuse," *Journal of Abnormal Psychology* 97(1988): 181–195.

R. E. Vuchinich, J. A. Tucker, and E. J. Rudd, "Preference for Alcohol Consumption as a Function of Amount and Delay of Alternative Reward," *Journal of Abnormal Psychology* 96(1987): 259–263.

83 T. Egan, "Youthful Binge Drinking Fueled by Boredom of the Open West," *The New York Times* (September 2, 2006): A1, A12.

G. Shohat-Ophir, K. R. Kaun, R. Azanchi, and U. Heberlein, "Sexual Deprivation Increases Ethanol Intake in *Drosophila*," *Science* 335(2012): 1351–1355.

84 Nurnberger and Bierut, "Seeking the Connections."

85 Rosenzweig, *The Book of Proverbs*, p. 66.

86 K. D. Brownell, G. A. Marlatt, E. Lichtenstein, and G. T. Wilson, "Understanding and Preventing Relapse," *American Psychologist* 41(1986): 765–782.

George and Marlatt, "Alcoholism."

G. A. Marlatt, "Craving for Alcohol, Loss of Control, and Relapse: A Cognitive-Behavioral Analysis," in *Alcoholism: New Directions in Behavioral Research and Treatment*, eds. P. E. Nathan, G. A. Marlatt, and T. Loberg, New York: Plenum, 1978.

87 C. Holden, "Is Alcoholism Treatment Effective?" *Science* 236(1987): 20–22.

W. R. Miller and R. K. Hester, "Inpatient Alcoholism Treatment: Who Benefits?" *American Psychologist* 41(1986): 794–805.

88 M. B. Sobell and L. C. Sobell, *Behavioral Treatment of Alcohol Problems: Individualized Therapy and Controlled Drinking*, New York: Plenum, 1978.

89 G. A. Marlatt, "The Controlled-Drinking Controversy," *American Psychologist* 38(1983): 1097–1110.

M. B. Sobell and L. C. Sobell, "Controlled Drinking: A Concept Coming of Age," in *Self-Control and Self-Modification of Emotional Behavior*, eds. K. R. Blankstein and J. Polivy, New York: Plenum, 1982.

90 B. Leach and J. L. Norris, "Factors in the Development of Alcoholics Anonymous (AA)," in *Treatment and Rehabilitation of the Chronic Alcoholic*, eds. B. Kissin and H. Begleiter, New York: Plenum, 1977.

S. Peele, "All Wet," *The Sciences* (March/April 1998): 17–21.

91 C. B. De Soto, W. E. O'Donnell, and J. L. De Soto, "Long-Term Recovery in Alcoholics," *Alcoholism: Clinical and Experimental Research* 13(1989): 693–697.

92 A. K. Davis and H. Rosenberg, "Acceptance of Non-Abstinence Goals by Addiction Professionals in the United States," *Psychology of Addictive Behaviors* 27(2013): 1102–1109.

S. Higuchi and T. Saito, "Reduction in Alcohol Consumption: Therapeutic Goal in Alcohol Dependence Treatment," *Japanese Journal of Alcohol Studies and Drug Dependence* 48(2013): 17–31.

N. Kimura, T. Shirasake, T. Shirasaka, Y. Sasaki, C. Kawazoe, and T. Saito, "A Survey of Alcoholics and Their Families on Controlled Drinking as a Treatment Goal: Discussions on New Treatment Approaches," *Japanese Journal of Alcohol Studies and Drug Dependence* 48(2013): 76–84.

H. Klingemann and H. Rosenberg, "Acceptance and Therapeutic Practice of Controlled Drinking as an Outcome Goal by Swiss Alcohol Treatment Programmes," *European Addiction Research* 15(2009): 121–127.

A. Luquiens, M. Reynaud, and H. J. Aubin, "Is Controlled Drinking an Acceptable Goal in the Treatment of Alcohol Dependence? A Survey of French Alcohol Specialists," *Alcohol and Alcoholism* 46(2011): 586–591.

93 J. Koerkel, "Behavioural Self-Management with Problem Drinkers: One-Year Follow-Up of a Controlled Drinking Group Treatment Approach," *Addiction Research and Theory* 14(2006): 35–49.

H. Rosenberg, "Prediction of Controlled Drinking by Alcoholics and Problem Drinkers," *Psychological Bulletin* 113(1993): 129–139.

94 S. Bujarski, S. S. O'Malley, K. Lunny, and L. A. Ray, "The Effects of Drinking Goal on Treatment Outcome for Alcoholism," *Journal of Consulting and Clinical Psychology* 81(2013): 13–22.

95 W. R. Miller, J. M. Brown, T. L. Simpson, N. S. Handmaker, T. H. Bien, L. F. Luckie, et al., "What Works? A MethodologicalAnalysis of the Alcohol Treatment Outcome Literature," in *Handbook of Alcoholism Treatment Approaches: Effective Alternatives*, 2nd ed., eds. R. K. Hester and W. R. Miller, Boston: Allyn and Bacon, 1995.

96 N. Heather, "Brief Intervention Strategies," in *Handbook of Alcoholism Treatment Approaches: Effective Alternatives*, 2nd ed., eds. R. K. Hester and W. R. Miller, Boston: Allyn and Bacon, 1995.

97 P. M. Monti, D. J. Rohsenow, S. M. Colby, and D. B. Abrams, "Coping and Social Skills Training," in *Handbook of Alcoholism Treatment Approaches: Effective Alternatives*, eds. R. K. Hester and W. R. Miller, Boston: Allyn and Bacon, 1995.

98 W. R. Miller, "Increasing Motivation for Change," in *Handbook of Alcoholism Treatment Approaches: Effective Alternatives*, 2nd ed., eds. R. K. Hester and W. R. Miller, Boston: Allyn and Bacon, 1995.

99 J. E. Smith and R. J. Meyers, "The Community Reinforcement Approach," in *Handbook of Alcoholism Treatment Approaches: Effective Alternatives*, 2nd ed., eds. R. K. Hester and W. R. Miller, Boston: Allyn and Bacon, 1995.

100 Miller et al., "What Works?"

101 J. D. Duffy, "The Neurology of Alcoholic Denial: Implications for Assessment and Treatment," *Canadian Journal of Psychiatry* 40(1995): 257–263.

102 R. L. Elkins, "An Appraisal of Chemical Aversion (Emetic Therapy) Approaches to Alcoholism Treatment," *Behaviour Research and Therapy* 29(1991): 387–413.
　　　　C. T. Rinmele, M. O. Howard, and M. L. Hilfrink, "Aversion Therapies," in *Handbook of Alcoholism Treatment Approaches: Effective Alternatives*, 2nd ed., eds. R. K. Hester and W. R. Miller, Boston: Allyn and Bacon, 1995.

103 A. W. Logue, "Taste Aversion and the Generality of the Laws of Learning," *Psychological Bulletin* 86(1979): 276–296.

104 A. W. Logue, K. R. Logue, and K. E. Strauss, "The Acquisition of Taste Aversions in Humans with Eating and Drinking Disorders," *Behaviour Research and Therapy* 21(1983): 275–289.

105 C. S. Mellor and H. P. White, "Taste Aversions to Alcoholic Beverages Conditioned by Motion Sickness," *American Journal of Psychiatry* 135(1978): 125–126.

106 Miller et al., "What Works?"

107 Ayerst Laboratories Inc., *Antabuse® Brand of Disulfiram in Alcoholism*, New York: Ayerst Laboratories Inc., 1986.

108 www.nlm.nih.gov/medlineplus/druginfo/meds/a682602.html.

109 Ayerst Laboratories Inc., *Antabuse® Brand of Disulfiram in Alcoholism*.

110 G. Bigelow, D. Strickler, I. Liebson, and R. Griffiths, "Maintaining Disulfiram Ingestion among Outpatient Alcoholics: A Security-Deposit Contingency Contracting Procedure," *Behaviour Research and Therapy* 14(1976): 378–381.

111 D. Donovan and K. Witkiewitz, "Relapse Prevention: From Radical Idea to Common Practice," *Addiction Research and Theory* 20(2012): 204–217.

112 Miller et al., "What Works?"

113 A. N. C. Campbell, E. V. Nunes, A. G. Matthews, M. Stitzer, G. M. Miele, D. Polsky, et al., "Internet-Delivered Treatment for Substance Abuse: A Multisite Randomized Controlled Trial," *American Journal of Psychiatry* (published online April 4, 2014). DOI: 10.1176/appi.ajp.2014.13081055.
　　　　R. K. Hester and H. D. Delaney, "Behavioral Self-Control Program for Windows: Results of a Controlled Clinical Trial," *Journal of Consulting and Clinical Psychology* 65(1997): 686–693.
　　　　R. K. Hester, H. D. Delaney, and W. Campbell, "ModerateDrinking.com and Moderation Management: Outcomes of a Randomized Clinical Trial with Non-Dependent Problem Drinkers," *Journal of Consulting and Clinical Psychology* 79(2011): 215–224.

114 Miller et al., "What Works?"
115 B. S. McCrady and S. I. Delaney, "Self-Help Groups," in *Handbook of Alcoholism Treatment Approaches: Effective Alternatives*, 2nd ed., eds. R. K. Hester and W. R. Miller, Boston: Allyn and Bacon, 1995.
      Personal communication from Alcoholics Anonymous Information Office, August 1990.
116 www.aa.org/pdf/products/m-24_aafactfile.pdf.
117 B. S. McCrady, E. E. Epstein, and L. S. Hirsch, "Maintaining Change after Conjoint Behavioral Alcohol Treatment for Men: Outcomes at 6 Months," *Addiction* 94(1999): 1381–1396.
118 M. Ferri, L. Amato, and M. Davoli, "Alcoholics Anonymous and Other 12-Step Programmes for Alcohol Dependence," *The Cochrane Library* (published online July 19, 2006). DOI: 10.1002/14651858.CD005032.pub2.
119 Peele, "All Wet."
      Project MATCH Research Group, "Matching Alcoholism Treatments to Client Heterogeneity: Project MATCH Posttreatment Drinking Outcomes," *Journal of Studies on Alcohol* 58(1997): 7–29.
120 D. A. Dawson, "Correlates of Past-Year Status among Treated and Untreated Persons with Former Alcohol Dependence: United States, 1992," *Alcoholism: Clinical and Experimental Research* 20(1996): 771–779.
      Peele, "All Wet."
121 Peele, "All Wet."
122 L. A. Rone, S. I. Miller, and R. J. Frances, "Psychotropic Medications," in *Handbook of Alcoholism Treatment Approaches: Effective Alternatives*, 2nd ed., eds. R. K. Hester and W. R. Miller, Boston: Allyn and Bacon, 1995.
123 R. F. Anton, S. S. O'Malley, D. A. Ciraulo, R. A. Cisler, D. Couper, D. M. Donovan, et al., "Combined Pharmacotherapies and Behavioral Interventions for Alcohol Dependence," *JAMA* 295(2006): 2003–2017.
      Bujarski, O'Malley, Lunny, and Ray, "The Effects of Drinking Goal on Treatment Outcome for Alcoholism."
      G. Miller, "Tackling Alcoholism with Drugs," *Science* 320(2008): 168–170.
      W. van den Brink, P. Sørensen, L. Torup, K. Mann, and A. Gual for the SENSE Study Group, "Long-Term Efficacy, Tolerability and Safety of Nalmefene as-Needed in Patients with Alcohol Dependence: A 1-Year, Randomised Controlled Study," *Journal of Psychopharmacology* (published online March 26, 2014). DOI: 10.1177/0269881114527362.
124 W. R. Miller and S. A. Brown, "Why Psychologists Should Treat Alcohol and Drug Problems," *American Psychologist* 52(1997): 1269–1279.
125 http://core.siu.edu/results/index.html.
126 http://pubs.niaaa.nih.gov/publications/CollegeFactSheet/CollegeFactSheet.pdf.
127 J. E. Brody, "Curbing Binge Drinking Takes Group Effort," *The New York Times* (September 9, 2008): F7.
      B. Busteed, "The Mistake Colleges Make about Student Drinking," *The Chronicle of Higher Education* (May 2, 2008): A34–A35.
      N. DeSantis, "Appeals Court Allows Alcohol Ads in Virginia College Newspapers," *The Chronicle of Higher Education* (published online September 25, 2013): http://chronicle.com/blogs/ticker/appeals-court-allows-alcohol-ads-in-virginia-college-newspapers/66629.
      www.ufsa.ufl.edu/faculty_staff/committees/alcohol_drug_education/uf_alchohol_policy/supervision_and_control_policies/.
      D. E. Fierberg, "To End Fraternity Hazing, End Boozing First," *The Chronicle of Higher Education* (May 4, 2012): A25–A26.

S. Kolowich, "The Anti-Amethyst Initiative," *Inside Higher Ed* (published online April 13, 2010): www.insidehighered.com/news/2010/04/13/drinking#sthash.eVvHVy4m.dpbs.

A. Miller, "New Insights on College Drinking," *Monitor on Psychology* (October 2013): 46–51.

D. Ziff, "UW-Madison Will Require Students Cited for Drinking to Take Course on Alcohol Risks," *Wisconsin State Journal* (posted online September 9, 2011): http://host.madison.com/news/local/education/university/uw-madison-will-require-students-cited-for-drinking-to-take/article_bb9046ec-da69-11e0-9432-001cc4c002e0.html.

128 www.theamethystinitiative.org.

129 T. Parker-Pope, "Drinking to Extremes to Celebrate 21," *The New York Times* (posted online April 8, 2008): http://well.blogs.nytimes.com/2008/04/08/drinking-to-extremes-to-celebrate-21/.

K. Sack, "21," *The New York Times Education Life* (November 2, 2008): 20–23, 41.

A. Tilsey, "Experts Discuss How to Address 'Butt-Chugging' on Campus," *Inside Higher Ed* (published online October 2, 2012): www.insidehighered.com/news/2012/10/02/experts-discuss-how-address-butt-chugging-campus#sthash.W3SiOozT.dpbs.

130 J. M. Angelo, "The Wasted Years," *University Business* (June 2004): 31–36.

131 D. Hawks, "Prevention and the Locus of Control: Internal, External or Somewhere in Between?" in *Self-Control and the Addictive Behaviours*, eds. N. Heather, W. R. Miller, and J. Greeley, New York: Maxwell Macmillan, 1991.

Musto, "Alcohol in American History."

M. Kuo, H. Wechsler, P. Greenberg, and H. Lee, "The Marketing of Alcohol to College Students: The Role of Low Prices and Special Promotions," *American Journal of Preventive Medicine* 25(2003): 204–211.

132 M. Massing, "Strong Stuff," *The New York Times* (March 22, 1998): 36–41, 48, 58, 72, 73.

12 HOW SWEET IT IS

1 www.cdc.gov//diabetes/pubs/factsheet11.htm.

2 Ibid.

3 N. R. Kleinfield, "Modern Ways Open India's Doors to Diabetes," *The New York Times* (September 13, 2006): A1, A12–A13.

D. Yach, S. R. Leeder, J. Bell, and B. Kistnasamy, "Global Chronic Diseases," *Science* 307(2005): 317.

4 D. M. Nathan and R. Frishman, *Diabetes*, Boston: Harvard Medical School Health Publications Group, 1999.

5 P. Björntorp, "The Importance of Body Fat Distribution," in *Eating Disorders and Obesity: A Comprehensive Handbook*, eds. K. D. Brownell and C. G. Fairburn, New York: The Guilford Press, 1995.

6 Ibid., p. 1.

7 www.cdc.gov//diabetes/pubs/factsheet11.htm.

8 Yach, Leeder, and Kistnasamy, "Global Chronic Diseases."

9 Nathan and Frishman, *Diabetes*.

10 W. Shakespeare, *Othello* in *The Complete Works of William Shakespeare*, ed. W. A. Wright, Garden City, NY: Garden City Books, 1623/1936, p. 634.

11 S. Basu, P. Yoffe, N. Hills, and R. H. Lustig, "The Relationship of Sugar to Population-Level Diabetes Prevalence: An Econometric Analysis of Repeated Cross-Sectional Data," *PLoS ONE* 8(2013): e57873. DOI: 10.1371/journal. pone.0057873.

S. Holt, J. Brand, C. Soveny, and J. Hansky, "Relationship of Satiety to Postprandial Glycaemic, Insulin, and Cholecystokinin Responses" *Appetite* 18(1992): 129–141.

K. L. Morris and M. B. Zemel, "Glycemic Index, Cardiovascular Disease, and Obesity," *Nutrition Reviews* 57(1999): 273–276.

12 J. Albu, D. Allison, C. N. Boozer, S. Heymsfield, H. Kissileff, A. Kretser, et al., "Obesity Solutions: Report of a Meeting," *Nutrition Reviews* 55(1997): 150–156.

Björntorp, "The Importance of Body Fat Distribution."

S. M. Haffner, "Are There People Who Do Not Need to Lose Weight: The Role of Body Fat Distribution and Implications from Diabetes Research," in *Obesity Treatment: Establishing Goals, Improving Outcomes, and Reviewing the Research Agenda*, eds. D. B. Allison and F. X. Pi-Sunyer, New York: Plenum, 1995.

M. W. Schwartz, "Staying Slim with Insulin in Mind," *Science* 289(2000): 2066–2067.

G. Taubes, "Prosperity's Plague," *Science* 325(2009): 256–260.

13 M. Wei, L. W. Gibbons, T. L. Mitchell, J. B. Kampert, C. D. Lee, and S. N. Blair, "The Association between Cardiorespiratory Fitness and Impaired Fasting Glucose and Type 2 Diabetes in Men," *Annals of Internal Medicine* 130(1999): 89–96.

14 P. H. Bennett, "Type 2 Diabetes among the Pima Indians of Arizona: An Epidemic Attributable to Environmental Change?" *Nutrition Reviews* 57(1999): S51–S54.

C. Gonzalez, M. P. Stern, E. Gonzalez, D. Rivera, J. Simon, S. Islas, and S. Haffner, "The Mexico City Diabetes Study: A Population-Based Approach to the Study of Genetic and Environmental Interactions in the Pathogenesis of Obesity and Disease," *Nutrition Review* 57(1999): S71–S77.

R. A. Hegele, "Lessons from Genetic Studies in Native Canadian Populations," *Nutrition Reviews* 57(1999): S43–S50.

15 P. Tessari, "Changes in Protein, Carbohydrate, and Fat Metabolism with Aging: Possible Role of Insulin," *Nutrition Reviews* 58(2000): 11–19.

16 M. Elchebly, P. Payette, E. Michaliszyn, W. Cromlish, S. Collins, A. L. Loy, et al., "Increased Insulin Sensitivity and Obesity Resistance in Mice Lacking the Protein Tyrosine Phosphatase-1B Gene," *Science* 283(1999): 1544–1548.

17 Nathan and Frishman, *Diabetes*.

18 Diabetes Genetics Initiative of Broad Institute of Harvard and MIT, Lund University, and Novartis Institutes for BioMedical Research, "Genome-Wide Association Analysis Identifies Loci for Type 2 Diabetes and Triglyceride Levels," *Science* 316(2007): 1331–1336.

L. J. Scott, K. L. Mohlke, L. L. Bonnycastle, C. J. Willer, Y. Li, W. L. Duren, et al., "A Genome-Wide Association Study of Type 2 Diabetes in Finns Detects Multiple Susceptibility Variants," *Science* 316(2007): 1341–1345.

E. Zeggini, M. N. Weedon, C. M. Lindgren, T. M. Frayling, K. S. Elliott, H. Lango, et al., "Replication of Genome-Wide Association Signals in UK Samples Reveals Risk Loci for Type 2 Diabetes," *Science* 316(2007): 1336–1341.

19 J. Diamond, "Sweet Death," *Natural History* (February, 1992): 2–4, 6.

G. M. Reaven, "Insulin Resistance: A Chicken that Has Come to Roost," in *The Metabolic Syndrome X: Convergence of Insulin Resistance, Glucose Intolerance, Hypertension, Obesity, and Dyslipidemias—Searching for the Underlying Defects*, eds. B. C. Hansen, J. Saye, and L. W. Wennogle, New York: The New York Academy of Sciences, 1999.

20 Bennett, "Type 2 Diabetes among the Pima Indians of Arizona."

21 Nathan and Frishman, *Diabetes.*

22 B. J. Rolls and E. T. Rolls, *Thirst*, Cambridge, UK: Cambridge University Press, 1982.

23 J. Rodin, "Insulin Levels, Hunger, and Food Intake: An Example of Feedback Loops in Body Weight Regulation," *Health Psychology* 4(1985): 1–24.

24 P. J. Geiselman, "Sugar-Induced Hyperphagia: Is Hyperinsulinemia, Hypoglycemia, or Any Other Factor a 'Necessary' Condition?" *Appetite* 11(1988): 26–34.

25 K. Ackroff, A. Sclafani, and K. V. Axen, "Diabetic Rats Prefer Glucose-Paired Flavors over Fructose-Paired Flavors," *Appetite* 28(1997): 73–83.

26 R. G. Settle, "The Chemical Senses in Diabetes Mellitus," in *Smell and Taste in Health and Disease*, eds. T. V. Getchell, L. M. Bartoshuk, R. L. Doty, and J. B. Snow, New York: Raven Press, 1991.

27 H. N. Haan, "The Role of *APOE* 4 in Modulating Effects of Other Risk Factors for Cognitive Decline in Elderly Persons," *JAMA* 282(1999): 40–46.

28 D. Benton, "The Impact of the Supply of Glucose to the Brain on Mood and Memory," *Nutrition Reviews* 59(2001): S20–S21.

J. E. Morley, "Nutritional Modulation of Behavior and Immunocompetence," *Nutrition Reviews* 52(1994): S6–S8.

29 S. Tavernise and D. Grady, "For Diabetics, Health Risks Fall Sharply," *The New York Times* (April 17, 2014): A1, A15.

30 Nathan and Frishman, *Diabetes.*

31 A. L. Peters, "Diabetic's Olympian Triumph," *The New York Times* (October 31, 2000): F7.

32 R. R. Wing, "Treatment of Obesity in the Diabetic Patient," in *Eating Disorders and Obesity: A Comprehensive Handbook*, eds. K. D. Brownell and C. G. Fairburn, New York: The Guilford Press, 1995.

33 F. X. Pi-Sunyer, "How Effective Are Lifestyle Changes in the Prevention of Type 2 Diabetes Mellitus," *Nutrition Reviews* 65(2007): 101–110.

34 R. M. Lampman, J. T. Santinga, P. J. Savage, D. R. Bassett, C. R. Hydrick, J. D. Flora, and W. D. Block, "Effect of Exercise Training on Glucose Tolerance, in Vivo Insulin Sensitivity, Lipid and Lipoprotein Concentrations in Middle-Aged Men with Mild Hypertriglyceridemia," *Metabolism* 34(1985): 205–211.

35 R. M. Sanchez-Quesada, J. Ordonez-Llanos, T. Prat, A. Caixas, O. Jorba, J. R. Serra, et al., "Effect of Physical Exercise on Lipoprotein(a) and Low-Density Lipoprotein Modifications in Type 1 and Type 2 Diabetic Patients," *Metabolism* 49(2000): 640–647.

36 T. S. Church, S. N. Blair, S. Cocreham, N. Johannsen, W. Johnson, K. Kramer, et al., "Effects of Aerobic and Resistance Training on Hemoglobin A_{1c} Levels in Patients with Type 2 Diabetes," *JAMA* 304(2010): 2253–2262.

37 Tessari, "Changes in Protein, Carbohydrate, and Fat Metabolism with Aging."

38 M. Wei, L. W. Gibbons, J. B. Kampert, M. Z. Nichaman, and S. N. Blair, "Low Cardiorespiratory Fitness and Physical Inactivity as Predictors of Mortality in Men with Type 2 Diabetes," *Annals of Internal Medicine* 132(2000): 605–611.

Wei, Gibbons, Mitchell, Kampert, Lee, and Blair, "The Association between Cardiorespiratory Fitness and Impaired Fasting Glucose and Type 2 Diabetes in Men."

39 S. H. A. Holt and J. B. Miller, "Increased Insulin Responses to Ingested Foods Are Associated with Lessened Satiety," *Appetite* 24(1995): 43–54.

M. McIntosh and C. Miller, "A Diet Containing Food Rich in Soluble and Insoluble Fiber Improves Glycemic Control and Reduces Hyperlipidemia among Patients with Type 2 Diabetes Mellitus," *Nutrition Reviews* 59(2001): 52–57.

R. J. Wood and M. L. Fernandez, "Carbohydrate-Restricted Versus Low-Glycemic-Index Diets for the Treatment of Insulin Resistance and Metabolic Syndrome," *Nutrition Reviews* 67(2009): 179–183.

40 F. M. Silva, C. K. Kramer, J. C. Almeida, T. Steemburgo, J. L. Gross, and M. J. Azevedo, "Fiber Intake and Gycemic Control in Patients with Type 2 Diabetes Mellitus: A Systematic Review with Meta-Analysis of Randomized Controlled Trials," *Nutrition Reviews* 71(2013): 790–801.

41 Nathan and Frishman, *Diabetes.*

42 J. Alper, "New Insights into Type 2 Diabetes," *Science* 289(2000): 37, 39.

43 Elchebly et al., "Increased Insulin Sensitivity and Obesity Resistance in Mice Lacking the Protein Tyrosiac Phosphatose-1B Gene."

44 Nathan and Frishman, *Diabetes.*

45 D. Clery, "A Pancreas in a Box," *Science* 343(2014): 133–135.

E. Rosenthal, "Even Small Medical Advances Can Mean Big Jumps in Bills," *The New York Times* (April 6, 2014): 1, 20.

46 G. Mingrone, S. Panunzi, A. De Gaetano, C. Guidone, A. Iaconelli, L. Leccesi, et al., "Bariatric Surgery Versus Conventional Medical Therapy for Type 2 Diabetes," *The New England Journal of Medicine* 366(2012): 1577–1585.

P. R. Schauer, D. L. Bhatt, J. P. Kirwan, K. Wolski, S. A. Brethauer, and S. D. Navaneethan, "Bariatric Surgery Versus Intensive Medical Therapy for Diabetes—3-Year Outcomes," *The New England Journal of Medicine* (published online March 31, 2014). DOI: 10.1056/NEJMoa1401329.

47 G. H. Brody, S. M. Kogan, V. M. Murry, Y.-F. Chen, and A. C. Brown, "Psychological Functioning, Support for Self-Management, and Glycemic Control among Rural African American Adults with Diabetes Mellitus Type 2," *Health Psychology* 27(2008): S83–S90.

A. Cynkar, "Sugar-Free Solutions," *Monitor on Psychology* (October 2007): 62–63.

48 D. A. Galuska, J. C. Will, M. K. Serdula, and E. S. Ford, "Are Health Care Professionals Advising Obese Patients to Lose Weight?" *JAMA* 282(1999): 1576–1578.

H. Jones, and L. C. Liburd, "Reversing the Tide of Type 2 Diabetes among African Americans through Interdisciplinary Research," in *Urban Health and Society: Interdisciplinary Approaches to Research and Practice,* eds. N. Freudenberg, S. Klitzman, and S. Saegert, San Francisco: Jossey-Bass, 2009.

C. C. Wee, E. P. McCarthy, R. B. Davis, and R. S. Phillips, "Physician Counseling about Exercise," *JAMA* 282(1999): 1583–1588.

13 STRICTLY ABOUT FEMALES

1 P. Zareba, D. S. Colaci, M. Afeiche, A. J. Gaskins, N. Jørgensen, J. Mendiola, et al., "Semen Quality in Relation to Antioxidant Intake in a Healthy Male Population," *Fertility and Sterility* 100(2013): 1572–1578.

2 P. J. Brown and M. Konner, "An Anthropological Perspective on Obesity," in *Human Obesity*, eds. R. J. Wurtman and J. J. Wurtman, New York: New York Academy of Sciences, 1987.

3 C. M. Logue and R. H. Moos, "Perimenstrual Symptoms: Prevalence and Risk Factors," *Psychosomatic Medicine* 48(1986): 388–414.

M. A. McVay, A. L. Copeland, H. S. Newman, and P. J. Geiselman, "Food Cravings and Food Cue Responding Across the Menstrual Cycle in a Non-Eating Disordered Sample," *Appetite* 59(2012): 591–600.

P. J. Rogers and P. Jas, "Menstrual Cycle Effects on Mood, Eating and Food Choice," *Appetite* 23(1994): 289.

D. A. Zellner, A. Garriga-Trillo, S. Centeno, and E. Wadsworth, "Chocolate Craving and the Menstrual Cycle," *Appetite* 42(2004): 119–121.

4 American Psychiatric Association, *Diagnostic and Statistical Manual of Mental Disorders*, 5th ed., Washington, DC: APA, 2013.

5 "Energy Expenditure during the Menstrual Cycle," *Nutrition Reviews* 45(1987): 102–103.

6 M. S. Kurzer, "Women, Food, and Mood," *Nutrition Reviews* 55(1997): 268–276.

E. T. S. Li, L. B. Y. Tsang, and S. S. H. Lui, "Menstrual Cycle and Voluntary Food Intake in Young Chinese Women," *Appetite* 33(1999):109–118.

Rogers and Jas, "Menstrual Cycle Effects on Mood, Eating and Food Choice."

7 "Energy Expenditure during the Menstrual Cycle."

L. A. Leiter, N. Hrboticky, and G. H. Anderson, "Effects of L-Tryptophan on Food Intake and Selection in Lean Men and Women," *Human Obesity*, eds. R. J. Wurtman and J. J. Wurtman, New York: New York Academy of Sciences, 1987.

S. T. St. Jeor, M. R. Sutnick, and B. J. Scott, "Nutrition," in *Handbook of Behavioral Medicine for Women*, eds. E. A. Blechman and K. D. Brownell, New York: Pergamon, 1988.

8 R. J. Wurtman and J. J. Wurtman, "Carbohydrates and Depression," *Scientific American* 260(January 1989): 68–75.

9 C. S. Pomerleau, A. W. Garcia, A. Drewnowski, and O. E. Pomerleau, "Sweet Taste Preference in Woman Smokers: Comparison with Nonsmokers and Effects of Menstrual Phase and Nicotine Abstinence," *Pharmacology Biochemistry and Behavior* 40(1991): 995–999.

10 T. Engen, *The Perception of Odors*, New York: Academic Press, 1982.

R. G. Mair, J. A. Bouffard, and T. Engen, "Olfactory Sensitivity during the Menstrual Cycle," *Sensory Processes* 2(1978): 90–98.

11 J. M. Hormes and P. Rozin, "Perimenstrual Chocolate Craving. What Happens After Menopause?" *Appetite* 53(2009): 256–259.

S. A. Tucci, L. E. Murphy, E. J. Boyland, L. Dye, and J. C. G. Halford, "Oral Contraceptive Effects on Food Choice During the Follicular and Luteal Phases of the Menstrual Cycle. A Laboratory Based Study." *Appetite* 55(2010): 388–392.

12 R. E. Frisch, "Fatness and Fertility," *Scientific American* 258(March 1988): 88–95.

13 J. L. Cameron, "Nutritional Determinants of Puberty," *Nutrition Reviews* 54(1996): S17–S22.

B. R. Olson, "Effects of Nutrition on Reproductive Capacity," in *Food Intake and Energy Expenditure*, eds. M. S. Westerterp-Plantenga, E. W. H. M. Fredrix, and A. B. Steffens, Boca Raton, FL: CRC Press, 1994.

14 J. A. McLean and S. I. Barr, "Cognitive Dietary Restraint Is Associated with Eating Behaviors, Lifestyle Practices, Personality Characteristics and Menstrual Irregularity in College Women," *Appetite* 40(2003): 185–192.

15 F. M. Biro, L. C. Greenspan, M. P. Galvez, S. M. Pinney, S. Teitelbaum, G. C. Windham, et al., "Onset of Breast Development in a Longitudinal Cohort," *Pediatrics* 132(2013): 1019–1027.

16 M. May, "Battles over Body Fat," *Science* 260(1993): 1592–1593.

17 R. E. Frisch, *Female Fertility and the Body Fat Connection*, Chicago: University of Chicago Press, 2002.

18 Olson, "Effects of Nutrition on Reproductive Capacity."

19 K. D. Brownell, "History of Obesity," in *Eating Disorders and Obesity: A Comprehensive Handbook*, eds. K. D. Brownell and C. G. Fairburn, New York: The Guilford Press, 1995.

20 J. E. Schneider and G. N. Wade, "Availability of Metabolic Fuels Controls Estrous Cyclicity of Syrian Hamsters," *Science* 244(1989): 1326–1328.

21 Cameron, "Nutritional Determinants of Puberty."

22 P. M. Dubbert and J. E. Martin, "Exercise," in *Handbook of Behavioral Medicine for Women*, eds. E. A. Blechman and K. D. Brownell, New York: Pergamon, 1988.
   P. Ellison, "American Scientist Interviews," *American Scientist* 75(1987): 622–627.
   Logue and Moos, "Perimenstrual Symptoms."

23 Frisch, "Fatness and Fertility."
   Dubbert and Martin, "Exercise."

24 L. P. Morin, "Effects of Various Feeding Regimens and Photoperiod or Pinealectomy on Ovulation in the Hamster," *Biology of Reproduction* 13(1975): 99–103.

25 K. Brownell, "The Yo-Yo Trap," *American Health* (March 1988): 78, 80–82, 84.
   St. Jeor et al., "Nutrition."

26 G. Miller, "Hungry Ewes Deliver Offspring Early," *Science* 300(2003): 561–562.

27 K. Hawkes, J. F. O'Connell, and N. G. Blurton Jones, "Hadza Women's Time Allocation, Offspring Provisioning, and the Evolution of Long Postmenopausal Life Spans," *Current Anthropology* 38(1997): 551–565.
   K. Hawkes, J. F. O'Connell, N. G. Blurton Jones, H. Alvarez, and E. L. Charnov, "Grandmothering, Menopause, and the Evolution of Human Life Histories," *Proceedings of the National Academy of Sciences* 95(1998): 1336–1339.

28 M. Cooper, *Pica*, Springfield, IL: Charles C. Thomas, 1957.
   B. Knox, J. Kremer, and J. Pearce, "Food Fads during Pregnancy: A Question of Taste?" *Appetite* 23(1994): 288.
   P. Rosso, "Regulation of Food Intake during Pregnancy and Lactation," in *Human Obesity*, eds. R. J. Wurtman and J. J. Wurtman, New York: New York Academy of Sciences, 1987.
   W. Verbeke and I. De Bourdeaudhuij, "Dietary Behaviour of Pregnant Versus Non-Pregnant Women," *Appetite* 48(2007): 78–86.

29 J. Le Magnen, *Neurobiology of Feeding and Nutrition*, New York: Academic Press, 1992.

30 M. E. Mercer and M. D. Holder, "Food Cravings, Endogenous Opioid Peptides, and Food Intake: A Review," *Appetite* 29(1997): 325–352.
   P. T. B. Starks and B. L. Slabach, "The Scoop on Eating Dirt," *Scientific American* (June 2012): 30, 32.

31 E. J. Callahan and L. Desiderato, "Disorders in Pregnancy " in *Handbook of Behavioral Medicine for Women*, eds. E. A. Blechman and K. D. Brownell, New York: Pergamon, 1988.
   K. Uvnäs-Moberg, "Gastrointestinal Tract in Growth and Reproduction," *Scientific American* 261(July 1989): 78–83.

32 H. A. Guthrie, *Introductory Nutrition*, Saint Louis, MO: Mosby, 1975.

33 M. Erick, "Hyperolfaction and Hyperemesis Gravidarum: What Is the Relationship?" *Nutrition Reviews* 53(1995): 289–295.

34 R. M. Nesse and G. C. Williams, "Evolution and the Origins of Disease," *Scientific American* (November 1998): 86–93.

   M. Profet, "Pregnancy Sickness as Adaptation: A Deterrent to Maternal Ingestion of Teratogens," in *The Adapted Mind: Evolutionary Psychology and the Generation of Culture*, eds. J. H. Barkow, L. Cosmides, and J. Tooby, New York: Oxford University Press, 1992.

   P. W. Sherman and S. M. Flaxman, "Protecting Ourselves from Food," *American Scientist* 89(March–April 2001): 142–151.

35 T. M. Bayley, L. Dye, S. Jones, M. DeBono, and A. J. Hill, "Food Cravings and Aversions during Pregnancy: Relationships with Nausea and Vomiting," *Appetite* 38(2002): 45–51.

36 S. R. Crystal and I. L. Bernstein, "Morning Sickness: Impact on Offspring Salt Preference," *Appetite* 25(1995): 231–240.

   S. R. Crystal and I. L. Bernstein, "Infant Salt Preference and Mother's Morning Sickness," *Appetite* 30(1998): 297–307.

37 Uvnäs-Moberg, "Gastrointestinal Tract in Growth and Reproduction."

38 Ibid.

39 http://iom.edu/~/media/Files/Report%20Files/2009/Weight-Gain-During-Pregnancy-Reexamining-the-Guidelines/Report%20Brief%20-%20Weight%20Gain%20During%20Pregnancy.pdf

40 P. J. Bradley, "Conditions Recalled to Have Been Associated with Weight Gain in Adulthood," *Appetite* 6(1985): 235–241.

41 M. Mannan , S. A. R. Doi, and A. A. Mamun, "Association between Weight Gain During Pregnancy and Postpartum Weight Retention and Obesity: A Bias-Adjusted Meta-Analysis," *Nutrition Reviews* 71(2013): 343–352.

42 St. Jeor et al., "Nutrition."

43 T. O. Scholl, M. L. Hediger, C.-S. Khoo, M. F. Healey, and N. L. Rawson, "Maternal Weight Gain, Diet and Infant Birth Weight," *Journal of Clinical Epidemiology* 44(1991): 423–428.

44 A. Gibbons, "What's for Dinner? Researchers Seek Our Ancestors' Answers," *Science* 326(2009): 1478–1479.

   M. Hult, P. Tornhammar, P. Ueda, C. Chima, A.-K. E. Bonamy, B. Ozumba, and M. Norman, "Hypertension, Diabetes and Overweight: Looming Legacies of the Biafran Famine," *PLoS ONE* (published online October 22, 2010). DOI: 10.1371/journal.pone.0013582.

   P. James, "Marabou 2005: Nutrition and Human Development," *Nutrition Reviews* 5(2006): S1–S11.

   G.-P. Ravelli, Z. A. Stein, and M. W. Susser, "Obesity in Young Men after Famine Exposure in Utero and Early Infancy," *The New England Journal of Medicine* 295(1976): 349–353.

   A. L. Sawaya, P. A. Martins, L. P. Grillo, and T. T. Florêncio, "Long-Term Effects of Early Malnutrition on Body Weight Regulation," *Nutrition Reviews* 62(2004): S127–S133.

45 S. Song, "Does Famine Influence Sex Ratio at Birth? Evidence from the 1959–1961 Great Leap Forward Famine in China," *Proceedings of the Royal Society B* 279(2012): 2883–2890.

   D. St Clair, M. Xu, P. Wang, Y. Yu, Y. Fang, F. Zhang, et al., "Rates of Adult Schizophrenia Following Prenatal Exposure to the Chinese Famine of 1959–1961," *JAMA* 294(2005): 557–562.

46 B. Laraia, E. Epel, and A. M. Siega-Riz, "Food Insecurity with Past Experience of Restrained Eating Is a Recipe for Increased Gestational Weight Gain," *Appetite* 65(2013): 178–184.

47 L. M. Belzer, J. C. Smulian, S.-E. Lu, and B. J. Tepper, "Food Cravings and Intake of Sweet Foods in Healthy Pregnancy and Mild Gestational Diabetes Mellitus. A Prospective Study," *Appetite* 55(2010): 609–615.

A. E. Evenson, "Update on Gestational Diabetes Mellitus," *Primary Care: Clinics in Office Practice* 39(2012): 83–94.

D. M. Nathan and R. Frishman, *Diabetes*, Boston: Harvard Medical School Health Publications Group, 1999.

B. L. Silverman, L. Landsberg, and B. E. Metzger, "Fetal Hyperinsulinism in Offspring of Diabetic Mothers: Association with the Subsequent Development of Childhood Obesity," *Annals of the New York Academy of Sciences* 699(1993): 36–45.

48 G. M. Shaw, E. M. Velie, and D. Schaffer, "Risk ofNeural Tube Defect— Affected Pregnancies among Obese Women," *JAMA* 275(1996): 1093–1096.

M. M. Werler, C. Louik, S. Shapiro, and A. A. Mitchell, "Prepregnant Weight in Relation to Risk of Neural Tube Defects," *JAMA* 275(1996): 1089–1092.

49 E. L. Abel, "Fetal Alcohol Syndrome: Behavioral Teratology," *Psychological Bulletin* 87(1980): 29–50.

"Fetal Alcohol Syndrome," *Science* 258(1992): 739.

E. Hunt, A. P. Streissguth, B. Kerr, and H. Olson, "Mothers' Alcohol Consumption during Pregnancy: Effects on Spatial–Visual Reasoning in 14-Year-Old Children," *Psychological Science* 6(1995): 339–342.

A. P. Streissguth, J. M. Asase, S. K. Clarren, S. P. Randels, R. A. LaDue, and D. F. Smith, "Fetal Alcohol Syndrome in Adolescents and Adults," *JAMA* 265(1991): 1961–1967.

A. P. Streissguth, F. L. Bookstein, P. D. Sampson, and H. M. Barr, "Neurobehavioral Effects of Prenatal Alcohol: Part III. PLS Analyses of Neuropsychological Tests," *Neurotoxicology and Teratology* 11(1989): 493–507.

A. P. Streissguth, S. Landesman-Dwyer, J. C. Martin, and D. W. Smith, "Teratogenic Effects of Alcohol in Humans and Laboratory Animals," *Science* 209(1980): 353–361.

50 B. M. Altura, B. T. Altura, A. Carella, M. Chatterjee, S. Halevy, and N. Tejani, "Alcohol Produces Spasms of Human Umbilical Blood Vessels: Relationship to Fetal Alcohol Syndrome (FAS)," *European Journal of Pharmacology* 86(1983): 311–312.

51 C. R. Goodlett, D. J. Bonthius, E. A. Wasserman, and J. R. West, "An Animal Model of Central Nervous System Dysfunction Associated with Fetal Alcohol Exposure: Behavioral and Neuroanatomical Correlates," in *Learning and Memory: The Behavioral and Biological Substrates*, eds. I. Gormezano and E. A. Wasserman, Hillsdale, NJ: Lawrence Erlbaum Associates, 1992.

C. Ikonomidou, P. Bittigau, M. J. Ishimaru, D. F. Wozniak, C. Koch, K. Genz, et al., "Ethanol-Induced Apoptotic Neurodegeneration and Fetal Alcohol Syndrome," *Science* 287(2000): 1056–1060.

52 D. Kuehn, S. Aros, F. Cassoria, M. Avaria, N. Unanue, C. Henriquez, et al., "A Prospective Cohort Study of the Prevalence of Growth, Facial, and Central Nervous System Abnormalities in Children with Heavy Prenatal Alcohol Exposure," *Alcoholism: Clinical and Experimental Research* 36(2012): 1811–1819.

53 "Fetal Alcohol Syndrome."

A. P. Streissguth, H. M. Barr, P. D. Sampson, F. L. Bookstein, and B. L. Darby, "Neurobehavioral Effects of Prenatal Alcohol: Part I," *Neurotoxicology and Teratology* 11(1989): 461–476.

54 S. J. Lewis, L. Zuccolo, G. D. Smith, J. Macleod, S. Rodriguez, E. S. Draper, et al., "Fetal Alcohol Exposure and IQ at Age 8: Evidence From a Population-Based Birth-Cohort Study," *PLoS ONE* (published online November 14, 2012). DOI: 10.1371/journal.pone.0049407.

A. P. Streissguth, H. M. Barr, F. L. Bookstein, P. D. Sampson, and H. C. Olson, "The Long-Term Neurocognitive Consequences of Prenatal Alcohol Exposure: A 14-Year Study," *Psychological Science* 10(1999): 186–190.

55 P. D. Sampson, A. P. Streissguth, H. M. Barr, and F. L. Bookstein, "Neurobehavioral Effects of Prenatal Alcohol: Part II. Partial Least Squares Analysis," *Neurotoxicology* 11(1989): 477–491.

Streissguth et al., "Neurobehavioral Effects of Prenatal Alcohol: Part III."

56 G. B. Kolata, "Fetal Alcohol Advisory Debated," *Science* 214(1981): 642, 643, 645.

U.S. Department of Health and Human Services, *The Surgeon General's Report on Nutrition and Health: Summary and Recommendations* (DHHS Publication No. 88–50211), Washington, DC: U.S. Government Printing Office, 1988.

57 M. Frezza, C. Di Padova, G. Pozzato, M. Terpin, E. Baraona, and C. S. Lieber, "High Blood Alcohol Levels in Women: The Role of Decreased Gastric Alcohol Dehydrogenase Activity and First-Pass Metabolism," *The New England Journal of Medicine* 322(1990): 95–99.

B. Wuethrich, "Does Alcohol Damage Female Brains More?" *Science* 291(2001): 2077, 2079.

58 D. F. Musto, "Alcohol in American History," *Scientific American* (April 1996): 78–83.

59 www.cdc.gov/NCBDDD/fasd/data.html.

60 "ACOG Committee Opinion No. 462: Moderate Caffeine Consumption During Pregnancy," *Obstetrics and Gynecology* 116(2010): 467–468.

61 B. Weiss, "Behavior as a Common Focus of Toxicology," in *Nutrition and Behavior*, ed. S. A. Miller, Philadelphia: Franklin Institute, 1981.

62 G. K. Beauchamp, B. J. Cowart, and H. J. Schmidt, "Development of Chemosensory Sensitivity and Preference," in *Smell and Taste in Health and Disease*, eds. T. V. Getchell, L. M. Bartoshuk, R. L. Doty, and J. B. Snow, New York: Raven Press, 1991.

L. Cooke and A. Fildes, "The Impact of Flavor Exposure in Utero and Druing Milk Feeding on Food Acceptance at Weaning and Beyond," *Appetite* 57(2011): 808–811.

L. P. Lipsitt and G. Behl, "Taste-Mediated Differences in the Sucking Behavior of Human Newborns," in *Taste, Experience, and Feeding*, eds. E. D. Capaldi and T. L. Powley, Washington, DC: American Psychological Association, 1990.

L. Marlier, B. Schaal, and R Soussignan, "Bottle-Fed Neonates Prefer an Odor Experienced in Utero to an Odor Experienced Postnatally in the Feeding Context," *Developmental Psychobiology* 33(1998): 133–145.

J. A. Mennella, "Ontogeny of Taste Preferences: Basic Biology and Implications for Health," *American Journal of Clinical Nutrition* 99(suppl.) (2014): 704S–711S.

63 J. C. Molina, N. E. Spear, L. P. Spear, J. A. Mennella, and M. J. Lewis, "The International Society for Developmental Psychobiology 39th Annual Meeting

Symposium: Alcohol and Development: Beyond Fetal Alcohol Syndrome," *Developmental Psychobiology* (2007). DOI: 10.1002/dev.

64 A. A. Abrahamian, "The Placenta Cookbook," *New York* (August 29, 2011): 46–49, 154.

M. B. Kristal, J. M. DiPirro, and A. C. Thompson, "Placentophagia in Humans and Nonhuman Mammals: Causes and Consequences," *Ecology of Food and Nutrition* 51(2012): 177–197.

65 P. Wright, "Hunger, Satiety and Feeding Behavior in Early Infancy," in *Eating Habits: Food, Physiology and Learned Behavior*, eds. R. A. Boakes, D. A. Popplewell, and M. J. Burton, Chichester, UK: Wiley, 1987, p. 75.

66 R. M. Gilbert, "Caffeine: Overview and Anthology," in *Nutrition and Behavior*, ed. S. A. Miller, Philadelphia: Franklin Institute, 1981.

St. Jeor et al., "Nutrition."

67 J. Newman, "How Breast Milk Protects Newborns," *Scientific American* (December 1995): 76–79.

68 J. Protzko, J. Aronson, and C. Blair, "How to Make a Young Child Smarter: Evidence From the Database of Raising Intelligence," *Perspectives on Psychological Science* 8(2013): 25–40.

69 E. M. Blass, "The Ontogeny of Motivation: Opioid Bases of Energy Conservation and Lasting Affective Change in Rat and Human Infants," *Current Directions in Psychological Science* 1(1992): 116–120.

70 Uvnäs-Moberg, "Gastrointestinal Tract in Growth and Reproduction."

71 R. Von Kries, B. Koletzko, T. Sauerwald, E. Von Mutius, D. Barnert, V. Grunert, and H. Von Voss, "Breast Feeding and Obesity: Cross Sectional Study," *British Medical Journal* 319(1999): 1–9.

72 Wright, "Hunger, Satiety and Feeding Behavior in Early Infancy."

73 A. Palou and C. Picó, "Leptin Intake during Lactation Prevents Obesity and Affects Food Intake and Food Preferences in Later Life," *Appetite* 52(2009): 249–252.

74 L. M. Bartoshuk and G. K. Beauchamp, "Chemical Senses," *Annual Review of Psychology* 45(1994): 419–449.

Beauchamp et al., "Development of Chemosensory Sensitivity and Preference."

R. H. Porter, "Human Reproduction and the Mother-Infant Relationship: The Role of Odors," in *Smell and Taste in Health and Disease*, eds. T. V. Getchell, L. M. Bartoshuk, R. L. Doty, and J. B. Snow, New York: Raven Press, 1991.

75 J. A. Mennella and G. K. Beauchamp, "The Early Development of Human Flavor Preferences," in *Why We Eat What We Eat: The Psychology of Eating*, ed. E. D. Capaldi, Washington, DC: American Psychological Association, 1996.

J. A. Mennella and G. K. Beauchamp, "The Human Infants' Response to Vanilla Flavors in Mother's Milk and Formula," *Infant Behavior and Development* 19(1996): 13–19.

S. Nicklaus, "Development of Food Variety in Children," *Appetite* 52(2009): 253–255.

76 J. A. Mennella, C. P. Jagnow, and G. K. Beauchamp, "Prenatal and Postnatal Flavor Learning by Human Infants," *Pediatrics* 107(2001): E88.

77 L. J. Stein, B. J. Cowart, A. N. Epstein, L. J. Pilot, C. R. Laskin, and G. K. Beauchamp, "Increased Liking for Salty Foods in Adolescents Exposed during Infancy to a Chloride-Deficient Feeding Formula," *Appetite* 27(1996): 65–77.

78 S. J. Cheslock, E. I. Varlinskaya, E. S. Petrov, M. M. Silveri, L. P. Spear, and N. E. Spear, "Ethanol as a Reinforcer in the Newborn's First Suckling Experience," *Alcoholism: Clinical and Experimental Research* 25(2001): 391–402.

79 J. A. Mennella and G. K. Beauchamp, "Smoking and the Flavor of Breast Milk," *The New England Journal of Medicine* 339(1998): 1559–1560.

80 J. A. Mennella, "Infants' Suckling Responses to the Flavor of Alcohol in Mothers' Milk," *Alcoholism: Clinical and Experimental Research* 21(1997): 581–585.

J. A. Mennella, "Short-Term Effects of Maternal Alcohol Consumption on Lactational Performance," *Alcoholism: Clinical and Experimental Research* 22(1998): 1389–1392.

81 C. H. Kinsley and K. G. Lambert, "The Maternal Brain," *Scientific American* (January 2006): 72–79.

E. S. Mezzacappa, "Breastfeeding and Maternal Stress Response and Health," *Nutrition Reviews* 62(2004): 261–268.

82 St. Jeor et al., "Nutrition."

83 Rosso, "Regulation of Food Intake during Pregnancy and Lactation."

84 K. Uvnäs-Moberg, "Endocrinologic Control of Food Intake," *Nutrition Reviews* 48(1990): 57–63.

85 "Postprandial Thermogenesis in Lactating Women," *Nutrition Reviews* 49(1991): 209–210.

86 M. A. McCroy, "Does Dieting during Lactation Put Infant Growth at Risk?" *Nutrition Reviews* 59(2001): 18–21.

87 Uvnäs-Moberg, "Gastrointestinal Tract in Growth and Reproduction."

88 W. Shakespeare, *Antony and Cleopatra* in *The Complete Works of William Shakespeare*, ed. W. A. Wright, Garden City, NY: Garden City Books, 1623/1936, p. 1101.

89 S. A. Lederman, "Influence of Lactation on Body Weight Regulation," *Nutrition Reviews* 62(2004): S112–S119.

90 Shakespeare, *Antony and Cleopatra*, p. 1101.

14 WHEN AND WHY SMOKING
AFFECTS YOUR WEIGHT

1 www.cdc.gov/tobacco/index.htm.
www.lung.org/.

2 P. Hui, C. Rui, Y. Liu, F. Xu, J. Wu, L. Wu, et al., "Remodeled Salt Appetite in Rat Offspring by Perinatal Exposure to Nicotine," *Appetite* 52(2009): 492–497.

J. A. Mennella, L. M. Yourshaw, and L. K. Morgan, "Breastfeeding and Smoking: Short-Term Effects on Infant Feeding and Sleep," *Pediatrics* 120(2007): 497–502.

3 R. C. Klesges and L. M. Klesges, "Cigarette Smoking as a Dieting Strategy in a University Population," *International Journal of Eating Disorders* 7(1988): 413–419.

H. G. Pope, K. A. Phillips, and R. Olivardia, *The Adonis Complex: The Secret Crisis of Male Body Obsession*, New York: The Free Press, 2000.

C. A. Tomeo, A. E. Field, C. S. Berkey, G. A. Colditz, and A. L. Frazier, "Weight Concerns, Weight Control Behaviors, and Smoking Initiation," *Pediatrics* 104(1999): 918–924.

4 A. Seierstad, *The Bookseller of Kabul*, New York: Little, Brown, and Company, 2003, pp. 236–237.

5 N. E. Grunberg, "Nicotine, Cigarette Smoking, and Body Weight," *British Journal of Addiction* 80(1985): 369–377.

6 R. W. Foltin, M. W. Fischman, and M. F. Byrne, "Effects of Smoked Marijuana on Food Intake and Body Weight of Humans Living in a Residential Laboratory," *Appetite* 11(1988): 1–14.

7 K. M. Flegal, "Trends in Body Weight and Overweight in the U.S. Population," *Nutrition Reviews* 54(1996): S97–S100.
Grunberg, "Nicotine, Cigarette Smoking, and Body Weight."
R. C. Klesges, M. DeBon, and A. Meyers, "Obesity in African American Women: Epidemiology, Determinants, and Treatment Issues," in *Body Image, Eating Disorders, and Obesity: An Integrative Guide for Assessment and Treatment*, ed. J. K. Thompson, Washington, DC: American Psychological Association, 1996.
R. C. Klesges and A. W. Meyers, "Smoking, Body Weight, and Their Effects on Smoking Behavior: A Comprehensive Review of the Literature," *Psychological Bulletin* 106(1989): 204–230.
R. C. Klesges, K. D. Ward, J. W. Ray, G. Cutter, D. R. Jacobs, and L. E. Wagenknecht, "The Prospective Relationships between Smoking and Weight in a Young, Biracial Cohort: The Coronary Artery Risk Development in Young Adults Study," *Journal of Consulting and Clinical Psychology* 66(1998): 987–993.

8 N. E. Grunberg, K. A. Popp, and S. E. Winders, "Effects of Nicotine on Body Weight in Rats with Access to 'Junk' Foods," *Psychopharmacology* 94(1988): 536–539.

9 Grunberg, "Nicotine, Cigarette Smoking, and Body Weight."

10 J. B. Beckwith, "Eating, Drinking, and Smoking and Their Relationship in Adult Women," *Psychological Reports* 59(1986): 1075–1089.

11 K. A. Perkins, J. E. Sexton, A. DiMarco, and C. Fonte, "Acute Effects of Tobacco Smoking on Hunger and Eating in Male and Female Smokers," *Appetite* 22(1994): 149–158.

12 E. R. Gritz, A. Ippoliti, M. E. Jarvik, J. E. Rose, S. Shiffman, A. Harrison, and H. Van Vunakis, "The Effect of Nicotine on the Delay of Gastric Emptying," *Alimentary Pharmacology and Therapeutics* 2(1988): 173–178.

13 S. A. Wager-Srdar, A. S. Levine, J. E. Morley, J. R. Hoidal, and D. E. Niewoehner, "Effects of Cigarette Smoke and Nicotine on Feeding and Energy," *Physiology and Behavior* 32(1984): 389–395.

14 S. P. Kamdi, K. T. Nakhate, M. P. Dandekar, D. M. Kokare, and N. K. Subhedar, "Participation of Corticotropin-Releasing Factor Type 2 Receptors in the Acute, Chronic and Withdrawal Actions of Nicotine Associated with Feeding Behavior in Rats," *Appetite* 53(2009): 354–362.
Y. S. Mineur, A. Abizaid, Y. Rao, R. Salas, R. J. DiLeone, D. Gündisch, et al., "Nicotine Decreases Food Intake through Activation of POMC Neurons," *Science* 332(2011): 1330–1332.

15 Grunberg, "Nicotine, Cigarette Smoking, and Body Weight."

16 N. E. Grunberg and D. E. Morse, "Cigarette Smoking and Food Consumption in the United States," *Journal of Applied Social Psychology* 14(1984): 310–317.

17 N. E. Grunberg, "The Effects of Nicotine and Cigarette Smoking on Food Consumption and Taste Preferences," *Addictive Behaviors* 7(1982): 317–331.

18 H. B. Hubert, R. R. Fabsitz, M. Feinleib, and K. S. Brown, "Olfactory Sensitivity in Humans: Genetic versus Environmental Control," *Science* 208(1980): 607–609.

19 M. Y. Pepino and J. A. Mennella, "Effects of Cigarette Smoking and Family History of Alcoholism on Sweet Taste Perception and Food Cravings in Women," *Alcoholism: Clinical and Experimental Research* 31(2007): 1891–1899.

20 A. J. Jaffe and A. G. Glaros, "Taste Dimensions in Cigarette Discrimination: A Multidimensional Scaling Approach," *Addictive Behaviors* 11(1986): 407–413.

21 Grunberg, "Nicotine, Cigarette Smoking, and Body Weight."

22 K. A. Perkins, L. H. Epstein, B. L. Marks, R. L. Stiller, and R. G. Jacob, "The Effect of Nicotine on Energy Expenditure during Light Physical Activity," *The New England Journal of Medicine* 320(1989): 898–903.

23 A. Hofstetter, Y. Schutz, E. Jéquier, and J. Wahren, "Increased 24-Hour Energy Expenditure in Cigarette Smokers," *The New England Journal of Medicine* 314(1986): 79–82.

24 Klesges et al., "The Prospective Relationships between Smoking and Weight in a Young Biracial Cohort."

25 S. M. Hall, D. Ginsberg, and R. T. Jones, "Smoking Cessation and Weight Gain," *Journal of Consulting and Clinical Psychology* 54(1986): 342–346.

    R. S. Manley and F. J. Boland, "Side-Effects and Weight Gain Following a Smoking Cessation Program," *Addictive Behaviors* 8(1983): 375–380.

26 M. B. Cantor and J. F. Wilson, "Feeding the Face: New Directions in Adjunctive Behavior Research," in *Affect, Conditioning, and Cognition: Essays on the Determinants of Behavior,* eds. F. R. Brush and J. B. Overmier, Hillsdale, NJ: Lawrence Erlbaum Associates, 1985.

    J. Green and W. N. Tapp, "Feeding Cycles in Smokers, Exsmokers and Nonsmokers," *Physiology and Behavior* 36(1986): 1059–1063.

    Grunberg, "Nicotine, Cigarette Smoking, and Body Weight."

    N. E. Grunberg, D. J. Bowen, V. A. Maycock, and S. M. Nespor, "The Importance of Sweet Taste and Caloric Content in the Effects of Nicotine on Specific Food Consumption," *Psychopharmacology* 87(1985): 198–203.

    S. M. Hall, R. McGee, C. Tunstall, J. Duffy, and N. Benowitz, "Changes in Food Intake and Activity after Quitting Smoking," *Journal of Consulting and Clinical Psychology* 57(1989): 81–86.

    Klesges and Meyers, "Smoking, Body Weight, and Their Effects on Smoking Behavior."

    M. A. Sayette and D. J. Parrott, "Effects of Olfactory Stimuli on Urge Reduction in Smokers," *Experimental and Clinical Psychopharmacology* 7(1999): 151–159.

    B. Spring, J. Wurtman, R. Gleason, R. Wurtman, and K. Kessler, "Weight Gain and Withdrawal Symptoms after Smoking Cessation: A Preventative Intervention Using D-Fenfluramine," *Health Psychology* 10(1991): 216–223.

27 Jaffe and Glaros, "Taste Dimensions in Cigarette Discrimination."

    Hall et al., "Changes in Food Intake and Activity after Quitting Smoking."

    J. Rodin, "Weight Change Following Smoking Cessation: The Role of Food Intake and Exercise," *Addictive Behaviors* 12(1987): 303–317.

28 Hofstetter et al., "Increased 24-hour Energy Expenditure in Cigarette Smokers."

29 K. A. Perkins, C. Denier, J. A. Mayer, R. R. Scott, and P. M. Dubbert, "Weight Gain Associated with Decreases in Smoking Rate and Nicotine Intake," *International Journal of the Addictions* 22(1987): 575–581.

    Rodin, "Weight Change Following Smoking Cessation."

30 Klesges and Meyers, "Smoking, Body Weight, and Their Effects on Smoking Behavior."

    Hall et al., "Smoking Cessation and Weight Gain."

31 K. Doherty, F. S. Militello, T. Kinnunen, and A. J. Garvey, "Nicotine Gum Dose and Weight Gain after Smoking Cessation," *Journal of Consulting and Clinical Psychology* 64(1996): 799–807.

J. Gross, M. L. Stitzer, and J. Maldonado, "Nicotine Replacement: Effects on Postcessation Weight Gain," *Journal of Consulting and Clinical Psychology* 57(1989): 87–92.

Klesges and Meyers, "Smoking, Body Weight, and Their Effects on Smoking Behavior."

32 Grunberg et al., "Effects of Nicotine on Body Weight in Rats with Access to 'Junk' Foods."

33 Gross et al., "Nicotine Replacement."

34 L. H. Epstein and J. J. Leddy, "Food Reinforcement," *Appetite* 46(2006): 22–25.

35 K. O. Fagerström, N. G. Schneider, and E. Lunell, "Effectiveness of Nicotine Patch and Nicotine Gum as Individual versus Combined Treatments for Tobacco Withdrawal Symptoms," *Psychopharmacology* 111(1993): 271–277.

36 S. L. Frederick, S. M. Hall, G. L. Humfleet, and R. F. Muñoz, "Sex Differences in the Relation of Mood to Weight Gain after Quitting Smoking," *Experimental and Clinical Psychopharmacology* 4(1996): 178–185.

37 A. J. Stunkard and T. A. Wadden, "Restrained Eating and Human Obesity," *Nutrition Reviews* 48(1990): 78–86.

38 K. L. Schneider, B. Spring, and S. L. Pagoto, "Affective Benefits of Exercise While Quitting Smoking: Influence of Smoking-Specific Weight Concern," *Psychology of Addictive Behaviors* 21(2007): 255–260.

B. Spring, D. Howe, M. Berendsen, H. G. McFadden, K. Hitchcock, A. W. Rademaker, and B. Hitsman, "Behavioral Intervention to Promote Smoking Cessation and Prevent Weight Gain: A Systematic Review and Meta-Analysis," *Addiction* 104(2009): 1472–1486.

39 B. Hitsman, R. Pingitore, B. Spring, A. Mahableshwarker, J. S. Mizes, K. A. Segraves, et al., "Antidepressant Pharmacotherapy Helps Some Cigarette Smokers More than Others," *Journal of Consulting and Clinical Psychology* 67(1999): 547–554.

15 WE DO NOT LIVE BY BREAD ALONE

1 A. Waters, "How You Eat," *Chronicle of Higher Education* (June 15, 1994): B3.

2 N. R. Fitch, *Appetite for Life: The Biography of Julia Child*, New York: Doubleday, 1997.

3 K. Collins, *Watching What We Eat: The Evolution of Television Cooking Shows*, New York: Continuum, 2009.

D. Kamp, *The United States of Arugula: How We Became a Gourmet Nation*, New York: Broadway Books, 2006.

4 E. Rozin, *Ethnic Cuisine: The Flavor-Principle Cookbook*, Brattleboro, VT: The Stephen Greene Press, 1983.

5 A. Davidson, *The Oxford Companion to Food*, New York: Oxford University Press, 1999.

6 L. Abdallah, M. Chabert, B. Le Roux, and J. Louis-Sylvestre, "Is Pleasantness of Biscuits and Cakes Related to Their Actual or to Their Perceived Sugar and Fat Contents?" *Appetite* 30(1998): 309–324.

7 M. Clark, "The Rich Little Secret of Top Chefs: Fat," *The New York Times* (April 28, 1999): F1, F9.

8 S. H. Katz, "Fava Bean Consumption: A Case for the Co-Evolution of Genes and Culture," in *Food and Evolution: Toward a Theory of Human Food Habits*, eds. M. Harris and E. B. Ross, Philadelphia: Temple University Press, 1987.

9 S. Dickerman, "The Big Chill," *Saveur* (May 2010): 40–44, 46–47.

K. Wong, "The First Cookout," *Scientific American* (September 2013): 66–69.

10 Wong, "The First Cookout."

11 M. Enserink, "The Joy of Evidence-Based Cooking," *Science* 314(2006): 1235–1236.

12 D. Glenn, "Cook Up a Science Course, and Students Will Devour the Lessons," *The Chronicle of Higher Education* (November 19, 2010): A8.

13 S. H. Katz, "Food Behavior and Biocultural Evolution," in *The Psychobiology of Human Food Selection*, ed. L. M. Barker, Westport, CT: AVI Publishing, 1982.

14 L. L. Birch, J. Billman, and S. S. Richards, "Time of Day Influences Food Acceptability," *Appetite* 5(1984): 109–116.

15 C. Nemeroff and P. Rozin, "Sympathetic Magic in Kosher Practice and Belief at the Limits of the Laws of Kashrut," *Jewish Folklore and Ethnology* 9(1987): 31–32.

16 R. K. Oniang'o and A. Komokoti, "Food Habits in Kenya: The Effects of Change and Attendant Methodological Problems," *Appetite* 32(1999): 93–96.

17 L. E. Grivetti, "Food Prejudices and Taboos," in *The Cambridge World History of Food*, eds. K. F. Kiple and K. C. Ornelas, New York: Cambridge University Press, 2000.

18 L. Brown, J. Edwards, and H. Hartwell, "A Taste of the Unfamiliar. Understanding the Meanings Attached to Food by International Postgraduate Students in England," *Appetite* 54(2010): 202–207.

M. D. Guendelman, S. Cheryan, and B. Monin, "Fitting In but Getting Fat: Identity Threat and Dietary Choices among U.S. Immigrant Groups," *Psychological Science* 22(2011): 959–967.

19 A. Brillat-Savarin, 1825, quoted in *The Oxford Dictionary of Quotations* (Rev. ed.), 4th ed., ed. A. Partington, New York: Oxford University Press, 1996, p. 141.

20 E. Rozin and P. Rozin, "Culinary Themes and Variations," *Natural History* (February 1981): 6, 8, 12, 14.

21 C. Stallberg-White and P. Pliner, "The Effect of Flavor Principles on Willingness to Taste Novel Foods," *Appetite* 33(1999): 209–221.

22 Y.-Y. Ahn, S. E. Ahnert, J. P. Bagrow, and A.-L. Barabasi, "Flavor Network and the Principles of Food Pairing," *Scientific Reports* 1(196)(2011): 1–7.

C. P. des Gachons, E. Mura, C. Speziale, C. J. Favreau, G. F. Dubreuil, and P. A. S. Breslin "Opponency of Astringent and Fat Sensations," *Current Biology* 22(2012): R829–R830.

23 Rozin, *Ethnic Cuisine.*

24 M. Burros, "Vietnam: A Taste Trip from North to South," *The New York Times* (May 4, 1994): C1, C6.

M. Burros, "As Cultures Meet in South Africa, So Do the Cuisines," *The New York Times* (January 31, 1996): C4.

25 C. Claiborne, "Cajun and Creole: French at Heart," *The New York Times* (April 1, 1987): C1, C6.

R. Sokolov, *Fading Feast*, New York: E. P. Dutton, 1983.

26 B. Greene, "Cajun Country," *Cuisine* (September 1979): 42–54.

J. B. Harris, *High on the Hog: A Culinary Journey From Africa to America*, New York: Bloomsbury, 2011.

27 G. M. Story and L. Cruz-Orengo, "Feel the Burn," *American Scientist* 95(2007): 325–333.

28 C. E. Martin, "Appalachian House Beautiful," *Natural History* 91(2)(1982): 4, 6–8, 10, 12, 14–16.

A. C. Revkin, "Need Elephant Repellant? Try This Hot Pepper Brew." *The New York Times* (June 20, 2000): F3.

UDAP Industries, *Pepper Power*, December 3, 2003. Available online at: www.udap.com/faq.htm.

29 K. F. Kiple and K. C. Ornelas, eds., *The Cambridge World History of Food*, New York: Cambridge University Press, 2000.

L. Perry, R. Dickau, S. Zarrillo, I. Holst, D. M. Pearsall, D. R. Piperno, et al., "Starch Fossils and the Domestication and Dispersal of Chili Peppers (*Capsicum* spp. L.) in the Americas," *Science* 315(2007): 986–988.

30 B. G. Galef, "Enduring Social Enhancement of Rats' Preferences for the Palatable and the Piquant," *Appetite* 13(1989): 81–92.

31 P. Rozin and K. Kennel, "Acquired Preferences for Piquant Foods by Chimpanzees," *Appetite* 4(1983): 69–77.

32 M. J. Caterina, A. Leffler, A. B. Malmberg, W. J. Martin, J. Trafton, K. R. Petersen-Zeitz, et al., "Impaired Nociception and Pain Sensation in Mice Lacking the Capsaicin Receptor," *Science* 288(2000): 306–313.

33 L. M. Bartoshuk, "Psychophysical Advances Aid the Study of Genetic Variation in Taste," *Appetite* 34(2000): 105.

B. J. Tepper, "PROP Taster Status Is Related to Fat Perception and Preference," in *Olfaction and Taste XII: An International Symposium*, ed. C. Murphy, New York: New York Academy of Sciences, 1998.

34 R. J. Stevenson and M. R. Yeomans, "Does Exposure Enhance Liking for the Chili Burn?" *Appetite* 24(1995): 107–120.

35 P. Rozin, "Human Food Selection: The Interaction of Biology, Culture and Individual Experience," in *The Psychobiology of Human Food Selection*, ed. L. M. Barker, Westport, CT: AVI Publishing, 1982.

P. Rozin, "Getting to Like the Burn of Chili Pepper: Biological, Psychological, and Cultural Perspectives," in *Chemical Sense: Vol. 2. Irritation*, eds. B. G. Green, J. R. Mason, and M. R. Kare, New York: Marcel Dekker, 1990.

36 Rozin, "Getting to Like the Burn of Chili Pepper."

37 P. Rozin, M. Mark, and D. Schiller, "The Role of Desensitization to Capsaicin in Chili Pepper Ingestion and Preference," *Chemical Senses* 6(1981): 23–31.

38 Rozin, "Human Food Selection."

39 P. Rozin, D. Reff, M. Mark, and J. Schull, "Conditioned Opponent Responses in Human Tolerance to Caffeine," *Bulletin of the Psychonomic Society* 22(1984): 117–120.

40 J. Billing and P. W. Sherman, "Antimicrobial Functions of Spices: Why Some Like It Hot," *The Quarterly Review of Biology* 73(1998): 3–49.

P. W. Sherman and S. M. Flaxman, "Protecting Ourselves from Food," *American Scientist* 89(March–April 2001): 142–151.

41 L. H. R. J. Pilou, R. Hursel, and M. S. Westerterp-Plantenga, "Capsaicin Increases Sensation of Fullness in Energy Balance, and Decreases Desire to Eat After Dinner in Negative Energy Balance," *Appetite* 77C(2014): 44–49.

   S. Whiting, E. J. Derbyshire, and B. Tiwari, "Could Capsaicinoids Help to Support Weight Management? A Systematic Review and Meta-Analysis of Energy Intake Data," *Appetite* 73(2014): 183–188.

42 J. S. Henderson, R. A. Joyce, G. R. Hall, W. J. Hurst, and P. E. McGovern, "Chemical and Archaeological Evidence for the Earliest Cacao Beverages," *Proceedings of the National Academy of Sciences* 104(2007): 18937–18940.

43 H. Schmitz and H.-Y. Shapiro, "The Future of Chocolate," *Scientific American* (February 2012): 60–65.

44 C. M. Gibb, P. T. G. Davies, V. Glover, T. J. Steiner, F. C. Rose, and M. Sandler, "Chocolate Is a Migraine-Provoking Agent," *Cephalalgia* 11(1991): 93–95.

45 P. Rozin, E. Levine, and C. Stoess, "Chocolate Craving and Liking," *Appetite* 17(1991): 199–212.

   H. P. Weingarten and D. Elston, "Food Cravings in a College Population," *Appetite* 17(1991): 167–175.

   D. A. Zellner, A. Garriga-Trillo, E. Rohm, S. Centeno, and S. Parker, "Food Liking and Craving: A Cross-Cultural Approach," *Appetite* 33(1999): 61–70.

46 M. M. Hetherington and J. I. MacDiarmid, "'Chocolate Addiction': A Preliminary Study of Its Description and Its Relationship to Problem Eating," *Appetite* 21(1993): 233–246.

47 M. B. Engler and M. M. Engler, "The Emerging Role of Flavonoid-Rich Cocoa and Chocolate in Cardiovascular Health and Disease," *Nutrition Reviews* 64(2006): 109–118.

48 G. Desideri, C. Kwik-Uribe, D. Grassi, S. Necozione, L. Ghiadoni, D. Mastroiacovo, et al., "Benefits in Cognitive Function, Blood Pressure, and Insulin Resistance through Cocoa Flavanol Consumption in Elderly Subjects with Mild Cognitive Impairment: The Cocoa, Cognition, and Aging (CoCoA) Study," *Hypertension* 60(2012): 794–801.

   A. Scholey and L. Owen, "Effects of Chocolate on Cognitive Function and Mood: A Systematic Review," *Nutrition Reviews* 71(2013): 665–681.

   F. A. Sorond, S. Hurwitz, D. H. Salat, D. N. Greve, and N. D. L. Fisher, "Neurovascular Coupling, Cerebral White Matter Integrity, and Response to Cocoa in Older People," *Neurology* 81(2013): 904–909.

49 P. J. Geiselman, C. F. Smith, D. A. Williamson, C. M. Champagne, G. A. Bray, and D. H. Ryan, "Perception of Sweetness Intensity Determines Women's Hedonic and Other Perceptual Responsiveness to Chocolate Food," *Appetite* 31(1998): 37–48.

   P. Rozin, "Sweetness, Sensuality, Sin, Safety, and Socialization: Some Speculations," in *Sweetness*, ed. J. Dobbing, New York: Springer-Verlag, 1987.

50 B. L. Gelb, *The Dictionary of Food*, New York: Ballantine Books, 1978.

   E. L. Gibson and E. Desmond, "Chocolate Craving and Hunger State: Implications for the Acquisition and Expression of Appetite and Food Choice," *Appetite* 32(1999): 219–240.

51 A. Drewnowski, "The Science and Complexity of Bitter Taste," *Nutrition Reviews* 59(2001): 163–169.

P. M. Fedorchak, J. Mesita, S. A. Plater, and K. Brougham, "Caffeine-Reinforced Conditioned Flavor Preferences in Rats," *Behavioral Neuroscience* 116(2002): 334–346.

G. K. Mumford, S. M. Evans, B. J. Kaminski, K. L. Preston, C. A. Sannerud, K. Silverman, and R. R. Griffiths, "Discriminative Stimulus and Subjective Effects of Theobromine and Caffeine in Humans," *Psychopharmacology* 115(1994): 1–8.

52 T. G. Benedek, "Food as Aphrodisiacs and Anaphrodisiacs?" in *The Cambridge World History of Food*, eds. K. F. Kiple and K. C Ornelas, New York: Cambridge University Press, 2000.

S. D. Coe and M. D. Coe, *The True History of Chocolate*, New York: Thames and Hudson, Ltd., 1996.

53 E. Tomaso, M. Beltramo, and D. Piomelli, "Brain Cannabinoids in Chocolate," *Nature* (August 22, 1996): 677–678.

54 C. K. Billings, "Effect of Bupropion on Chocolate Craving," *American Journal of Psychiatry* 146(1989): 119–120.

D. Lester and D. Bernard, "Liking for Chocolate, Depression, and Suicidal Preoccupation," *Psychological Reports* 69(1991): 570.

K. Palczewski and P. D. Kiser, "As Good as Chocolate," *Science* 340(2013): 562–619.

55 E. Smeets, A. Roefs, and A. Jansen, "Experimentally Induced chocolate Craving Leads to an Attentional Bias in Increased Distraction but Not in Speeded Detection," *Appetite* 53(2009): 370–375.

M. Tiggemann, E. Kemps, and J. Parnell, "The Selective Impact of Chocolate Craving on Visuospatial Working Memory," *Appetite* 55(2010): 44–48.

56 J. Lacaille, J. Ly, N. Zacchia, S. Bourkas, E. Glaser, and B. Knäuper, "The Effects of Three Mindfulness Skills on Chocolate Cravings," *Appetite* 76(2014): 101–112.

H. Oh and A. H. Taylor, "A Brisk Walk, Compared with Being Sedentary, Reduces Attentional Bias and Chocolate Cravings among Regular Chocolate Eaters with Different Body Mass," *Appetite* 71(2013): 144–149.

57 M. Harris, "India's Sacred Cow," in *Issues in Nutrition for the 1980s: An Ecological Perspective*, eds. A. L. Tobias and P. J. Thompson, Monterey, CA: Wadsworth, 1980.

C. Henderson, "The Great Cow Explosion in Rajasthan," in *Advances in Historical Ecology*, ed. W. Balée, New York: Columbia University Press, 1998.

D. Jacobson, "A Reverence for Cows," *Natural History* (June 1999): 58–63.

A. Roosevelt, "The Evolution of Human Subsistence," in *Food and Evolution: Toward a Theory of Human Food Habits*, eds. M. Harris and E. B. Ross, Philadelphia: Temple University Press, 1987.

58 K. Hill and A. M. Hurtado, "Hunter-Gatherers of the New World," *American Scientist* (September/October 1989): 436–443.

59 W. Arens, *The Man-Eating Myth: Anthropology and Anthropophagy*, New York: Oxford University Press, 1979.

60 W. J. Carr, J. T. Hirsch, B. E. Campellone, and E. Marasco, "Some Determinants of a Natural Food Aversion in Norway Rats," *Journal of Comparative and Physiological Psychology* 93(1979): 899–906.

61 D. R. Harris, "Aboriginal Subsistence in a Tropical Rain Forest Environment: Food Procurement, Cannibalism, and Population Regulation

in Northeastern Australia," in *Food and Evolution: Toward a Theory of Human Food Habits*, eds. M. Harris and E. B. Ross, Philadelphia: Temple University Press, 1987.

G. Kolata, "Anthropologists Suggest Cannibalism Is a Myth," *Science* 232(1986): 1497–1500.

P. Villa, C. Bouville, J. Courtin, D. Helmer, E. Mahieu, P. Shipman, et al., "Cannibalism in the Neolithic," *Science* 233(1986): 431–438.

62 A. Defleur, T. White, P. Valensi, L. Slimak, and E. Crégut-Bonnoure, "Neanderthal Cannibalism at Moula-Guercy, Ardèche, France," *Science* 286(1999): 128–131.

Y. Fernández-Jalvo, J. C. Díez, J. M. B. De Castro, E. Carbonell, and J. L. Arsuaga, "Evidence of Early Cannibalism," *Science* 271(1996): 277–278.

C. G. Turner and J. A. Turner, *Man Corn: Cannibalism and Violence in the Prehistoric American Southwest*, Salt Lake City: The University of Utah Press, 1999.

T. D. White, "Once Were Cannibals," *Scientific American* (August 2001): 58–65.

63 J. A. Darling, "Mass Inhumation and the Execution of Witches in the American Southwest," *American Anthropologist* 100(1999): 732–752.

64 M. J. Kohn, "You Are What You Eat," *Science* 283(1999): 335–336.

65 J. M. Diamond, "Archaeology: Talk of Cannibalism," *Nature* 407(2000): 25–26.

C. Holden, "Molecule Shows Anasazi Ate Their Enemies," *Science* 289(2000): 1663.

R. A. Marlar, B. L. Leonard, B. R. Billman, P. M. Lambert, and J. E. Marlar, "Biochemical Evidence of Cannibalism at a Prehistoric Puebloan Site in Southwestern Colorado," *Nature* 407(2000): 74–78.

K. J. Reinhard, "A Coprological View of Ancestral Pueblo Cannibalism," *American Scientist* 94(2006): 254–261.

J. N. Wilford, "New Data Suggests Some Cannibalism by Ancient Indians," *The New York Times* (September 7, 2000): A2, A22.

66 W. J. Carr, S. Y. Choi, E. Arnholt, and M. H. Sterling, "The Ontogeny of a Natural Food Aversion in Domestic Rats (*Rattus norvegicus*) and house Mice (*Mus musculus*), *Journal of Comparative and Physiological Psychology* 97(1983): 260–268.

67 N. J. Richardson, R. Shepherd, and N. A. Elliman, "Current Attitudes and Future Influences on Meat Consumption in the U.K.," *Appetite* 21(1993): 41–51.

M. L. S. Santos and D. A. Booth, "Influences on Meat Avoidance among British Students," *Appetite* 27(1996): 197–205.

68 H. Rothgerber, "A Meaty Matter. Pet Diet and the Vegetarian's Dilemma," *Appetite* 68(2013): 76–82.

69 M. A. Amerine and E. B. Roessler, *Wines: Their Sensory Evaluation*, San Francisco: W. H. Freeman, 1976.

J. Durac, *Wines and the Art of Tasting*, New York: E. P. Dutton, 1974.

B. Ensrud, *Wine with Food: A Guide to Entertaining through the Seasons*, New York: Congdon & Weed, 1984.

70 Amerine and Roessler, *Wines*.

T. Hummel, J. F. Delwiche, C. Schmidt, and K.-B. Hüttenbrink, "Effects of the Form of Glasses on the Perception of Wine Flavors: A Study in Untrained Subjects," *Appetite* 41(2003): 197–202.

71 J. Chandrashekar, D. Yarmolinsky, L. von Buchholtz, Y. Oka, W. Sly, N. J. P. Ryba, and C. S. Zuker, "The Taste of Carbonation," *Science* 326(2009): 443–446.

72 Amerine and Roessler, *Wines.*

73 A. V. Cardello, "The Role of the Human Senses in Food Acceptance," in *Food Choice, Acceptance and Consumption,* eds. H. L. Meiselman and H. J. H. MacFie, London: Blackie Academic & Professional, 1996.

74 Amerine and Roessler, *Wines.*

75 J.-X. Guinard, A. Souchard, M. Picot, M. Rogeaux, and J.-M. Sieffermann, "Sensory Determinants of the Thirst-Quenching Character of Beer," *Appetite* 31(1998): 101–115.

76 Amerine and Roessler, *Wines.*

77 A. Mantonakis, P. Rodero, I. Lesschaeve, and R. Hastie, "Order in Choice: Effects of Serial Position on Preferences," *Psychological Science,* 20(2009): 1309–1312.

78 Amerine and Roessler, *Wines.*

79 M. Siegrist and M.-E. Cousin, "Expectations Influence Sensory Experience in a Wine Tasting," *Appetite* 52(2009): 762–765.

80 H. Plassmann, J. O'Doherty, B. Shiv, and A. Rangel, "Marketing Actions Can Modulate Neural Representations of Experienced Pleasantness," *Proceedings of the National Academy of Sciences,* 105(2008): 1050–1054.

81 A. C. North, D. J. Hargreaves, and J. McKendrick, "In-Store Music Affects Product Choice," *Nature* 390(1997): 132.

82 B. Wallace, *The Billionaire's Vinegar: The Mystery of the World's Most Expensive Bottle of Wine,* New York: Three Rivers Press, 2009.

83 M. Gaillet-Torrent, C. Sulmont-Rossé, S. Issanchou, C. Chabanet, and S. Chambaron, "Impact of a Non-Attentively Perceived Odor on Subsequent Food Choices," *Appetite* 76(2014): 17–22.

C. Jacob, "Styles of Background Music and Consumption in a Bar: An Empirical Evaluation," *International Journal of Hospitality Management,* 25(2006): 716–720.

B. Scheibehenne, P. M. Todd, and B. Wansink, "Dining in the Dark. The Importance of Visual Cues for Food Consumption and Satiety," *Appetite* 55(2010): 710–713.

Q. Wang, "Music, Mind, and Mouth: Exploring the Interaction between Music and Flavor Perception," Master's Thesis (September 2013), Massachusetts Institute of Technology, http://alumni.media.mit.edu/~janiwang/thesis/janice_wang_ms_thesis.pdf.

B. Wansink, M. Shimizu, A. V. Cardello, and A. O. Wright, "Dining in the Dark: How Uncertainty Influences Food Acceptance in the Absence of Light," *Food Quality and Preference* 24(2012): 209–212.

F. Zampollo, B. Wansink, K. M. Kniffin, M. Shimizu, and A. Omori, "Looks Good Enough to Eat: How Food Plating Preferences Differ Across Cultures and Continents," *Cross-Cultural Research: The Journal of Comparative Social Science* 46(2012): 31–49.

D. A. Zellner, C. R. Loss, J. Zearfoss, and S. Remolina, "It Tastes as Good As It Looks! The Effect of Food Presentation on Liking for the Flavor of Food," *Appetite* 77C(2014): 31–35.

84 S. Kershaw, "Using Menu Psychology to Entice Diners," *The New York Times* (December 23, 2009): D1.

"Menu Mind Games," *New York* (December 14, 2009): 92–93.

85 R. Rivera, "New York City Reintroduces Calorie Rule," *The New York Times* (published online October 25, 2007): www.nytimes.com/2007/10/25/nyregion/25calories.html?_r=0.
86 N. Freudenberg, *Lethal But Legal*, New York: Oxford University Press, 2014.
87 G. Meredith, 1859, quoted in *The Oxford Dictionary of Quotations* (Rev. ed.), 4th ed., ed. A. Partington, New York: Oxford University Press, 1996, p. 458.
88 E. R. B. Lytton, 1860, quoted in *The Oxford Dictionary of Quotations* (Rev. ed.), 4th ed., ed. A. Partington, New York: Oxford University Press, 1996, p. 458.

AUTHOR INDEX

SUBJECT INDEX

Note: page numbers in **bold** refer to illustrations.

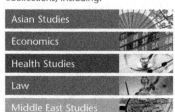

CPSIA information can be obtained
at www.ICGtesting.com
Printed in the USA
BVOW06s1931100417
480832BV00003B/3/P